ALABAMA GOVERNORS

Chattahoochee Valley Libraries
One Card...a World of Possibilities!

*Generously donated to the
collection by the
Columbus Ledger Enquirer*

A POLITICAL HISTORY

OF THE STATE

ALABAMA

GOVERNORS

EDITED BY

Samuel L. Webb *and*
Margaret E. Armbrester

Foreword by Albert P. Brewer

The University of Alabama Press
Tuscaloosa and London

Copyright © 2001
The University of Alabama Press
Tuscaloosa, Alabama 35487–0380
All rights reserved
Manufactured in the United States of America
9 8 7 6 5 4 3 2 1
09 08 07 06 05 04 03 02 01
Designed by Gary Gore
Set in Electra and CastellarMT

Library of Congress Cataloging-in-Publication Data

    Alabama governors : a political history of the state / edited by Samuel L. Webb
and Margaret E. Armbrester ; foreword by Albert P. Brewer.
      p. cm.
    Includes bibliographical references and index.
    ISBN 0–8173-1082–7 (alk. paper) — ISBN 0–8173-1083–5 (pbk. : alk. paper)
     1. Governors—Alabama—History. 2. Governors—Alabama—Biography. 3.
Alabama—Politics and government. I. Webb, Samuel L., 1946— II. Armbrester,
Margaret E. (Margaret England), 1943—
    F326 .A543 2001
    976.1'009'9—dc21   00–012559

British Library Cataloguing-in-Publication Data available

Dedicated to the Comer Foundation,
whose generosity in providing honoraria for
the contributors and funding for the photographs
and cover helped to make this book possible.

CONTENTS

Foreword by Albert P. Brewer   ix
Acknowledgments xi
Political Maps of Alabama xiii
Introduction 1

I. Territorial and Early Statehood, 1798–1847

Territorial Governors
Winthrop Sargent 7
William C. C. Claiborne 8
Robert Williams 9
David Holmes 10
William Wyatt Bibb 11

State Governors
William Wyatt Bibb 13
Thomas Bibb 16
Israel Pickens 17
John Murphy 21
Gabriel Moore 24
Samuel B. Moore 28
John Gayle 31
Clement Comer Clay 34
Hugh McVay 38
Arthur P. Bagby 41
Benjamin Fitzpatrick 45
Joshua L. Martin 48

II. Crises, Civil War, and Reconstruction, 1847–1874

Reuben Chapman 53
Henry W. Collier 57
John A. Winston 61
Andrew B. Moore 65
John Gill Shorter 70
Thomas H. Watts 73
Lewis E. Parsons 77
Robert M. Patton 80
Wager Swayne 83
William Hugh Smith 87
Robert B. Lindsay 90
David P. Lewis 94

III. The Bourbon Era, 1874–1900

George S. Houston 101
Rufus W. Cobb 106
Edward A. O'Neal 109
Thomas Seay 113
Thomas G. Jones 116
William C. Oates 122
Joseph F. Johnston 127

IV. The Progressive Era through World War II, 1900–1947

William J. Samford 137
William D. Jelks 140

Russell M. Cunningham 147
Braxton Bragg Comer 150
Emmet O'Neal 157
Charles Henderson 162
Thomas E. Kilby 166
William W. Brandon 170
Bibb Graves 173
Benjamin M. Miller 180
Frank M. Dixon 185
Chauncey M. Sparks 190

V. Post–World War II to 1987

James E. Folsom 197
Gordon Persons 206
John Patterson 210
George C. Wallace 216
Lurleen B. Wallace 230
Albert P. Brewer 235
Jere Beasley Sr. 239

VI. The Post-Wallace Era

Forrest ("Fob") James Jr. 243
Guy Hunt 249
James E. Folsom Jr. 254
Don Siegelman 257

Appendix: Governors of Alabama 261
Select Bibliography 263
Contributors 267
Index 271

FOREWORD

Fifty-four people have served as governor of Alabama: one was a woman, one was a military governor, two served as acting governors in the absence from Alabama of the elected chief of state, and one became governor upon the felony conviction of the incumbent. All have been white, some wealthy, others almost impoverished. In addition to being its chief executive, Alabama's governor is also the chief legislator, the chief ambassador, and the chief spokesperson for the state. Alabama's past and present circumstances reflect the personality, character, political philosophy, programs, and policies of each of its governors. This work studies the administrations of all of Alabama's governors—from the most obscure to the most famous or infamous, as the case may be—and from it we learn about this unique place called Alabama.

The reader of this volume discovers an interesting consistency in the actions of Alabama's governors, both in positive and negative ways. Most have genuinely, and a few disingenuously, tried to represent the great majority of people in the state who were small landowners, farmers, and laborers. In appealing politically to these groups, however, the state's governors have demonstrated an unfortunate willingness to subordinate discussion about the real issues that affect our lives—education, roads, prisons, public health—to appeals to fear and emotionalism for the purpose of political gain. Among the common themes used to arouse the populace's emotions has been to portray the federal government as the enemy of the state. Governors, from Alabama's earliest days to recent times, have found it politically useful to position themselves as protectors of the state's citizenry from the actions of those in Washington. In the 1830s it was Governor Gayle who threatened to use the state militia against federal troops during an Indian removal crisis. In the 1960s it was Governor Wallace's stand in the schoolhouse door and, more recently, Governor James's brief suggestion that he might use the state militia to keep the federal government from removing a display of the Ten Commandments from the walls of a Gadsden courthouse.

Other themes course through this volume, demonstrating that the more things appear to change in Alabama, the more they seem to stay the same. In Alabama's infancy, sectional division between north and south Alabama influenced much of the political direction of state government, and this continues, if somewhat more weakly, even to our day. Early political factions aligned around issues of class and race, and these factors continue to affect the state's politics. As Alabama decides policy on compelling public issues—whether slavery, prohibition, or lotteries—moral and religious concerns affect the actions of our state leaders. From early banking and currency issues to more recent state incentive packages to lure businesses to Alabama, economic issues rank high on the agendas of Alabama's governors. Women, although almost invisible in the politics of the state until World War II, are, nonetheless, observed throughout its history as objects of political gossip in the campaigns and administrations of their husbands.

Alabama has had its share of wise and gifted governors and its fair share of flawed ones. All have sought and received public approval for some of their actions, and all have had other actions rejected by the public. These political biographies tell of governors exhibiting wisdom and generosity of spirit under harsh circumstances. They also chronicle how these public servants reacted politically and personally to both fortune and misfortune. The masses of people of the state have been affected for good and for ill by the shenanigans, as well as by the honorable deeds, of their leaders.

This study of Alabama's governors provides a much needed overview of Alabama's political experience and, within that grid, its social, economic, and cultural experience. Through the lives, words, and deeds of its chief executives, one gains a real sense of the state's history—not just what happened but, more important, why it happened. This book fills a void in the literature of Alabama's history, and it is a fascinating read.

Margaret Armbrester and Sam Webb are to be congratulated for gathering the most gifted researchers of the Alabama scene to write about the lives and actions of the state's governors. The editors have harmonized the variety of participating voices, producing a highly readable volume that is a useful reference for information about individual governors and an important resource to students of Alabama history. There is much to learn much from this superb account.

ALBERT PRESTON BREWER
Forty-ninth Governor of the State of Alabama, 1968–1971,
and Distinguished Professor of Law and Government,
Cumberland School of Law, Samford University

ACKNOWLEDGMENTS

In producing this book, we became indebted to a host of people, many obvious and others less apparent. Our essayists, leading scholars in the area of southern history and political science, provided us with dense, well-researched, and interestingly told stories about the administrations of Alabama's five territorial governors and its fifty-four state governors. Their task was not easy, and our gratitude to them for joining us in this project is boundless.

We are also indebted to Nicole Mitchell, director of the University of Alabama Press, who recognized the need for this work, encouraged it, and exercised infinite patience throughout the editing and publishing process.

Because we wanted to express our appreciation to our essayists by offering them a small honorarium and because we also wanted to include features in the book that neither we nor an academic press could underwrite, we approached the Comer Foundation for funding. Located in Sylacauga, Alabama, and established by the family of former governor Braxton Bragg Comer, the foundation regularly supports the arts and humanities. We gratefully acknowledge the foundation's enormous contribution to this project, which was provided with absolutely no stipulations or restrictions.

Former governor Albert Preston Brewer graciously agreed to provide the foreword. Respected for his lifetime of service to the state, this good man took the office of governor of Alabama under difficult circumstances and served the state with dignity and intelligence. Governor Brewer is the author of numerous essays and articles on Alabama history and law and is presently Distinguished Professor of Law and History at the Cumberland School of Law at Samford University. He continues to be actively involved in the public affairs of the state. We deeply appreciate his participation and are honored by his involvement in this work.

Dr. Tennant S. McWilliams, dean of the School of Social and Behavioral Sciences at the University of Alabama at Birmingham (UAB), and Dr. Raymond A. Mohl, chair of the UAB Department of History, encouraged this project. The department's administrative assistant, Debra Givens, provided us support with her usual competence and good sense. Lindsey Humphries and Mary Ashley were helpful in moving our copying and mailing needs to the finish line. Our sincere thanks also go to Howard Fox, Kurt Kinbacher, and Jeremy Soileau, graduate assistants in the UAB Department of History, who provided excellent research and editing services.

Finally, we are deeply indebted to our spouses for their support. The process of producing this book took longer than we originally anticipated, and our mates endured our carping and complaining with grace. Thank you, Ann and Rodger. We owe you.

POLITICAL MAPS *of Alabama*

An intrastate geographic division played a major role in Alabama's politics from the antebellum period to the middle of the twentieth century. The Black Belt, where the state's largest plantation owners and a majority of its black population lived, usually differed in its choices of candidates from north Alabama's hill country and southeast Alabama's Wiregrass region. This was particularly true in controversial elections where the issues were relatively clear.

The hill and Wiregrass regions were home to the state's small white farmers, referred to in many texts as "yeomen." These yeomen were fiercely independent people who resented the power of the Black Belt planters, opposed special privileges for the wealthy, and voted for candidates who championed the common white man. In the nineteenth century they were Jacksonian Democrats and Populists, and in the twentieth century they supported candidates most closely identified with those at the lower end of the economic scale.

The first three maps demonstrate the extraordinary continuity of that north-south political division in the 1855, 1892, and 1946 Alabama gubernatorial elections. The fourth map, from the results of the 1990 election, suggests that as the state's economy moved away from agriculture and became more industrial, the post-1960s political scenery changed, dividing along urban and rural lines rather than north-south.

Map 1 reflects the areas of strongest support for Alabama's most obstinate Jacksonian Democrat, John A. Winston, in the 1855 general election. Map 2 reveals the areas where the populist Reuben Kolb won majorities over his Democratic opponent in 1892. Map 3 points out areas where the neopopulist Democrat James E. Folsom won his largest majorities in the 1946 Democratic primary runoff. Map 4 includes interstate highway 65, which runs the full length of the state. Readers will note the unusual support for Republican candidate Guy Hunt in 1990 in the areas nearest to I-65, which are more heavily urban and industrial, and the strength of his opponent, Paul Hubbert, as you move away from I-65.

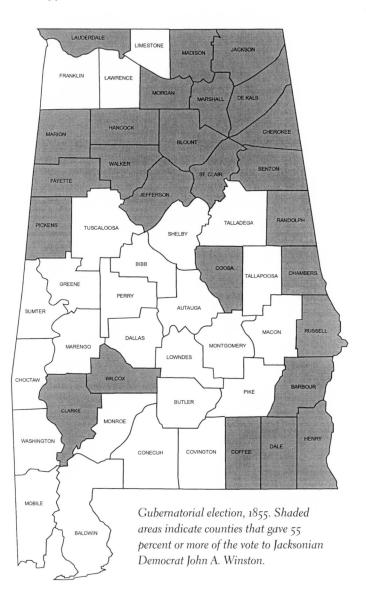

Gubernatorial election, 1855. Shaded areas indicate counties that gave 55 percent or more of the vote to Jacksonian Democrat John A. Winston.

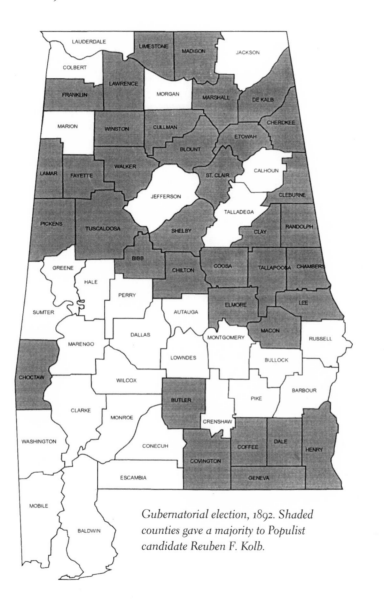

Gubernatorial election, 1892. Shaded counties gave a majority to Populist candidate Reuben F. Kolb.

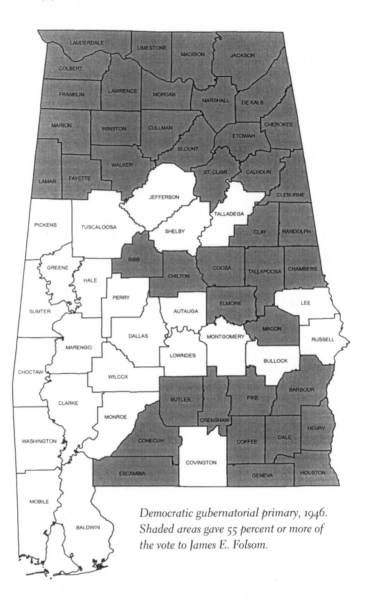

xvi
◇

Democratic gubernatorial primary, 1946.
Shaded areas gave 55 percent or more of
the vote to James E. Folsom.

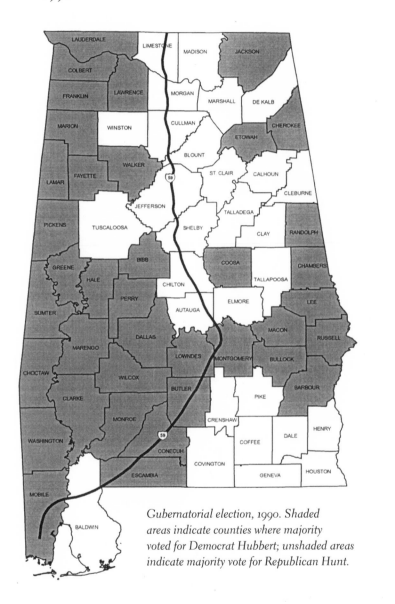

Gubernatorial election, 1990. Shaded areas indicate counties where majority voted for Democrat Hubbert; unshaded areas indicate majority vote for Republican Hunt.

ALABAMA GOVERNORS

INTRODUCTION

The easiest way to explain the need for a political history of Alabama's governors is to reflect upon the impact of their actions or failures to act. The influence of post-Reconstruction governors who returned Alabama to white supremacy or the demagoguery of later segregationist governors such as George Wallace quickly come to mind. But it may give readers a better sense of the importance of what a governor does or does not do to recall one incident in the career of a man whom many historians remember fondly.

On Monday afternoon, February 6, 1956, Alabama governor James Elisha Folsom and a group of friends sailed contentedly on the state's yacht in the Gulf of Mexico near Mobile. They drank and fished with carefree abandon even though the governor knew that a potential crisis threatened the state. While the yacht drifted, a dramatic set of events was unfolding at the University of Alabama in Tuscaloosa. Folsom knew that the first attempt to integrate the university racially in accord with the 1954 U.S. Supreme Court decision in *Brown v. Board of Education* had been set in motion with the registration of a black woman named Autherine Lucy for the 1956 spring term. In the days leading up to actual integration, school officials sought cooperation from the governor, who expressed a willingness to enforce the law and thus avoid mob rule. Yet on the day he should have been available to carry out this duty, he disappeared into the gulf and took no action to avoid trouble.

On that Monday in Tuscaloosa, word spread that Lucy was attending classes. Hundreds of students and as many other whites from the surrounding community gathered near the university administration building and became a screaming, violent mob. They threatened and pursued university officials and blacks who happened to appear on campus. With no leadership or action provided by the governor, administrators feared for Lucy's safety and whisked her off campus. Fearful of escalating violence and unwilling to uphold the *Brown* decision, the university's board of trustees expelled the young woman from school.

The second attempt to integrate the University of Alabama succeeded in 1963 but only after President Kennedy sent in a federalized Alabama National Guard unit to insure success and national television cameras appeared on campus to provide the publicity that fueled the national political career of

Governor George C. Wallace. None of the 1963 events would have been necessary if Folsom had acted decisively. If he had actively supported the peaceful integration of Alabama's schools during his second term in office (1955–59), the burning political issue that dominated Alabama politics from then until the 1970s might have been diffused.

People unfamiliar with Folsom might conclude that he was just another southern bigot, fundamentally no different from Wallace, and that his failure to act on that February day was to be expected. But Folsom was no racist. No Alabama public official since Reconstruction had shown more sympathy for the plight of black Alabamians, and none did more to encourage their uprising during the 1950s. The governor appointed registrars willing to put black citizens on the voter rolls, spoke out for racial tolerance, refused to sign legislative acts and resolutions that defied the Supreme Court, and privately assisted the leaders of the Montgomery bus boycott. He was a spokesman for the downtrodden and the opponent of special privilege, but when confronted with this opportunity to extend equal rights, he was unavailable. His inaction was a failure of judgment and personal weakness that portended ominous future possibilities. The English philosopher Sir Isaiah Berlin writes that it is an "indispensable ingredient of good political judgement" for politicians to understand that "the tremors" they set off "sometimes run through the entire depth of our society; levels to which we pay no conscious attention are stirred, and all kinds of unintended results ensue." Certainly, we in Alabama wonder what a governor determined to enforce the law and see simple human justice done might have spared us.

Once a person is elected or appointed to public office there is an automatic juxtaposition of power and responsibility that is at the heart of our national civic culture, and the story of Folsom and the Autherine Lucy crisis is just one in a long line of dramatic incidents in which Alabama's governors failed to act responsibly. There have also been times in which governors have acted so decisively, forcefully, and shrewdly that the public good has been served. When Governor Benjamin M. Miller (1931–35) fought to create the state's first income tax law during the depths of the Great Depression, he created great consternation but saved the state's school system and other public services from destruction. Today's governor and those who follow him would do well to remember the extraordinary consequences of their public behavior.

Recognizing the broad effect of the state's governors on Alabama, we often found ourselves needing an accessible, up-to-date, and easy-to-use source that provided us with accurate information about their administrations. We envisioned a work that would be useful not only to academics but also to students and teachers in secondary schools and university settings, local historians, patrons of local libraries, journalists, and others. We invited the leading historians and political scientists of the state to write essays on each of Alabama's governors. They gratified us with their enthusiastic responses. We provided our contributors with a brief outline of elements to include and asked them to concentrate on their subject's years as governor rather than on the biographical or family data normally available in other published books and encyclopedias.

With the excellent work of the contributors in hand, we began the editing process. Issues of selection and rejection of material, of objectivity and interpretation, of completeness, of including necessary factual details while maintaining an interesting and readable document—all of these concerns and others were in our minds as we did our work. The reader will find a small amount of repetition from essay to essay because we wanted each one to stand alone; but, together, they provide a unified history of the state. The essays are scholarly, and each contributor provided a bibliography of references on his or her subject. The editors furnished a selected bibliography of the standard works on Alabama's political past.

The state's political experience has sometimes been bizarre, occasionally wonderful, and never dull. Several of the state's governors fought duels; one killed his wife's lover; one at age thirty-nine married a sixteen-year-old; another barricaded himself in his administrative office and refused to give it up when voters failed to reelect him; one (a Yale alumnus) married his first cousin and was an officer in the Ku Klux Klan; at least one was a chronic drunk; and one was elected first as a Democrat and then as a Republican. All but one of Alabama's governors has been Protestant; one entered state politics when his father was assassinated; two sets of governors were father and son; one was a professional football player; one was only five feet, one inch in height and another six feet, eight inches. Several died in office; one was removed from office after a felony conviction.

Although the central focus of the essayists is on the public policy decisions of the men and one woman who governed our state, they recognized that in order to understand many of our governors they needed to examine and discuss the campaigns and elections that sent the officials to the capital. The ideology expressed on the stump, the geographic areas of the state that supported or opposed candidates (see the maps on pages xiv–xvii), the interest groups that participated in the campaigns, and the emotions and demands of the particular times in which the candidates ran affected and informed gubernatorial administrations. The authors tell us something about who these officials were, the important decisions they made, the issues that dominated their time in office, and the policy initiatives they took. The contributors also review the governors' accomplishments and failures and examine, in the brief space available, the complex factors that led to their action or inaction.

Antebellum nineteenth-century state government was small, and the areas in which governors could make policy were constricted. The 1901 constitution centered enormous political power in Montgomery, and those who served during the twentieth century enjoyed longer terms and enhanced influence. Thus, the essays on antebellum governors are usually shorter than those on some of the later chief executives. The length of the essays says nothing about the personal feelings or biases of the editors or authors toward the subjects. Additional space is naturally given to governors who served more than one term, and longer pieces are accorded those whose policies had a greater impact on the state's people.

The editors take full responsibility for decisions that may have created weaknesses in this work. The essayists deserve full credit for the book's strengths.

I

Territorial and Early
Statehood, 1798–1847

In 1798 America's western boundary extended only to the Mississippi River, and Spain still held a foothold in the southern part of what became the states of Mississippi and Alabama. When Congress created the Mississippi Territory out of lands in the Old Southwest, the United States was a mere twenty-two years old with a recently formed constitutional government. Arguments at the 1787 constitutional convention exposed issues that soon became crises in Alabama's experience: federal versus state authority, banking and currency, slavery, taxation, and tariffs.

Between 1815 and 1850 thousands of people left the states of Virginia, North Carolina, South Carolina, Tennessee, and Georgia for Alabama. Few were aristocrats; most strongly resembled the settlers William Faulkner described as entering the state of Mississippi at about the same time:

They brought no slaves and no Phyfe and Chippendale highboys, indeed, what they did bring most of them could (and did) carry in their hands. They took up land and built one- and two-room cabins and never painted them, and married one another and produced children. . . . They supported their own churches and schools, they married and committed infrequent adulteries and more frequent homicides among themselves and were their own courts, judges, and executioners. They were Protestants and Democrats and prolific. (Quoted in Cleanth Brooks, William Faulkner: The Yoknapatawpha Country)

By 1819, when Alabama became a state, the United States had won its second war of independence and was a maturing nation enjoying a political era of "good feelings." Over the first three decades of Alabama's statehood, Indians were removed from the area, national and state banking systems were created and destroyed, roads remained primitive, railroads were almost unknown in Alabama, and slavery was becoming the topic of greatest interest to the citizens of the state.

The Territorial Governors of the Alabama Area, 1798–1819

KIT CARSON CARTER III

A T THE end of the American Revolution, Alabama's neighbor to the east, like many of the older colonies, held colonial claims that reached to the Mississippi River. Georgia's territory ostensibly spanned all of present-day Mississippi and Alabama except for the Mobile area below the thirty-first parallel, which was held by Spain. Much of this Old Southwest region, however, was also claimed by indigenous Indian nations and the new United States government. The constant intrigue among these interests made exercising actual jurisdiction over the land by the United States difficult, if not impossible. Georgia's attempts to sell much of its alleged territory through the Yazoo deals of 1789 and 1795 were rife with fraud and threatened serious conflict with the federal government. Spain's claim above the thirty-first parallel, but not the Spanish presence, was eliminated by the Pinckney Treaty of 1795. During the first third of the nineteenth century, most of the Indian lands in the territory (and then states) were absorbed by the United States by treaty or conquest.

7
◇

By congressional act on April 7, 1798, the United States formed the Mississippi Territory out of the present-day states of Mississippi and Alabama above the thirty-first parallel. Georgia's land claims were yet to be purchased by the federal government, and the high-handed machinations of Georgia land speculators, especially in light of the Yazoo frauds, resulted in considerable hostility toward anyone from that state being appointed to positions of power. As a result, George Mathews, a Georgia land speculator and President John Adams's first appointee to be governor of the new territory, met with such opposition in the seat of government at Natchez that he was quickly removed. Until a new appointment could be made, there was military rule under General James Wilkinson, whose federal troops occupied the area for four months.

The first Mississippi territorial governor actually to hold office was Winthrop Sargent of Gloucester, Massachusetts. Born on May 1, 1753, he became a New England Federalist of strong convictions. Sargent held two degrees from Harvard and served with distinction as an officer in major battles of the revolutionary war. Despite, or perhaps because of, his distinguished career during America's revolution, this imperious man was plagued with a haughty demeanor, poor health, and harsh and intolerant ways toward the rustic Jeffersonian Republicans of the Old Southwest. His difficulties in governing the new territory began when opposition gathered against his imposed law code of 1799. The code was to function as a kind of governing directive until the territory had enough voters to elect a legislature. That same year, Sargent by executive fiat divided the Natchez district into Adams (which included Natchez proper), Pickering, and Washington Counties, a decision that also met opposition.

Sargent   Sargent was strongly attached to the Natchez community and remained in the area at his plantation, Gloucester, named for his place of birth, after his dismissal by newly elected president Thomas Jefferson in 1801. One personal bright spot of his term as territorial governor was his marriage in 1798 to Mary McIntosh Williams, a wealthy young widow. This union produced a son, William Fitz Winthrop Sargent. Private citizen Winthrop Sargent prospered and helped to organize the Bank of Mississippi at Natchez. He died in 1820 and was buried at his plantation.

John Steele, a native of Virginia and a revolutionary war veteran, was secretary of the Mississippi Territory and acted as its governor during Sargent's many trips out of the frontier area. Steele served as chief executive from April 1801 until the arrival of Jefferson's new appointee, William C. C. Claiborne, in November.

William Charles Cole Claiborne was born in Sussex County, Virginia, in August 1775. Educated at the Richmond Academy and at William and Mary College, at the age of sixteen he read law while serving as a clerk in the United States House of Representatives. Subsequently he was admitted to the Virginia bar and later moved to Nashville, Tennessee, to practice law. Governor John Sevier appointed him judge in the Tennessee territorial supreme court, and in 1796 Claiborne helped to frame the state constitution of Tennessee. In 1797, despite the fact that he was not yet twenty-five years old and thus did not meet the

Claiborne   age requirement mandated by the Constitution, Claiborne was elected to Congress, where he served until 1801.

Claiborne was only twenty-six when Jefferson appointed him governor of the Mississippi Territory. The energetic young governor organized a militia and used it to reduce the incidences of robbery along the Natchez Trace, which by 1800 was a major route into and through the territory. He moved the territorial capitol from Natchez to the neighboring village six miles north at Washington, where he also founded Jefferson College. He established a mail route along the trace and formally incorporated the town of Natchez, creating for it a mayor's court with extensive jurisdiction.

Claiborne presided over negotiations for a treaty with the Choctaws, securing for the United States the tribe's earlier cessions of lands to the British, which included portions of what became southwest Alabama. The treaty, solemnized in 1802 at Fort Confederation, was signed for the United States by General James Wilkinson and for the Choctaws by Pushmataha. The Alabama portion of the territory, inhabited almost entirely by Indians, held little interest for the Natchez government and even less following the Louisiana Purchase of 1803.

President Jefferson chose Governor Claiborne and General Wilkinson to receive the formal transfer of the Louisiana Territory from the French on December 20, 1803. While continuing to serve as governor of the Mississippi Territory, Claiborne also served as governor-general of Louisiana until a permanent government was established. On October 2, 1804, Jefferson appointed him governor of the Territory of Orleans, and he served in that capacity until 1812, when he became governor of the state of Louisiana. During his second term as governor of Louisiana, Claiborne participated in Andrew Jackson's 1815 defense of New Orleans against the British. In 1817, the thrice married Claiborne was elected to the United States Senate but never served. He died in New Orleans on November 3, 1817, at age forty-two and was buried in Metairie Cemetery.

During Governor Claiborne's absences from the Mississippi Territory, the capable secretary of the territory, Cato West, functioned as acting governor and indeed governor *ad interim*. West, a native of Fairfax, Virginia, migrated to Mississippi by way of Georgia and helped to lead the opposition to Governor Sargent. As acting governor from 1803 to 1805, West was instrumental in opening a land office at Washington Town in present-day Alabama, and he pushed for a more comprehensive slave code. West also secured an act that legalized the marriages of those territorial citizens whose unions had not enjoyed the benefit of licensed clergy or government officials.

Jefferson finally appointed Robert Williams to be Claiborne's successor as governor of the Mississippi Territory in 1805. Born in Prince Edward County, Virginia, in 1768, he was taken by his parents to North Carolina at an early age. Williams grew up in Nottingham County, read law, and began its practice. He married Elizabeth Winston, served in the North Carolina Senate, and was elected to the U.S. House of Representatives, where he served from 1797 to 1802. In 1802 he and Thomas Rodney of Delaware were appointed commissioners to ascertain the rights of land claimants in the Mississippi Territory west of the Pearl River. This position led to his appointment to the governorship.

Williams

During Williams's tenure as governor, which lasted from March 1805 to March 1809, former vice president Aaron Burr was accused of conspiring to establish an independent government in the southwest United States by separating Kentucky and perhaps the Mississippi Territory from the United States and joining them with New Spain (Mexico and much of the western United States). In 1807 Burr, the brilliant and adventurous son and grandson of presidents of the College of Princeton, was arrested in the south Alabama (east Mississippi Territory) community of Wakefield near present-day McIntosh in Washington County. He was held for trial at Fort Stoddert and was later acquitted.

In an act of great importance to the Alabama portion of the Mississippi Territory, President Jefferson in 1804 appointed Harry Toulmin to be U.S. judge of what formally became known as the Tombigbee District of the huge Washington County. Toulmin had previously served as president of Transylvania University in Lexington, Kentucky, and as secretary of state of Kentucky. He is remembered as the compiler of Mississippi's territorial laws in 1806 and for his similar work later in codifying the laws of the infant state of Alabama in 1823.

In 1808 Williams received lands in the Tennessee Valley from the Chickasaws and Cherokees from which Madison County was created. By 1810 this large county, which held the blossoming settlement of Huntsville, contained half the population of the Mississippi Territory. In the southern part of the territory, another grant from the Choctaws provided a narrow band of land that connected the Bigbee and Natchez Districts. In the eastern portion of the territory, the Federal Military Road—the old Three-Chopped-Way, shuttled settlers through Creek territory into the Alabama River valley. The population of the Mississippi Territory continued to grow, particularly in the Bigbee District in present southwest Alabama. As the first decade of the nineteenth century drew to a close, territorial population totaled 40,532. Constant conflicts over land claims and Williams's frequent extended visits back to North Carolina made him an unpopular chief executive and forced his resignation on March 3, 1809. Williams died on January 25, 1836, with many people still convinced that he was a co-conspirator in the Burr plot.

The last appointee to the governorship of the Mississippi Territory was David Holmes, who was born in York County, Pennsylvania, on March 10, 1769. Holmes's family moved to Winchester, Virginia, where David clerked in his father's store until taking up the study of law. He practiced law first in Harrisburg, Pennsylvania, and later in Virginia, where he served as a congressman from 1797 to 1809. On March 1, 1809, he was appointed to the governorship of the Mississippi Territory by President James Madison. Late in that same year Governor Holmes signed an act creating Baldwin County in the Alabama area from land taken from the southern part of Washington County. That act reflected the growing population of white settlers who were arriving in that general location on foot, by boat, on horses, mules, and wagons. The settlers met a thriving culture of indigenous Indians, particularly Creeks, who would be reckoned with in some manner by this immigrant population.

The outbreak of a second war with England in 1812 with its inclusive Creek Indian War produced a violent time during Holmes's administration. Spain surrendered Mobile to American military forces in 1813, and the lower portions of Alabama and Mississippi were added to the United States as a result of the war. Andrew Jackson received a large cession of land from the defeated Creeks in 1814, causing hordes of white settlers to move into the central and southeastern portions of eastern Mississippi. Montgomery, first called New Philadelphia and then Alabama Town, gained its first settler, Arthur Moore, in 1814. A treaty negotiated with the Choctaws in 1816 at Fort Tombecbe meant

Holmes

that almost all of present-day Alabama was opened to settlement. Cherokees held a small amount of land in the lower Tennessee Valley; Creeks maintained an area east of the Coosa River; and Choctaws held small parcels of land in the Fort Tombecbe area.

By 1820 the Mississippi Territory contained just under 220,000 settlers, an amazing leap in population matched in American history only by the rush to California two decades later. The Alabama half of the Mississippi Territory, which persistently had urged division from its western counterpart, now more aggressively moved for creation of a separate government. This eastern population had few ties with the Natchez-based government, and it was too distant from them, as war with the Creeks had so clearly demonstrated.

In early March 1817, Congress passed legislation creating the state of Mississippi and a separate territory of Alabama. Alabama's name was chosen from the main river in its central area. The popular and capable Holmes was elected the first governor of the state of Mississippi, and William Wyatt Bibb, former U.S. senator from Georgia, was appointed by President James Monroe to be the one and only governor of the Alabama Territory. The new territory's legislature met temporarily at St. Stephens on the lower Tombigbee River. Existing Mississippi officers, laws, and institutions remained in effect. The territorial legislature met only twice during Alabama's short, two-year existence as a separate territory—both times in 1818.

William Wyatt Bibb was born in Virginia on October 2, 1781, but spent all but three years of his life in Georgia. Bibb's term as territorial governor was in many ways successful. Elections were called, land was surveyed and divided, relations with Indian populations were formalized, and the immigrant population grew to almost 100,000. Two-thirds of these new settlers were white, and one-third were black. Between 1816 and 1818, Montgomery, Limestone,

Lauderdale, Clarke, Tuscaloosa, Shelby, Dallas, Cahaba (later Bibb), St. Clair, and numerous other counties were created.

During the two territorial sessions held before Alabama joined the Union, actions were taken that affected Alabama's early state history. Bibb objected to Mississippi's proposal that Congress move its eastern boundary to a line marked by the Tombigbee and Mobile Rivers. The Alabama assembly added its objections, and the motion was defeated in Congress. Bibb oversaw the territorial assembly's repeal of the Mississippi Usury Act, recommended chartering a state university, advocated increased road and bridge construction, and called for improved water transportation. In a highly controversial move he used his authority to reject a legislative commission recommendation to place the capital of the state at Tuscaloosa, a location that was convenient to north Alabama legislators. Rather, he pushed through the selection of Cahawba as the site for a "permanent" capital, a location unfriendly to north Alabama legislators. Bibb's tenure as territorial governor raised thorny issues of sectionalism between north and south Alabama and between rich and poor populations of the territory over this and equally contentious banking issues.

In 1819 Congress passed enabling legislation to allow Alabama to hold a constitutional convention as a preliminary step to entering the Union as a state. A convention met at Huntsville on July 5, 1819, and by August 2 the delegates approved a constitution for the state of Alabama. Territorial governor William Wyatt Bibb was elected the first governor of the state of Alabama, which was admitted to the Union as its twenty-second state by an act approved by Congress on December 14, 1819.

References

Carter, Clarence E., ed. *Territorial Papers of the United States.* Washington: U.S. Government Printing Office, 1938.

Claiborne, John F. H. *Mississippi as a Province, Territory and State, with Biographical Notices of Eminent Citizens.* 1880. Reprint, Baton Rouge: Louisiana State University Press, 1964.

Hamilton, Peter J. *Colonial Mobile.* 1910. Reprint, University: University of Alabama Press, 1976.

Rowland, Dunbar, and Albert Godfrey Sanders, eds. *Mississippi Provincial Archives, 1701–1729, French Dominion.* 5 vols. Jackson: Mississippi Department of Archives and History, 1929.

William Wyatt Bibb, 1819–1820, and Thomas Bibb, 1820–1821

DANIEL S. DUPRE

L IKE thousands of other restless migrants in the early nineteenth century, Alabama's first two governors came to the frontier seeking new opportunities for personal advancement. The successes of William Wyatt Bibb (1781–1820) and Thomas Bibb (1784–1838), however, depended heavily on connections they forged in the more stable and advanced environment of Georgia. The impulse to resettle may have been instilled in the brothers early in life when the Bibb family left Amelia County, Virginia, where Bibb was born on October 2, 1781, to start anew in Elbert County, Georgia. Their father, Captain William Bibb, was an officer in the revolutionary army and a member of the Virginia legislature. Captain Bibb and his family probably migrated to Georgia in 1784 with a large number of Virginians who followed General George Mathews, hero of the Battle of Brandywine. Most of the general's followers were families of veterans like himself who took advantage of the new nation's offer of land bounties to former soldiers. They established tobacco farms on the rich lands around the confluence of the Broad and Savannah Rivers in northeastern Georgia. The Bibbs are recorded as one of the earliest pioneer families in Elbert County.

Captain Bibb died in 1796, leaving his widow to care for eight children. The family was not left destitute, and both William, the oldest, and his younger brother Thomas were able to receive educations. After attending William and Mary College for two years and then receiving his medical degree from the University of Pennsylvania in 1801, William returned to Petersburg, the bustling commercial center of Elbert County, Georgia, to practice medicine.

William Bibb

Politics, not doctoring, captured William Bibb's attention, and his ambition extended beyond Petersburg. In 1802 at the age of twenty-one, he was elected to the Georgia state legislature, where he served four years. The voters of the Broad River region of Georgia rewarded that service by electing him to Congress in 1806, though he barely met the age requirement. After a stint of six years in the House of Representatives, where he proved a consistent supporter of President James Madison, Bibb joined his Petersburg neighbor, Charles Tait, in the United States Senate. Bibb was only thirty-two years old.

What accounts for Bibb's rapid rise to power? One nineteenth-century historian noted William Bibb's "dignified but easy bearing" and suggested that "his uniform courtesy and kindness . . . won the respect of all classes." He was a skillful politician, able to maintain both an aura of statesmanship and a relaxed rapport with the voters. Still, the alliances he forged with prominent Georgians such as Tait and Senator William H. Crawford certainly helped Bibb's political career. He was popular enough for a Georgia county to be named for him. That popularity evaporated in the spring of 1816 when Bibb joined a majority of his fellow congressmen in passing the Salary Act, which effectively doubled congressional pay. This unpopular action caused Bibb to lose his bid for reelection that fall to George M. Troup. He resigned his Senate seat in humiliation in the fall of 1816.

With his political future in Georgia looking dim, Bibb turned his attention westward. His brother Thomas had already migrated to north Alabama in 1811, and William's Georgia connections allowed him to follow. When the Alabama Territory was separated from Mississippi in 1817, President James Monroe, on the advice of Secretary of Treasury William Crawford, appointed William Bibb territorial governor. That April, William and his wife, Mary Freeman, joined thousands of others who were struck by "Alabama land fever." The Bibbs traveled to Alabama to settle briefly at the territorial capital of St. Stephens on the Tombigbee River.

Governor Bibb's Georgia roots not only linked him to powerful friends in the federal government but also provided an extensive political base in Alabama itself. Former Petersburg neighbors, including his brother Thomas, were prospering in the Tennessee Valley through land speculation, planting, commerce, and their creation of the Planters and Merchants Bank of Huntsville. Less well-to-do settlers in north Alabama designated that Broad River group the "Royal Party." A second migratory stream led more Georgians into the Black Belt regions of central Alabama. The alliance between those two groups of Georgia settlers, working in concert with William Crawford and other federal officers to guide Alabama to statehood in 1819, gave William Bibb tremendous clout in his new home.

Although William Bibb created a political base that briefly transcended sectional divisions, a critical reality confronted the new governor. A mountain barrier isolated the Tennessee Valley, the wealthiest and most populated region at that time, from the southern portion of the state, which benefited from the river systems that flowed south into Mobile Bay. Bibb addressed this problem in his annual message to the Alabama Territory general assembly in February

14
◇

1818 when he called for investments in transportation improvements that would not only facilitate the flow of goods and people but also bind together divided regions. He recognized that economic prosperity and political stability required such an effort.

But Governor Bibb's own high-handed actions in selecting a capital for the new state of Alabama exacerbated the very sectional tensions he sought to ease and eroded his political popularity. A commission appointed in early 1818 by the territorial legislature to determine the capital's location chose Tuscaloosa, a site far enough north on the Black Warrior River to make it accessible to the residents of the Tennessee Valley. Bibb overrode that decision in favor of a location to the south, where the Cahawba flowed into the Alabama River. Flexing his political muscle in Washington, Bibb arranged a federal land grant in that area and promised, in his message to the stunned assembly in November 1818, that the new town of Cahawba would "vie with the largest inland towns in the Country" in population and prosperity.

William Bibb's decision to buck the legislative commission generated intense resentment, especially in the Tennessee Valley. Marmaduke Williams of Tuscaloosa challenged Bibb's claim to the governor's office of the new state of Alabama, campaigning through the summer of 1819 almost solely on the Cahawba issue. Thomas Bibb's popularity in northern Alabama helped to deflect the challenger's complaints against his brother, and friends elsewhere reminded voters of William Bibb's useful political connections in the federal government and the role played by the Georgia faction in Alabama's statehood. In the September elections, Bibb narrowly defeated Williams by a vote of 8,342 to 7,140.

The office claimed by Bibb late in 1819 afforded him less power than he had enjoyed as territorial governor. Alabama's constitution limited the state's governors to two, two-year terms and allowed the legislative branch to override gubernatorial vetoes with a simple majority vote. The assembly also elected state judges and the heads of executive departments. The constitutional convention delegates who voted for those general restrictions also inserted in the document a more pointed rejoinder to Bibb's autocratic decision on the capital. Although they accepted Cahawba, they granted the assembly the power to select a permanent seat of government in 1825 without the involvement of the governor.

In his message to the first meeting of Alabama's state legislature, Bibb called for support for education and improved transportation. The legislature enacted penalties for dueling and for helping slaves to escape and reestablished a limit on usury rates in the state. Weakened by tuberculosis even before the election, Bibb devoted much of his limited energies to solidifying Cahawba's claim to the government by creating a flourishing capital city on the banks of the Alabama River. When the legislature appropriated a mere $10,000 for the construction of a capitol building, enough for only a temporary structure, Bibb persevered, collecting money from the public auctioning of lots in Cahawba into a substantial building fund. Construction began in 1820, but Governor Bibb did not live to see the completion of the capitol for which he had fought so ardently. While riding near his plantation in Autauga County, he was thrown from his horse, bruising his head and kidney. He spent much of early 1820 bedridden and in "as much pain . . . as ever fell to the lot of any man." William Bibb died in July 1820 at the age of thirty-nine, leaving behind his wife and two children. Legislators who convened in the unfinished state house honored the man by changing the name of Cahawba County to Bibb County.

The 1819 constitution provided that a governor who was no longer able to serve was to be replaced by the president of the state senate, which meant that William Wyatt Bibb's brother Thomas became governor of Alabama in 1820. Although Thomas Bibb had dabbled in politics since his arrival in Alabama in 1811 and had served as a delegate to the constitutional convention and in the state senate, for the most part this Bibb had concentrated on his own personal economic affairs. Associates agreed that Thomas did not have his brother's political skills, and most legislators viewed him as a caretaker governor, which limited his impact on several pressing issues. Legislators from north and south Alabama, for example, were deeply divided over whether to pass an apportionment bill to reallocate seats in the legislature before the state census was completed, a decision fraught with implications for the vote in 1825 on the location of the state capital.

Thomas Bibb

Economic hardship that came in the wake of the Panic of 1819 also contributed to political pressures. Popular resentment toward private banks exacerbated antagonism toward Georgians who controlled many of the banks and enjoyed large profits from the temporarily high usury rates made possible by Bibb's support for repeal of the Mississippi Usury Act. When the privately owned banks offered depreciated bank notes in lieu of suspended specie payments, popular support for the creation of a state bank to alleviate the hard times grew even more. Thomas Bibb outlined a plan for the creation of a state banking institution but lacked the political will or power to pursue that goal to fruition. He refused to run for election in 1821, returning instead to Belle Mina, his plantation in Limestone County, where he died in 1838.

As William Wyatt Bibb lay dying in 1820, Charles Tait, his old colleague from Georgia and fellow migrant to Alabama, mused about the future in a letter to Alabama's U.S. senator John Williams Walker. Alabama would "be exposed to great agitation and peril" if Bibb succumbed, Tait believed, but if he lived, the governor's "talents and his conciliatory manners" would "silence the pretensions of little men and promote our general prosperity." What might have happened if Bibb had carried out his term in office? Perhaps the legislature would have resolved its apportionment difficulties and confronted the economic problems of the day under the guidance of a seasoned political leader. But the political culture of Alabama was changing in the years after the Panic of 1819, and economic hardship sharpened resentments. The Georgia faction that afforded William Bibb so much goodwill as Alabama moved into statehood became tainted by its association with private banking misdeeds and land speculation. Had he lived, Bibb almost certainly would have found his Georgia connections to be a political liability by the early 1820s.

References

Abernethy, Thomas Perkins. *The Formative Period in Alabama, 1815–1828.* 2d ed. University: University of Alabama Press, 1965.

Brantley, William H. *Three Capitals: A Book about the First Three Capitals of Alabama: St. Stephens, Huntsville, and Cahawba.* 1947. Reprint, University: University of Alabama Press, 1976.

Brewer, Willis. *Alabama: Her History, Resources, War Record, and Public Men, From 1540 to 1872.* Montgomery: Barrett and Brown, 1872.

McIntosh, John. *The Official History of Elbert County, 1790–1935.* Elberton, Ga.: Stephen Heard Chapter, Daughters of the American Revolution, 1940.

Rogers, William Warren, Robert David Ward, Leah Rawls Atkins, and Wayne Flynt. *Alabama: The History of a Deep South State.* Tuscaloosa: University of Alabama Press, 1994.

17
◇

Israel Pickens, 1821–1825

Daniel S. Dupre

LIKE William Wyatt Bibb, Israel Pickens was an established politician who migrated to Alabama in search of greater opportunities. Born in Mecklenburg County, North Carolina, on January 30, 1780, Israel was the son of Captain Samuel Pickens, a veteran of the American Revolution, and Jane Carrigan Pickens. After first attending a local academy, he studied law at Jefferson College in Pennsylvania. In 1802 Pickens moved to Burke County, in western North Carolina, to practice law and was soon caught up in politics. His election to the state senate in 1808 was a stepping stone to higher office; North Carolina voters sent Pickens to the U.S. House of Representatives in 1811, where he served until 1817. A staunch supporter of President James Madison, Pickens was one of Congress's "War Hawks," an important group of southern

and western politicians who pushed the nation toward military conflict with England in 1812.

Politics and war were not the only things on Pickens's mind during this period; he courted and married Martha Lenoir, the daughter of one of North Carolina's wealthiest men, in 1814. Like countless other residents of the eastern seaboard, he was struck by "Alabama land fever" as cotton prices soared and new fertile lands opened in the Old Southwest in the post–War of 1812 period. He decided not to run for a fourth term to Congress and instead moved to St. Stephens in the spring of 1817 to take a job as register of the land office for

Pickens

Washington County. Wasting no time in establishing himself in his new home, Pickens purchased almost thirty-five hundred acres in southwest Alabama in less than a year and became the first president of the Tombigbee Bank of St. Stephens. Forging alliances with business elites in this burgeoning new community, he proved adept at finances and was instrumental in helping the bank maintain its specie reserves during the Panic of 1819.

18
◇ Despite his economic successes as a planter and financier, Pickens did not forsake politics with his move to Alabama. He returned to public service in 1819 as a delegate to Alabama's constitutional convention. At that time, he was aligned with Governor William Bibb's Georgia faction. But Pickens, sensitive to shifts in the popular mood, began to distance himself from the Georgians in 1820. He built his political fortune in Alabama by mounting a populist challenge to Bibb's political machine. During the boom period that preceded the Panic of 1819, many Alabamians had engaged in various kinds of speculations, and no group was more successful at these questionable actions than the transplanted Georgians of the Tennessee Valley. Associated with the Planters and Merchants Bank of Huntsville, Georgians amassed wealth and power commensurate with their title of the "Royal Party." When prosperity collapsed in 1819 and depression lingered into the 1820s, many Alabamians, struggling to stay afloat in a sea of debt, sought scapegoats for their predicament. None fit the bill so well as the "Royal Party" and its Huntsville bank, which had suspended specie payments during the economic crisis. In north Alabama, popular animosity toward the bank and its supporters tainted the Georgia faction, significantly weakening its power at the very same time as its leader, William Bibb, lay dying. Israel Pickens ran against the Georgians in the 1821 governor's race, defeating Dr. Henry Chambers, a director of the Planters and Merchants Bank, by a vote of 9,616 to 7,129.

Pickens used popular resentment toward the private monied interests of the "Royal Party" to ride into the governorship and crush the supremacy of the Georgia faction. He artfully used this resentment to push through the creation of Alabama's state bank, his greatest achievement. Although public support for such an institution was growing in the wake of the panic, Pickens still had to demonstrate great skill and patience in laying the groundwork for state involvement in the economy. He first countered a challenge by the legislative friends of the Planters and Merchants Bank, vetoing a bill in 1821 that would have committed substantial public funds to a state institution dominated by private banks.

In his message to the assembly the following year, Governor Pickens argued that the charter of a Bank of Alabama had to give the state control over its direction commensurate with its interest in invested capital. Pickens also went on the offensive against the Planters and Merchants Bank that year, although he moved cautiously. Because much of the economic activity of the state depended on the notes of that bank, destroying it before establishing a state-controlled substitute would prove economically and politically unsound. Pickens put pressure on the Huntsville bank by publicly announcing that he had ordered a court investigation into whether its suspension of specie payments to note holders violated the bank's charter. Supporters of the Planters and Merchants Bank in the legislature suddenly were willing to deal with the governor and declared that the bank would resume specie payments by the end of 1823 or voluntarily forfeit its charter. Pickens had achieved what he wanted; north Alabama would have a circulating currency for a year, and the Huntsville bank had essentially ratified the instrument of its own death. It never fully resumed specie payments and lost its charter early in 1825.

In 1823 Pickens again defeated Chambers while his allies gained control of both houses of the legislature. Those political fortunes were offset by personal tragedy when Pickens's wife and infant son died soon after the election. He dealt with his grief through hard work, redoubling his efforts to establish the state bank. With the "Royal Party" chastened by the election outcome, his bank legislation passed in 1823, and the Bank of Alabama opened in 1824. The bank had an initial capitalization of more than $200,000 and was to be managed by a president and board of directors elected annually by the legislature.

But Pickens actually had to amass the money needed to open the bank. He convinced the legislature in his first term to invest $100,000 of funds set aside for a state university. Pickens looked forward to the establishment of the University of Alabama, but the bank took first priority. He skillfully delayed the selection of a campus site and won the approval of the university's board of directors to invest the pledged funds in the bank rather than in the construction of classroom buildings. The rest of the bank's money came from state bonds sold on the New

York market and from the sale of federal land grants reserved for financing transportation improvements in Alabama. The governor's brother, Andrew Pickens, became the first president of the state bank. Although the Bank of Alabama later lost the confidence of the people and collapsed under charges of mismanagement during another national depression, its creation in 1824 marked a significant step in the development of state power over economic affairs. For many years its profits paid the cost of running Alabama's state government.

Israel Pickens used popular hostility toward the aristocratic pretensions of the Georgia "Royal Party" to his advantage. He failed, however, to anticipate the overwhelming popularity of Andrew Jackson among the people of Alabama when he supported Jackson's opponent, John Quincy Adams, in the election of 1824. Party alignments had not yet coalesced in this era, and several prominent politicians jockeyed for position in the presidential election, including William Crawford, the national leader of Alabama's Georgia faction. Still, Pickens was smart enough to praise Jackson's recent military exploits in Florida and downplayed his opposition to Old Hickory's presidential ambitions. Thus, Pickens's support of Adams did no real damage to the governor's reputation.

Governor Pickens played host to another famous military hero, the Marquis de Lafayette, who was touring the country in 1825 to the great acclaim of Americans grateful for his support in the Revolution. Lafayette, accompanied by his dog, Quiz, entered Alabama through Creek nation lands and was escorted across the Chattahoochee River by "fifty Indian warriors, who were stripped naked and finely painted." He then proceeded to Montgomery, where he was welcomed by the governor and entertained at a lavish ball. From Montgomery, Lafayette traveled to Cahawba, where he enjoyed another ball and a more informal barbecue, and then he journeyed on to Mobile. Governor Pickens supervised every detail of the visit, from hiring a New Orleans band to play at the ball to selecting the military officers who escorted the old general through the state. Lafayette's visit cost Alabama more than $15,000, and most citizens were pleased that he had honored them with his presence.

Israel Pickens's former opponent, Henry Chambers, died early in 1825 before claiming the Senate seat to which he had been elected. The following year, Pickens's personally chosen successor, Governor John Murphy, granted Pickens the interim appointment as Alabama's junior senator, thus violating the gentleman's agreement that the state's U.S. senators would be chosen from different sections of the state. Pickens's health was poor, and he spent much of the congressional session of 1826 bedridden. Tuberculosis and fevers forced his resignation at the end of the year and led him to Cuba, where he hoped warmer weather would ease his sufferings. Instead, Pickens's condition deteriorated, and he died there on April 24, 1827, leaving behind a daughter and two sons and a legacy as the "father" of many of the foundations of Alabama's young government.

References

Abernethy, Thomas Perkins. *The Formative Period in Alabama, 1815–1828.* 2d ed. University: University of Alabama Press, 1965.

Bailey, Hugh C. "Israel Pickens, Peoples' Politician." *Alabama Review* 17 (1964): 83–101.

Brantley, William H. *Three Capitals: A Book about the First Three Capitals of Alabama: St. Stephens, Huntsville, and Cahawba.* 1947. Reprint, University: University of Alabama Press, 1976.

Dupre, Daniel S. *Transforming the Cotton Frontier: Madison County, Alabama, 1800–1840.* Baton Rouge: Louisiana State University Press, 1997.

Rogers, William Warren, Robert David Ward, Leah Rawls Atkins, and Wayne Flynt. *Alabama: The History of a Deep South State.* Tuscaloosa: University of Alabama Press, 1994.

John Murphy, 1825–1829

Hugh C. Bailey

John Murphy was born in Robeson County, North Carolina, circa 1785 to first-generation Scottish immigrant Neil Murphy. As a child, Murphy moved with his family to South Carolina, where he completed his preparatory education and taught school to earn money for college. He attended South Carolina College in the same class with a future governor of Alabama, John Gayle, and another important antebellum political figure, James Dellet, both of whom later played important roles in Murphy's political career in Alabama. Following his graduation in 1808, Murphy read law, which he never practiced, and for the next ten years he served as clerk of the South Carolina Senate. He was also appointed a trustee of South Carolina College, which later became the University of South Carolina, a position he held from 1808 to 1818.

Murphy

Murphy was married twice, first to Sarah Hails in South Carolina, the mother of his son John Murphy Jr. After her death, he married Sarah Darrington Carter, a Clarke County, Alabama, widow. She bore him several children, including a second son, Duncan Murphy, who spent much of his life in California and served in its legislature. In 1818 Murphy moved to Monroe County in the southern portion of the newly created Alabama Territory. He bought land, began to create his own plantation, and quickly established himself as a man who commanded the respect of his peers. In 1819 he was elected a delegate to the constitutional convention, where he served on the Committee of Fifteen that drafted the constitution. He was elected as one of Monroe County's five members of the House of Representatives in 1820, and in 1822 he was chosen the county's only member of the Alabama Senate.

As an Alabama politician, Murphy quickly aligned himself with Israel Pickens's "popular" party, which opposed the "Royal Party" or Georgia faction. These "royalists," including Governors William Bibb and Thomas Bibb and U.S. senator John Williams Walker, were viewed as advocates of the territorial legislation that permitted the charging of unrestricted interest rates and as supporters of the privately owned and much disliked Planters and Merchants Bank of Huntsville. As a legislator, Murphy endorsed Pickens's efforts to establish a state bank as a means of providing adequate capital for the currency-starved state, and he and Pickens forged a strong alliance.

The dominance of the Pickens forces was so great that Murphy was twice elected governor without opposition in 1825 and 1827. The most important development in his first term was the decision to move the capital from Cahawba to Tuscaloosa. The 1819 Alabama Constitution provided for the first session of the legislature to be held in Huntsville and "all subsequent sessions at the town of Cahawba" until 1825 when legislators could "designate by law . . . the permanent seat of Government" without the need for concurrence by the governor. Understandably, most of the interest in the 1825 election focused on the selection of a site for the capital.

Travel to Cahawba was long and difficult for legislators from north and west Alabama; regular flooding in Cahawba and subsequent fevers gave the advocates of another location strong arguments. The southern site was associated with the arrogant actions of Governor William Wyatt Bibb who had ignored a legislative commission recommendation to place the capital at Tuscaloosa in 1819. Sectional interests were paramount when northern and west-central Alabama legislators gained a narrow ascendancy in the legislature in the 1825 election. Murphy, like Pickens, was a south Alabamian who opposed the move from Cahawba, but as a realist without a veto, he did not fight the effort, and Tuscaloosa was chosen. Cahawba continued to flourish for several decades, but by the late nineteenth century that community had all but vanished.

Tuscaloosa, it turned out, was also the locus of the most important development of Murphy's second term in office. Murphy's involvement in events that led to the opening of the University of Alabama began in 1821 when he was elected by the legislature to the university's first board of trustees. The board's chairman was Murphy's friend and colleague Governor Israel Pickens. Despite urgent requests from the trustees to move forward with the establishment of the institution, Pickens took no action and, in fact, used university endowment to raise capital for his state bank.

In his legislative message of November 1827, Murphy urged that the creation of a state university be addressed and that commissioners from each judicial district inspect proposed sites and report back to the legislature. His recommendation initiated the process through which the newly chosen capital city also became the site of Alabama's first state university. Buildings began to be constructed in Tuscaloosa, although the university did not officially open its doors until 1831.

During Murphy's term as governor, Congress granted the state 400,000 acres in north Alabama to be sold to finance the building of canals around the Muscle and Colbert shoals that interrupted transportation on the Tennessee River. Although some canals were built, they failed to serve their intended purpose because other of the river's shoals were untouched. In another disappointment and despite his vigorous efforts, Murphy failed to keep a branch of the Bank of the United States from opening in Mobile. This branch, as the governor had feared, ultimately provided disastrous competition to the state Bank of Alabama.

Murphy opposed passage of the "Tariff of Abominations" in 1828. Nevertheless, out of respect for President Jackson, he did not join South Carolina's call for nullification of the tariff law and instead worked for conciliation on this issue. Murphy's moderate posture on the tariff was, in part, responsible for his defeat by Dixon Hall Lewis, the leader of Alabama's more militant states' rights group, in a race for the U.S. House of Representatives in 1831.

In 1833 Murphy finally succeeded in winning a seat in Congress, defeating his former South Carolina College classmate James Dellet. Knowing the political cost of moderation, it is a measure of Murphy's character that he refused to be demagogic on such bitterly contested political issues as the question of Creek Indian removal. To avoid open conflict and perhaps bloodshed between the federal government and Alabama, Congressman Murphy cooperated with his fellow lawmakers in negotiating a peaceful settlement with the Jackson administration on the Indian question, a settlement that protected Alabama's claims to sovereignty and permitted removal of most of the Indians. His last race for public office, a contest for a U.S. House seat, came in 1839 when he was defeated by former opponent Dellet, who had become a leader of the emerging Whig Party in Alabama.

Until his death on September 21, 1841, Murphy spent the last years of his life in Clarke County on the plantation he carefully developed. He was an able political leader who took moderate stands on inflammatory states' rights issues. His years as governor are associated with the relocation of the state capital to

Tuscaloosa and the initiation of steps leading to the opening of the University of Alabama.

References

Abernethy, Thomas Perkins. *The Formative Period in Alabama, 1815–1828.* 2d ed. University: University of Alabama Press, 1965.

Brantley, William H. *Three Capitals: A Book about the First Three Capitals of Alabama: St. Stephens, Huntsville, and Cahawba.* 1947. Reprint, University: University of Alabama Press, 1976.

Owen, Thomas McAdory. *History of Alabama and Dictionary of Alabama Biography.* 4 vols. Chicago: S. J. Clarke, 1921.

Sellers, James B. *History of the University of Alabama, 1818–1902.* University: University of Alabama Press, 1953.

Gabriel Moore, 1829–March 1831

Harriet E. Amos Doss

24
◇

GABRIEL Moore won election without opposition as Alabama's fifth governor in 1829. His early public service in numerous offices and skillful championing of the common man earned Moore the popular support of the state's developing frontier constituency.

The son of Matthew and Letitia Dalton Moore, Gabriel Moore was born in Surry (presently Stokes) County, North Carolina, circa 1785. He received his education in Greensboro at David Caldwell's Academy, popularly known as the "Log College," a forerunner of the University of North Carolina. He read law in North Carolina before migrating in 1810 to Huntsville in Madison County, Alabama, the most populous county in the eastern part of the Mississippi Territory. He immediately entered public service with his appointment in 1810 as tax assessor and collector for Madison County. His duties included supervising the census for Madison County that helped to determine the apportionment of representatives for the Mississippi Territorial Assembly.

Gabriel Moore

Moore built his political career with appeals to the small farmers who populated Madison County and with attacks on that area's Broad River faction, whose members often resided in the county seat of Huntsville. This champion of the people owned almost five hundred acres of land and four slaves in 1815, property holdings that placed him closer to the typical pioneer settler of the county than the business elite in the town. An affluent attorney as well as small planter, Moore, observed a contemporary, was "a skillful election-eer [who] courted the lower stratum of society." He appealed to the common man by delivering stump speeches in which he declared that he came not from the "Royal Party" but from the poor. Known for his "insinuating address and ardent temperament," Moore was, as Willis Brewer noted, "a man of the people, public-spirited, hospitable, and firm in friendship as he was bitter in enmity."

Moore represented Madison County in the Mississippi Territorial Assembly from 1811 to 1817, and he served as its speaker from 1815 to 1817. When Alabama became a separate territory in 1817, Moore continued to represent the county in the assembly and served as speaker during its first session in January and February 1818. He did not seek election as speaker for the second session in November 1818, fearing the political consequences from the legislature's grant of a divorce to his wife and approval of her petition to resume using her maiden name of Mary Parham Caller. To compound the political fallout, Moore subsequently fought a duel with her brother, although neither suffered serious injury.

Moore survived his personal difficulties and in 1819 was one of eight Madison County representatives to the state constitutional convention that met in Huntsville. Moore then handily won election as the first state senator from Madison County, receiving almost four times as many votes as his opponent and predictably drawing most of his votes from residents of the county rather than from Huntsville proper. He served as president of the Alabama Senate in 1820.

For four terms from 1821 to 1829 Moore represented Alabama voters in the U.S. Congress. In his first term as Alabama's solitary congressman, he served as the state's representative at large. For the next three terms he represented the northern district, one of the state's three districts. In the Congress, Moore sought surveys of possible routes to connect the Alabama River and Tennessee River systems and ways to facilitate navigation on the Tennessee River. Moore ultimately proved successful in obtaining extensive federal aid for navigation improvements around Muscle Shoals.

Along the political way, Moore made powerful enemies, including Clement Comer Clay, a leader of the Broad River faction of Madison County and a future governor. In 1825 Moore won reelection to his seat in the U.S. Congress over a challenge from Clay. The following year, he refused to support Clay's quest for a Senate seat, insuring Clay's defeat. From that time forward, Clay despised Moore, and, years later, when the two men accidentally rode the same stagecoach for 170 miles, neither acknowledged the other's presence.

In 1829 Moore gave up his congressional seat to become governor of Alabama. As governor he gained widespread voter support for his long-time priorities for the state: internal improvements and land debt relief for citizens who were financially damaged by the Panic of 1819. Moore asked the legislature to pass measures to link the Alabama River and Tennessee River systems, thereby connecting north and south Alabama. If that link were developed, supporters believed that farm income and real estate values would rise and internal as well as external trade through the state's seaport in Mobile would increase. In 1830, as the navigational improvements he had helped to win as a congressman began at Muscle Shoals, Moore brought the Tennessee River–Alabama River project to the legislature again.

Moore's agenda also included an appeal to the small farmers in the state by seeking "a better and more equitable system of disposing of the public lands." Thousands of acres in Alabama were opened to settlement as Indians relinquished them to the federal government. Moore advocated changes in federal laws so that these lands were available in smaller parcels, preferably forty acres, and at graduated prices depending on the fertility of the soil. Without these changes in land policy, the governor argued, many Alabamians could not afford the high prices and would continue to migrate westward.

Moore promoted education during his administration, observing that "the increase of knowledge is the best security for sound public morality." In his 1830 address to the legislature he spoke eloquently about the imminent opening of the University of Alabama, which aimed to extend "the benefits of education to even the humblest of our citizens." He also advocated penal and judicial reform. He asked the legislature, without success, to establish a centralized state penitentiary system that could rehabilitate prisoners so that they might reenter society. Moore also sought a more enlightened criminal justice system and reminded the legislature that the state's constitution provided for "a penal code founded on principles of reformation, and not of vindictive justice." For the "vigorous and speedy administration of justice," he advocated the establishment of a separate, three-man state supreme court to augment the existing system of state circuit judges who were, as needed, called on to serve as a supreme court. The lawmakers enacted this system on January 14, 1832, after Moore's resignation as governor. Under the legislation, supreme court justices were elected by the legislature for six-year terms.

Moore praised the Bank of Alabama and asked the legislature to establish branches of the bank in both the Tennessee Valley and south Alabama to provide more efficient service to those regions of the state, but legislators declined to do so during his tenure as governor. Although praising the state bank, Moore, a dedicated Jacksonian, opposed the Bank of the United States as a "mammoth institution" with power "over our State institutions, not only unfriendly to their healthy existence, but our State sovereignty itself." He urged Alabama's congressional delegation to vote against rechartering the Bank of the United

States, and, if it were rechartered, Moore suggested that the state delegation seek restrictions on its operations within the state.

Almost immediately after he had won the governorship, Moore began to maneuver for a seat in the U.S. Senate. His pro-Jackson and anti–Bank of the United States rhetoric served him well as he spread rumors about incumbent senator John McKinley's loyalty to Jackson. In 1830 Moore formally announced his candidacy for the Senate seat. After a bitter campaign in which the *Huntsville Democrat* questioned Moore's own commitment to Jackson, he won election to the Senate. On March 3, 1831, he resigned the governorship.

Moore soon lost the popular support that had brought him to the Senate. Professing his support for Jackson, Moore nonetheless allied himself in 1832 with Vice President John C. Calhoun and voted against Senate confirmation of Martin Van Buren, Jackson's nominee as American minister to Great Britain. Vice President Calhoun's tie-breaking vote insured that Van Buren lost the position. President Jackson reacted to Moore's disloyalty by encouraging political opposition to him in Alabama. Public meetings in north Alabama in February and March of 1832 called for Moore's resignation. Despite his earlier professed belief in the practice of legislative instruction, when the Alabama legislature joined the public outcry and called for his resignation, Moore refused. He served the remainder of his full term until 1837. Aware that legislators would not give him a second term as senator, Moore ran in 1836 for his old seat in the U.S. House of Representatives. He suffered his first election defeat and never again held public office.

27
◇

Following his involuntary retirement from public office, Moore experienced financial setbacks that coincided with the Panic of 1837. Between 1841 and 1843 the Circuit Court of Madison County placed liens in favor of his creditors on more than two thousand acres of land and sixty slaves that Moore had pledged as collateral on loans. He left the state with a few slaves, and records show a sad migration to a rented plantation in Panola County, Mississippi, in 1843, then to the Republic of Texas in 1844. He died in Texas on August 6, 1844, and was buried near Caddo Lake in Harrison County. Moore's will and subsequent litigation provided freedom for some of the slaves he had transported to Texas. One of the slaves with whom he traveled and who won her freedom after his death was Mary Minerva, whom court records indicate was Moore's daughter.

Moore's death in relative obscurity and poverty contrasted sharply with the prominence he had enjoyed as a gifted politician who served the state for more than twenty years. He helped to shape Alabama's first constitution and influenced the early form and structure of the government of the new state. His greatest political successes came when he championed the concerns of the common people and professed Jacksonian rhetoric. When he challenged Jackson, even selectively, his popular following eroded.

References

Act Passed at the Second Session of the First General Assembly of the Alabama Territory, in the Forty-Third Year of American Independence, 1818.

Benton, Thomas Hart. *Thirty Years' View*. Vol. 1. New York: D. Appleton, 1854.

Brewer, Willis. *Alabama: Her History, Resources, War Record, and Public Men, from 1540 to 1872*. Montgomery: Barrett and Brown, 1872.

Carter, Clarence E., ed. *Territorial Papers of the United States*. Vol. 6, *The Territory of Mississippi, 1809–1817*. Washington, D.C.: U.S. Government Printing Office, 1938.

Doss, Harriet E. Amos. "The Rise and Fall of an Alabama Founding Father, Gabriel Moore." *Alabama Review* (July 2000): 163–76.

Dupre, Daniel. *Transforming the Cotton Frontier: Madison County, Alabama, 1800–1840*. Baton Rouge: Louisiana State University Press, 1997.

Journal of the House of Representatives, at a Session of the General Assembly of the State of Alabama, November 16, 1830. In *Records of the States of the United States of America: A Microfilm Compilation Prepared by the Library of Congress in Association with the University of North Carolina*, edited by William Sumner Jenkins. Washington, D.C.: U.S. Government Printing Office, 1949.

Martin, James M. "The Early Career of Gabriel Moore." *Alabama Historical Quarterly* 29 (fall/winter 1967): 89–105.

———. "The Senatorial Career of Gabriel Moore." *Alabama Historical Quarterly* 26 (summer 1964): 249–81.

Moore, Gabriel. Papers. Alabama Department of Archives and History, Montgomery.

Saunders, James E. *Early Settlers of Alabama*. New Orleans: L. Graham and Son, 1899.

Sentell, J. O. "The Supreme Court of Alabama, 1820–1970: A Glimpse." *Alabama Lawyer* 31 (April 1970): 144–46.

Samuel B. Moore, March–November 1831

MARY JANE McDANIEL

WHEN Gabriel Moore resigned as governor of Alabama in 1831 to take a seat in the United States Senate, Samuel Moore, not a relative, replaced him. Samuel Moore was born in Franklin County, Tennessee, in 1789. His family settled near Woodville in Jackson County, Alabama, when it was still part of the Mississippi Territory. After reading law at home, he received a law license and opened a practice in 1819. In 1823 he entered the

Alabama House of Representatives from Jackson County. In these early years he was a minor member of the state legislature, but gradually he added important committee assignments. The lifelong bachelor was neither brilliant nor a great orator, and he seems to have made few friends or enemies.

In 1828 Samuel Moore moved from the state house to the state senate representing Jackson County, and in 1830 he became president of that body, defeating Levin Powell of Tuscaloosa by a vote of ten to eight. By such two-vote margins, history is made. Governor Gabriel Moore began his duties as a U.S. senator from Alabama in March 1831, and Samuel Moore, as president of the state senate, succeeded to the governorship.

Early in Moore's brief tenure as governor, the University of Alabama opened to students. As chairman of the board of trustees, Samuel Moore made a brief address and presented keys to university president Henry A. Woods. From April 18 to November 21, a total of ninety-four students enrolled. Tuition for the full year was set at $20, but students who arrived that first fall paid only $10. The list of students kept by Henry Tutwiler, secretary of the faculty, read like a list of the prominent families in early Alabama and included Alexander Beaufort Meek, John G. Davenport, and George Shortridge, among others.

Like his predecessor, Samuel Moore was hostile to the national bank and opposed its rechartering. As a Jacksonian, he also believed that private or corporate banking was undemocratic and violated the principles of equal rights and republican government. State banking, on the other hand, was acceptable to Moore if the revenue it earned was put to public use.

Moore's strong states' rights mentality emerged again in his views on protective tariffs, which he opposed because they benefited northern states at the expense of southern states. Furthermore, he argued that such tariffs were unconstitutional because they were not uniform in their application. For such discriminatory and partial legislation to be legal, Moore asserted, the Constitution would have to be amended. If that did not occur and protective tariffs continued to do harm to southern farmers, southern states should reevaluate their membership in the Union and consider the possibility of secession. Despite such radical musings, there is no indication of any serious advocacy of secession by Moore in the 1830s.

Samuel Moore, as Gabriel Moore before him, took an interest in internal improvements, especially the idea of connecting the Tennessee and Warrior Rivers. This linkage, similar to those suggested by earlier governors, would serve to connect the northern and southern regions of the state, stimulate agriculture and industry, benefit commercial trade, and make Mobile a leading port. Improving navigation on the Coosa River was also on Moore's agenda, and at one point he advocated the improvement of most of the navigable rivers in Alabama.

Moore also repeated his predecessor's recommendation to the legislature for the construction of a state penitentiary. Cost concerns prevented passage of the penitentiary bill under the administrations of both Gabriel Moore and Samuel Moore. In a related issue, Samuel Moore endorsed legislative action to extend jurisdiction of Alabama's courts over the state's remaining Indian populations as a means of exercising control over them, similar to Georgia's actions with regard to its Cherokee population.

Even before he assumed office, Samuel Moore announced his candidacy for governor in the 1831 election. The other candidates were fellow Democrats John Gayle of Greene County and Nicholas Davis of Limestone County. Moore came in a distant third with a plurality in only three counties, and John Gayle emerged the victor.

Immediately after Gayle took office in November 1831, Moore retired to Carrollton in Pickens County to resume the practice of law. Missing the special appeal of politics, he soon came out of retirement. In 1834 he was elected to represent Pickens and Fayette Counties in the state senate, and he spent the next term trying to obtain internal improvements for Pickens County, especially the construction of a stagecoach road connecting Tuscaloosa to Carrollton.

In 1835 he became president of the state senate again. While Moore was the presiding officer, others in state government described him as "courteous and gentlemanly in his manners" and with "a good knowledge of parliamentary rules." When he was nominated for the presidency of the senate in 1836, however, he lost to a future governor, Hugh McVay. Moore lost his seat in the state senate in a failed reelection bid in 1838 and never held statewide office again. He served as the judge of the county court in Pickens County, a position he held for six years.

After losing a bid for reelection to the office of judge, he reopened his law office in Carrollton, but it was never profitable. Moore received little attention in life, and his death in Carrollton on November 7, 1846, went largely unnoticed. Poverty stricken, he left no estate and was buried in an unmarked grave. In 1918 the Masonic Society of Carrollton erected a plain monument in his memory.

References

Moore, Samuel. Administrative Files. Alabama Department of Archives and History, Montgomery.

Smith, Clyde M. "Life of Samuel B. Moore." Master's thesis, University of Alabama, 1938.

John Gayle, 1831–1835

SARAH WOOLFOLK WIGGINS

Gayle

JOHN Gayle, Alabama governor, U.S. congressman, and jurist, was born on September 11, 1792, in Sumter District, South Carolina, to Mary Rees and Matthew Gayle. At the opening of the American Revolution, Matthew Gayle served as a cavalryman in the army of the South Carolina "swampfox," Francis Marion. In 1812 the family moved to Mount Vernon, Alabama, and then to nearby Monroe County, where Matthew was a planter.

John Gayle attended Mt. Bethel Academy in Newberry District, South Carolina, then South Carolina College, where he was elected without opposition to be president of the Clariosophic Society, a literary and debating organization. When he was graduated in 1813, Gayle traveled through Creek Indian country and safely reached his parents' home near Fort Stoddert in what was to become Alabama. Travelers following that same route a few days later were not so fortunate, as many were killed and scalped in an Indian attack.

Gayle intended to return to South Carolina to resume the legal studies that he had begun in the office of Abraham Giles Dozier. The recent Fort Mims massacre and frequent clashes between white settlers and the Creeks, however, created terror on the frontier and gave Gayle deep concerns for the safety of his elderly parents and young sisters. He decided to remain in the area and organize troops to protect the settlers. He joined in the fight for several months until the war ended in 1814.

After the war Gayle completed his legal studies in the office of Judge Abner Smith Lipscomb in St. Stephens. He was licensed to practice in 1818 and opened a law office at Claiborne in Monroe County. In 1819 the young Presbyterian and prohibitionist married Sarah Ann Haynsworth, who bore him six children. By 1830 he owned ten slaves.

When the Alabama Territory was created in 1817, Gayle became a member of the legislature, which elected him in 1818 to be solicitor (criminal prosecutor) of the First Judicial Circuit in southwest Alabama. After two years, his booming law practice led him to resign as solicitor. Between 1822 and 1830, Gayle was elected to the Alabama House of Representatives first by Monroe County and later by Greene County, where he made his new home. In 1823 he was elected chairman of the House Ways and Means Committee, and in 1829 he was elected speaker of the house. Admired for his impartiality, in 1823 Gayle became judge of the Third Judicial Circuit and ex-officio judge of the Alabama Supreme Court. He resigned from the court in 1828.

Despite the continuing acrimony in Alabama over the protective tariff issue, in 1831 Gayle was elected governor as a strong antinullification, pro-Jackson candidate. He was reelected without opposition in 1833, leaving office in 1835. In his first speech to the legislature he denounced nullification and supported President Andrew Jackson's stand on the issue. He championed internal improvements in Alabama and pressed unsuccessfully for construction of a canal to link the Tennessee and Tombigbee Rivers. He was more successful in getting Alabama's first railroad built across north Alabama from Tuscumbia to Decatur. This forty-four miles of track permitted transportation to bypass the rapids on the Tennessee River at Muscle Shoals. While he was governor, the legislature also incorporated in 1833 the state's first cotton mill, the Bell Factory, which was located northeast of Huntsville.

The major crisis that Gayle faced as governor developed during 1832 and 1833 over the issue of lands previously ceded to the United States by the Creek Indians. Gayle clashed with his old friend, President Jackson, over this issue, an ironic turn of events because Jackson's enormous popularity in Alabama came in no small part from his breaking the power of the Creeks in the southeast at the battle of Horseshoe Bend. The 1832 Creek cession in Alabama was divided into counties by state legislative action before full surveys were completed. When squatters rushed in and were not careful to stay off land guaranteed by treaty to the Creeks, conflicts between whites and Indians occurred. The Indians appealed to Washington, and Jackson ordered federal troops to remove all white settlers from the Indian cession.

When federal troops attempted to remove Hardaman Owens, Russell County commissioner of roads and revenue and a flagrant land grabber, he was killed. A county grand jury indicted the soldier responsible for the murder, and Gayle insisted on his surrender to state officials. The governor championed the rights of the settlers, protested federal military presence on Alabama soil as an insult to the state's sovereignty, and ordered a militia to be organized in the newly formed counties in the eastern section. Governor Gayle was, thus, claiming the right to arrest, try, and, perhaps, convict a United States soldier for an act committed as part of his duties. It looked for a time as though civil conflict might occur between Alabama claiming state sovereignty and the United States government.

Alabama's congressional delegation worked tirelessly to convince Jackson to come to peaceful terms with Gayle. Recognizing the possibility of violence, the president dispatched Francis Scott Key to Tuscaloosa to resolve the quarrel. Key hurried to complete the survey of Creek lands, required the Indians immediately to choose the lands they wanted to keep, and met with Governor Gayle in an attempt to soothe hard feelings. The soldier accused of killing the white settler disappeared, no trial was held, and the army withdrew. Key arranged terms to solve the conflicting claims, stating that only those white settlers on lands expressly reserved for the Creeks would have to vacate. Titles to the lands vacated could be purchased from the Indians. Key's diplomacy succeeded, and a collision between state and federal authority was averted, although the terms of the treaty with the Indians were ignored.

The immediate crisis ended peacefully, but the incident had long-range effects on Alabama politics. Jackson's popularity was severely diminished, Alabamians were alarmed by the increasing power of the federal government, political parties in Alabama were realigned, and the foundation was laid for the states' rights movement in Alabama in the 1850s. Governor Gayle shifted from support of Jackson's nationalist views toward espousing support for states' rights. He insisted that the federal government had no legal jurisdiction to negotiate treaties that limited a state's authority over all the citizens and territory within its borders. He claimed that all people within the boundaries of the state, whether Indians, soldiers, whites, or blacks, were subject to the laws of the state.

Gayle's attitude on the protective tariff issue hardened after Jackson signed into law the Tariff of 1832 and threatened to use the military, if necessary, to enforce the law in states that nullified the act. When Jackson began to promote Vice President Martin Van Buren to succeed him, the Whig Party was born in Alabama. The division between the former friends was so deep that Gayle served as a Whig presidential elector for Judge Hugh White in 1836 and for William Henry Harrison in 1840, although he did not declare himself formally a Whig until 1840.

After his term as governor, Gayle returned to his law practice, this time in Mobile. His wife, Sarah, had died on July 30, 1835, and on November 1, 1837, he married Clarissa Stedman Peck, who bore him four additional children. After suffering defeat as a Whig candidate in an 1841 race for the U.S. Senate, in 1847 Gayle was elected to the U.S. House of Representatives as a Whig.

In Washington Gayle and his daughter Amelia lived in the same house as John C. Calhoun. Amelia became a favorite of Calhoun, accompanying him on his morning walks around the U.S. Capitol. In Congress Gayle focused primarily on matters of local and state concern, including getting federal land grants for railroads in Alabama. On national questions he seemed most interested in matters related to the expansion of slavery.

After only one term in Congress, Gayle did not seek reelection. He returned to Mobile and in 1849 was appointed judge of the U.S. District Court in Alabama and served in that position until his death in Mobile on July 21, 1859. He was buried in Magnolia Cemetery in Mobile.

References

Brewer, Willis. *Alabama: Her History, Resources, War Record, and Public Men, from 1540 to 1872.* Montgomery: Barrett and Brown, 1872.

Gorgas, Amelia Gayle. Sketch of John Gayle. Gorgas Family Papers, Hoole Special Collections Library, University of Alabama, Tuscaloosa.

Mobile Daily Register, July 22, 1859 (obituary).

Owen, Thomas McAdory. *History of Alabama and Dictionary of Alabama Biography.* 4 vols. Chicago: S. J. Clarke, 1921.

Thornton, J. Mills, III. *Politics and Power in a Slave Society: Alabama, 1800–1860.* Baton Rouge: Louisiana State University Press, 1978.

Clement Comer Clay, 1835–July 1837

J. MILLS THORNTON III

34

BEGINNING his political career in Alabama as a leading member of the wealthy Broad River political machine, Clement Comer Clay ultimately found favor with the voters of the state as a Jacksonian Democrat. His life and political career encompass much of Alabama's territorial and early state history — fighting Indians, helping to write the state's first constitution, serving as the state's first chief justice and later as legislator, congressman, governor, and U.S. senator.

Clay

C. C. Clay was born in Halifax County, Virginia, on December 17, 1789, the son of planter William Clay and Rebecca Comer Clay. Around 1795 the family moved to Grainger County, Tennessee, in the northeastern part of the state. Clay was graduated from Blount College, the future University of Tennessee, in 1807 and read law in Knoxville under Hugh Lawson White. He was admitted to the bar at the end of 1809 and moved to the new town of Huntsville in the Mississippi Territory in November 1811. Clay served under Andrew Jackson in the Creek War of 1813–14 and in 1815 married Susanna Claiborne Withers, who bore him three sons.

Clay quickly allied himself with the wealthy entrepreneurs from the Broad River area of Georgia, headed by Huntsville Bank (Planters and Merchants

Bank) president Leroy Pope and Pope's son-in-law John W. Walker, who dominated Huntsville's economy. Young Clay became a stockholder and director of the Huntsville Bank and, as a member of the Alabama territorial legislature, joined with Walker to fight for measures to strengthen the bank's position. One of their legislative victories eliminated all limits on interest rates that could be charged by lenders in the territory.

At the Alabama constitutional convention of 1819, Walker was chosen the convention's president, and he appointed Clay to chair the Committee of Fifteen that drafted the constitution. Clay fought successfully for life terms for judges, but was unsuccessful when he joined probank delegates in an effort to make it easier for the legislature to charter banks. The new state legislature elected Clay one of Alabama's five circuit judges, who also jointly constituted the state supreme court; the other judges then chose Clay as the state's first chief justice.

In the meantime, the Panic of 1819 plunged the state into depression. Virtually all of the cases decided by the supreme court during Clay's tenure involved actions to collect debts. Because of the territorial act that abolished usury limitations, which Clay had supported, many of these debts required enormous interest payments. At the end of 1823, Clay resigned from the bench to become an attorney for the creditors in the first of what became known as the "big interest" cases in which debtors challenged the validity of the exorbitant rates. In this case, the leader of Huntsville's antibank forces, U.S. senator William Kelly, succeeded in convincing the state supreme court to limit the interest payments demanded from the debtors.

In 1825 Clay ran for Congress, but because of his association with banking and creditor elements, he was defeated overwhelmingly by the small-farmer spokesman Gabriel Moore. He then began to alter his public positions to try to appeal to poorer voters. In 1826 he ran for the U.S. Senate against John McKinley, also a former supporter of the Huntsville Bank faction. Both Clay and McKinley now claimed to be ardent followers of Andrew Jackson, who had swept the state in the presidential election of 1824. But Clay also sought the votes of the handful of legislators who admired John Quincy Adams and thereby alienated a crucial number of Jacksonians. McKinley thus narrowly defeated Clay and won the Senate seat by a legislative vote of forty-one to thirty-eight.

At the same time that Clay and McKinley were opposing each other for the Senate, they were jointly the attorneys for the creditors in the second of the "big interest" cases. In this final round of the battle, the two men persuaded the state supreme court that the statute of limitations barred debtors from recovery of the usurious interest they had already paid.

In 1828 Clay was elected to the state house of representatives and was unanimously chosen its speaker. Ensconced in this new position, he proceeded

35
◇

to adopt a series of anti-small-farmer positions that were fraught with political danger for him. Alabama's small farmers, like good Jacksonian Democrats everywhere, were vigorously antiaristocratic, suspicious of the power of private corporations, and positively inflamed by any efforts to limit the effect of their franchise. Clay made several political mistakes, including his opposition to pricing the Muscle Shoals Canal land grant within the reach of poor squatters. He also opposed exempting nonslaveholders from slave patrol duty and amending the state constitution to limit the term of judges to six years. In other actions, he favored repealing the law that prohibited participants in duels from holding public office, opposed efforts to secure married women their separate estates, and voted to extend the state's jurisdiction over the Creek Indian territory.

Clay again ran for Congress in 1829. His legislative opposition to low prices for the Muscle Shoals Canal land grant became the principal issue of this campaign. His opponent carried the counties of the western Tennessee Valley, where most of the land grant was located, by championing reduced land prices and preference rights for the squatters. But Clay swept his own Madison County, where enthusiasm was high for getting as much money as possible from the lands in order to finance the building of the proposed canal. Once in Congress, however, Clay embraced the cause of squatters and public land debtors and was able to free himself from an identification with aristocratic beliefs. With the exception of his vote to override Andrew Jackson's veto of the Maysville Road Bill, he never again deviated from the Jacksonian line on national issues, and in later years he publicly recanted this single heterodox action. Clay strongly supported Jackson's crusade against the Bank of the United States, and though he opposed protective tariffs, he endorsed Jackson's denunciation of nullification. He continued to defend slavery, however, and asserted that even a program of compensated emancipation would lead to southern secession. By his final term in the House, he had become chairman of the Committee on Public Lands and a leading advocate of the graduation and reduction of land prices and permanent preemption rights for squatters.

In 1835 Alabama Democrats nominated Clay for governor, and he defeated the Whig candidate, Enoch Parsons, by nearly two to one. His first message to the legislature was devoted largely to warning of the danger of abolitionism; he demanded that northerners who had mailed abolitionist pamphlets to the South be punished, and he urged strengthening laws against slave insurrection.

In the spring of 1836, desperate economic conditions among the Creeks who remained on Alabama soil drove some three thousand of them to follow the lead of Nea-mathla into open revolt. Clay called out the state militia and took personal command of it. Most of the Creeks, however, joined in the effort to suppress the rebellion. When U.S. forces under General Thomas Jesup arrived in June, the revolt collapsed. Even though most of the Indians had remained loyal, Clay, in a gesture certain to appeal to the great majority of Alabama voters, insisted that the federal government compel all of the Creeks to leave the state immediately for Oklahoma; the government complied.

The following spring Alabama's people were feeling the terrible effects of the Panic of 1837. Demonstrating his recently acquired tendency toward demagoguery reflected in his prosquatter positions in Congress and in his heavy-handed actions toward the Creeks, Clay summoned the legislature into special session and recommended extreme measures that he hoped would aid hard-pressed debtors but that ultimately helped to drive the state bank into bankruptcy. The legislature enacted the Relief Act of (June) 1837, which required the bank and its branches to suspend immediate collection of debts owed them and provide their debtors with three additional years in which to pay. Furthermore, the bill ordered the issuance of $5 million in bonds that the bank's various branches were to sell to raise capital so that they could make additional loans to Alabamians in desperate financial circumstances. These extraordinarily foolish acts, although advancing Clay's political career, left the bank with a vast indebtedness and no means to service it. Grateful legislators—many of whom were themselves debtors to the Bank of Alabama—unanimously elected Clay to the U.S. Senate to succeed John McKinley, who had been appointed by President Martin Van Buren to the U.S. Supreme Court. Clay resigned as governor and took his Senate seat in September 1837.

In the Senate, Clay continued to affect a Jacksonian style. He renewed his crusade for preemption rights for squatters and the reduction of public land prices; pressed for the removal of the Cherokees to Oklahoma; and fought for the adoption of President Van Buren's independent subtreasury scheme. The deepening depression, however, created such a crisis in Clay's personal finances that he was forced to resign from the Senate in November 1841. In 1830 he had owned fifty-two slaves and shortly thereafter had purchased a second large plantation. In 1840 he was compelled to begin selling off his slaves to meet his debts, and he continued these sales throughout the coming decade.

These financial reverses were accompanied by political ones. In 1842 Governor Benjamin Fitzpatrick appointed Clay to prepare a digest of the state's laws, but Clay's political enemies in the legislature, led by future U.S. district judge William G. Jones, opposed the formal adoption of the digest when Clay submitted it. It was accepted only after a lengthy and embarrassing floor fight. In the summer of 1843, Fitzpatrick appointed Clay to a vacancy on the state supreme court, but the following December, Whig and Calhounite Democrat legislators joined to defeat Clay's election to the full term. In 1846 Governor Joshua L. Martin named Clay to the three-member board that was supervising the liquidation of the Bank of Alabama, but in 1848 the legislature abolished the board, in part to deprive Clay of the office. After these successive humiliations,

Clay retired from public life and devoted himself to his Huntsville law practice, in partnership with his sons. His eldest son, Clement Claiborne Clay, had launched a political career of his own, one that took him eventually to the U.S. and Confederate Senates.

Although Clay often adopted a partisan Jacksonian image, he never genuinely accepted the pro-small-farmer, anticapitalist ideology that went with it. Rather, he became Jacksonian almost entirely to advance his political career. With his withdrawal from public life he was freed to resume the pro-planter, pro-development attitudes that characterized his early career. He took a leading part in the creation of the Memphis and Charleston Railroad and became a large stockholder in it. He went as a delegate to two Southern Commercial Conventions, and on every possible occasion he spoke out strongly for the cause of southern rights. In the meantime, with the return of prosperity in the 1850s, his economic situation began to improve. By 1860 he owned eighty-four slaves, real estate worth $60,000, and personal property valued at $85,000.

Clay's advocacy of secession and his son's vigorous support of the Confederacy made the former governor a particular object of Unionist hostility during the Civil War. When federal forces occupied Huntsville at the end of 1864, Clay was imprisoned as a hostage to force Confederates to release Unionist leader David C. Humphreys. His time in jail broke Clay's health. By the summer of 1865 he was an invalid. His wife, Susanna, died at the beginning of 1866, and he survived her by only eight months, dying on September 6, 1866.

References

Nuermberger, Ruth Ketring. *The Clays of Alabama: A Planter-Lawyer-Politician Family.* Lexington: University of Kentucky Press, 1958.

Thornton, J. Mills, III. *Politics and Power in a Slave Society: Alabama, 1800–1860.* Baton Rouge: Louisiana State University Press, 1978.

Hugh McVay, August–November 1837

MARY JANE MCDANIEL

I N THE summer of 1837, Hugh McVay began his brief career as governor by a one-vote stroke of political fortune. He replaced Governor Clement C. Clay, who resigned the office to serve Alabama in the U.S. Senate. The gubernatorial election of 1837 had already been held, and Arthur P. Bagby of Monroe County had been elected. Thus McVay served only three months until Bagby took office in November. Most officials, especially those in the state legislature, understood that the interim governor was only a temporary custodian of the office and would wield little power. Nearly all of the surviving correspondence of his governorship refers to him either as "acting" governor or *ex officio* governor or does not address him by name at all.

Hugh McVay, the first governor of Alabama to come from Lauderdale County, was born near Greenville, South Carolina, in 1766. He married Polly Hawks in the 1780s, and they lived in Kentucky and Tennessee before moving to Alabama in 1807. The family became one of Madison County's earliest squatters. McVay bought land, became a surveyor, and was one of the first attorneys admitted to the Madison County bar, although   *McVay* he apparently never developed a law practice.

Polly McVay died in 1817, having produced nine children. Soon after this, McVay moved his family to Lauderdale County and settled near Florence. In 1827 he married Sophia W. Davison in Memphis, a marriage that did not survive. Sophia ran away with a man she claimed was her cousin while her husband was at the state capital in Tuscaloosa. McVay then obtained one of the few divorces ever granted by the state legislature. This domestic rift had no known adverse political consequences for the future governor.

39
◇

McVay maintained a strong, long-term interest in state politics. He represented Madison County in both the Mississippi and Alabama territorial legislatures and was the Lauderdale County delegate to the 1819 constitutional convention in Huntsville. Beginning in 1820, he represented Lauderdale in the state legislature, serving five years in the lower house and seventeen in the state senate. Because McVay was an early supporter of Andrew Jackson, the local aristocracy often opposed him, but ordinary farmers regularly supported him. In 1836 he became president of the senate by only a one-vote margin. From that position, he became Alabama's chief executive for a brief but difficult period.

McVay took office as the Panic of 1837 continued to wreak havoc in Alabama, especially on its overextended and badly administered state bank. McVay, a fearless Jacksonian Democrat known as a strong opponent of the banking system in Alabama, generally favored a *laissez faire* approach to the economy. Distrustful, probank legislators who benefited from their support of the bank decided that secrecy and noncooperation were the wisest strategies to use with this governor. They deliberately kept documents related to the bank's financial dealings from him. As he prepared to leave office, McVay admitted to the legislature and to the public that he had no information on how the banks were operating under Clay's Relief Act of 1837. He did not even know if any of the bonds issued by that legislation to provide capital for the moribund bank had sold at all. Furthermore, McVay told the legislature that he blamed the depression's impact in Alabama on the "heedless creation of banks and wild and prodigal issues of bank paper." On November 22, 1837, the interim governor left office.

In 1840 McVay returned to the Alabama Senate and again was elected its president. During this period he frequently played the maverick's role. He was the only member of his party in 1840 to vote against the General Ticket Bill, which called for congressmen to be elected statewide rather than by districts. The bill was introduced by Democrats in an attempt to diminish Whig strength in specific districts of Alabama. McVay cast the only opposition vote to a senate bill that provided for flogging anyone who embezzled from a bank, and he was the only senator from the Tennessee Valley to vote against establishing a state bank branch in that area. McVay remained in the senate until 1844, when he returned to his home in Lauderdale County.

In an age that admired flamboyant oratory, McVay's speeches were infrequent, generally short, and to the point. A contemporary described them as "plain, frank, and honest." His plain speech matched his appearance and simple style of dress. Although his lack of formal education produced numerous unfavorable comments, he was actually a shrewd, tough man who voted independently and worried little about his popularity. By the time of his retirement, McVay was a successful planter who owned more than a thousand acres and forty slaves. He died in 1851 and was buried in the family cemetery outside of Florence.

References

Bjurberg, Richard H. "A Political and Economic Study of Alabama's Governors and Congressmen, 1831–1861." Master's thesis, Auburn University, 1947.

Brantley, William H. *Banking in Alabama, 1816–1860.* 2 vols. Birmingham: Birmingham Printing Co., 1961.

Garrett, Jill. *A History of Lauderdale County, Alabama.* Columbia, Tenn.: N.p., 1964.

Garrett, William. *Reminiscences of Public Men in Alabama for Thirty Years.* Atlanta: Plantation Publishing, 1872.

McVay, Hugh. Administrative Files. Alabama Department of Archives and History, Montgomery.

Arthur P. Bagby, 1837–1841

MARY JANE MCDANIEL

ARTHUR Pendleton Bagby was born in 1794 in Louisa County, Virginia, where his family remained through Bagby's educational years. Financial problems ultimately caused his family to migrate to Claiborne, Monroe County, in the Alabama Territory. Here the future governor read law and, in 1819, opened a legal practice. Bagby married twice, first to Emily Steel of Georgia and then to Anne Elizabeth Connell of South Carolina in 1828, and he fathered nine children.

Bagby's first political office was as a representative of Monroe County in the state legislature in 1821. After his reelection in 1822, he became speaker of the house at the exceptionally young age of twenty-eight. Over the next fifteen years he served in both houses of the state legislature and was elected to several terms as president of the senate. In the early 1820s, Bagby was a National Republican who supported President John Quincy Adams. His loyalties soon changed, and by the end of the decade he became a committed Jacksonian Democrat. He supported President Andrew Jackson's stand against South Carolina's tariff nullification and openly opposed a bill committing Alabama to support an enlarged national bank.

Bagby served two terms as governor of Alabama. To many of his contemporaries, he looked and acted like a governor. Standing more than six feet tall, the handsome Bagby had a graceful walk and the demeanor of a gentleman that made his presence at public functions notable. He read widely and was a student of law and government. The governor's voice was clear and pleasant, and, although given to long-windedness, he was a gifted orator. In 1837 he defeated the former speaker of the house, Samuel W. Oliver, who ran as an independent on an anti–Van Buren platform. Bagby's immense popularity led to a decisive reelection victory in 1839 over a weak Whig opponent.

Bagby

Bagby spent most of his two administrations on economic issues. He inherited the most serious problems resulting from the depression of 1837 and its intertwined effect on the banking system in Alabama. Banks had suspended specie payment during the tenure of Governor Clay, and charges of mismanagement and corruption were leveled

41
◇

from all quarters. To add to the problems, banking executives and probank legislators kept information about the state's financial institutions from Bagby as they had from the previous administration. In his first year as governor, Bagby naively assumed the legislature would act seriously on his cautious and conservative agenda, and he failed to press actively for his program among the lawmakers. Bagby may not have understood fully the complex economic issues, and in pursuing his antibank program, he, as his predecessors, made far-reaching mistakes.

In 1838 Bagby allowed resumption of specie payment. Officials of the state bank proposed a plan to advance money to planters based on their cotton harvest, then sell the crop in Europe for specie. Whigs and most big planters favored this approach as a way to market their cotton and strengthen the bank, but Bagby opposed it. In addition, he tried to limit the sale of more state bonds to provide capital for the banks' continued operations, but the state legislature ignored his recommendations and approved a new $2.5 million issue. When Alabama cotton found only a small market in Europe, the state found itself going deeper into debt.

The banking issue was complicated by the fact that it cut across normal party loyalties. Legislators regularly investigated and debated the issue but were apparently satisfied with the approach of burdening the state with debt through unwise bond issues. Occasionally, they took more useful steps. In 1839 the lawmakers reduced the number of directors of each bank from twelve to six and required that directors not be indebted to the bank or any of its branches. They also enacted a provision that allowed the governor to appoint three commissioners to audit each bank twice a year and report back to the governor, not the legislature. This should have meant that Bagby and future governors would at last have dependable information regarding the banks' operation. In reality, personal and political intrigues kept this mechanism from working.

In 1840 the Merchants Bank of New York submitted a shocking financial report that disclosed that Alabama owed $11.5 million on state bonds with no apparent way of paying. Financial concerns in New Orleans and New York had acquired some of the bonds, but the overwhelming majority were sold in London, including some to Nathan Rothschild and Company. The state was struggling to pay the annual interest on these bonds, which was more than $600,000, a debilitating debt that remained a political issue for years.

As difficult as these economic issues were, Bagby, an ambitious and loyal Democrat, had to deal with another thorny problem. In the presidential election of 1840, Whig candidate William Henry Harrison was elected, and Democrats in Alabama won their narrowest majority ever in the legislature. To limit this new Whig popularity, Bagby signed the General Ticket Bill, which provided for the election of congressmen on a statewide basis rather than by congressional districts. Originally proposed by William Lowndes Yancey, editor of the *We-tumpka Argus*, this act was clearly a political maneuver designed to strengthen Alabama's Democratic Party. In recent statewide votes, Democratic candidates for Congress had won a majority of the total votes. Despite overall Democratic popularity, the Whigs won and controlled seats in Mobile, Montgomery, and Tuscaloosa, three of the state's five congressional districts. Whigs understandably fought the bill in both houses of the state legislature, asserting that it was unconstitutional and "an unrighteous attempt at disfranchisement." They also maintained that the more heavily populated northern counties were attempting to control the southern ones. Although the General Ticket Bill was enacted in January 1841, Whig outrage forced the legislature to include a rider that required a popular referendum on the bill in August.

When President William Henry Harrison called a special session of Congress for May 1841, Alabama found itself in a political dilemma. Under existing state law, the terms of Alabama congressmen expired in March and the next regular election was not until August. Bagby called a special congressional election to be conducted under the general ticket system, and both parties put up candidates for all five congressional positions. The Democrats won in the two northern districts, and Whig candidates received majorities in the three southern ones. The Democrats, however, with heavy support from the larger white population in north Alabama, had an overall majority of more than three thousand votes. Therefore, under the new general ticket system, all five congressmen elected in 1841 were Democrats. The new system was short lived. In the August referendum enough Democrats joined Whigs to restore the district system. In November 1841 the legislature repealed the general ticket legislation, but Bagby, ever the faithful Democrat, continued to support the failed system, devoting half of his last annual message before the legislature to its defense.

Among the accomplishments of Bagby's administration was the completion of Indian removal that began under Clay. In south Alabama, state troops were raised to help fight the Seminole War in Florida, a chancery court was introduced, and a commission appointed to mark the boundary between Alabama and Georgia did its work successfully. In 1839 the legislature finally authorized construction of a penitentiary, which opened in Wetumpka in 1841. Imprisonment for debt was abolished except in cases of fraud, and the penitentiary system abolished branding and whipping.

Bagby was a strong advocate of slavery, and his annual message to the legislature in November 1840 was one of the first public speeches in Alabama to defend slavery as a positive good. In a rationale that foretold the position of many in the later antebellum period, he favorably compared the condition of slaves to that of free laborers in other regions. Bagby asserted that slave laborers enjoyed more of the necessities of life than their free counterparts in the north and that the lives of slaves would deteriorate if they were emancipated. The governor averred that slavery had existed from earliest times, that the African was suited best to slavery, and that divine will did not prohibit it. In light of the "peculiar character of a portion of our population," asserted Bagby, county militia should be raised and maintained to deal with emergencies that involved slaves.

After completing his second term as governor, Bagby was selected to fill the vacancy in the U.S. Senate created by the resignation of Clement C. Clay, and in 1842 the legislature elected him to a full term. After struggling unsuccessfully with the bank dilemma for four years, Bagby left this seemingly intractable problem to his successor, Benjamin Fitzpatrick.

While a senator, Bagby supported Manifest Destiny, the annexation of Texas, and permitting slavery in the nation's territories. In 1848 President James K. Polk appointed him minister to Russia, a position he held briefly until he resigned after Whig candidate Zachary Taylor was elected president later that year. Bagby's last public activity was to serve on a committee to codify the laws of Alabama.

After retiring from public life, Bagby lived in Wilcox County for a few years and then moved to Mobile, where his financial problems continued, caused by a habit of living just beyond his means on borrowed money. At his death from yellow fever in the fall of 1858, he owed the Alabama bank at Mobile more than $3,000, and he had no property to cover the debt.

44
◇

References

Bagby, Arthur P. Administrative Files. Alabama Department of Archives and History, Montgomery.

Brantley, William H. *Banking in Alabama, 1816–1860.* 2 vols. Birmingham: Birmingham Printing Co., 1961.

Garrett, William. *Reminiscences of Public Men in Alabama for Thirty Years.* Atlanta: Plantation Publishing, 1872.

Sellers, James B. *Slavery in Alabama.* University: University of Alabama Press, 1950.

Benjamin Fitzpatrick, 1841–1845

J. Mills Thornton III

B ENJAMIN Fitzpatrick, like most of his predecessors in the governor's chair, was associated with the Jacksonian wing of the Alabama Democratic Party, but he also led a loosely organized faction of the party sometimes known as the "Montgomery Regency," whose members were united more around family and personal ties than ideology. Fitzpatrick's two terms as governor, like those of his three immediate predecessors, were dominated by questions surrounding the state-owned Bank of Alabama, which was still teetering on the verge of bankruptcy as a result of the depression that followed the Panic of 1837.

Fitzpatrick was born in Greene County, Georgia, on June 30, 1802, the son of William Fitzpatrick, who served as a Georgia state legislator for nineteen years, and Anne Phillips Fitzpatrick. Benjamin was orphaned when he was only seven and was reared by his older brothers and sisters. He received little formal schooling and led a rather knockabout youth. When he was just fourteen, he traveled alone to the newly opened former Creek territory of central Alabama, obtained work as a clerk in a Wetumpka store, was employed as a deputy sheriff, and, finally, read law under Montgomery mayor Nimrod E. Benson. He was admitted to the bar in 1821 at age nineteen and was immediately elected by the new state legislature as the circuit solicitor for the Montgomery area. He was reelected to this position in 1825, defeating future congressman Samuel W. Mardis.

Fitzpatrick

In 1827 Fitzpatrick married Sarah Terry Elmore, a member of the wealthy and prominent family for whom Elmore County was later named. Between his marriage in 1827 and his wife's death in 1837, she bore him six sons. This marriage brought Fitzpatrick a large plantation across the Alabama River from Montgomery, which caused him to decline reelection as circuit solicitor to devote more of his efforts to cotton planting. His slaveholding grew from 24 persons in 1830, to 50 in 1840, and to 106 in 1850. By 1860 his real estate was valued at $60,000 and his personal property at $125,000. A decade after his first wife's death, he married Aurelia Blassingame of Marion and by her had a seventh son.

45
◇

After the death of his first wife, he turned his attention increasingly to politics. In 1837, he was a candidate for the gubernatorial nomination in the Democratic legislative caucus but was narrowly defeated by Arthur P. Bagby. In 1840 he served as a Democratic candidate for presidential elector and conducted an impressive statewide canvass for Martin Van Buren. In 1841 the Democrats nominated him for governor, and he was elected over the Whig nominee, taking 57 percent of the vote.

During his campaign Fitzpatrick assured Alabama voters that he had never been either a director or a debtor of the bank and promised to approach the financial crisis without any probank bias. Fitzpatrick was by nature a cautious and conservative man, and he initially wanted to save the indebted bank. It was primarily the Jacksonian commitment to inactive government, rather than its hostility to corporate capitalism, that had attracted him to the Democratic Party. In Fitzpatrick's first message to the legislature, he urged the liquidation of the extraordinarily mismanaged branch at Mobile, but he sought merely the reform of the main bank and its three other branches. Radical Jacksonians, who hated all banks, joined with Whigs who opposed the state ownership of a bank to produce an incongruous legislative majority for more extreme action. In early 1843 Fitzpatrick reluctantly signed legislation to liquidate all four of the branches and to preserve only the main bank at Tuscaloosa.

46
◇
To Fitzpatrick's surprise, this action was greeted with widespread popular approbation, and in the summer of 1843 he was reelected to a second term without any opposition. He then moved to a much harder antibank line. When the bank's charter expired in January 1845, Fitzpatrick refused to support its renewal and signed a bill eliminating the state's support of the banking system altogether. He continued, however, adamantly to oppose radical Democrat efforts to repudiate the state debt, which had been contracted in large part to keep the banks in operation. When he left the governorship, the legislature chose him as one of the three commissioners to supervise the bank's final liquidation.

Although the bank issue dominated Fitzpatrick's two administrations, he also continued to advocate actions to limit the power of government. In his first inaugural address, Fitzpatrick succinctly stated the antebellum attitude toward taxation: "The essence of modern oppression is taxation. The measure of popular liberty may be found in the amount of money which is taken from the people to support the government; when the amount is increased beyond the requirement of a rigid economy, the government becomes profligate and oppressive." Consistent with this antigovernment view, Fitzpatrick championed a constitutional amendment that changed meetings of the legislature from annual to biennial sessions.

In November 1848 Governor Reuben Chapman appointed Fitzpatrick to the vacancy in the U.S. Senate created by the death of Dixon H. Lewis, and when the state legislature met in 1849, the Democratic caucus, under the influence of the Montgomery Regency, chose him as its nominee for the full term. A group of north Alabama Democrats led by Jeremiah Clemens of Huntsville, reflecting the abiding sectional divisions in Alabama, bolted the caucus on the contention that Fitzpatrick's election would unfairly give both Senate seats to south Alabama. On the sixth ballot, Whig members threw their votes to Clemens, and Fitzpatrick was defeated. In January 1853 Governor Henry W. Collier appointed Fitzpatrick to the Senate once again, this time to succeed William R. King, who had been elected vice president of the United States. Fitzpatrick was overwhelmingly elected to the seat by the legislature in November, and in 1855 he was reelected to a full term over a Know-Nothing candidate.

In the Senate, Fitzpatrick devoted most of his attention to public land policy. He strongly supported the reduction of public land prices and fought for preemption rights for squatters on lands the federal government had granted to railroads. He played an active role in obtaining the passage of the Homestead Bill of 1860 but, in an act of party loyalty, refused to vote to override President James Buchanan's veto of it. He was the U.S. Senate's president pro tempore from December 1857 to January 1861, when Alabama seceded from the Union.

In the late 1850s Fitzpatrick was whipsawed between those who supported immediate secession from the Union and those who wanted to take a more moderate course. He had long been an enthusiastic advocate of Stephen A. Douglas's doctrine of popular sovereignty in the territories, and this earned him the active opposition of William Lowndes Yancey and Yancey's following of young and ambitious southern rights Democrats. When Fitzpatrick sought early reelection to the Senate in 1859, Yanceyites in the state legislature blocked the resolution to call the election. Not surprisingly, this action made Fitzpatrick and Yancey bitter enemies.

In the summer of 1860 the Baltimore Democratic National Convention nominated Fitzpatrick for vice president on a ticket with the Unionist Douglas. Fitzpatrick initially gave his consent to the candidacy, but discovering on his return home how unpopular Douglas was in Alabama, he declined the nomination. The split among Alabama's Democrats, however, remained. In the election of delegates to the secession convention in December 1860, Fitzpatrick became one of the leaders of the opposition to the Yanceyite faction. The Yanceyites were advocating immediate, separate state secession, and Fitzpatrick sought to defeat them by endorsing instead the cooperative secession of all the southern states by joint action. Fitzpatrick, however, was able to generate substantial support for his proposal only in Alabama's northern counties. When the convention adopted the secession ordinance, Fitzpatrick resigned his Senate seat on January 21, 1861, and returned to his plantation. Two years later, when his name was placed in nomination for a seat in the Confederate Senate, southern rights radicals who remained irreconcilably opposed to Fitzpatrick helped to defeat him.

With the end of the Civil War, Fitzpatrick was elected to represent Autauga County in the constitutional convention of 1865, summoned under the terms of presidential Reconstruction. When the delegates met, Fitzpatrick was unanimously chosen the convention's president, but this proved to be his last participation in public life. The constitution produced by the convention was voided, and Fitzpatrick himself was disfranchised by the terms of the Military Reconstruction Acts of 1867. He died at his plantation on November 21, 1869.

References

Abrams, David L. "The State Bank of Alabama, 1841–1845." Master's thesis, Auburn University, 1965.

Duncan, William W. "The Life of Benjamin Fitzpatrick." Master's thesis, University of Alabama, 1930.

Thornton, J. Mills, III. *Politics and Power in a Slave Society: Alabama, 1800–1860.* Baton Rouge: Louisiana State University Press, 1978.

48
◇

Joshua L. Martin, 1845–1847

HUGH C. BAILEY

JOSHUA Lanier Martin, the Alabama governor who delivered the final blow to the state bank, was a descendant of a French immigrant, Louis Montaigne. Montaigne, who changed his name to Martin, immigrated to South Carolina in 1724 and then, like the ancestors of numerous other Alabama families, made the trek to Tennessee, where Joshua Martin was born near Maryville in Blount County on December 5, 1799. Martin received an excellent general education under the tutelage of two local ministers, and in 1819, at the age of twenty, he moved with his family to Alabama. He married twice—first to Mary Gillam Mason and later to Sarah Ann Mason—sisters who were members of the distinguished Mason family of Virginia. By his wives, Martin had seven children, five sons and two daughters.

Martin was a precocious young man who had an ingratiating personality and an aptitude for the law. After studying law with his brother in Russellville, he was admitted to the bar, opened a law office in Athens, and in 1822 was elected to the state legislature as a representative from Limestone County, a position he held, except for one year, until 1828. In assuming his seat in Tuscaloosa, Martin began a career of public service that was to encompass the remaining thirty-four years of his life.

In 1829 Martin was elected solicitor of the Fourth Judicial Circuit; five years later he defeated a former justice of the Alabama Supreme Court, Judge John White of Talladega, for a seat on the Circuit Court. In 1835 he was elected as one of Alabama's five representatives to the U.S. Congress, and he was reelected in 1837. At the end of his second term, Martin returned to private life and in 1841 was elected chancellor of the Middle Chancery Division of the state, a position he held until he became governor.

Martin's election as governor was directly related to his consistent opposition to the state bank, which was chartered in 1823 in the wake of the Panic of 1819. For more than a decade the bank won the almost universal approval of Alabamians, providing financing that was otherwise unavailable and in some *Martin* years, through its profits, paying the state's operating expenses and allowing the legislature to abolish direct taxes. When the depression of 1837 came, the imprudent actions of the bank and its branches led to serious consequences, and the bank's charter, which expired in 1845, was not renewed. Yet, powerful forces within both the Whig and Democratic Parties were in favor of renewing the charter and saving the bank. In 1845 antibank delegates were delayed in arriving at the Democratic convention at Tuscaloosa because their boats could not move through the surprisingly shallow levels in the Warrior and Tombigbee Rivers. In their absence, probank delegates constituted a majority and hurriedly nominated Nathaniel Terry of Limestone County, a legislator and large debtor to the bank, as the party's candidate for governor.

Martin, who was incensed by the Democratic convention's action, acceded to the request of many who shared his views on the bank and ran as an independent candidate. Like the national campaign of 1840, the 1845 Alabama gubernatorial contest was one of the most intense the state had yet seen. The Whigs did not field a candidate and were divided in their sentiment regarding Terry's fitness for office. Some of them supported Terry and his probank position, but others found him anathema because he had authored the general ticket law, soon repealed, that provided for the election of the state's congressional delegates "at large." The odiousness of the bank and Martin's intense campaigning led to his election by a five-thousand-vote margin.

As governor, Martin was often opposed and maligned by the "regular" Democrats who never forgave the disloyalty of his bolt from the party. Nevertheless, he pursued the dismantling of the bank with vigor. The legislature appointed Francis S. Lyons of Marengo County to collect as much of the debt owed to the bank as possible and to liquidate its assets and obligations. Lyons performed the mission with great ability until his retirement in 1853. Although the state lost millions of dollars, its credit was protected and economic disaster averted.

During the one-term governor's tenure the legislature acknowledged the growing population of the newly created counties that had emerged from former Creek lands in central and east Alabama by approving removal of the capital from Tuscaloosa to the more central location at Montgomery. The amendment to the constitution that accomplished this move was ratified by a narrow margin, and in 1846 Martin and the state government moved into the capitol that was built and paid for by the city fathers of Montgomery. The operation of the poorly managed state penitentiary, which had opened in Wetumpka in 1841, was privatized in 1846. A six-year lease provided that for $500 in annual rent and the payment of operating expenses, John Graham of Coosa County had the right to all profits that could be earned from inmates' labor. While these events were occurring, the Mexican War enjoyed popular support in Alabama, and many of the state's citizens volunteered for army service, although few saw actual battleground action during the brief conflict.

Although Martin would have liked a second term, he understood that he was a pariah to many within the party and that his candidacy would do irreparable damage to the Democrats and almost certainly insure a Whig victory. He finally chose not to run for a second term, and in 1847 resumed the practice of law in Tuscaloosa. He was again elected to the state legislature in 1853 and died three years later in Tuscaloosa on November 2, 1856. Martin's legacy was one of dedicated public service through the Democratic Party, which ironically reached its zenith when, as an independent governor, he did what other Democrats had feared to do and dismembered the state bank.

References

Moore, Albert B. *History of Alabama*. 1934. Reprint, Tuscaloosa: Alabama Book Store, 1951.

Neeley, Mary Ann. "Painful Circumstances: Glimpses of the Alabama Penitentiary, 1846–1852." *Alabama Review* 44 (January 1991): 3–16.

Owen, Thomas M. *A History of Alabama and Dictionary of Alabama Biography*. 4 vols. 1921. Reprint, Spartanburg, S.C.: Reprint Co., 1978.

Stewart, John Craig. *The Governors of Alabama*. Gretna, La.: Pelican Publishing, 1975.

II

Crises, Civil War, and Reconstruction, 1847–1874

In 1861 Alabama seceded from the Union, but the issues and circumstances that caused that event were in play from the first years of Alabama's statehood. During the state's first three decades, internal issues of banking, capital location, Indian removal, and partisan politics between largely sectional interests kept the population of the state from focusing entirely on the big "enemy"—the federal government and its protective tariffs, its monster banking system, and, worst of all, its interference in slavery. In the 1840s and 1850s, issues related to slavery occurred more often and with more acrimony. The admission of Texas and California to the Union, debates over the Wilmot Proviso and the Compromise of 1850, "Bleeding Kansas," and the Dred Scott decision kept the subject uppermost in the national dialogue. Strong emotions and forceful, if not always honorable, personalities exacerbated issues in the state.

Alabama was deeply divided over secession, and the northern half of the state was filled with many residents who never gave up their devotion to the Union. Secession led to civil war, and, although no major battles were fought in the state, much of Alabama's upcountry and portions of the south were decimated by raiding troops from both armies. Alabama soldiers fought for the Confederate cause elsewhere, and their losses of life and property were enormous. The Reconstruction era followed, and the state's sectional, racial, and class divisions widened during the "Tragic Era." Reconstruction had the effect of making the Republican Party so unpopular among whites that the state moved toward total Democratic Party control.

Reuben Chapman, 1847–1849

JOHN R. MAYFIELD

R EUBEN Chapman's one term as governor was not a time of legislative innovations or notable administrative initiatives. Rather, it served as a transition from Jacksonian-style politics concerned with internal issues such as state banking and Indian removal to politics increasingly dominated by national issues. During Chapman's tenure, Alabama's response to national events sped the process by which state issues became submerged beneath a wave of proslavery and prosecession rhetoric.

Reuben Chapman was born in Virginia on July 15, 1799, the son of Ann Reynolds and Reuben Chapman, a minor officer in the revolutionary war. In 1824, when young Reuben was twenty-five, he traveled on horseback to Alabama, where he read law in his brother Samuel's office. He then moved to Morgan County and ultimately to Huntsville in Madison County. He prospered and soon acquired a plantation in Black Belt Sumter County, thus forging connections in both sections of the state. He remained a bachelor until age thirty-nine, when he married a sixteen-year-old girl, Felicia Pickett. Together they reared two sons and four daughters. One nineteenth-century observer described Chapman as "bright, humorous and impressive in conversation, with courtly manners." On Sundays he took a pew in the Episcopal Church.

Chapman

In 1835 Chapman entered Congress from his north Alabama district and was reelected six times. He was a loyal Democrat, taking the usual Jacksonian line against a national bank, high tariffs, and such. There was nothing remarkable about his service until the introduction in 1846 of the Wilmot Proviso, a rider to an appropriations bill that, if passed, would bar slavery from any territories acquired from Mexico as a result of U.S. victory in its war with that nation. At that possibility Chapman came alive. He immediately voiced his opposition, and his public denunciations put him in line with a group of proslavery, southern disciples of South Carolina states' rights senator John C. Calhoun. A rising star among these Calhounites was Alabama's own William Lowndes Yancey, a fire-eating, proslavery editor and lawyer who presided over the Democratic convention in 1847 and placed Chapman's name in nomination for governor.

It was a timely and perhaps brilliant move. Incumbent Joshua Martin's bolt from the Democratic Party in 1845 made him unacceptable as a candidate in 1847. Nathanial Terry, who had won the Democratic nomination in 1845 only to be rejected by the voters, campaigned hard for another chance. Another contender for the nomination was Henry W. Collier, a Tuscaloosa lawyer who, like the Whigs, favored privately chartered banks that might ease the tight money supply. In Chapman, Alabama Democrats had a compromise choice: a regular party man who had not been directly involved in the Terry-Martin bank controversy of 1845, a man who was antibank and thus satisfied that important segment of the party, and a north Alabamian who was also a planter known to be friendly to the interests of the Black Belt.

In response to Terry's machinations at the 1845 convention, Democrats changed the party rules so that two-thirds of the delegate votes, rather than a simple majority, were necessary for nomination. The Terry forces at the convention stuck together through nineteen ballots, but after ten hours, an exhausted crowd finally nominated Chapman by acclamation. Whigs, noting the Democratic factionalism, sensed victory and nominated their own north Alabama candidate, Nicholas Davis, a Limestone County planter, but Chapman defeated him handily by more than six thousand votes. He promptly threw a festive and opulent inaugural ball.

Behind the gaiety lay a darker reality. Chapman saw Alabama's important challenges as being almost entirely external. In a pattern that would become almost a gubernatorial *sine qua non* over the coming decades and even to the present, Chapman took the many real and hard problems of the state—in this case debtor relief and an inadequate money supply—and simply ignored them. Rather, he preferred to attack "outside interference," calling on his fellow Alabamians to resist all northern attempts to prevent slaveholders from taking their property wherever they pleased. To do otherwise, he asserted, would make Alabamians "serfs where we were equals, and equals only with our serfs." It was rhetoric that delighted Yancey and the great mass of Alabamians.

Chapman's inaugural speech was a harbinger of the political atmosphere to come. Of seven pages of printed text, the new governor spent only two on state issues, and there he dealt primarily with the evils of banks. He offered no initiatives, announcing only his firm opposition to "the policy of chartering banks of any description" and warned that the state was too much in debt to contemplate improvements in public works or enhanced education. The rest of the speech was a diatribe against the "General Government." Chapman opened his address with a vague warning about states' rights, which he quickly narrowed to a single subject: the Wilmot Proviso. The proviso, he warned, was not simply a proposition to bar slavery from territories won in the war; it was a first step toward "other still more direct measures in Congress to abolish slavery." In language that was astonishingly blunt for 1847, Chapman declared the Missouri Compromise a mistake *"in law"* that was tolerable only because slaveholders would not want to take their property into colder climates anyway. But he conceded that, if the Missouri Compromise line kept passions at bay, "it ought to be faithfully and honestly observed." Still, he argued, slaveholders must never allow an act of Congress to prohibit slavery in any other territory. To do so would be to make the constitution and the Union "the instrument of our degradation and final destruction." To Chapman and the South's relief, although the Wilmot Proviso passed in the House of Representatives, it was defeated in the U.S. Senate. Over the next decade the sentiments expressed by Chapman evolved into something like a southern mantra for the fire-eaters.

More mundane matters awaited Chapman when the state legislature met. There he had little time or inclination to innovate. He did veto a bill that would have chartered the Mobile and Ohio Railroad in Alabama on the simple grounds that buried in the act was language that would make the parent company tax exempt. A similar, but less offensive, measure ultimately passed. Chapman was deeply interested in the affairs of the University of Alabama and especially in an important professorship in geology and agriculture that existed there. He did not win his argument to split the position into two separate professorships, but happily secured the appointment of a gifted state geologist. In 1848 the legislature chose Michael Tuomey to teach at the university and to serve as the state's geologist. His study of the mineral deposits of the state is still considered a classic.

Chapman ultimately made a number of political mistakes that led to his downfall. He proposed taxing land that had recently been purchased from the federal government, although previous law and tradition left such lands tax free for five years. He remained firmly opposed to banks, which left the state with no settled policy on banking and currency. Alabamians were forced to rely either on specie, of which there was too little, or on paper money from other states, of which there was too much. As the price of cotton began to rise and influential men in both parties began to press their schemes for railroads to transport their crops, pressure for a rational banking system mounted. The still-ambitious gubernatorial candidate Collier, though a Democrat, co-opted Whigs and called for private banks. By 1849 he had won over a fair number of the anti–state bank Democrats. Chapman's intransigent stand against chartering banks of any description became a lonely one. His one wise act in dealing with the financial problems of the state was to reduce the bank commission from three members to one, leaving the extremely capable and hard-nosed Francis S. Lyons to finish dismantling the Bank of Alabama before he retired in 1853.

To add to his problems, Chapman had blundered badly early in his term. Through death and resignation, both of Alabama's U.S. Senate seats fell open in 1848. Despite the fact that north Alabama newspapers called for a convention to select two new senators, Chapman refused and appointed two south Alabamians to serve out the unexpired terms. This violated the unwritten rule that senate seats must be shared sectionally. This gaffe, added to the growing appeal of private banking, eliminated any chance Chapman had for renomination. At the convention he fell short of the same two-thirds vote that had earned him the nomination two years earlier. Henry Collier won, and he won again in the general election. Chapman's failure to win the convention in 1849 marked the first time that a Democratic incumbent failed to get a chance for a second term. (Joshua Martin, who had been elected governor as an independent, was not technically a Democrat.) In quiet acceptance of the inevitable, Chapman, in his last message to the legislature, gave his blessing to Collier's bank plans.

In that same message Chapman returned again to a discussion of the national landscape that had changed dramatically during his two-year tenure as governor. The nation was engulfed in controversy over the question of what to do about the territories taken by the United States during the Mexican War, and Congress was torn between extremists and those who hoped to fashion a compromise. In a harder, more threatening version of his inaugural, Chapman protested any attempt to exclude slavery from the Mexican cession, even California. More to the point, he attacked anyone who would attempt to make the defense of slavery a partisan issue within the state. "There is no division of sentiment among [the people of Alabama], and dangerous would be the spirit which, for party purposes, would represent the people composing one party as less sensitive to such wrongs and less disposed to redress them, than those of the other. We are one on this subject." Considering the rabid partisanship of the Jacksonian era, this call for unity was an extraordinary statement and one that signaled the ground shift occurring in southern politics.

Chapman remained involved in state politics until his death, but his only other run for office was to defeat Jeremiah Clemens, a Know-Nothing and former Whig-turned-nativist, for a seat in the state legislature in 1855. By 1860 southern Democrats such as Yancey had become proslavery zealots, and it was impossible for them to compromise. Too late, Chapman saw the probable disintegration of his party. When the Charleston convention of 1860 split over the nomination of Stephen A. Douglas, he traveled to Baltimore to plead for reconciliation and compromise. He failed. During the war that ensued, Chapman lost a son in battle, his home was burned, and he was imprisoned by northern troops. Like many of his fellow Confederates, he recovered and prospered after the war. His estate in Huntsville was considerable when he died on May 16, 1882.

References

Brantley, William H. *Banking in Alabama, 1816–1860.* 2 vols. Birmingham: Birmingham Printing Co., 1961.

Huntsville Democrat

Inaugural Address of Governor Chapman, Delivered December 16, 1847. Montgomery: McCormick and Walsh, 1847.

Journal of the House of Representatives, State of Alabama, 1849.

Montgomery Tri-Weekly Flag and Advertiser

Northern Alabama: Historical and Biographical Illustrated. Birmingham: N.p., 1888.

Owen, Marie Bankhead. *Our State: Alabama.* Birmingham: Birmingham Printing Co., 1927.

Thornton, J. Mills, III. *Politics and Power in a Slave Society: Alabama, 1800–1860.* Baton Rouge: Louisiana State University Press, 1978.

Henry W. Collier, 1849–1853

LEAH RAWLS ATKINS

IN THE aftermath of the U.S. war with Mexico (1845–48), sectional politics raged not only in Washington but also in Alabama, where the state Democratic Party was divided between the states' rights (Chivalry) and Unionist (Hunker) factions. Incumbent governor Reuben Chapman erred badly when he ignored public sentiment and tradition by appointing south Alabamians to finish the unexpired terms of Alabama's two U.S. senators. Opposition to Chapman's renomination was vigorous in north Alabama, where Unionist sentiment was strongest, especially because one of his appointees was the pro-secessionist ex-governor Benjamin Fitzpatrick. The Democratic Party needed a compromise candidate, and Henry Collier was its choice.

Henry Watkins Collier, the son of James Collier and Elizabeth Bouldin, was born on the family plantation in Lunenburg County, Virginia, on January 17, 1801. His father moved the family to the Abbeville district of South Carolina when Collier was a baby, and as a boy he was regularly taken to the Methodist

Collier

Church and educated in the classical tradition at the log-cabin academy of Dr. Moses Waddel. Collier traveled with his parents to the Alabama Territory in 1818, settled in Huntsville, and read law with Judge John Haywood of the

Tennessee Supreme Court in Nashville. He began practicing law in Huntsville but soon moved to Tuscaloosa, where he established a law practice with Simon (Sion) L. Perry.

In 1826 Collier—a handsome man with a dignified bearing, gray wide-set eyes, and a high forehead—married Mary Ann Battle, a descendant of wealthy and influential North Carolina families. The marriage produced four children who lived to adulthood. For several years Mrs. Collier's niece, Virginia Tunstall, lived with the family following her mother's death in North Carolina. On February 1, 1843, at the Collier home, eighteen-year-old Virginia married a young legislator, Clement Comer Clay Jr., son of former governor Clay. The alliance of these two families strengthened the political careers of both Collier and the younger Clay.

In 1827, after Tuscaloosa became the capital of Alabama, Collier ran for the legislature, advocating the construction of a new capitol in Tuscaloosa. He served one term in the state house of representatives, where he built a reputation for fairness, hard work, an astute understanding of the law, and a judicious disposition. The legislature elected him a judge of the Third Circuit Court, which had the effect of making Collier a member of the ad hoc Alabama Supreme Court. When the legislature constituted a separate and distinct supreme court in 1836, Collier was elevated to that court and made its chief justice, a position he held for twelve years. During his tenure on the courts, he wrote some 1,165 thoughtful, well-reasoned opinions, which caused William Garrett to note in his 1872 reminiscences that Collier's opinions "form his most enduring monument."

In June 1849 the Democratic Party, with the states' rights group in control, met in Montgomery. Although many delegates expected they would nominate Governor Chapman for a second term, the party ultimately decided to support Collier as a compromise candidate to ensure victory in the August elections. Two diverse factions supported Collier: those who followed Clay, the leader of the north Alabama states' rights group, and those who listened to south Alabama Unionist (at that time) William Rufus King, whose nephew and adopted son was to marry Collier's daughter in 1856. The Whigs, satisfied that Collier agreed with their attitude that government should be used to stimulate economic growth, did not nominate a candidate. Although there were scattered votes for other candidates, Collier won the governorship with 37,221 votes, and his opponents jointly mustered only 704. Historian Mills Thornton noted that Whig faith in Collier was justified when Collier adopted and endorsed that party's policies on private banking. During the 1850s this Democratic governor created the statewide system of private banks about which the Whigs had long dreamed.

Three years earlier in 1846, the legislature had moved the seat of government to Montgomery, where a new capitol was constructed on Goat Hill. There the legislature certified Collier's election on November 16, 1849. On December 14, three days before his inauguration, the capitol burned, and Collier took his oath of office at the Montgomery Methodist Church.

During his tenure as governor, Collier promoted educational reform. He supported a state public education system and advocated more equitable funding for county schools. In 1850 he proposed the creation of a state superintendent's office to provide leadership and oversight, but the legislature rejected this idea. Collier attacked Alabama's inadequate funding of schools, calling it a "blighting apathy that pervades the community." The governor was equally progressive on other issues as well. During the 1849–50 legislative session, he supported judicial reforms, especially a constitutional amendment giving the people the right to elect circuit and probate judges. In 1850 Collier entertained Dorothea L. Dix when she visited Montgomery. Her advocacy of reform in the treatment of mentally ill and prison populations and Collier's support of her ideas led to the founding of the state hospital for the insane by the legislature in 1851, although it was 1860 before the facility opened. Collier also promoted prison reform, visited the state penitentiary regularly, and kept an eye on its supervision. Furthermore, Collier championed economic diversification and encouraged investment in textile mills. He recognized the importance of agriculture to the state's economy and petitioned the legislature to establish a professorship of agriculture at the University of Alabama, but no action was taken.

Despite the support for southern rights that he articulated in his inaugural address on December 17, 1849, Collier had a reputation for being a moderate, more in the Hunker wing than the Chivalry wing of the state Democratic Party. Divisive sectional issues that began when Chapman was governor had an impact on Collier's tenure, and his gubernatorial years were played out under a cloud of bitter debates over slavery and its expansion. The Compromise of 1850 was intensely debated in Alabama, and although Collier supported the compromise, he encouraged Alabama to send delegates to the June 1850 Nashville Convention to discuss southern rights and the South's loss of political power within the Union. Following that meeting he differed with the more radical states' righters when he refused their demand to call a separate convention to discuss the state's status in the Union, correctly understanding that the majority of Alabama's citizens did not yet favor secession.

Collier was renominated in 1851 and ran on the record of his first term. He so effectively occupied the middle ground that his token opposition came only from both the extremes—dissatisfied, fire-eating states' righters and Benjamin G. Shields, a staunch Unionist. His campaign was helped when the state's most outspoken secessionist, William L. Yancey, refused to run, forcing the southern rights faction to accept Collier as a compromise. Shields polled

59

only 5,747 votes, and Collier won handily. Although Collier's moderation held the Democratic Party together, within a few years it fractured as states' rights advocates moved toward the Southern Rights Party.

Governor Collier supervised the rebuilding of the capitol, which was completed and occupied before he left office in 1853. The capitol remains the central antebellum architectural structure in Montgomery. When his term of office ended, Collier retired from public life. His health was not good, and he refused the legislature's offer of a seat in the U.S. Senate. By June 1855 he was virtually bedridden but followed his doctors orders to travel to the springs. He journeyed first to Blount Springs and then to Lauderdale County's Bailey Springs, where he died on August 28, 1855, of cholera morbus, an early term for gastroenteritis. Collier's moderate and conservative leadership provided a period of calm before slavery issues and sectional politics fully captured the state in the storms that led to secession.

References

Alabama Court Reports. Reports of the Cases of the Alabama Appellate Courts, 1819—.

Brewer, Willis. *Alabama: Her History, Resources, War Record, and Public Men, from 1540 to 1872.* Montgomery: Barrett and Brown, 1872.

Collier, Henry Watkins. Papers. Alabama Department of Archives and History, Montgomery.

Dictionary of American Biography. American Council of Learned Societies, 1929.

Dorman, Lewy. *Party Politics in Alabama from 1850 through 1860.* Montgomery: Alabama State Department of Archives and History, Historic and Patriotic Series, no. 13, 1935.

Garrett, William. *Reminiscences of Public Men in Alabama for Thirty Years.* Atlanta: Plantation Publishing, 1872.

Owen, Thomas M. *History of Alabama and Dictionary of Alabama Biography.* 4 vols. Chicago: S. J. Clarke, 1921.

Riley, Benjamin F. *Makers and Romance of Alabama History.* N.p., [1915?].

Stewart, John Craig. *The Governors of Alabama.* Gretna, La.: Pelican Publishing, 1975.

Thornton, J. Mills, III. *Politics and Power in a Slave Society, Alabama, 1800–1860.* Baton Rouge: Louisiana State University Press, 1978.

John A. Winston, 1853–1857

WILLIAM L. BARNEY

A LABAMA'S first native-born governor, John Anthony Winston, was born on September 4, 1812, in the Tennessee Valley region of Madison County. Educated in private schools, he attended Cumberland College in Nashville, Tennessee, before his marriage in 1832 to Mary Agnes Walker. In 1835 the couple settled in Sumter County, where Winston had purchased a large plantation. Although this area of the western Black Belt was normally Whig in its politics, Winston repeatedly gained public office as a states' rights Democrat. After his election to the Alabama House of Representatives in 1840 and again in 1842, he served in the state senate from 1843 to 1853. He emerged as a leader of the southern rights wing of the Democrats when he served as president of the senate from 1845 to 1849.

Winston was successful in his public life but led a vexing private life. Since 1844 he had operated a cotton commission firm in Mobile, and he owned extensive plantations in Alabama, Mississippi, Arkansas, and Texas. Following the death of his first wife in 1842, he married Mary W. Longwood, but this marriage ended in a divorce granted by the legislature in 1850. The marriage effectively ended in 1847 when Winston discovered that his wife was having an affair with Sidney S. Perry, the family physician. Winston promptly shot the doctor to death. He suffered no penalty when county magistrates declared his action "justifiable homicide."

Winston

However stormy Winston's private life, his initial public image was one of political moderation. He was instrumental in preventing the Alabama delegation at the 1848 Baltimore convention of the Democratic Party from walking out with William Lowndes Yancey over the refusal of the convention to accept Yancey's Alabama Platform, which demanded congressional protection of slavery in the territories. Two years later during the sectional crisis provoked by debates leading to the Compromise of 1850, Winston again rejected the extreme prosecession, southern rights stand of Yancey and those who supported his position. When north Alabama Democrats joined south Alabama Whigs in a coalition Unionist Whig party in 1850–51, Winston became an architect of the reorganization of the Democrats along

61
◇

traditional partisan lines. He frequently reminded north Alabama Democrats of Whig snobbery and the value of Democratic patronage under the spoils system. As a reward for his party loyalty, he gained the Democratic gubernatorial nomination in 1853. He won that position with no opposition when his Whig opponent's poor health forced him to drop out.

In his inaugural address on December 20, 1853, Winston outlined his states' rights philosophy. Like a good Jacksonian Democrat, he deplored the use of state funds—the people's money—to assist private corporations in banking and transportation. Whatever economic benefits might result from state-supported development were more than offset, in Winston's mind, by the corrupting influence of corporate power and the dangers it posed to the individual liberties of the people. Winston offered those who sought to unify north and south Alabama along an axis of state-funded railroads only a hedged statement that if the state debt were completely eliminated, state funds might then be used for internal improvements from a treasury surplus through adequately secured loans. Apart from favoring "a judicious system of popular education," he pledged to keep the state out of the affairs of its citizens.

For all his talk of a strict construction of the state's constitution, Winston was not previously viewed as a doctrinaire ideologue on the issue of internal improvements. After all, he had attended the Mobile Internal Improvements Convention of 1851 and indicated during his gubernatorial campaign that he was open to limited state aid for railroads. Moreover, proponents of state aid, a loosely organized group centered in Tennessee Valley and eastern hill counties that stood to benefit most from projected routes for railroads, were confident that the governor would not defy the clearly expressed will of the legislature if aid bills were passed. Previous Alabama governors had been reluctant to veto legislation and generally had done so only on technical, constitutional grounds. When differences emerged over policy issues, governors usually deferred to the legislature. Thus, the state-aid men were genuinely surprised when Winston vetoed the railroad bills they pushed through the legislature. The only aid bills he approved in his first term were a loan of $400,000 to the Mobile and Ohio Railroad and a more limited offer of assistance to the Tennessee and Coosa line.

The most significant legislation to pass during Winston's first term was the Education Act of 1854, which inaugurated state aid for free public schools in Alabama. Sponsored by Mobile representative Alexander B. Meek and fashioned after that county's school system, the act provided for the state to divide $100,000 a year among the counties and allowed counties to collect real estate and personal property taxes for educational purposes. The act also created a state superintendent of education and was later amended to establish county superintendents. The state's timing was unfortunate, and little progress was made before the Civil War began.

Although Democratic politicians in Montgomery resented Winston's opposition to their railroad schemes, the average voter appreciated his stand against raiding the state treasury. He was easily nominated by his party in 1855 for a second term. His opponent was George D. Shortridge of the new Know-Nothing (American) Party, an amalgam of former Whigs and some Union Democrats. Shortridge ran as the candidate of progress and prosperity by coming out in favor of state financing for internal improvements. Winston, who had already politicized the issue, was delighted with the opportunity to center his campaign on the question of state aid. As he noted after the election, "I took the ground, emphatically, that under no circumstances would I sanction any measure using or pledging the credit of the State for any purpose whatever." He won reelection with nearly 60 percent of the vote, and more ballots were cast for him than for any antebellum governor of Alabama. In an ironic twist, the loser, George Shortridge, polled more votes against Winston than any candidate to that time had garnered against a Democrat, which demonstrated the intense interest of the public in the railroad aid issue.

In his biennial message to the legislature in November 1855, a triumphant Winston praised the "sober common sense of the people" for "correct[ing] the [railroad] mania that pervaded the minds of many, but a few months since. We should rejoice that for the future, there is hope that the acts of the State will be confined to the few simple legitimate purposes of a republican government." But he misread the temperament of the new legislature. In an effort to stem defections to the Know-Nothings, Democrats in north Alabama and the eastern hill counties had nominated prorailroad men for the legislature. These Democrats, along with the Know-Nothing members, constituted a legislature that was even more committed to state aid than its predecessor. Winston refused to give any ground.

In his second term Winston vetoed thirty-six bills passed in the 1855–56 legislative session, most of them dealing with grants of corporate privilege and the lending of state funds. He repeatedly held, as he put it in his veto of a bill providing a loan to the Memphis and Charleston Railroad, that "the only purpose for which the government has a right to exact the means of the citizen, is to carry on the affairs of the government, and to pay obligations already existing." He insisted that any straying from this core principle "brings, as inevitably as a departure from physical and moral law, a speedy punishment, and admonishes those who have fixed ideas of public policy of the dangers of any abandonment of principle in legislation and matters of government."

Although the legislature overturned twenty-seven of the vetoes, Winston used other methods to block the use of state funds for internal improvements. With political skills sharpened by years of infighting in the legislature, Winston was a formidable adversary, and, when challenged by the legislature, he knew how to turn the technicalities of the law to his advantage. Thus, when the railroad politicians attempted to get around Winston's prohibition on the use of state taxes for aid by turning to the retired notes of the Bank of Alabama as a source for loans, the governor stymied them by securing an opinion from the state attorney general that such use violated the prohibition in the U.S. Constitution against the emission of bills of credit by the states.

Winston's anticorporate stand on behalf of the people's money made him an undeniable popular hero, but it cost him the party support he needed to gain a U.S. Senate seat in 1857. In the words of future Reconstruction governor Robert M. Patton, a staunch opponent of Winston in the legislature of the 1850s, the problem was not just Winston's "mulish opposition to the legislature" but also his derailment of the promotional agenda so obviously favored by the railroad and commercial interests in the Democratic Party. His fellow Democrats succeeded in keeping Winston out of the Senate, and in 1859 they pushed a railroad bill through the legislature that provided the general aid Winston had so staunchly opposed. Passage of this bill established a dangerous precedent for state aid to railroads that would be important during the Reconstruction era.

Winston's hope for a Senate seat was also damaged by the perception that his southern rights credentials were not as strong as those of his opponent, although

Winston, as governor, repeatedly warned white Alabamians of a northern "war on our rights" and predicted that northern aggression "will inevitably drive us to dissolve the political ties which have heretofore existed between us and our assailants." Still, his southern rights credentials were not as strong as those of incumbent Clement Claiborne Clay, who held on to his Senate seat in 1857. Winston needed to strengthen his credentials as an advocate of southern rights if he hoped to win a seat in the Senate. Although he wanted his old enemy Yancey to look like the responsible person, it was Winston who actually caused the Alabama delegation to walk out of the 1860 Democratic Party convention in Charleston. He returned to Montgomery, where he made speeches accusing Yancey of having pursued a reckless course and of using rhetoric that created the environment that made the walkout necessary, destroying the party and insuring the election of Lincoln. Yancey's reputation suffered little; in fact, he became the man of the hour in Alabama when he led the state out of the Union. Winston, before his game playing, had supported the candidacy of Stephen A. Douglas, whose election he believed would save the Union. He miscalculated terribly, and his stand on behalf of cooperative action by the southern states was rejected at Alabama's secession convention in favor of immediate and separate state secession.

After serving as Governor Moore's appointee as Alabama's commissioner to Louisiana to consult on the secession crisis, Winston raised troops and fought in the Civil War as colonel of the Eighth Alabama Infantry. He saw action during the Virginia peninsula campaign in 1862, but poor health soon forced him to resign. After the war, he was a delegate to the state constitutional convention of 1865. Although he was elected finally to the U.S. Senate for the 1867–73 term, the Republican Congress refused to seat him when he would not take the oath of allegiance to the United States. Thoroughly committed to white supremacy, he remained a bitter enemy of Radical Reconstruction until his death.

Complications from rheumatism contributed to his death in Mobile on December 21, 1871. By then, Alabama was in the midst of an ambitious and expensive program of state aid for railroads, a far cry from the limited role of state government championed by Winston during his tenure as governor. No other antebellum governor so forcefully voiced the fears of the people's interests being corrupted by an alliance of public and corporate power. But John A. Winston's vision of an agrarian Alabama bound by the strict states' rights doctrines of Jacksonian democracy was now as much a relic of the past as the slave society he had so ardently defended.

References

Brewer, Willis. *Alabama: Her History, Resources, War Record, and Public Men, from 1540 to 1872*. Montgomery: Barrett and Brown, 1872.

Garrett, William. *Reminiscences of Public Men in Alabama for Thirty Years*. Atlanta: Plantation Publishing, 1872.

Sisk, Glenn N. "John Anthony Winston: Alabama's Veto Governor." Master's thesis, University of Alabama, 1934.

Thornton, J. Mills, III. *Politics and Power in a Slave Society: Alabama, 1800–1860*. Baton Rouge: Louisiana State University, 1978.

Andrew B. Moore, 1857–1861

LEAH RAWLS ATKINS

A NDREW Barry Moore is remembered in the state's history as the governor who took Alabama out of the Union. Ironically, he was elected as the moderate, nonsecessionist choice of Alabama voters. The son of a revolutionary war and War of 1812 veteran, Moore discovered by the end of his second term as governor that events beyond his control had moved his state to abandoning the Union it had joined only forty-two years before.

Andrew B. Moore
1857–1861

Moore, the son of Charles and Jane Barry Moore, was born on March 7, 1801, in the Spartanburg district of South Carolina. Although no information about his early education has survived, Moore evidently received a good one.

His father registered land in Perry County in 1820 where he joined an older son, Thomas W. B. Moore, who was the first of the family to settle in Perry County. The elder Moore established a plantation west of Marion near the old Fairview Presbyterian Church and became a successful cotton planter.

In 1826 young Andrew Moore arrived in Marion, which was still a frontier town with log cabins. One account suggests that he had remained in South Carolina to complete his education and another that he came to Marion on business and had no intention of remaining permanently. Whatever the reason, he was convinced by townspeople to stay and teach at a local school

Andrew Moore

for two years. He then read law with Elisha Young and Sidney M. Goode and was admitted to the bar in 1833. On December 5, 1832, Moore, a Presbyterian, married Mary Ann Goree, the daughter of a neighboring cotton planter, and the couple had four children.

Moore was six feet tall, well built, with sharp facial features. Although sometimes rigid, he was generally frank and cordial, a master at political party maneuvering, and possessed of a logical mind. One legislative contemporary described Moore as "a clever fellow but scary" who "has a good opinion of himself."

Moore served as a justice of the peace for eight years and in 1839 was elected to the state house of representatives on the Democratic ticket. The Whig Party was strong in Perry County, and Moore was defeated in 1840 but regained his legislative seat in 1842. In the legislative session the following year, Moore supported using only the white population to determine representation in the legislature despite the preference in his Black Belt community for counting all people, including slaves, which would have increased the legislative power of those counties. Nonetheless, Moore retained the confidence of his constituency and held his seat for three more sessions.

Moore was elected speaker of the state house in 1843, 1844, and 1845. From this powerful position he supported Governor Benjamin Fitzpatrick in his campaign to liquidate the Alabama state bank. Moore considered the bank to be a cancer destroying the credibility of state government, "eating into the very vitals of the body politic." He favored the removal of the capital from Tuscaloosa and its relocation in Montgomery, and he supported a constitutional amendment providing for biennial sessions of the legislature. When the house was in session, Moore often called for another member to take the speaker's chair so he could mingle on the floor and participate in the debate. The future governor was the last person to speak in the old statehouse in Tuscaloosa when he responded to a resolution of appreciation for his service as speaker.

In 1846 Moore returned to his law practice in Marion but remained active in the Democratic Party, often serving as a peacemaker between the Hunkers (moderate) and the Chivalry (states' rights) factions. In 1848 Moore was a presidential elector for the Democratic ticket, and in 1850 he represented Alabama as a delegate to the controversial Nashville Convention, which debated secession. In 1851 Governor Henry W. Collier appointed him to a vacancy on the First Circuit Court, where Moore served until 1857, when he accepted the Democratic Party's nomination for governor. His nomination occurred after twenty-six ballots and a spirited contest between several candidates. Moore was conservative, and although he supported southern rights, he was moderate on the issue of secession, whereas three of his opponents were extremists. Moore did not think the people of Alabama were ready for secession, and he believed the South's grievances did not yet justify disunion. The national Democratic Party, Moore argued, was the best protector of the South's rights within the Union. The Know-Nothing and Whig Parties were weak in Alabama, and there was no opposition to Moore's candidacy in the general election.

Moore's first years in office were relatively quiet and reflected a reformist attitude. He supervised the construction of the state hospital for the insane in Tuscaloosa and saw it opened under the supervision of Dr. Peter Bryce. Moore took a special interest in the hospital because his wife experienced mental problems. The school for the deaf and blind in Talladega was completed during this time. Moore pushed for completion of the Alabama and Tennessee River Railroad, which would connect north and south Alabama and provide transportation from the Tennessee River to the Alabama River. Unfortunately, the railroad was completed only to Blue Mountain near Talladega by the time war began in 1861. Moore supported increased appropriations for Alabama schools and a separate state prison for female inmates.

In 1859 Moore was renominated, but in this election he faced spirited opposition from William F. Samford, who represented the extreme southern rights faction and was a strong secessionist. Samford's poor health kept him from campaigning in person, but he circulated flyers and wrote hundreds of letters to newspapers and political leaders portraying Moore as too weak in defending the South. Moore won reelection by a comfortable margin and continued a cautious course, still convinced that Alabamians were not yet ready for secession. John Brown's raid at Harper's Ferry, Virginia, in October 1859 changed his mind, and in his second inaugural speech, delivered in December 1859, he addressed the issue of southern rights forcefully.

During the 1859–60 session of the legislature, Governor Moore recommended, and the legislature approved, various acts to prepare the state to defend itself. A military bill provided for a volunteer corps in every county and a $200,000 appropriation to equip the troops. Two scholarships were funded for each county to send students to military schools. Moore recommended that the mineral district of Alabama be developed and that construction of the South and North Railroad be expedited so that the vast mineral resources of Alabama could be connected with the rest of the South. Although during the campaign he advocated reducing taxes, Moore shifted his position after the election and advised the legislature to address first the reduction of the state's debt.

Moore refused, however, to go along with South Carolina governor William H. Gist's request for a southern convention to consult on secession. He preferred, instead, a resolution pending in the Alabama legislature that instructed him to call an election of delegates to a secession convention should a "black Republican" be elected president. This was the conservative alternative because Moore was still convinced that the Democratic Party candidate would win in 1860 and thus a crisis would be averted one more time. When the results of the presidential votes in the North began to reach Montgomery in early November, people became excited, and a mass meeting was called. Moore spoke to the crowd, finally admitting that he saw secession as the only way the South could protect itself after the election of a Republican candidate. The crowd cheered when he said that Alabama should protect its sovereignty.

68
◇   The somewhat reluctant governor called for a special election to select delegates to a secession convention. He sent letters to state banks asking that they suspend specie payments and hold reserves for the state. Moore dispatched agents into northern states to purchase arms and ammunition for the state's militia and sent commissioners to other southern states to consult on the issue of secession. On January 3, 1861, four days before the secession convention was to meet, Governor Moore ordered Alabama troops to seize federal installations in the state: the arsenal at Mount Vernon and Fort Morgan and Fort Gaines at the entrance to Mobile Bay. In this executive order, both praised and condemned, Moore took control of federal property while Alabama was technically still in the Union.

On January 11 the Alabama secession convention adopted an ordinance that dissolved "the Union between the State of Alabama and other States united under the compact styled 'The Constitution of the United States of America.'" In the remaining months of his term, Moore welcomed delegates to the Confederate Congress and arranged through his daughter's mother-in-law, Mrs. Napoleon Lockett, to have Nicola Marschall design a Confederate flag. This flag, the "Stars and Bars" and not the well-known Confederate battle flag, was raised over the capitol in Montgomery for the first time while President Abraham Lincoln was making his inaugural address. Publicly, Moore took a back seat during the months when Montgomery was the capital of the

Confederacy, but he appointed both an adjutant general and a quartermaster general for the state and took steps to prevent speculators from benefiting from the scramble for supplies and food.

Moore's term of office ended on December 2, 1861. Although he turned the responsibility of government over to his successor, John Gill Shorter, he continued to support the war effort as a special aide to the new governor. In this capacity Moore traveled to north Alabama to recruit troops and supplies, and throughout the war he worked to supply salt and food to the state's indigent and to the widows and wives of Confederate soldiers.

At war's end in the spring of 1865, Moore was imprisoned by federal troops at Fort Pulaski, Georgia, along with several other southern governors and political leaders. Because of his poor health, he was released from prison in August and returned to his home in Marion. In the years after the war, he practiced law as his health allowed. Moore died at his home on April 5, 1873. Obituaries in the *Selma Times* and the *Mobile Register* gave no cause of death, but they praised his integrity, charity, courage, and leadership for the state during the crisis of secession and war.

References

Brewer, Willis. *Alabama: Her History, Resources, War Record, and Public Men, from 1540 to 1872*. Montgomery: Barrett and Brown, 1872.

Dorman, Lewy. *Party Politics in Alabama from 1850 through 1860*. Montgomery: Alabama State Department of Archives and History, Historic and Patriotic Series, no. 13, 1935.

Garrett, William. *Reminiscences of Public Men in Alabama for Thirty Years*. Atlanta: Plantation Publishing, 1872.

Knapp, Virginia. "William Phineas Browne, Business Man and Pioneer Mine Operator of Alabama." *Alabama Review* 3 (April 1950): 116.

McMillan, Malcolm C. *The Alabama Confederate Reader*. University: University of Alabama Press, 1963.

McMillan, Malcolm C. *The Disintegration of a Confederate State: Three Governors and Alabama's Wartime Home Front, 1861–1865*. Macon, Ga.: Mercer University Press, 1986.

Moore, Andrew Barry. Papers. Alabama State Department of Archives and History, Montgomery.

Owen, Thomas M. *History of Alabama and Dictionary of Alabama Biography*. 4 vols. Chicago: S. J. Clarke, 1921.

Stewart, John Craig. *The Governors of Alabama*. Gretna, La.: Pelican Publishing, 1975.

Thornton, J. Mills, III. *Politics and Power in a Slave Society: Alabama, 1800–1860*. Baton Rouge: Louisiana State University Press, 1978.

John Gill Shorter, 1861–1863

HENRY M. MCKIVEN

OHN Gill Shorter inherited the governor's chair just as Civil War hardships began to be felt by the people of Alabama. A Jackson Democrat, Shorter had entered state politics in 1845 and was deeply affected by the debate that arose in the nation later that decade over the right of southerners to carry their slaves into new territories acquired by the United States. He and other "Young Democrats" put aside Jacksonian policies for what they considered to be a more modern and forward-looking ideology based on the sectional considerations espoused by Alabama's impassioned orator William Lowndes Yancey.

Shorter was born in Monticello, Georgia, on April 3, 1818, and remained there when his father moved in 1833 to east Alabama, where the elder Shorter began to acquire property in and around Irvinton, later Eufaula, in Barbour County. After his graduation from the University of Georgia, young John followed his family to Alabama in 1837. By the mid-1840s, Shorter's family had acquired enough land to rank them among the wealthiest families in Barbour County. In addition, John and his brother Eli created one of the most successful

law practices in that part of the state. John Gill, a Baptist, married Mary Jane Battle, also of Eufaula, in 1843, and they had one daughter who lived to maturity.

John and Eli, who later served as an Alabama congressman, parlayed their local influence into successful political careers. As the son of a man devoted to the tenets of Jacksonian democracy, John Gill joined the Barbour County Democratic Party. In 1845 he won election to the state senate, where he served one term, but chose not to run for a second. He returned to active politics in 1851 when he won a seat in the state house. Shorter, however, left the legislature when Governor Henry Collier appointed him circuit judge of the Eufaula district. He

Shorter

won election to that judgeship in 1852 and remained in that position until his election as governor in 1861.

Moving from Jacksonian nationalism to Yancey's states' rights sectionalism, Shorter and his fellow Alabama delegates to the 1850 Nashville Convention sought to push the issue of slavery in the territories to the forefront of southern political discourse. Although in 1850 he did not yet believe that secession was the way to deal with threats to southern rights, Shorter and others among the elitist Eufaula Regency (a group of lawyer-planters both Whig and Democrats) clearly believed that the region should prepare for that possibility should other means of redressing southern grievances fail. Throughout the 1850s, Shorter attempted to persuade his constituents that their personal independence rested on a determined resistance to those in the nation who would reduce the South to a state of inequality within the Union.

Shorter's political goals were not limited to agitation of the southern rights issue. Influenced by the *laissez-faire* doctrines coming out of Britain during the 1850s and concerned about the economic future of the South, he joined other young Alabama Democrats in linking southern sectionalism to a vision of economic development quite different from their Jacksonian forbears. These young Democrats endorsed free trade, state investment in education, and internal improvements as ways to move the state's economy forward and to free the South from northern dependence.

Secession appeared to offer Shorter an opportunity to build a government and society more consistent with southern ideals as he understood them. His initial service to the Confederacy was to act as commissioner to his native Georgia on behalf of Governor Andrew B. Moore. In this capacity, he urged the people of that state to cooperate in secession. He was one of only two Yanceyites from Alabama to be elected to the provisional Confederate Congress, where he assisted in writing the Confederate constitution and urged the congress to pass a provision that states owned all the public land within their borders. In May 1861 Shorter and other members of the Confederate Congress left Montgomery to convene in Richmond, Virginia, the permanent capital of the Confederacy.

In August 1861 at age forty-three, Shorter defeated former Whig Thomas Hill Watts of Montgomery and three other candidates to become the first governor elected under the flag of the Confederate states. The candidates ran limited formal campaigns, and Shorter's reputation as an all-out secessionist along with his name recognition as a Confederate congressman led to his easy victory by a margin of almost ten thousand votes. Ironically, the secessionist Shorter won with the votes of nonsecessionist north Alabamians; the former Whig Unionist Watts carried most of south Alabama's Black Belt.

Shorter's inaugural address sought to unite Alabamians as a people distinct from and superior to the "Yankee race." He spoke of the need to end commercial, social, and political dependence on "a people who appreciate neither the value of liberty nor the sanctity of compacts." Shorter expressed hope that Alabamians would steel themselves for the sacrifice required to complete their revolution.

John Gill Shorter
1861–1863

The realities of the war soon intruded, however, forcing Shorter to compromise virtually every principle he had endorsed in the 1850s. A man who had devoted much of his political life to defending states' rights and limited government, Shorter oversaw an enormous expansion of power to both the Confederate government in Richmond and the state government in Montgomery. Not long after his inaugural in December 1861, the Confederate States of America enacted its conscription law, and Shorter, after protesting the law's broad and illogical exemptions, assisted in its enforcement. To Alabamians and most other Americans north and south, no greater violation of individual liberty existed than to require that a man serve in the army. Voters remembered Shorter's support of this measure and held him accountable when he ran for reelection in 1863.

Shorter was forced, albeit reluctantly, to expand the power and role of state government. Faced with a critical shortage of manpower for the construction of defenses at Mobile, he sought legislation to allow him to impress slaves into forced labor for the state. Until the legislation was passed in October 1862, the governor forced slaves into service under his emergency war powers. For the remainder of his term, he faced withering criticism from slave owners over this policy. They bitterly complained about the poor care slaves received in Mobile and on defense projects in other locations. Once again, harsh reality forced Shorter to abandon his own strongly held principles.

During Shorter's tenure as governor, much of north Alabama fell into Union hands, and Union raids moved into central Alabama as well. He appointed former governor Moore as his military aide to raise troops in north Alabama to fight the Union invaders. Volunteers were told to bring their own horses and rifles, reflecting the desperate arms scarcity among southern troops as early as spring 1862. Shorter issued an order to make the University of Alabama a military training school, although it had been offering its students military training since John Brown's raid in 1859. Flexible when faced with military exigencies, Shorter invested more of the state's dwindling resources in defending Mobile.

Although generous to the military, Shorter remained steadfastly consistent in his prewar hostility toward government action to meet individual needs. With the exception of helping soldiers' families, Shorter opposed legislation to provide food or housing for the thousands of other Alabamians who suffered excruciating deprivation during the war. When the legislature began consideration of laws to control the soaring prices of goods, Shorter warned against violation of the laws of the market, arguing that such legislation would make matters only worse. The governor finally signed a compromise price control bill that, due to his opposition, was much weaker than originally written. By 1863 circumstances were so horrific that Shorter could no longer ignore the need for government action, and he finally supported a measure that appropriated funds to be distributed to counties to provide aid to indigent citizens. To this welcome but inadequate assistance, Shorter also employed state agents to purchase foodstuffs for distribution throughout the state.

By the election of 1863, a man who had professed the value of *laissez-faire* and free trade doctrines had reluctantly overseen the greatest expansion of state government in Alabama history. Without doubt, some in the state survived the war because of his "big government" programs for the state's needy. But his help was too little and too late and did not translate into votes for Shorter in 1863. The state had suffered invasion by northern troops, taxes and prices had soared, the war dragged on much longer than originally anticipated, and those left in the state were desperate. Shorter ran a low-key reelection campaign, but men who thought the government had done too much joined men who thought the government had done too little to elect Thomas Hill Watts governor by an almost three-to-one vote. Shorter did not even carry his own Barbour County and joined the ranks of the few Alabama governors of this era who failed to win election to a second term. His all-out secessionism and wartime hardships cost him dearly. He was a graceful loser who cooperated with his successor and, after the war, quietly returned to his law practice in Eufaula, where he died on May 29, 1872.

References

Fleming, Walter Lynwood. *Civil War and Reconstruction in Alabama.* New York: Columbia University Press, 1905.

McMillan, Malcolm C. *The Disintegration of a Confederate State: Three Governors and Alabama's Wartime Home Front, 1861–1865.* Macon, Ga.: Mercer University Press, 1986.

Thornton, J. Mills, III. *Politics and Power in a Slave Society: Alabama, 1800–1860.* Baton Rouge: Louisiana State University Press, 1978.

73
◇

Thomas H. Watts, 1863–May 1865

HENRY M. MCKIVEN

ALTHOUGH Thomas Hill Watts refused to campaign for governor in 1863, he agreed to serve if the people of Alabama elected him. He remained in Richmond during most of the campaign, performing his role as the Confederacy's attorney general, and won a landslide victory over the unpopular incumbent, John Gill Shorter.

Thomas H. Watts
1863–1865

Watts was born in the Alabama Territory on January 3, 1819, to a prominent planter family. He grew up in Butler County in south Alabama and returned there after graduating with honors in 1840 from the University of Virginia. Young Watts actively supported Whig candidate William Henry Harrison in the 1840 election. In 1841 he began to practice law in Greenville, and a year later he

made his own initial foray into politics when he won election to the state house as a Whig, representing Butler County. He served in that capacity through 1845. In 1848 he moved his law practice to Montgomery, where he began to acquire considerable holdings in land and slaves. Montgomery County citizens elected him first to the lower house of the legislature and then, in 1853, to the state senate.

Watts's position on sectional issues in the early 1850s differed little from mainstream southern Whigs. He supported the Compromise of 1850, believing that continued agitation of the slavery issue would certainly disrupt the Union and ultimately lead to the destruction of the South's "peculiar institution."

Watts

This moderate Unionist posture served Watts well over the short term, but this middle-ground position ultimately destroyed the Whig Party in Alabama and across the nation. In 1855 Watts ran as a Know-Nothing candidate for Congress but lost this bid. Although several Alabama districts elected Know-Nothing representatives, Watts could not overcome skillful manipulation by his Democratic opponent of the ongoing crisis in "bleeding" Kansas, where conflict between proslavery and antislavery forces had openly erupted.

As late as 1860 Watts still held a relatively moderate position on southern rights. In the election of 1860 he supported the Constitutional Unionist candidate, John Bell, not Yancey's candidate, Southern Democrat John Breckenridge. After Lincoln and the Republicans won, however, Watts began to advocate immediate secession. He and Yancey both ran as Montgomery County secessionist delegates to the Alabama secession convention, and Watts received more votes than Yancey. As a leader of the immediate secessionists at the convention, Watts, to no avail, attempted to forge an accommodation between the Yanceyites and the cooperationists.

Later that summer Watts was a late entry into the governor's race but was defeated by John Gill Shorter in the gubernatorial election of 1861. He then lost his bid for a seat in the Confederate Senate to secessionist Clement Claiborne Clay. During both campaigns, his opponents raised questions about Watts's devotion and loyalty to the Confederate cause.

Watts helped to organize the Seventeenth Alabama Regiment and served in its ranks until Confederate president Jefferson Davis appointed him attorney general in April 1862. In his brief tenure in that office, Watts helped to organize the Confederate Supreme Court and wrote opinions defending increased centralization of government authority in Richmond. As attorney general he reversed an earlier decision and allowed the Confederate president to appoint officers from within state regiments to Confederate positions, a controversial and legalized version of impressment of state soldiers into Confederate service. Of more importance, Watts upheld the constitutionality of the Confederate Conscription Act of 1862.

Watts, the former Unionist Whig, easily defeated incumbent governor Shorter in the 1863 gubernatorial race. Given Watts's role in the expansion of Confederate government power, it is ironic that his campaign benefited from discontent over Shorter's similar interventionist policies within the state. Watts also received support from war-weary voters who thought he shared their desire for a quick end to the fighting. During his single term in office, however, Watts railed at those in the state who advocated immediate peace and reconstruction at any cost and dispelled any doubts about his commitment to the Confederate cause. "Let us prefer death to a life of cowardly shame," he told the legislature. He assured citizens of Alabama that he was a "war man all over," and he spent much of his term struggling with an obstructionist "Peace Party" clique within the legislature. His conflict with this group limited Watts's ability to strengthen the defense of Mobile as well as to deal with the deteriorating economic and social conditions in Alabama.

Confederate money was worthless by 1864, and "in-kind" taxation—whereby the government took a percentage of product in lieu of worthless currency—was placed on southerners by both the state and the Confederacy. The legislature approved Watts's request for continued aid for the indigent, but the amounts available for that purpose were insufficient to meet the desperate need. By executive proclamation in 1864, Watts suspended state taxes in nine enemy-occupied north Alabama counties in hopes of relieving some of the burden caused by the much-hated tax-in-kind. Exacerbating the awful conditions were Confederate impressment agents who came into the state to secure foodstuffs and Confederate calvary who also foraged goods from farms. Watts's suspension of state taxes may have silenced some of his most vocal legislative opponents, but it won him little support from that body for his efforts to deal with other issues facing the state.

By 1864 Alabamians were weary of the war, its brutality, and its economic hardships. Civil order no longer existed in Alabama as Confederate and Union deserters roamed the countryside, plundering farms and attacking vulnerable targets. Unionists fought with secessionists, and the people of the state yearned for peace at almost any price. Watts urgently requested an increase in the state militia so he could restore order and strengthen the defense of Mobile, but the legislature refused to act. Watts could only issue a proclamation ordering all foreign-born noncitizens to enlist in the militia, but this did not generate enough additional manpower to police the state and defend Mobile.

Watts was no more successful in his relationship with the Confederate government. Upon entering office, he confronted a serious problem with the Confederate conscription policy, which Watts as Confederate attorney general had favored. The much-expanded Confederate conscription policy allowed the Confederate States of America to pull soldiers from the depleted ranks of Alabama's state militia. Watts, now on the other side of the issue, threatened conflict with Confederate agents who tried to take men from state units. To make matters worse, bogus impressment officers were handing out counterfeit government notes in exchange for farm produce. Watts understood that such practices contributed to the extreme suffering of the state's citizenry and to the deterioration of law and order and pleaded with the Confederate government to curb the offenses, but his requests were unheeded.

When Union general James H. Wilson approached Montgomery in April 1865, Watts, carrying state documents, and other state officials abandoned the city and fled to Union Springs. The "Cradle of the Confederacy" offered no resistance and surrendered to Wilson's troops. In May 1865 federal troops arrested Governors Watts, Moore, and possibly Shorter, along with other state and Confederate officials. Watts was sent to a Union prison for a very brief period. By the time he returned to Alabama, Union soldiers had burned his plantation home, his slave houses, and his entire cotton crop. He lost much of the land he had owned prior to the war and was forced into bankruptcy.

Watts lived twenty-seven years after the war during which time he reopened his Montgomery law offices and began again to acquire property. He assisted in the "redemption" of the state from Radical Republicans, and the former Whig became a prominent figure in the affairs of the renamed Democratic and Conservative Party. Watts served briefly in the state legislature from 1880–81 and ran unsuccessfully for the U.S. Senate in 1891. He died in Montgomery on September 16, 1892.

References

Fleming, Walter Lynwood. *Civil War and Reconstruction in Alabama.* New York: Columbia University Press, 1905.

McMillan, Malcolm C. *The Disintegration of a Confederate State: Three Governors and Alabama's Wartime Home Front, 1861–1865.* Macon, Ga.: Mercer University Press, 1986.

Thornton, J. Mills, III. *Politics and Power in a Slave Society: Alabama, 1800–1860.* Baton Rouge: Louisiana State University Press, 1978.

Lewis E. Parsons, June–December 1865

SARAH WOOLFOLK WIGGINS

L EWIS Eliphalet Parsons, who was appointed provisional governor of Alabama by President Andrew Johnson in June 1865, was politically active in Alabama before the Civil War, first as a Whig and then as a Know-Nothing. He served as an Alabama elector for Whig presidential candidate Millard Fillmore in 1856. In 1859 Parsons was elected to represent Talladega County in the Alabama House of Representatives (1859–1861), where he advocated state aid for internal improvements.

Parsons was born in Lisle, New York, on April 28, 1817, the eldest son of Jennett Hepburn and Erastus Bellamy Parsons. His father was a farmer and a descendant of Jonathan Edwards of Massachusetts. Educated in New York public schools, Lewis Parsons read law with Frederick Tallmadge in New York and afterward with G. F. Woodward in Philadelphia. He moved to Talladega, Alabama, in 1840 and formed a successful law partnership with Alexander White. He married Jane Ann Boyd McCullough Chrisman of Kentucky on September 16, 1841, by whom he had seven children. Parsons was both a Presbyterian and a Mason and, according to William Lowndes Yancey, the ablest and most resourceful Union debater that Yancey had ever encountered.

By 1860 Parsons owned $12,000 in real property and $66,000 in personal property, which included no slaves. A wealthy man in his adopted state, he was also an influential political leader. In 1860 in an attempt to save the Union by unifying support around the Democratic candidate, the former Whig switched party loyalty to support Stephen A. Douglas. Even after the states of the lower South left the 1860 Democratic National Convention, Parsons believed secession still might be avoided in Alabama. Despite his and other Unionists' efforts, Alabama voted to secede from the Union on January 11, 1861.

Parsons

During the Civil War many Unionists fled Alabama or decided to serve in the Confederate army, but Parsons did neither. Too old to be drafted, he continued practicing law in Talladega during the war, although two of his sons fought for the Confederacy. In 1863, as opposition to the Civil War mounted in Alabama, voters elected a governor and legislature that they believed would

77
◇

lead the state to a swift and separate peace. Parsons was returned to the Alabama House of Representatives, where in 1863 he supported the Confederacy's use of slaves as soldiers but opposed the Confederate government's attempt to control the state militia system.

On May 29, 1865, President Andrew Johnson announced a plan of Reconstruction for the states of the former Confederacy, and on June 21 he appointed Parsons — a respected, moderate Unionist — as provisional governor of Alabama. He served as governor until December 20, 1865. Parsons declared all Alabama laws enacted before January 11, 1861, except those regarding slavery, to be in force, and he retained Confederate public servants in their offices. Johnson's Reconstruction plan specified that prospective southern voters must take a loyalty oath to regain their citizenship, and those who were disfranchised were to apply for a presidential pardon. While the registration process was under way, Parsons called for an election to choose delegates to a convention to write a new state constitution. In a proclamation Parsons reminded Alabamians that the slave code was a dead issue and that former slaves were free and must be governed by the laws of Alabama as free men.

Following the provisions of Johnson's plan, a constitutional convention convened on September 12, 1865, with former governor Benjamin Fitzpatrick as its president. The convention abolished slavery, repealed the ordinance of secession, and repudiated the state's $20 million wartime debt, leaving the state with only its 1861 debt of less than $3.5 million. Although these issues were settled with little debate, the matter of legislative reapportionment caused a great controversy. Through various machinations, south Alabama had dominated the antebellum legislature and was likely to do so again if freed blacks were counted for apportioning seats in the postwar legislature. After bitter argument, the 1865 convention apportioned representation on the basis of the white population instead of the whole population of the state, giving north Alabama white counties political control during presidential Reconstruction in Alabama. Years later, Parsons reflected that he had erred by not urging the convention to adopt qualified black suffrage. Had that step been taken, he believed, Alabama would have been recognized as a state and admitted to representation in Congress in 1865 or 1866, thereby avoiding the later turmoil of congressional Reconstruction.

The 1865 constitutional convention adopted the new constitution by proclamation and called an election for governor, legislature, and congressmen for November. Robert Miller Patton won the governor's office in December 1865, and the legislature elected Parsons to the U.S. Senate. He was never seated because Congress rejected southern representatives.

Parsons resumed his Talladega law practice and continued to be politically influential. He was a delegate to the National Union Convention organized in

1866 to mobilize support for Johnson's conservative approach to Reconstruction. In September 1867 when the Democratic and Conservative Party was organized in Alabama, Parsons joined and became a party leader. In 1868 he led Alabama's delegation to the Democratic National Convention.

In early 1867 Congress passed three acts that took control of Reconstruction away from President Johnson. The new congressional plan abolished the state government established under presidential Reconstruction. A new constitutional convention met on November 5, 1867, to write another state constitution. By this document blacks were enfranchised, and significant numbers of whites were disfranchised with no pardon available. The convention reapportioned the state legislature, basing representation on the whole population. In one of the state's most interesting ironies, dominance in the legislature now returned to the Black Belt counties of the state.

Former governor Parsons devised a plan to help the Democratic and Conservative Party of Alabama defeat ratification of the radical document. If white conservatives boycotted the election and the Ku Klux Klan intimated blacks from voting, the proposed constitution would not receive the majority necessary for ratification. Parsons's plan worked, delaying Alabama's readmission to the Union until July 1868.

The November 1868 Republican victory convinced Parsons that further opposition to congressional Reconstruction was futile. In September 1869 he stunned contemporaries by defecting to the Republican Party. Parsons later explained his decision by saying that the 1868 election had ensured Republican control of the presidency and the Congress for the next four years. Having opposed Republicans as long as it was beneficial, Parsons conceded it "was better to make terms with them," work with them, and "acquire their confidence."

Parsons became an instant leader among the native white southern Republicans (scalawags) and engaged in factional fights for power within the party. He returned to the Alabama House of Representatives in 1872, where he served as speaker and assisted in defeating proposed civil rights bills. Also in 1872 Parsons represented Alabama as a delegate to the Republican National Convention, was chairman of the convention's platform committee, and was a presidential elector for Ulysses S. Grant.

After Democrats "redeemed" Alabama from Republican rule in the 1874 election, Parsons continued to be politically active as a Republican, although many other white Alabama Republicans rejoined the Democrats. His nomination in 1877 as U.S. attorney for the Northern District of Alabama provoked a storm of opposition from his political enemies. He held this office while awaiting confirmation from the U.S. Senate. Despite numerous endorsements, including a strong public recommendation from Alabama's U.S. senator John Tyler Morgan, a Democrat, the Senate rejected his nomination in March 1878, and Parsons relinquished the office. His political career at last concluded, Parsons directed his attention again to practicing law in Talladega. He continued there until his death on June 8, 1895.

References

Owen, Thomas M. *History of Alabama and Dictionary of Alabama Biography.* 4 vols. Chicago: S. J. Clarke, 1921.

Parsons, Henry. *Parsons Family Descendants of Comet Joseph Parsons, Springfield, 1636–Northhampton, 1655.* N.p., 1912.

Talladega (Alabama) Our Mountain Home. June 12, 1895 (obituary).

Wiggins, Sarah Woolfolk. *The Scalawag in Alabama Politics, 1865–1881.* University: University of Alabama Press, 1977.

Robert M. Patton, December 1865–March 1867

WILLIAM WARREN ROGERS JR.

80
◇

THE Civil War had ended only eight months before Robert Miller Patton was inaugurated governor of Alabama on December 13, 1865. The popularly elected Patton succeeded Lewis E. Parsons who was the state's appointed provisional governor. Congress refused to seat southern delegations, so Alabama continued in limbo outside the Union with no representation in the Congress. When Patton left office two years later, Alabama was poised to resume its place within the ranks of the states.

Patton

Robert Patton was born on July 10, 1809, in Virginia but spent almost his entire childhood in Alabama's Tennessee Valley at Sweetwater, near Florence in Lauderdale County. He was educated at Green Academy in Huntsville. In 1829 Patton moved to Florence, where he became a merchant and a planter, owning more than four thousand acres of land and three hundred slaves. In 1832 he married Jane Locke Braham, who bore him nine children.

Patton was elected to the Alabama state legislature in 1832 and served with distinction as a Whig in both legislative houses until the eve of the Civil War. He was twice elected president of the state senate. As an opponent of secession, he voted for Stephen Douglas in the presidential election of 1860. Yet, as with many other reluctant Confederates, he supported Alabama's course after the conflict began.

Three of Patton's sons served with Confederate military forces, and two of them were killed.

In the summer of 1865, Patton resumed his public career and helped draft the new state constitution. To conform with President Andrew Johnson's guidelines, an election was held in November, and Patton easily defeated two opponents and became the state's twentieth governor. The fifty-seven-year-old Patton was tall, with gray hair and a beard that gave him a distinguished appearance.

His most pressing task involved restoring order and a measure of prosperity where there was little of either. In Alabama, as in every southern state, despair and adversity prevailed. Farms lay in disrepair, and livestock had disappeared. Freedmen were reluctant to enter labor contracts, and white landowners offered inadequate compensation. The severe economic realities gave few industrial alternatives to an overwhelmingly agricultural state such as Alabama. In his inaugural address Patton admitted that the state's economic circumstances were "peculiarly embarrassing," although fertile land remained, and he reminded them of cotton's continued value to the world.

In that first official speech, Patton also noted that most ex-Confederates could be pardoned by taking a simple oath of allegiance to the Union. White Alabamians who had accepted the Thirteenth Amendment freeing the slaves nevertheless opposed extending the privileges of citizenship to blacks as congressional Republicans endorsed. Patton resisted black enfranchisement and frequently averred that the state "must be guided and controlled by the superior intelligence of the white man." A majority of Alabamians took comfort in this assertion. Although a Whig, Patton held views consistent with state Democrats when he assured his constituents that "politically and socially, ours is a white man's government."

While in office Patton received countless plaintive appeals from desperate Alabamians. Patton pronounced the situation of foreclosures and families losing their homes and land at sheriff sales to be "absolutely appalling." He supported relief legislation and urged the legislature to find an "equitable compromise" between creditors and debtors. Patton cooperated with General Wager T. Swayne, commissioner of the Bureau of Refugees, Freedmen, and Abandoned Lands for Alabama (i.e., the Freedmen's Bureau), in the bureau's work to feed, clothe, and provide subsistence for blacks and some whites during this critical period. Patton urged repeal of the federal cotton tax—a three cents tax on every pound of processed cotton—on the grounds it was crippling one of the state's few sources of income. Impoverished Alabama farmers needed no extra burden to overcome. Patton labeled the tax oppressive and unjust, imposed and enforced with the state having no representation in Congress. Patton's outcries brought little response, but this burdensome tax was discontinued in 1868 in response to protests from poor black cotton farmers.

Robert M. Patton
1865–1867

Putting Alabama's finances in order was a high priority for Patton. He succeeded in lowering the state's debt and steered a responsible financial course. In the years preceding the war, railroad construction increased. With the return of peace, Patton strongly supported use of state credit to subsidize and underwrite land grants and generous tax and incorporation laws to encourage renewed railroad construction in the state. Corrupt implementation of that policy later caused enormous economic problems for the state.

A statewide system of public education was just beginning at the war's onset, and Patton urged the state to again expend money on education in counties where funds were not available. Similarly, the governor encouraged increased support for the hospital for the insane at Tuscaloosa. The idea of saving the state money by leasing prisoners in the state penitentiary to private interests appealed to Patton, and, unmindful of ethical considerations, the governor became a silent partner in the state's first convict-leasing company. The governor recommended using the inmates on railroad construction and in the state's coal mines.

In these and other ways, Patton had the mind of future Bourbon politicians. He assumed a classic paternalist attitude regarding the more than 437,000 emancipated slaves. In language that was progressive for its time, Patton asserted, "We have a high moral duty to perform towards the freedmen." He advocated opening the hospital for the insane to black patients as well as white, promoted the education and welfare of the emancipated population, and vetoed "black code" legislation that would have limited their movement and in other ways discriminated against the freedmen.

In 1866 Congress began to require southern states to ratify the Fourteenth Amendment as a condition for readmission to the Union. At first, Patton advised against ratification. The amendment created a common national citizenship regardless of a person's race and extended to all Americans the guarantees of due process and equal protection of the law in the state of their residence as well as nationally. Soon, however, he changed his mind, realizing that Alabama's ratification seemed to promise congressional readmission in 1868. With President Johnson urging nonratification, Alabama's legislature ignored Patton's logic and declined to ratify the amendment.

In March 1867 Congress, over President Andrew Johnson's veto, passed the Military Reconstruction Acts and took over the Reconstruction process. By this act, Patton remained governor in name only; real power was effectively organized by General Swayne, with whom Patton enjoyed a cordial and workable relationship. The measure divided the South into military districts with Alabama, Georgia, and Florida composing the Third District. In addition, Congress officially made ratification of the Fourteenth Amendment a requirement for the end of military rule and readmission to the Union.

Patton served as governor of Alabama during one its most critical and uncertain times. During his tenure, the financial status of the state improved "as much as could be reasonably expected." On leaving the governor's office, Patton was free to pursue various business ventures, and he promoted and invested in railroad development and served as trustee of several state colleges. Patton never approved of the subsequent Republican administration and lived to see it replaced by Democratic and Conservative governors.

General Swayne once described Patton as a "practical, conscientious, economical old merchant who I thought would neither deceive nor be deceived." It was a fair judgment. Patton's administration was a transitional bridge between a turbulent social, political, and economic period to restoration within the Union. He died on February 29, 1885, at age 75 at his Sweetwater home.

References

Carter, Dan T. *When the War Was Over: The Failure of Self-Reconstruction in the South, 1865–1867.* Baton Rouge: Louisiana State University Press, 1985.

Fleming, Walter Lynwood. *Civil War and Reconstruction in Alabama.* New York: Columbia University Press, 1905.

Rogers, William Warren, Robert David Ward, Leah Rawls Atkins, and Wayne Flynt. *Alabama: The History of a Deep South State.* Tuscaloosa: The University of Alabama Press, 1994.

Summers, Mark W. *Railroads, Reconstruction, and the Gospel of Prosperity: Aid under the Radical Republicans, 1865–1877.* Princeton: Princeton University Press, 1984.

Wiggins, Sarah Woolfolk. *The Scalawag in Alabama Politics, 1865–1881.* University: University of Alabama Press, 1977.

83
>

Wager Swayne, March–December 1867

Michael W. Fitzgerald

G ENERAL Wager T. Swayne, often referred to as Alabama's military governor, never formally held that title. Nonetheless, he wielded substantial executive authority as assistant commissioner of the Freedmen's Bureau for Alabama during the early years of Reconstruction under the provisional governor, Lewis E. Parsons, and his successor, Governor Robert M. Patton.

Wager Swayne was born on November 10, 1834, in New York City. His parents, Noah Haynes Swayne and Sarah Ann Swayne, were native Virginians who liberated their slaves and relocated to Ohio, where Noah Swayne became

Swayne

prominent in Republican politics and eventually was appointed to the U.S. Supreme Court by Abraham Lincoln. Thus young Wager Swayne fell heir both to antislavery convictions and to influential Republican connections.

Swayne was graduated from Yale University in 1856 and the Cincinnati Law School in 1859, then entered the practice of law with his father. At the outbreak of the Civil War, he joined the army and commanded the Forty-third Ohio Volunteer Regiment through much of the war. He rose to the rank of brigadier general and eventually won the Congressional Medal of Honor. Late in the war, Swayne lost his right leg at Rivers Bridge in South Carolina. A committed Episcopalian, the general's religious bearing under duress won the admiration of his equally devout superior officer, General Oliver O. Howard. On Howard's appointment to head the Freedmen's Bureau, he appointed his convalescing subordinate to the post of assistant commissioner for Alabama.

Arriving in Montgomery in July 1865, Swayne discovered his underfunded new agency in disorder. He promptly decided to cooperate with Alabama's civil officials under presidential Reconstruction and disavowed confiscation. He urged emancipated slaves to sign contracts and go back to work, even prodding them with the threat of arrest. Authorized by law to establish army courts to protect the newly emancipated population, he instead offered to acknowledge the authority of civil tribunals but only if they agreed to accept black testimony. He also appointed Alabama officials as local Freedmen's Bureau agents if they agreed to these terms. Provisional governor Lewis E. Parsons endorsed Swayne's approach and termed his conduct "eminently satisfactory." This characterization was borne out when Swayne lobbied behind the scenes during the constitutional convention of September 1865 to forestall some of the extreme racial legislation adopted in other southern states. Parsons and Swayne also cooperated on political matters such as facilitating state efforts at famine relief, and Swayne assisted the governor in lobbying President Johnson for recognition of the new Alabama constitution.

Swayne continued to collaborate with Parsons's elected successor, Governor Robert M. Patton. Swayne's early optimism about the prospects for black progress soon faded, however. Violence in the countryside toward the newly freed people escalated, and the civil authorities he had approved seemed less than vigilant in protecting them. Furthermore, the newly elected legislature, once recognized by the president, ignored Swayne's advice. The general convinced Governor Patton to veto several of the state's more stringent "black codes," pointing out the negative impact on northern public opinion.

By early 1866 Swayne accepted conflict with conservative whites as inevitable. Stymied in the political sphere, Swayne turned his attention toward providing education to the emancipated slave. He approached northern benevolent societies and churches for support, concluding that if black schools could be opened at no cost, the civil government would fund teachers rather than allow outsiders to fill those positions. Swayne, contrary to law, actually expended Freedmen's Bureau money for the schools with the covert approval of General Howard. "In the present decadence of our powers," Swayne observed, education was "the principal means of usefulness remaining."

As the struggle between President Johnson and Congress intensified and with the Republican triumph in the 1866 congressional races, Swayne recognized that changes were coming. He hoped the legislature might be intimidated and pushed for ratification of the pending Fourteenth Amendment as a way to avoid even more drastic measures from the Congress. Despite the endorsement of Governor Patton, state legislators rejected the new constitutional amendment. This defeat persuaded Swayne that only black suffrage could force necessary changes, and continuing violence toward blacks provided him the "fullest evidence" that Alabama was "not very fit for a free government at all."

When Congress enacted its military Reconstruction in March 1867 and seized control of the Reconstruction process from President Johnson, Swayne, now military commander as well as bureau chief, enjoyed enhanced authority. He outlawed local governments' use of the chain gang and released those who had been jailed as "vagrants" under Alabama's black codes. He also utilized the restoration of martial law to punish violent offenders. With the encouragement of his superior, General John Pope, commander of the Third Military District, Swayne encouraged organization of the new black electorate. He appeared at numerous conventions and helped to create the Republican Party of Alabama at a state convention in June. Swayne's office became forthrightly partisan: the state Republican Party's Union League was organized by one of his employees, and Swayne's superintendent of voter registration, William H. Smith, became the first Republican governor of the state. In addition, three of the six Alabama congressmen elected under the initial Reconstruction elections were bureau agents, and Swayne "half permitted" his name to be placed in consideration for one of the state's U.S. Senate seats.

Swayne's political intervention, especially at the constitutional convention of November 1867, drew the ire of conservatives and the attention of President Johnson. In December, the president ordered the removal of both Pope and Swayne. The general's successor, General Julius Hayden, came to power on January 11, 1868, and moved to "purge the Bureau from all party affiliations." The confusion of leadership facilitated the white conservative boycott of the constitutional ratification election of 1868, thus preventing the constitution from receiving the required majority. Congress, nonetheless, admitted Alabama under the Republican constitution in July 1868.

In December 1868 Swayne married Ellen Harris of Louisville, Kentucky. After being reassigned to his army unit, he served in the west until 1870, when he retired from the military. He returned to the practice of law in Toledo, Ohio, and became a highly successful corporate attorney. Swayne relocated to New York City in 1881 and died there in 1902, a Republican to the end.

The reputation of Wager Swayne has enjoyed an odd fate at the hands of historians, who have generally stressed his early conciliatory policies toward Alabama's postwar white government. At the turn of the century, Walter Lynwood Fleming praised his bureau as "probably the least harmful of all in the South," whereas more recent scholars have seen him as insufficiently protective of the emancipated slave. Taking his career in Alabama as a whole, however, one should not overemphasize Swayne's initial moderation. He was committed to the bureau's goal of securing civil rights and moved toward more drastic means as increased obstructions blocked his efforts. He helped to create the Alabama Republican Party, and his activist policies laid the groundwork for expansion of public education to black children.

86 References

Bethel, Elizabeth. "The Freedmen's Bureau in Alabama." *Journal of Southern History* 14 (February 1948): 49–92.

Fitzgerald, Michael W. "Wager Swayne, the Freedmen's Bureau, and the Politics of Reconstruction in Alabama." *Alabama Review* 48 (July 1995): 188–218.

Fleming, Walter Lynwood. *Civil War and Reconstruction in Alabama.* New York: Columbia University Press, 1905.

White, Kenneth B. "Wager Swayne: Racist or Realist?" *Alabama Review* 31 (April 1978): 92–105.

William Hugh Smith, July 1868–December 1870

MICHAEL W. FITZGERALD

W ILLIAM Hugh Smith, the state's first Republican governor elected under the terms of military reconstruction, remains a controversial figure. For all of his support for Reconstruction, Smith occupied an anomalous position at the head of a Republican Party composed primarily of freedmen. Before the war, Smith had owned slaves, and he opposed secession on the grounds it would imperil slave property. Practical considerations, rather than enthusiasm for emancipation and civil rights, motivated his political course, and once elected governor he quickly sought accommodation with the ex-Confederate white majority. He left office under suspicions of corruption because of his handling of state aid to railroads.

Smith was born in Fayette County, Georgia, on April 26, 1826, the son of Jeptha Vinnen Smith and Nancy Dickson Smith. He had two sisters and six brothers, several of whom became his political allies. In his teens, Smith moved with his family to Wedowee, in Randolph County. After an "academic education," Smith read law and was admitted to the bar in 1850. In 1856 he married Lucy Wortham, who bore him three sons and five daughters.

After some years as a lawyer, Smith moved into a political career. From 1855 through 1859 he served in the Alabama House of Representatives as a states' rights Democrat but gradually evolved into a strong Union man. In 1860 he ran as an elector on the presidential ticket of Stephen A. Douglas and, in the ensuing crisis, opposed immediate secession. After the war began, criticism of Smith's Unionist position became so intense that he heard reports that he was about to be arrested as a traitor. In December 1862, he fled behind Union lines with his father and three of his brothers. Smith spent the remainder of the war recruiting soldiers for the First Alabama Cavalry, a Union regiment, and he accompanied that regiment during General Sherman's "march to the sea."

Smith

After Appomattox, Smith was a leading candidate of the "Unconditional Unionists" for appointment as provisional governor under presidential Reconstruction. The more conciliatory Lewis Parsons received the post instead. Parsons appointed Smith to the Alabama circuit court. Smith soon resigned the position on the grounds that no Union man could, in good conscience, serve under the postwar circumstances that existed in Alabama. In concert with other disaffected Unionists, he lobbied Congress to overturn presidential Reconstruction and enact black suffrage. He also devoted himself to his entrepreneurial interests in mining and railroad promotion.

With the emergence of military Reconstruction, Smith emerged as a leading political figure in Alabama, chairing the first statewide Republican convention in June 1867. He pledged to carry out the work of Reconstruction "on the basis of equality and justice for all, without respect to race or color." Smith's service as head of General Wager Swayne's voter registration bureau, established to implement the Military Reconstruction Acts, helped him win the Republican nomination for governor in the February 1868 election, which was also called to ratify the Reconstruction constitution.

When a conservative boycott appeared to have defeated the ratification of the Reconstruction constitution, Smith opposed Republican efforts to declare the document in effect without the stipulated majority. He thus opposed his own inauguration as governor, but Congress placed him in office in July 1868. Among his first actions in office was to secure the abandonment of the constitution's provisions that disfranchised Confederate public officials and military officers. Despite Republican arguments that terrorism made a fair election impossible, Smith vetoed the proposal of the Republican legislature to cast the state's presidential electoral vote in 1868 without holding an election. Governor Smith also publicly denounced "Carpetbag" influence within the party, specifically that of Alabama's "Radical" senator George E. Spencer, a stand that won him considerable praise in the Democratic press.

The most striking aspect of Governor Smith's conservative proclivities was his minimizing the need for drastic action against the terrorism of the Ku Klux Klan. His term coincided with that group's worst violence, but Smith did not invoke the constitution's provisions for a state militia because such a force would be overwhelmingly composed of newly freed black men, and this might have led to a racial bloodbath. He argued that local law enforcement could deal effectively with the situation, and he publicly opposed federal legislation against the Klan. In a published interview, Smith downplayed the Klan and told an interviewer that "if such an organization ever existed in this state [he] was not aware of it." Only in 1870, in the face of spectacular public violence, did Smith exert his power to place terrorists on trial and to publicize their atrocities. His cautious position endeared him to conservative opinion in the state but antagonized the freedmen and white Republicans to whom he owed his office.

Smith also cooperated with conservative Democrats on less emotional issues. His major goal was the economic development of the state, and railroad promotion was a popular issue with bipartisan appeal. During presidential Reconstruction, the conservative Democratic legislature had already passed a general subsidy act for railroads built within the state. With Smith's support, the Republican legislature expanded the government endorsement of company railroad bonds from $12,000 to $16,000 per mile. "We should do everything consistent with the ability of the State, to encourage works of internal improvement, and develop our material resources," he observed. The state subsidy legislation also encouraged local grants to railroads, resulting in a dramatic increase in railroad mileage and potential government liability. Governor Smith participated personally in this activity, serving on one railroad's board of directors along with several legislative allies.

As the railroad bond endorsements swelled the potential state debt, Smith finally suggested scaling back the public's liability. His actions were fiscally dubious, especially with respect to the strategic Alabama and Chattanooga line, whose directors hoped would penetrate the mineral district around modern Birmingham. These directors contributed substantial sums to the governor and reportedly financed Smith's own separate railroad corporation. The Alabama and Chattanooga clearly benefited from the governor's special solicitude. Smith signed a $2 million direct aid bill primarily for the benefit of the A and C despite his awareness that legislators had been bribed by agents of that company. Of more note, the governor endorsed hundreds of thousands of dollars in bonds to the A and C above the amount authorized by law, leaving his successors with nightmarish fiscal difficulties that culminated in the state's insolvency. Smith later admitted his negligence in this matter, and a recent study of southern railroads singles Smith out among southern governors as one of several "fools" of the era who engaged in "slovenly" record keeping.

As Smith's reelection campaign approached, he faced numerous challenges. The newly freed blacks and many white Republicans resented his inaction on the Klan and his lack of enthusiasm for civil rights. Furthermore, the state's increasing fiscal woes undermined the Republicans' ambitious desire for more free public schools. Smith was renominated by a divided party, and although the freedmen had little choice but to back him, other white elements around Senator Spencer reportedly colluded in his defeat. Smith's support among white Democrats evaporated as the election neared and the scope of railroad bond abuse became evident. By a narrow margin of 77,721 to 76,292, Smith was defeated by Democratic candidate Robert Burns Lindsay. In November 1870 Smith, surprised by the outcome, contested the election on the grounds of fraud and intimidation, citing Klan outbreaks of violence in several counties. After barricading himself in his office for some weeks and surrounded by still-present units of the federal army, Smith eventually conceded defeat and withdrew.

After Smith left the governorship, disclosures of his official misconduct effectively ended his political career. He returned to Randolph County and resumed the practice of law, was appointed circuit judge by Republican governor David P. Lewis in 1873, and later served as federal district attorney under President James Garfield. He remained active in Republican patronage matters, maintaining for decades his opposition to carpetbag influence in the party. Smith eventually relocated to Birmingham, where he died on January 1, 1899, at the age of seventy-two.

In recent decades, scholars have applauded Republican efforts during Reconstruction to implement equal justice under the law. As governor, William Hugh Smith supported ratification of the Fifteenth Amendment securing equal suffrage, and his government oversaw creation of a free school system that for the first time included Alabama's black children. Beyond this, his accomplishments in the field of civil rights were limited, and the other complaints of his various critics—white and black—appear all too valid.

References

Parnell, Ralph Erskine. "The Administration of William Hugh Smith: Governor of Alabama, 1868–1870." Master's thesis, Auburn University, 1958.

Summers, Mark W. *Railroads, Reconstruction, and the Gospel of Prosperity: Aid under the Radical Republicans, 1865–1877.* Princeton: Princeton University Press, 1984.

Trelease, Allen. *White Terror: The Ku Klux Klan Conspiracy and Southern Reconstruction.* New York: Harper and Row, 1971.

Wiggins, Sarah Woolfolk. *The Scalawag in Alabama Politics, 1865–1881.* University: University of Alabama Press, 1977.

90
◇

Robert B. Lindsay, 1870–1872

MICHAEL W. FITZGERALD

ROBERT Burns Lindsay faced unprecedented difficulties as governor of Alabama, and despite his Democratic affiliation, he became nearly as unpopular as any Republican of the era. Born on July 4, 1824, in Lochmaben, Scotland, Lindsay was the son of John and Elizabeth McKnight Lindsay. Raised as a Presbyterian, he received an extensive education and won academic prizes at the University of St. Andrews. In 1844, Lindsay immigrated to North Carolina, where he joined his brother in the teaching profession. Five years later, he relocated to Tuscumbia, Alabama, where he read the law and was admitted to the bar in 1852. He was elected to represent Franklin County in the Alabama House of Representatives as a Democrat in 1853 and moved up to the state senate soon thereafter. In 1854, he married Sarah Miller Winston, the half-sister of then-governor John Winston. She bore him nine children. This fortunate marriage assisted his political career, and he emerged as a prominent supporter of Governor Winston's campaign against railroad subsidies.

In the campaign of 1860 Lindsay took a strong Unionist position, resigning a place on the John C. Breckenridge electoral ticket in order to serve on that of Stephen A. Douglas. In his own words, he "opposed secession on every hill and every valley in North Alabama." In the crisis of 1861 he opposed immediate secession and continued to denounce it even after war began. Lindsay eventually took "a slight part in the rebellion" and later observed that he "never was much of a soldier; it did not suit [me]." His tepid Confederate loyalties proved popular locally, and after Appomattox, voters returned him to the state senate in 1865.

Lindsay

Lindsay opposed the Reconstruction Acts of 1867, but with the election of President Grant he publicly called on Democrats to accept political reality. To some Alabamians, this suggested Lindsay's potential defection to the Republican Party, but in 1870, the Democratic and Conservative Party chose him as its nominee for governor, primarily because of his moderate stance toward Reconstruction. He had "no known Klan associations," as one historian observed, and he appealed to the antisecession, white "swing" voters of north Alabama, many of whom might otherwise approve of Republican governor William H. Smith's Unionist credentials. Lindsay won election by a narrow margin, and after several weeks of Smith disputing the result, he assumed the governorship in December 1870.

Governor Lindsay immediately faced a financial crisis. On January 1, 1871, Alabama's most ambitious state-supported railroad, the Alabama and Chattanooga, proved unable to pay the interest on its bonds, claiming a short-term cash flow problem. The managers of the railroad turned to the state to pay the interest, as called for in earlier subsidy legislation. The governor discovered, however, that his predecessor in the governor's office had issued several hundred thousand dollars in bonds beyond that authorized by law to the A and C, which was known for corrupt practices. Lindsay pledged to honor all bonafide bonds but delayed payment because "not a line of a record" had been kept of the number of bonds issued. He sought a legislative inquiry into this corruption and asked legislators to approve payments to the innocent purchasers of fraudulently issued bonds.

This plausible course of action proved disastrous. The default on the state-endorsed bonds sent a shock wave through Wall Street. The Alabama and Chattanooga managers found themselves without funds to continue operation.

Worse still, the default imperiled several other half-finished railroad projects statewide. The legislature temporized for months over the issue of which bonds to acknowledge, hoping to pay only those people who had unknowingly purchased unauthorized securities. The resulting delay raised speculation about the state's ability to redeem the other securities it had endorsed. By the time the legislature gave Lindsay wide latitude to decide which bonds should be paid, all Alabama railroad securities, endorsed by either the state or local governments, were impaired. Several railroad companies halted construction and ultimately went bankrupt during the Panic of 1873, an event that left the state unable to pay its other obligations as well.

Lindsay's effort to distance himself from railroad corruption while attempting to protect the state's credit satisfied no one. His revelation of Governor Smith's misdeeds undermined Alabama's whole railroad program. When Lindsay seized control of the defaulting Alabama and Chattanooga, as required under the aid law, his woes were compounded. The state lacked the legal authority and expertise to finish construction, and the railroad ran at a ruinous loss and could not be sold until completed. The seizure also subjected the state to litigation, which further complicated the situation. At one point, railroad workers commandeered the bankrupt line to force payment of back wages. The most embarrassing development, however, was Governor Lindsay's implication in bribery. The directors of the A and C paid hundreds of thousands of dollars in cash and securities to one of Lindsay's friends, Nathaniel McKay, who gave them promises that they would retain control of the railroad. This attempted bribe, in which Lindsay's personal role is unclear, left the governor's reputation in shreds.

In other areas, however, Governor Lindsay could claim some accomplishments, with perhaps the most important one a decline in Ku Klux Klan activity. The statewide Democratic victory eliminated some of the partisan reasons for terrorism. Enhanced national scrutiny of the Klan and the threat of federal intervention against it may also explain the decrease in Klan violence. Lindsay's policy toward the Klan was complex: he often tried to stop violence in Klan-ridden localities by encouraging beleaguered Republican local officials to resign, whereupon he then appointed Democrats who were more acceptable to the white population. Thus, Lindsay was less committed to the rule of law than he was to the elimination of the Republican Party in Alabama. Still, he publicly denounced "crime and lawlessness," arguing that it was "condemned by the leading and influential citizens of the country." Such avowals may have contributed to the decline of Klan activity.

Some Democratic constituents applauded Lindsay's retrenchment measures, but cuts in education funding that closed schools prematurely undermined the governor's support. These school funding problems resulted from the fiscal difficulties created by the railroad scandals. Within the Democratic Party, Lindsay had antagonized not only those interested in railroad projects but also those who favored the wholesale repudiation of the railroad bonds. His most vocal critic was Robert McKee of the *Selma Argus*, who editorialized that Lindsay diverted school money to "Wall Street Gamblers and foreign speculators" and warned that the people risked being "robbed by corrupt combinations for the benefit of private corporations." At the 1872 Democratic state convention, Lindsay's announcement that he would not be a candidate reportedly evoked applause, and only the chairman's timely intervention prevented hisses at his name. The Democratic gubernatorial candidate, ex-secessionist Thomas H. Herndon of Mobile, ran poorly. His opponent, David P. Lewis, won by a substantial margin, with eight previously Democratic north Alabama counties voting Republican. Thus Governor Lindsay had dispirited his party and paved the way for a Republican resurgence, ironically abetted by the decline of terrorist violence that once supported Democratic candidates.

Two months after leaving office, Lindsay was stricken with paralysis. He returned to his law practice at a limited level, but "took no interest in politics" beyond occasional defenses of his administration in the press. He remained an invalid until his death in Tuscumbia in 1902. As governor, Robert Burns Lindsay was faced with difficult fiscal challenges for which no attractive solution existed. His response to the crisis exacerbated the situation, with ruinous result to his party and the state as well.

93
◇

References

Fleming, Walter Lynwood. *Civil War and Reconstruction in Alabama*. New York: Columbia University Press, 1905.

Owen, Thomas M. *History of Alabama and Dictionary of Alabama Biography*. 4 vols. Chicago: S. J. Clarke, 1921.

Riley, Mary Danley. "The Heritage of Colbert County, Alabama." Alabama Heritage Series, no. 17. Clanton, Ala.: N.p., 1999.

Summers, Mark W. *Railroads, Reconstruction, and the Gospel of Prosperity: Aid under the Radical Republicans, 1865–1877*. Princeton: Princeton University Press, 1984.

Webb, Samuel L. "A Jacksonian Democrat in Postbellum Alabama: The Ideology and Influence of Journalist Robert McKee, 1869–1896." *Journal of Southern History* 62 (May 1996): 239–74.

David P. Lewis, 1872–1874

SARAH WOOLFOLK WIGGINS

AVID Peter Lewis was born circa 1820 in Charlotte County, Virginia, the son of Mary Smith Buster and Peter C. Lewis, who then owned thirty-five slaves. The family moved in the 1820s to Madison County, Alabama, where the future governor's father became a county commissioner.

After studying law in Huntsville with Judge Robert Brickell, Judge Daniel Coleman, and attorney Luke Pryor, David Lewis attended lectures in law at the University of Virginia. He was admitted to the bar and moved to Lawrence County, Alabama, in 1843, where he developed a successful law practice. By 1860 Lewis was a wealthy man, owning $20,000 in real property and more than $40,000 in personal property, including thirty-four slaves. Despite his affluent circumstances the future governor never married.

Lewis supported Stephen A. Douglas for president in 1860 and represented Lawrence County in the 1861 Alabama constitutional convention that voted to take Alabama out of the Union. He opposed disunion but signed the secession ordinance under instructions sent to him by his constituents from a public meeting in Moulton. In 1861 he was elected to the provisional Confederate Congress and was appointed to the Patents and Indian Affairs Committees. His service in the congress was brief, lasting only from February 8 until April 29, when he resigned to join a volunteer Confederate company that soon disbanded. He later declined appointment as lieutenant colonel in General Philip Roddey's unit, thus reflecting his growing distaste with the war. In 1862 Lewis and other north Alabama Unionists organized a secret Peace Society, which advocated seeking ways for Alabama unilaterally to end its involvement in the war and return to the Union. In 1863 Governor John Gill Shorter appointed Lewis as judge of the Fourth Judicial Circuit, where he remained until January 1, 1864. Although exempt from conscription as the owner of a public mill, he was, nonetheless, ordered to report for military service in the fall of 1864. Lewis refused and crossed through the federal lines to Nashville, where he remained until the end of the Civil War.

Lewis returned to Alabama in July 1865 and opened a law practice in Huntsville. On May 29, 1865, President Andrew Johnson announced a plan of

Lewis

Reconstruction for the states of the former Confederacy that required prospective voters to take a loyalty oath and required disfranchised southerners to apply for a presidential pardon. As a former member of the provisional Confederate Congress as well as one who had owned property valued at $20,000 in 1860, Lewis was among those specifically disfranchised in the federal law. He applied for a pardon and was certified as a registered voter on August 25. Between 1865 and 1868, Lewis quietly practiced law, remained out of politics, and was known as a learned and respected attorney.

Presidential Reconstruction ended with the passage of the Reconstruction Acts of March 1867, and control of Reconstruction passed to the Congress. In 1868 Lewis returned to politics when he attended the Democratic National Convention as a delegate. After the Republicans won the presidency and control of Congress in November 1868, Lewis reevaluated his political allegiances and in 1869 joined the Republican Party. Unlike many others, Lewis did not publicly explain his change of political parties.

In Alabama, as in many southern states, newcomers to the South (carpetbaggers) controlled congressional Reconstruction, but the situation in Alabama was different. Although outnumbered in the Republican Party by a coalition of newcomers and blacks, southern white Republicans (scalawags) such as Lewis dominated political activities of the party in Alabama. Despite the success of the scalawags, Lewis was outraged by congressional treatment of southern Unionists. He was livid that a man who had "sincerely grieved at the success of secession, and whose only crime was a fatherly sympathy for his son, who had joined the rebel army to avoid the disgrace of conscription" was viewed to be as guilty as a man who had actively supported the idea of secession. He was particularly offended by the officeholding disability in the Fourteenth Amendment, whereby men who had sworn to uphold the federal Constitution and subsequently aided the Confederacy could not hold office until Congress voted to remove the disability. Lewis advocated a general amnesty to remove the disabilities of those who had opposed secession in 1860. Political neglect of the Unionists was the only issue about which Lewis spoke in the late 1860s and early 1870s. He was not embroiled in the bitter quarrels between natives and newcomers within the Alabama Republican Party in this period.

Having lost the governorship in 1870, Republicans realized that their party's success in 1872 required the support of the state's Unionists of 1860. Republican leaders agreed to compose a state electoral ticket entirely of native Unionists, especially those from north Alabama, an area that had been rife with opposition to secession. As a well-known north Alabama Unionist with few political enemies in 1872, Lewis was an attractive candidate for governor and won by a decisive majority over Democratic candidate Thomas Hord Herndon of Mobile.

David P. Lewis
1872–1874

The outcome of the 1872 election was in doubt, however, when conflicting returns were reported in many legislative races. Both political parties claimed victory, and each organized a separate legislature on November 18, 1872. The Democratic-controlled body met in the state capitol, and the Republican-controlled body met at the federal courthouse. Both claimed a working majority. Governor Lewis recognized the Republican-controlled legislature on November 29, 1872, and requested that federal troops be dispatched to Montgomery to protect the lawmaking body.

The governor then sent three prominent Alabama Republicans to Washington to explain the situation to President Ulysses S. Grant and to ask for his assistance. The president referred the problem to U.S. Attorney General George H. Williams, who directed Lewis to allow both legislatures to continue as they were until he could arrange a compromise. Then he sent elaborate instructions to merge the two legislative bodies, and his plan organized a fusion legislature on December 17, 1872. Republicans held a majority of two in the house and Democrats a majority of one in the senate, gained after the death of a Republican senator in early 1873. After reorganization of the legislature, the laws passed earlier by the Republican legislature that had met at the federal courthouse were legalized on February 28, 1873.

The almost equal division between Democrats and Republicans paralyzed legislative action. The Panic of 1873 wreaked havoc on a state already suffering from earlier reckless railroad development. Lewis was unfairly blamed for the state's near-bankruptcy condition by 1874. Actually, the damage had been done between 1868 and 1872 when Governors Smith and Lindsay, a Republican and a Democrat, respectively, used the state's credit to build first a Republican-backed railroad and then a Democratic-backed one.

The most important legislation considered during Lewis's administration was an effort to enact a civil rights bill. On February 2, 1873, a black representative introduced such a bill in the Alabama House of Representatives, where it was referred to the Judiciary Committee. The bill forbade racial discrimination on common carriers and in hotels, schools, and theaters. The scalawag chairman of the committee permitted no action on the bill until black legislators on the house floor moved to force committee action. The committee, under pressure, reported the bill adversely and proposed a milder substitute bill. This offering provided for separate first-class accommodations on common carriers and integrated second-class accommodations. It did not mention hotels, schools, or theaters, and after stormy debate, the original bill died on March 10, as the full house concurred with the adverse report of the Judiciary Committee.

The Democratic-controlled senate also faced the civil rights issue when a black senator introduced a bill similar to that first introduced in the house. The bill was referred to the senate Judiciary Committee, which reported a substitute, stating that all citizens were entitled to equal accommodations in hotels and on common carriers. The substitute passed on April 4, but the legislature adjourned before the house acted on the senate bill. The acrimonious debate over these bills exposed the dilemma of Alabama's white Republicans on the civil rights issue: endorse any civil rights bill and risk losing north Alabama whites; oppose any civil rights bill and risk alienating black Republicans. Alabama Republicans faced the unenviable task of explaining to their constituents how a Republican-controlled house had defeated civil rights bills while a Democratic-controlled senate had passed one. It was clear for all to see that Republican political success in Alabama hinged on how well the party could play both white ends of the state against the black middle, and it was also clear that the race issue had the potential to destroy the party in Alabama. Through all of the uproar in the legislature over civil rights, Governor Lewis remained aloof and silent.

In 1874 Alabama Republicans hoped to repeat their 1872 success and nominated Lewis for a second term. Unfortunately for the Republicans, the wounds were still raw from the debate on a state civil rights law and over internal party patronage battles between native Republicans and carpetbaggers. In addition, debates had begun in Congress over a proposed Republican federal civil rights bill. Alabama Democrats seized the initiative and made race the leading issue of the 1874 campaign. Black Republicans attacked their white party leaders, calling Governor Lewis a man with an "utter lack of backbone" who had betrayed black Republicans into the hands of their enemies. As the race issue, economic policy, and corruption inflamed an Alabama electorate, whites deserted the Republicans, and Democrats won both the governor's chair and the legislature in a landslide.

After the defeated Lewis failed in his attempt to win appointment to a federal judgeship in 1874, he retired from politics. When Democrats rewrote the Alabama constitution in 1875, the former governor endorsed its ratification. By the fall of 1876 Lewis, like many other disillusioned Alabama scalawags, had returned to the Democratic Party. He explained that Republican Reconstruction was a "disgraceful failure," and he saw no hope among Republicans for southern men of conservative views.

After leaving public office Lewis practiced law in Huntsville and accumulated considerable property, including a plantation of 1,600 acres near Hillsboro in Lawrence County, another 940 acres in that county, and several lots in the city of Decatur. An Episcopalian, he died in 1884 and was buried in Maple Hill Cemetery in Huntsville.

References

Brewer, Willis. *Alabama: Her History, Resources, War Record, and Public Men, from 1540 to 1872.* Montgomery: Barrett and Brown, 1872.

David P. Lewis
1872–1874

Huntsville Southern Advocate, July 4, 1884 (obituary).

Huntsville Weekly Democrat, July 9, 1884 (obituary).

Montgomery Daily Advertiser, July 5, 1884 (obituary).

Owen, Thomas M. *History of Alabama and Dictionary of Alabama Biography*. 4 vols. Chicago: S. J. Clarke, 1921.

Wiggins, Sarah Woolfolk. *The Scalawag in Alabama Politics, 1865–1881*. University: University of Alabama Press, 1977.

Woolfolk, Sarah Van V. "Amnesty and Pardon and Republicanism in Alabama." *Alabama Historical Quarterly* 26 (1964): 240–48.

III

The Bourbon Era, 1874–1900

Twelve years after the Civil War ended, the last remnant of Union troops finally left the South, and Democrats were installed in power in the region's states. Southerners during this time were of a mixed mind: they hallowed the "Old South" but understood that their futures rested on a new, more industrialized economy—one more like the North's. It was an era of weak, noncharismatic presidents and a Congress content with the status quo. The national representatives entered into comfortable, if not ethically desirable, relationships with business, and southern governors and legislators did likewise. Southern governors boasted of their cheap labor and offered tax breaks and land grants to bring business to their desperate states.

In Alabama's factories and furnaces, laborers competed for jobs with convicts and children who worked long hours in unhealthy circumstances, and sharecroppers took the place of slaves on the farms. Few in power seemed to notice or care. Economic stringency was the hallmark of the "Bourbon" governors of the state, who saw little or no role for government in helping the common man, that is, until the Populist Party came into the picture. With this third party's success in drawing voters, governors had to become more active in addressing the needs and demands of the state's poorer population. Populism drew black support, but their votes were counted out by whites at the polls. On the other hand, thousands of black men did hold and exercise the right to vote. After 1901, few could.

George S. Houston, 1874–1878

WILLIAM WARREN ROGERS

EORGE Smith Houston had important political careers both before and after the Civil War. His grandparents emigrated from Ireland to South Carolina in 1760. A son, John Houston, married Hannah Pugh Reagan, and together they moved to Virginia, then to Williamson County, Tennessee, near the town of Franklin, where George Smith Houston was born on January 17, 1811. When he was sixteen the family moved to Alabama's Tennessee Valley and settled near Florence in Lauderdale County. Houston worked on the family farm and attended school at a local academy. Early on, he developed a fondness for books, read law in the office of Judge George Coalter of Florence, and completed his studies in a judge's private law school at Harrodsburg, Kentucky.

Houston returned to Florence and parlayed his lawyer's credentials into a political career. In 1831 he was elected from Lauderdale County to the state house of representatives as a Jacksonian Democrat. Houston was appointed a district solicitor in 1834, but when he sought popular election to that office the next winter, he was defeated. He then moved one county east to Limestone and opened a law office in the county seat of Athens. In May he married a local woman, Mary I. Beatty, and they had a large family of eight children, four of whom died before 1860. After his wife Mary died, Houston married Ellen Irvine of Florence in 1861, and they had two additional children.

Successful in his 1837 effort to recapture the solicitor's position, Houston held the office until 1841, when he was elected to Congress as a Democrat. Houston began an influential career as a member of the House, where with the exception of *Houston* one two-year term, he remained until 1861. During his long tenure, Houston served on the Committee on Territories and as chairman of three powerful committees: Military, Ways and Means, and Judiciary. He lost popularity temporarily by leading the opposition in north Alabama to Senator John C. Calhoun's 1849 "Address of the Southern Delegates In Congress to their Constituents," which questioned the federal government's right to limit slavery in territories gained from war with Mexico. As a Unionist, Houston was one of only four southern Democrats who refused to sign the document, and he asserted that those who supported it were exacerbating mounting sectional tensions. Because of his stand on this issue, opposition to him grew. After judiciously sitting out one term, he ran in the 1851 election and won.

In his private life Houston was a successful cotton farmer, and by 1860 he owned real estate worth $84,000 and held a personal estate valued at $150,000. His nineteen-hundred-acre plantation in Limestone County was worked by seventy-eight slaves. The crops were diversified, but like other planters, Houston concentrated on a money crop, and in the year before the Civil War produced 123 bales of cotton.

Still, Houston was a professional politician whose political longevity was attributable to several factors. He was an impressively built man who, a contemporary noted, had "a thoughtful face and [was] one of the few men who passed a long Congressional term in the maintenance of temperate and sturdy habits." An Alabama newspaper declared that, although not an "orator," Houston was "wise, prudent and discreet." Furthermore, the union Democrat shared ideas with Whigs, which helped explain his long political strength in the Tennessee Valley.

Houston campaigned for Democrat Stephen A. Douglas for president in 1860 and opposed secession. He was a member of the House of Representatives "Committee of Thirty-three" that proposed a constitutional amendment in December 1860 forbidding Congress ever to abolish slavery. Ironically, if ratified it would have been the Thirteenth Amendment. Later in December, Houston refused to sign a statement by southern congressmen denouncing the Republicans and advocating secession. Yet in 1861, after his state seceded from the Union, he joined the Alabama delegation who resigned their offices and returned home.

Houston retired to Athens, and when the Civil War began he took no part in it. Even so, two of his sons served in the Confederate army, and Houston, sympathetic to his state and region, refused to take an oath of allegiance to federal authority. In 1862 his property was overrun by Union colonel John Basil Turchin's troops as they sacked and plundered Athens.

After the war ended and Andrew Johnson attempted to install presidential Reconstruction in the South, Houston was elected by the postwar legislature to the United States Senate. Shortly afterward, Johnson's Radical Republican opponents gained control of Congress and refused to seat Houston and other southerners. In 1866 he served as a delegate to the National Union Convention in Philadelphia, which was an abortive attempt by President Johnson to create a new political party to oppose the Radical Republicans. He was defeated for a

Senate seat in 1867 by former governor John A. Winston and returned to his law practice. Houston played no role in Alabama's Reconstruction political wars between 1867 and 1874.

Republican strength in Alabama during that period was based on native white (scalawags) voters, newly arrived whites (carpetbaggers), and freedmen who comprised the largest voting block among Alabama Republicans. This coalition made the Republican Party a strong political force in the state, and voters elected two Republican governors, in 1868 and 1872. Democrats, on the other hand, relied on white voters in all regions of the state, including former Whigs who had been without a party since the 1850s. In order to avoid offending Whigs, Democrats called their organization the Democratic and Conservative Party.

The election of 1874 was significant for both parties. It determined which party would control state government and the state's political and economic future. Democrats felt a sense of urgency about regaining the state from the racially integrated Republican Party. They persuaded white Alabamians to put aside historic differences and unite to "redeem" the state. To effect this alliance, they chose a man acceptable to both Unionists and south Alabamians: George Smith Houston, whose sobriquet was the "Bald Eagle of the Mountains." Democrats reinforced their single-minded appeal to white supremacy by promising honesty and economy as opposed to Republican profligacy. To insure success, some Democrats resorted to violence and intimidation against Republicans, particularly blacks. In a record turnout Houston defeated David Lewis 107,118 to 93,934 votes. Victory was explained by the increase in white voters, particularly in north Alabama, where Unionists voted overwhelmingly for Houston.

Houston's two administrations set the agenda for the "Bourbon" Democrats. The word "Bourbon" referred to the return of the royal house in France following the French Revolution and the Napoleonic wars. Republicans used it pejoratively to mean reactionary and unenlightened. To Democrats it meant conservatism, limited government, honesty, frugality, and white supremacy. As governor, Houston acted on the Bourbon promises of economy by refusing to spend some $10,000 of a contingency fund set aside by the legislature. In the interest of economy, if not humanity, he expanded the state's practice of leasing its prisoners to private contractors. Convict leasing, combining profits for corporations and revenues for the state, was a barbaric practice and a dark stain on Alabama's reputation.

In an unexpected bright spot for this conservative era, the not-yet-fully Bourbon legislature finally approved creation of a state public health board in 1875 after years of debate. Alabama was one of the first states in the nation to establish such a board, but no monies were appropriated for its work until 1879, when legislators approved $3,000 annually. Alabama's Board of Health wisely gave complete control of public health issues to the state's medical association and the physicians who were its members, thus freeing it to a large degree from political influence.

Although yellow fever and other diseases regularly caused loss of life, Alabama's declining population was caused more by a migration of blacks and whites from the troubled state during the war and Reconstruction. With the increased need for industrial labor, Houston strongly promoted immigration but with limited success. Nor was he able to accomplish much in the way of educational progress, concluding sorrowfully that "the problem, how to confer the best practical educational advantages to the greatest number, consistent with justice and duty, is of more difficult solution than many suppose."

The foremost reason for Houston's failure in education was the acute financial situation that he inherited. He declared in his inaugural address, "Alabama is embarrassed; her indebtedness is great, and her people are impoverished. . . . We must restore the credit of the State to its former high and honorable position; preserve inviolate her good faith, and at the same time protect our people against excessive, unjust and improper taxation." Railroad bonds were the most controversial part of the state's debt problem, which some put at $30 million.

With legislative authorization, Houston named himself to head a three-man commission to study the bonded debt issue and to recommend a program for retiring it. He named Tristam B. Bethea, a Mobile financier, and Levi W. Lawler, a Talladega planter, as the other commission members. Bethea was not a stockholder in any company affected by the debt question, but Lawler had been a director of a railroad. Houston also had been a director of the Louisville and Nashville Railroad, and his law partner had been a director of another, a circumstance that in later times would have made the commission's makeup unlawful because of conflict-of-interest restrictions. The members had the alternatives of recognizing the state's obligation for the entire debt, repudiating the debt as fraudulent—an action Houston had always opposed—or "scaling down" the debt and paying only a portion of it. After a year of study and review, the commission came up with a complicated settlement. They decided to set the legitimate debt at $18 million, which they later reduced to $12.5 million. Bondholders of the Republican-controlled Alabama and Chattanooga Railroad were the most adversely affected. Some interpreted the commission's action as draconian, but in the long run it proved beneficial to the state, and Houston deserves major credit for the settlement. As he said, "The only mode by which the credit of the State could have been restored and maintained untarnished, and the people saved from intolerable burdens, was a frank, fair and just compromise."

Another major reform that Houston and the Democrats contemplated was replacing the constitution adopted during the Republican regime in 1868.

Legislators set a vote for the summer of 1875 to decide whether to have a constitutional convention and to elect delegates to it. In general the Republicans opposed the convention, and the Democrats favored it. The campaign was less tense than the governor's election of 1874, and voter turnout was smaller, but bitterness and disputation abounded. Alabama voters favored the convention by a vote of 77,763 to 59,928. Ninety-nine delegates were elected—eighty Democrats, twelve Republicans of whom four were black, and seven independents. Among the Democratic delegates were political leaders from the antebellum period and former secessionists, some of whom were destined for future political positions as well. At the convention, rivalry between Black Belt planters and the rising industrial and railroad leaders of Alabama resulted in victories for each side. Later, an alliance between the two groups would give them economic and political power that lasted well beyond the first half of the twentieth century.

The new constitution declared that no state could secede, but debated all other questions. In summary, the 1875 constitution provided the following: state and county aid to internal improvements was prohibited; immigration was encouraged; educational and property qualifications for voting or holding office were forbidden; federal and state elections were to be held at different times to exclude Washington from monitoring statewide contests; and various offices, including that of lieutenant governor, were abolished. State officeholders were limited to two two-year terms, and many had their salaries reduced. Limits were placed on state taxes; a person could exempt $1,000 and eight acres of land from taxes, although exemptions could be waived. Separate schools for blacks and whites were required.

A popularly elected judiciary and general incorporation provisions were retained from the old constitution. No mention was made of disfranchising blacks; to have done so would have brought down the wrath of Washington. Besides, Black Belt planters controlled the votes of former bondsmen in order to counter white voter strength in north Alabama. No convention vote was taken on the constitution, but it was submitted to the voters and won approval by a margin of almost sixty thousand votes. Only four Black Belt counties, where black males voted in huge numbers, rejected the document.

Even though blacks continued to vote, the 1874 election and the new constitution had made Alabama once again the white man's state. Houston was reelected in 1876, easily defeating his Republican opponent and setting a two-term precedent for his Bourbon successors. He was elected to the United States Senate in 1878 and served from March 4, 1879, until his death in Athens on December 31 of that year.

As he left the governor's office in 1878, Houston boasted of his accomplishments and credited the "untiring efforts and wise policy of the Democratic-Conservative Party [that] caused [past] wrongs to be righted." He noted that "with a continuance of that party's rule we may reasonably expect to enjoy the blessings it has secured." The verdict of history has been less kind, but without doubt Houston was an archetypal "Bourbon" Democrat, and his administration reflected that philosophy. In his own time Houston was considered a hero by most of Alabama's white voters.

References

Fleming, Walter Lynwood. *Civil War and Reconstruction in Alabama*. New York: Columbia University Press, 1905.

Going, Allen J. *Bourbon Democracy in Alabama, 1874–1890*. University: University of Alabama Press, 1951.

Koart, Virgil Paul. "The Administration of George Smith Houston, Governor of Alabama, 1874–1878." Master's thesis, Auburn University, 1963.

McMillan, Malcolm C. *Constitutional Development in Alabama, 1798–1901: A Study in Politics, the Negro, and Sectionalism*. 1955. Reprint, Spartanburg, S.C.: Reprint Co., 1978.

Owen, Thomas M. *History of Alabama and Dictionary of Alabama Biography*. 4 vols. Chicago: S. J. Clarke, 1921.

Wiggins, Sarah Woolfolk. *The Scalawag in Alabama Politics, 1865–1881*. University: University of Alabama Press, 1974.

Rufus W. Cobb, 1878–1882

ROBERT DAVID WARD

IT SHOULD come as no surprise that Rufus Willis Cobb, second in the line of Bourbon succession, was from the coal mining county of Shelby. From the beginning, the Bourbon establishment represented both the cotton-growing Black Belt planters and the north Alabama entrepreneurs of railroads and mining. The form of their protective laws and policies might vary with the nature of particular interests, but their common and binding intent was the protection of property and the advancement of wealth.

Cobb was born on February 25, 1829, into a plantation family that lived near Asheville in St. Clair County, Alabama. He was graduated from the University of Tennessee in 1850, returned to Asheville to read law, and was admitted to the bar in 1855. He joined the Confederate army as an officer in 1861 and served throughout the war, first with Forney's brigade in Virginia and then with General Joseph Wheeler's cavalry in Tennessee. After the war he resumed his law practice and moved to neighboring Shelby County in 1867. From this new location he established the relationships and the interests that marked his public life.

Cobb was a perfect exemplar of a New South Democrat. He became the president of the Central Iron Works in Helena, was a staunch ally of rising mining and manufacturing interests, and served as an attorney for the powerful Louisville and Nashville Railroad. After his election to the state senate in 1872 and again in 1876, he performed essential services for Governor Houston, most notably in leading the fight in the 1875 constitutional convention against repudiation of the state's corrupt and tainted railroad debt and in structuring the terms of a debt settlement that was favorable to the Louisville and Nashville Railroad. Cobb established his reputation as a trustworthy guardian of Bourbon interests, and his election as president of the senate marked his elevation to the leadership ranks of the Democratic Party.

Cobb

In 1878 the state Democratic convention met in Montgomery to nominate its candidates. Cobb's name was entered for the governorship, and although he initially ran second in a field of three, on the fifteenth ballot he won the nomination. There were at least two defining moments in this convention. The first came when the convention refused to seat two black members of the Montgomery County delegation; the second occurred with the passage of a resolution that "congratulated both races that white supremacy had been firmly established." Democratic victories in 1874 and 1876 left the Republican Party in disarray, and Cobb's election was preordained. But the election hinted at the rapid growth of independents and Greenbackers in Alabama. Indeed, in 1880, when Cobb was reelected, the Greenback candidate polled 46,386 votes to the incumbent's 100,591. This opposition to the Bourbons was generated by the earlier Panic of 1873 and the continuing contraction of the currency nationwide.

107
◇

In many respects, Governor Cobb was a mainline Bourbon in his support for tax reductions and economy in government. When he left office in 1882, the state surplus was $150,000 more than he had inherited from Governor Houston. It said nothing for fiscal responsibility, however, when the legislature in 1879 rescinded the requirement for annual audits of the state treasurer. Cobb was lucky that his treasurer, "Honest Ike" Vincent, was not exposed for stealing $250,000 until Cobb had finished his second term.

Cobb's greatest fight as governor, and his major defeat, centered on the administration of the state's convict lease system. Forsaking the penitentiary system, both postwar Alabama Republicans and Democrats leased convicts in a variety of occupations. Governor Cobb's conscience had no quarrel with squeezing state revenue from prisoners, but he was firmly committed to the state receiving its fair share from the bounty of cheap labor.

Governor Cobb inherited Warden J. G. Bass from Governor Houston. Bass pleased his patrons with a trickle of revenue to the state treasury and received glowing reports on his splendid treatment of prisoners from the prison inspectors. Governor Cobb was not impressed and correctly believed that Bass had signed contracts for much less than their true value. Cobb removed the warden from the bidding process and greatly increased state revenue from the leasing of convicts. The governor demonstrated strong executive prowess when he refused to reappoint Bass as warden, but there was a second act to this drama. With doubts and many reservations, Cobb bowed to statewide pressure for the appointment of John Hollis Bankhead as warden, a pressure manufactured by Bankhead himself. The governor was now simply outmaneuvered. Bankhead had state medical officers investigate mines that used convict labor and supported their reports of unhealthy and hazardous conditions. Posing as a reformer, Bankhead used public opinion in support of his own convict plan: the Pratt Consolidated Mines would receive all the convicts and build a prison at the mines. Governor Cobb opposed the plan and pointed out that Bankhead could have improved conditions himself if he had been truly interested in the welfare of the convicts. Bankhead defended the monopoly he was trying to bestow on the Pratt mines by arguing that it was not the business of the state to inquire as to who benefited from convict leasing as long as the state received its revenue. The governor lost this fight against special privilege, and the legislature under Cobb's successor gave Bankhead most, if not all, of what he wanted.

The other major issue of Cobb's administration was railroad regulation, which, given his railroad associations, one might think he would oppose. In fact there was growing public pressure to curb the abuses of the railroads. As a contemporary said, "The adjustment of the relations of the railroad property to the rights of the local patrons had become imperative." Cobb understood political reality, and in his message to the legislature in 1880 he announced that it was time to act. In 1881 legislators established a railroad commission but gave it little power. The commission could not initiate new rates on its own even in demonstrated cases of inequity; it could only respond to complaints raised by shippers. The commission was weaker than proponents had wanted and was susceptible to influence, pressure, and domination from those it sought to regulate. Nonetheless, it was at least a beginning in the very long fight to protect the public interest.

Noteworthy educational actions occurred in the legislature during Cobb's two terms. Building on previous legislative actions that supported vocational training for white and black postsecondary students, two Macon County state legislators pressed their colleagues for a school for blacks in their county—a measure that rewarded blacks who supported their election. In the spring of 1881, with a state appropriation of $2,000, Tuskegee Normal and Industrial School opened with a student body of twenty-five. Under Booker T. Washington's leadership, the reputation of the school rose to national recognition.

Moral concerns were also debated during Cobb's tenure. The prohibition issue became so prominent in Alabama and throughout the nation during this period that a minor third-party movement developed around it during the 1880s. During Cobb's administration, prohibition forces attempted to push a statewide local option law through the legislature, but they failed.

After his second term as governor, Cobb returned to Shelby County, where he continued to serve as president of the Central Iron Works and was involved with the development of an iron mine in north Alabama. In 1888, Governor Thomas Seay appointed him probate judge of Shelby County, and he remained in that office until 1892. Cobb continued to be active in politics through the 1890s, although he never ran for public office again. Throughout his career and until his death in Birmingham on November 26, 1913, he was a perfect New South Democrat.

References

DuBose, John Witherspoon. "Forty Years of Alabama, 1861–1901." Chapter 37, Administration of Governor Cobb manuscript, John Witherspoon DuBose Papers. Alabama Department of Archives and History, Montgomery.

Going, Allen J. *Bourbon Democracy in Alabama, 1874–1890.* University: University of Alabama Press, 1951.

Moore, Albert Burton. *History of Alabama.* 1934. Reprint, Tuscaloosa: Alabama Book Store, 1951.

Owen, Thomas M. *History of Alabama and Dictionary of Alabama Biography.* 4 vols. Chicago: S. J. Clarke, 1921.

Edward A. O'Neal, 1882–1886

MARY JANE MCDANIEL

EDWARD Asbury O'Neal continued the line of prosecession, faithful Confederate, "redeeming" Bourbon governors who controlled the executive branch of Alabama in the late nineteenth century. His administration was similar in many ways to those of his predecessors, Governors Houston and Cobb, but one embarrassing event—over which he had little control—made his tenure memorable.

Edward A. O'Neal
1882–1886

O'Neal's parents moved to Madison County, Alabama, from South Carolina shortly before he was born in September 1818. Edward, whose father died when he was young, attended Green Academy in Huntsville and in 1836 was graduated with honors from LaGrange College. In that same year, he married Olivia Moore, the daughter of a prominent Madison County family. Together they established a home in Florence and had nine children.

In the decades before the Civil War, O'Neal became increasingly active in politics. He was slight in stature, and his youth was marked by tremendous energy and enthusiasm for his causes, although his political opponents described him as lacking "force of mind and character." He loved pomp and parade, and most described him as an excellent speaker. Everyone agreed on his integrity and honesty. O'Neal studied law in Huntsville with James W. McClung, was admitted to the bar, and in the 1840s established a successful practice in Florence, serving as legal representative for northwest Alabama's large plantation and textile mill owners. Before making an unsuccessful run for Congress in 1848, O'Neal served as solicitor of the Fourth Circuit. He was a states' rights Democrat who actively encouraged secession and celebrated the firing on Fort Sumter.

Edward O'Neal

After that event, O'Neal raised a company for the Ninth Alabama Infantry. In April 1862, he received a commission as colonel of the Twenty-sixth Alabama, which was assigned to Lee's Army of Northern Virginia and participated in many of the major battles of the Civil War. The Twenty-sixth Regiment was famous for its valor and bravery and suffered very high casualty rates. Its colonel, described by Confederate contemporaries as "indulgent, impetuous, and fearless, and much beloved by his troops," was wounded twice in two separate battles. O'Neal was one of the original commanders of the guards at the infamous Andersonville Prison, and he and the Twenty-sixth later joined southern troops in the defense of Atlanta during Sherman's attack. The decimated company consolidated with other Alabama regiments who surrendered at Greensboro, North Carolina, in 1865. Only after O'Neal's surrender did the Confederacy award him a commission as brigadier general, but he never received it nor officially accepted it. The state of Alabama later issued him a legitimate commission as brigadier general.

Four years to the day after O'Neal left Florence for the war, he returned, resumed his law practice, and became a tireless worker in the Democratic Party. He nominated Robert Burns Lindsay for governor at the state Democratic convention in 1870, contributed to the "redemption" of Alabama from Republican rule in 1874, and played a prominent role in the state constitutional convention of 1875, where he chaired the Committee on Education. In the

1880 presidential election, he served as a statewide elector for the Democratic Party candidate.

In a carefully managed campaign conducted over several months, General O'Neal's name was placed in newspapers as a possible candidate for the 1882 gubernatorial nomination. He was touted for his role in redeeming the state from "radicalism and reconstruction," and north Alabama voters insisted that it was their time to hold the governorship again. O'Neal's Confederate military activities also received wide attention, and at the June convention he received the nomination.

In July 1882 a coalition of independents and Greenbackers met in Birmingham and nominated a slate of candidates for state offices, including James Lawrence Sheffield of Marshall County for governor. Although both white and black Republicans agreed to endorse Sheffield and the other Greenback nominees, O'Neal won the 1882 election easily. The *Mobile Daily Register* characterized the election as "a quiet day" with "no disturbances in the state."

The only event attracting national attention during O'Neal's administration involved Isaac ("Honest Ike") Harvey Vincent, who in 1882 was reelected for an unprecedented third term as Alabama's state treasurer. In late January 1883 Vincent's clerk informed him that the state auditor's office would begin an examination of his records the next day. Vincent took the first train out of town that night because he knew that more than $200,000 was missing from state funds. At first the governor did not seem to realize that Vincent was a fugitive, but when he learned of an $8,000 overdraft in the state's bank account, he hired the Pinkerton Detective Agency to locate Vincent. The agency failed to locate him despite following leads from Canada to Mexico, but several years later Vincent was discovered in Texas and returned to Alabama for trial, during which he was convicted of embezzlement. O'Neal began legal proceedings to recover the lost funds, but because of mishandled or lost paperwork dealing with Vincent's bond, the state recovered only a small portion of the monies. Bourbon claims of fiscal responsibility suffered an enormous blow.

During this affair, additional accounting irregularities were discovered in other departments, which led the legislature to create the office of Examiner of Accounts. The first state examiner, J. W. Lapsley, found and corrected numerous errors and saved the state thousands of dollars. O'Neal recommended that a bond be required of all future state treasurers, but the state did not regularly require this process until 1898.

O'Neal's first term was marked by a small increase in state spending and by the use of state troops to put down labor unrest in Opelika and Birmingham, which earned him criticism. Still, despite south Alabama support for John M. McKleroy of Barbour County, in a show of party unity O'Neal received the nomination of his party for a second term by acclamation. The renomination showed both the wish to maintain the two-term precedent and the desire to reward O'Neal's loyalty to the Democratic Party. Despite some censure of him because of the Vincent affair. O'Neal easily won a second term in 1884. Republicans put up no opposition and in some counties, such as Montgomery, instructed its black members not to vote at all.

O'Neal took a particular interest in education, but he was equally determined to limit state spending. During his terms, the Agricultural and Mechanical College at Auburn expanded its departments, and state normal schools for the training of white teachers opened at Jacksonville and Livingston. The number of elementary and secondary public schools expanded, and, according to O'Neal, more Alabama children were receiving an education than at any time since the establishment of public education. Yet, in 1883 the total state budget for education was $130,000, and spending per child in Alabama remained among the lowest of any state in the nation.

A mortality rate of 7 percent at state mines using convict labor led O'Neal to request health inspections in 1883. Reportedly, convicts lived in unsanitary conditions that bred diseases, were treated with cruelty, and were provided with insufficient food. As a result of these inspections, circumstances improved, and the state health officer described conditions in 1884 as "tolerable."

112
◇ O'Neal's administrations were sympathetic toward farmers, and he established Alabama's State Department of Agriculture, appointing Judge E. B. Betts of Huntsville as its first commissioner. To improve rural life, the state tried to control yellow fever and introduced health and hygiene studies in the curriculum of rural schools.

In the latter part of his administration, O'Neal addressed the problem of state control of local issues. He noted that local legislation absorbed so much of legislators' time that they neglected the general interest. In addition, many local laws passed without serious consideration, and O'Neal asserted that it was "possible that no two precincts in the state are living under the same laws." The legislature did not act on his requests, and the problem of state control of local issues grew worse in the next century.

O'Neal served at a time when the prevailing political ideology opposed strong chief executives, and he was neither an innovative nor controversial governor. The Democratic Party and apparently the state desired leaders who represented the old order and maintained a safe status quo. O'Neal comfortably fit those requirements. His terms represent a transition between Bourbon redemption and the social and political upheavals of the early 1890s.

O'Neal was the first, and so far the only, governor in Alabama history to have his son (Emmet) also elected governor. ("Little" Jim Folsom served briefly in the position once held by his famous father but was not elected to that office.)

After leaving office, O'Neal returned to Florence, where he lived in retirement. He died at his home in November 1890 and is buried in Florence Cemetery.

References

Going, Allen J. *Bourbon Democracy in Alabama, 1874–1890*. University: University of Alabama Press, 1951.

O'Neal, Edward A. Administration Papers and Clipping Files. Alabama Department of Archives and History, Montgomery.

Palmer, Mark A. "The Political Career of Alabama Treasurer Isaac Harvey Vincent." Master's thesis, Auburn University, 1994.

Twenty-sixth Alabama Infantry. Compiled Service Records of Confederate Soldiers Who Served in Organizations from the State of Alabama. Microfilm copies. Florence Public Library, Florence, Alabama.

Thomas Seay, 1886–1890

ROBERT DAVID WARD

FOR those Alabamians who believed in signs and portents, 1886 did not begin auspiciously. It rained in Alabama, and kept raining, and the state's rivers rose to unprecedented heights. The bridge at Wetumpka was swept away. Reginald H. Dawson, president of the Board of Convict Commissioners, was fearful for the safety of some of his charges and rose from his sick bed to paddle to the rescue of convicts perched on the roof of a flooded building. Braxton Bragg Comer, later one of Alabama's most notable governors, survived a series of misadventures in flooded waters and observed the rare sight of five rabbits lined up on a tree limb as he paddled a canoe into downtown Montgomery. The waters receded, and if it was not catastrophe that marked the next few years, it was at least a time when change and turmoil were abroad in the land.

Alabama's governor during the four years from 1886 to 1890, when anger at Bourbon rule began to boil over, was Thomas Seay. Born to Reuben and Ann McGee Seay on November 20, *Seay* 1846, the future governor spent his boyhood days on a plantation in Greene (later Hale) County. In 1858 his family moved to Greensboro, where he began his higher education at Southern University (which later merged with Birmingham College to create Birmingham-Southern College). Secession and war interrupted his studies. In 1863 sixteen-year-old Seay enlisted and served as a private in the Confederate army. He saw action in skirmishes around Mobile and had the ill fortune of being captured and imprisoned on Ship Island near Alabama's port city.

Having survived war and brief captivity, young Seay returned to his studies at Southern University and was graduated in 1867. He read law, was admitted to the bar, and settled down to the dual pursuits of a southern gentleman — practicing law and growing cotton. In 1874, at the age of twenty-eight, he was defeated in a race for the state senate, but two years later he was elected to that body, where he remained for ten years and served as its president from 1884 to 1886. He married Ellen Smaw of Greene County in 1875, and she bore him two children before her death in 1879. Two years later he remarried, this time to Clara de Lesdernier, by whom he had four more children.

By the time the Democratic convention met in June 1886, delegates confronted a four-man race for the governorship. Private Thomas Seay was a dark horse who nonetheless had support among the politicians and industrial interests of Birmingham, Anniston, and Sheffield. After the tenth ballot Seay gained strength, and on the thirtieth ballot the other candidates withdrew, and Seay was nominated for governor by acclamation. The divisive Democratic convention revealed a growing factionalism within the party between the state's industrial-planter interests and the small farmer. Seay was elected governor with 145,095 votes against 37,118 for Republican Arthur Bingham and 576 for the Prohibition candidate, John T. Tanner. Although Seay's political views did not differ substantially from his recent predecessors, his nomination was reported to be a "victory for the young men of the convention" against the older and more famous Bourbon "Generals." He earned the same $3,000 salary his predecessors had received, making the Alabama governor's salary the lowest in the South along with those of North Carolina and Georgia.

There were signs that the times were changing and that the new governor represented a more flexible approach to public affairs. Seay compiled an interesting and sometimes ambiguous record. He took an aggressive stance against lynching, angering the sheriff of Lauderdale County with his protest of an incident there. He opposed the prohibition movement and asserted that the issue was a moral one that should not be politicized. In another area Seay appeared not so much Bourbon as ineffective. In 1887 Senator Daniel Smith of Mobile led a legislative fight endorsed by Seay that enacted a law regulating the labor of women and children under age eighteen to eight hours a day, the first such act passed by a southern state. Legislators in the next session exempted two textile mill counties from the act, and in 1894 the never-enforced bill was repealed. Seay was the first Alabama governor to loosen state funds to provide small pensions for disabled Confederate veterans or the widows of slain

Confederates. In a remarkable event for the time, the legislature in 1886 chose Miss Gem Weakly of Florence as senate enrolling clerk, and she became the first woman to hold public office in the state of Alabama.

Ultimately, Governor Seay is best remembered for his support of education. He endorsed the controversial Blair Education Bill, a proposal in the U.S. Congress to grant federal funds for education to states on the basis of their illiteracy rates. His position countered that of Alabama's powerful and popular senator John Tyler Morgan, who opposed it, fearing that it would lead to federal control of education. Seay further supported an appropriation "to introduce technical teaching of agriculture at the State Agricultural and Mechanical College" (Auburn); urged the founding of a black school for the deaf, which the legislature approved in 1891; and oversaw the establishment of the Normal School at Troy (Troy State University) and the Normal School for Colored Students in Montgomery (Alabama State University). While he supported increased but cautious expenditures to education, he simultaneously and in good Bourbon fashion lowered the tax rate and ended his term of office with a surplus in the treasury from added revenues that came from the increased value being placed on property in the state.

Had these actions comprised the total of Seay's administrations, the young governor would be remembered for sharing many of the same progressive instincts of the U.S. president at that time, Grover Cleveland, who visited Alabama in 1887. In counterpoint to these apparently progressive stands, however, Seay took positions that were typically Bourbon. Although he appointed Reuben F. Kolb, who later emerged as Alabama's most famous Populist, as state commissioner of agriculture, Seay was no friend to the agrarians, who looked to the state for relief from their desperate economic plight. Kolb's appointment was an inadvertent action that provided "Genial Reuben" with the base necessary to build his power and influence. In fact, Seay demonstrated his abiding conservatism when he reconsidered his acceptance of an invitation to speak to the 1889 Farmers' Alliance convention in Montgomery in a pointed display of his unhappiness with that group's drift toward politics.

In a similarly Bourbon-like action, Seay backed the interest of one of the state's largest companies in a dispute over the convict lease system. In 1888 a ten-year exclusive contract for convict labor was awarded to the Tennessee Coal, Iron, and Railroad Company (TCI), new owners of the Pratt mines where the state's prisoners were normally leased. Losing bidders protested the award, and a legislative committee found that TCI had not made the highest bid, nor were they taking the requisite number of convicts. Legislators recommended that the governor nullify the contract that cost the state badly needed revenue, but Seay backed the company when it promised to live by the terms of its contract with the state. TCI increased its payment for the convicts, but the state never required the company to follow all the terms of the contract. The state's largest city was also the scene of a riot in 1888 when two thousand men stormed the Birmingham jail with the intent of hanging Richard Hawes for murdering his wife and two small daughters. Seay sent state troops to the city to maintain law and order. The developing and prospering mineral district of Birmingham and Bessemer applauded his strong action.

Governor Seay was an interesting blend of old values and new directions. The reign of the Bourbons was about to undergo its first major challenge—not an ephemeral changing of the guard but a major effort to alter the content and beneficiaries of public action. At the very time when Alabama's mining and manufacturing concerns grew and prospered, its small farmers struggled for survival. In reaction and counterpoint to their economic woes, those farmers cast about for causes and for cures. With that search came organization—the Grange, the Wheel, and the Farmers' Alliance and then political alignment with the Populist Party and the Jeffersonian Democrats. As the winds of the Populist revolt blew around him, Seay bent with the wind but was never swept away from the old moorings of the state Democratic Party.

References

DuBose, John Witherspoon. "Forty Years of Alabama, 1861–1901." Chapter 39, Administration of Governor Seay manuscript, John Witherspoon DuBose Papers. Alabama Department of Archives and History, Montgomery.

Going, Allen J. *Bourbon Democracy in Alabama, 1874–1890.* University: University of Alabama Press, 1951.

Rogers, William Warren. *The One-Gallused Rebellion: Agrarianism in Alabama, 1865–1896.* Baton Rouge: Louisiana State University Press, 1970.

Rogers, William Warren, Robert David Ward, Leah Rawls Atkins, and Wayne Flynt. *Alabama: The History of a Deep South State.* Tuscaloosa: University of Alabama Press, 1994.

116
◇

Thomas G. Jones, 1890–1894

PAUL MCWHORTER PRUITT JR.

THOMAS Goode Jones enjoyed a reputation as a committed Bourbon Democrat. Closer study shows him to be a complicated and perhaps conflicted personality who had congenial associations with Radical Republicans and held liberal attitudes on race issues. Yet he is remembered for winning the governorship of Alabama in one of the state's most racist elections through the manipulated votes of blacks.

Jones was born November 26, 1844, in Macon, Georgia. He was the eldest child of Samuel Goode Jones (1815–1886) and Martha Goode Jones, both descendants of old Virginia families. Samuel Jones was graduated from Williams College and came south in 1839, where he made a notable career as a railroad builder in Georgia. He moved his family to Montgomery, Alabama, in 1849 where, during the Civil War, he served as captain of the home guard.

From his father, Thomas Jones learned not only ambition but also devotion to the South. The latter was tempered by faith in a Whig nationalism that served industrial development with national programs such as railroad building. Jones was prepared

Jones

for a gentleman's career, attending preparatory schools in Virginia. By the fall of 1860 he was a cadet at the Virginia Military Institute, where both his aptitude and his loyalties would be put to the test. Like his father, the teenaged Jones supported the Confederacy—drilling volunteers in Richmond, serving with Stonewall Jackson in the Valley campaign, and as an aide to Georgia's general John B. Gordon, and finally with Lee's Army of Northern Virginia. He was wounded several times, earned promotion to major, and survived to carry a flag of truce through the lines at Appomattox.

117
◇

Jones's wartime service with Gordon was an important influence on his future life. A southern industrial promoter and a future governor of Georgia, Gordon affirmed the values of Jones's father and became a role model for Thomas's future behavior. Gordon and Jones both chose careers in law and politics, worked for the Louisville and Nashville Railroad, and maintained a close friendship.

After the war Jones returned to Montgomery and began his postwar life as a southern gentleman, farming cotton on land provided by his father. In 1866 he married Georgena Bird of Montgomery, who bore him thirteen children. Jones soon left agriculture to concentrate on his legal career, studying under Chief Justice A. J. Walker. He was admitted to practice in 1868. Jones edited a short-lived journal for laboring men, the *Daily Picayune*, in which he was critical of Reconstruction but avoided making vitriolic attacks on Republicans. An unsuccessful Democratic candidate for Montgomery alderman in 1869, Jones was hired by the Republican-dominated supreme court in 1870 as its official reporter, a post that gave him steady work over the next ten years.

It was fortunate that he had that income; by 1870 the unstable cotton market had buried Jones under heavy debt, and he lost his land. During the 1870s and early 1880s, he established himself as a successful lawyer who became a trusted advocate for the Louisville and Nashville Railroad and other important clients. At the same time he was gaining a reputation as a moderate politician who was loyal to the Democrats but willing to work with Republicans. From 1875 to 1884 he served as a Montgomery alderman, concerning himself with technical issues such as public health and quarantine. He served as aide-de-camp to Governor George S. Houston, the Redeemer Democrat whose 1874 election overturned Republican power and restored white supremacy. Jones also was involved in the organization of state militia units, and by 1880 had risen to command of the Second Infantry Regiment of state troops. Throughout his life he retained a military bearing and a prickly sense of personal honor.

In 1884 Jones was elected to the state legislature. As he was making a name for himself, he was also sorting out a personal philosophy made up of diverse elements: the nationalism and opportunism of a New South railroad man, a lawyer's profound respect for legal rights, and a self-conscious paternalism toward black citizens. Years later he explained his racial views by citing Robert E. Lee, who had expressed concern for the welfare of a seemingly worthless soldier "because he is under me."

As a legislator, Jones was committed to the rule of law. He risked the wrath of white landowners by opposing bills that would have subjected defaulting black farmers to peonage or imprisonment for debt. He also opposed the "fee" system by which sheriffs and other officers were paid according to the number of black convicts they were able to lease out. He understood that under Alabama's convict lease system, the state profited because law enforcement officials hustled black prisoners, many convicted of minor offenses, into Tennessee Coal, Iron, and Railroad Company's Pratt mines or other work camps. The same officials also winked at the brutal practices of local magnates or gave way to lynch mobs. Jones's legalistic response to such events was aimed chiefly at insuring order and due process for all citizens. Thus he was a willing commander of state troops called out to suppress mobs.

In 1886 Jones was elected speaker of the house; thereafter his political rise was rapid. The times were tense for the state's Democrats as they tried to retain the loyalties and votes of small farmers caught in a trap of falling cotton prices and high interest rates. Jones knew what it was to be a frustrated farmer; yet he would not challenge the prevailing political order. Like many Democrats, he was unprepared for the rise of the Farmers' Alliance and kindred organizations, which attracted tens of thousands of white and black Alabamians in the late 1880s. Jones further disapproved of alliance ties to the Knights of Labor and other labor groups, which, in his view, were foes of the corporations that he served as legal counsel and that he credited with returning prosperity to Alabama.

In 1890, when the Farmers' Alliance rallied behind the Democratic gubernatorial candidacy of Commissioner of Agriculture Reuben F. Kolb, Jones was one of four conservatives who ran in an attempt to stop him. At the state convention in May, Kolb was close to victory when the anti-Kolb managers decided to pool their votes. Jones was the least well known of the challengers, but his delegates were judged the most likely to bolt to Kolb. For this reason and perhaps for his youthful vigor, after three days and thirty-three ballots Jones was given the nomination. Having secured a difficult nomination, he won easily against his Republican opponent. He took office declaring overconfidently that Alabama was "singularly free from agrarianism and communism."

As governor, Jones encountered difficulties with the legislative branch of the state's government, which rarely shared his desire to pass laws to make sheriffs more accountable for lynchings. Nor did legislators appreciate Jones's opposition to their efforts to limit funds available to black schools. To his mind, such actions were clearly against the spirit and intent of the Fourteenth Amendment. The governor and the legislature nonetheless agreed on a bill requiring separate but equal accommodations in railroad passenger cars, which passed in 1891.

Jones's reform tendency was not unique among white Alabamians—educator Julia Tutwiler, clergyman Edgar Gardner Murphy, and Populist Joseph C. Manning come to mind—but it was unusual among mainline Democrats. In his second term, Jones tried but failed to end the convict lease system. On this issue, he was a relentless lobbyist who enjoyed the support of labor unions, the Women's Christian Temperance Union, Reuben F. Kolb, and a considerable segment of the general public who agreed with his stance. In 1893 the legislature passed a measure by which the state convict authority began to acquire farmland with a view to making state prisons self-supporting. The plan was to transfer all prisoners from the mines by January 1, 1895, but it was not to be. The fiscal crisis that followed the Panic of 1893, which Jones met by borrowing money and approving a modest tax increase, was so intense that his successor, William C. Oates, persuaded the legislature to repeal the convict lease legislation. Indeed, Alabama would not end its convict lease system until the 1920s, the last state in the Union to do so.

Working on these reforms had little to do with Jones's main task as a party leader—namely, to keep Kolb and the agrarians out of power. Kolb had been a good loser in the 1890 Democratic convention nomination intrigue. Two years later he was determined either to win the Democratic gubernatorial nomination or to break the party apart. That spring saw fierce battles for delegates in which Jones, mindful of and resorting to the Democrats' long-time racial strategy, spoke of preserving "the walls of our civilization, which can be guarded only by a united white race." In June, rather than face a second convention defeat, Kolb's supporters proclaimed him the nominee of the "Jeffersonian" Democrats. Their organization, supported openly by the newly formed People's Party and tacitly by Republicans, challenged Bourbon control of the Black Belt by promising to protect the political rights of blacks.

Predictably, Democratic journalists and stump speakers responded with a campaign for white supremacy similar to that of 1874. It was bitterly ironic that Jones should have been the standard bearer in such a racist campaign. It likewise was ironic that Kolb, whose party was reaching out to blacks, criticized Jones's zealous opposition to lynch mobs. The saddest aspect of the election may have been that Jones won it as he did—by the narrow margin of 126,959 to 115,524, his victory provided by overwhelming majorities in the Black Belt. It was generally agreed that Kolb was "counted out" by Democratic election officials who stole the votes of black men. Jones reacted to mounting evidence of fraud with anger and denial, filing libel charges against one of his harshest critics, Populist editor Frank Baltzell. Plagued by shame, poor health, and financial problems, he considered returning to work for the Louisville and Nashville Railroad. Yet, for all his humane impulses, Jones believed in the superiority of white people. Although he lacked rancor toward Republicans, he was furious with the agrarians, and he believed that the Democratic Party was the rightful, if flawed, guardian of the southern way of life. In 1893, Jones supported passage of the Sayre Act, which provided for the governor to appoint county registrars and poll officials, insuring they would all be Democrats. These officials would maintain voting rolls and "assist" in marking the ballots of illiterate voters. Passage of the Sayre Act made the 1894 election instantly easier for Democrats.

In the summer of 1894 Governor Jones repeatedly sent troops to the Birmingham area to oppose violent strikes by miners and railroad workers whose political loyalties were decidedly Jeffersonian. State convicts and black "scabs" kept the mines operating. The strike was broken by Jones's actions, and the link between farm and labor forces was strengthened.

By endorsing William C. Oates's gubernatorial candidacy in 1894, Jones stood by the Bourbon and Hard Money faction of his party. In fact, in 1896 he supported the "goldbug" Democratic presidential candidate, Simon Buckner. After leaving office Jones continued to mix power politics with paternalism and regard for legal niceties. As governor he had opposed calling a constitutional convention, but in the wake of the 1892 and 1894 elections he changed his mind and began campaigning for a new document. As a delegate to the 1901 convention, he supported the concept of suffrage restrictions, yet in an eloquent speech he opposed the "grandfather clause" as an unconstitutional voting provision aimed solely at enfranchising whites.

In 1901, thanks in part to his warm relationship with Booker T. Washington, Jones was appointed by President Theodore Roosevelt to be federal judge of Alabama's northern and middle districts. Beginning in 1903 he presided over a series of trials brought by the United States government aimed at ending the corrupt arrangements among certain local officials, landlords, and employers that held many black laborers and poor whites in peonage. These arrangements outraged Jones, but he meted out mild punishments, convinced that the threat of exposure and future prosecution would end the practice.

Jones's last great public enterprise was his involvement in the twentieth-century rate-making controversy between the railroads, especially the Louisville and Nashville, and the state during the administration of Governor Braxton Bragg Comer. Unable to admit that he lacked objectivity with respect to his long-time employer, Jones freely granted injunctions blocking enforcement of state regulation of the railroad. The case, which began in 1907, dragged on until the two sides compromised in February 1914. Throughout, Jones withstood popular anger, defending to the last the railroad he had served for so long. He died two months after the settlement of the case, on April 28, ending a career that was in many respects full of contradictory actions.

References

Aucoin, Brent Jude. "Thomas Goode Jones, Redeemer and Reformer: The Radical Policies of a Conservative Democrat in Pursuit of a 'New' South, 1874–1914." Master's thesis, Miami University, 1993.

Daniel, Pete. *The Shadow of Slavery: Peonage in the South, 1901–1969.* New York: Oxford University Press, 1973.

Freyer, Tony, and Timothy Dixon. *Democracy and Judicial Independence: A History of the Federal Courts of Alabama, 1820–1994.* Brooklyn, N.Y.: Carlson Publishing, 1995.

Huggings, Carolyn Ruth. "Bourbonism and Radicalism in Alabama: The Gubernatorial Administration of Thomas Goode Jones, 1890–1894." Master's thesis, Auburn University, 1968.

Journal of the [Alabama] Senate, 1890–91.

Marston, Allison. "Guiding the Profession: The 1887 Code of Ethics of the Alabama State Bar." *Alabama Law Review* 49 (winter 1998).

Rogers, William Warren. *The One-Gallused Rebellion: Agrarianism in Alabama, 1865–1896.* Baton Rouge: Louisiana State University Press, 1970.

William C. Oates, 1894–1896

PAUL McWHORTER PRUITT JR.

W ILLIAM Calvin Oates held none of the contradictory philosophies that marked his predecessor, Thomas G. Jones. Neither did he enjoy Jones's comfortable childhood or excellent preparatory education. The eldest child of William and Sarah Sellers Oates, William was born on November 30, 1835, in Pike County. His father, who had migrated to the Wiregrass region from South Carolina, was a poor farmer who had little to offer his wife and children but a life of isolation and endless toil. Young William was ambitious, but his father had no money with which to educate him. In the end he attended a few school sessions after scraping together tuition by working on neighboring farms. As a child, Oates developed a penchant for getting into trouble, and in 1851, after committing a violent act, he decided to leave home and see more of the world.

122
◇ Oates embarked on a three-year picaresque adventure. Earning his keep as a cigar seller, house painter, deckhand, shingle maker, and, above all, a gambler, Oates made brief stays in northern Florida, Louisiana, and various Texas towns. In an autobiography written in his later years, he remembered himself as a lover of women and a brawler who specialized in gouging eyes. Few men have risen so far from such a rough beginning.

Oates

Early in 1854 Oates returned to Alabama. Cured of wanderlust though not of restlessness, the teenaged Oates traveled deeper into the Wiregrass to Henry County, where he found a job teaching school. Beginning in 1855 Oates began alternating teaching with study at Lawrenceville Academy, where schoolmaster William A. Clark and his staff schooled the young man in English composition, mathematics, Latin, and debate. He worked hard and excelled, becoming a fair classical scholar and graduating in just two years. As a debater Oates became interested in public affairs and not surprisingly turned to the study of law as a ladder upward. In 1858 he traveled to Eufaula to read law with the firm of James L. Pugh, Edward C. Bullock, and Jefferson Buford, lawyers who strongly supported secession and were associated with the "Eufaula Regency." In October he earned his license and two months later opened an office in the nearby town of Abbeville.

By 1860 Oates was supplementing his income by editing a Democratic newspaper. Although not an enthusiastic secessionist, he supported the action of Alabama's January 1861 convention. When the Civil War began, he understood that future rank and social position would follow military glory. Accordingly, he raised an infantry company, the Henry (County) Pioneers, and worked hard to provide them uniforms and equipment. The company left Abbeville in July 1861 and was soon in Virginia as Company G of the Fifteenth Alabama. In May and June of 1862, Oates and his men were with Stonewall Jackson in his Valley campaign and other significant battles. By January 1863, twenty-eight-year-old Oates was in command of the regiment, a reward he gained not only for bravery but also for the intelligent care with which he led his troops.

At Gettysburg on July 2, 1863, Oates and the Fifteenth Alabama fought themselves into legend by repeatedly assaulting Little Round Top, defended by the men of the Twentieth Maine. In a homeric duel, the 400 Alabamians suffered 138 casualties in a long day's struggle that ended in defeat for the southern forces. Following Gettysburg, Oates's regiment was one of several transferred to Tennessee that performed well at the Battle of Chickamauga, where Oates was shot in the thigh. By March 1864 he had returned to his command and was ordered north for the battles of Wilderness and Cold Harbor.

In August Oates was the victim of an intrigue when his subordinate, Major Alexander Lowther, secured a colonel's commission and supplanted him. Oates's most recent biographer suggests that he may have damaged his career by advocating, as early as February 1863, that the Confederacy enlist slaves to offset the Union edge in manpower. Years later, Oates was still angry that Confederate leaders had, in effect, preserved slavery at the cost of victory. He was given command of the Forty-eighth Alabama as a consolation prize, but on August 16, 1864, near Petersburg, Virginia, he was wounded seriously in his right arm and an amputation was necessary. When Lee surrendered to Grant, Oates was at home in Abbeville, recuperating from the injury that became his political badge of honor.

Upon his return to health Oates picked up the pieces of his life. He reopened his legal practice, which allowed him to harness his combative streak in civilian life. Like many ex-Confederates, Oates applied wartime attitudes to Reconstruction politics. He was loyal to the Democratic Party and viewed Republicans, especially scalawags, as enemy despoilers of the public treasury, and as such they were to be outmaneuvered and defeated. Oates disapproved of the violent methods of the Ku Klux Klan but did not hesitate to endorse ballot-box stuffing, bribery, or other means of controlling the votes of the freedmen in the name of white supremacy. Forced to accept the suffrage of black men, he became an architect of the system by which Bourbon Democrats could usually produce majorities sufficient to overcome

Republicans or independents. Service in the state house of representatives in 1870, where he served as chairman of the Ways and Means Committee, and as a delegate to the constitutional convention of 1875 brought Oates an enduring conviction that taxes should be low and government limited.

In 1880 Oates was rewarded for his service to the Confederacy and loyalty to the Democratic Party with a seat in Congress from the Third District. Backed by a network of veterans and former Regency politicians, he was unbeatable, winning reelection an additional six times. A large part of his success in Washington was due to the charm and ability of Sarah Toney Oates, whom he married in 1882. The daughter of a Eufaula family, she was twenty-seven years younger than Oates. Despite her youth, she was a natural-born political hostess. With his social acceptance assured, Oates won respect in Congress as a skilled parliamentarian and determined conservative. In the House he was conspicuous for his efforts to secure the return of funds collected under the Reconstruction-era cotton tax. In addition he opposed both the Blair bill, which would have spent federal funds on public education, and the Interstate Commerce Act. By the early 1890s, he was known as an uncompromising foe of measures to increase the money supply of the nation as a way to relieve agrarian distress. Oates remained a staunch supporter of the gold standard.

Oates's chief ambition was to advance to a Senate seat, but his plans changed as a result of the swirling state politics of the 1890s. For years, declining prices had threatened the independence of small farmers. As agrarian reform movements gained thousands of followers, Democratic leaders split over the stance of the party toward such organizations as the Farmers' Alliance. Alliance leader Reuben F. Kolb was denied the Democratic gubernatorial nomination in 1890 by a classic Bourbon combination of Black Belt and probusiness delegates. In 1892, Kolb broke with the party and ran as the candidate of the Jeffersonian Democrats, openly soliciting the votes of black farmers. His campaign against incumbent governor Thomas Jones and his effort to bypass the politics of white supremacy were both infuriating and frightening to conservatives such as Oates.

Kolb lost to Jones by approximately eleven thousand votes, almost certainly as a result of ballot fraud in the Black Belt. Democratic bosses, certain that Kolb was planning to run again in 1894, united behind Oates as a man who held the right stands against the Farmers' Alliance and who could best fight off the challenge of a growing quasi-Populist "Silverite" wing within the party. Backed by Jones and the *Montgomery Advertiser*, Oates ran for governor, defending his record of support for Grover Cleveland's antisilver policies. At the Democratic convention in May 1894 he defeated Birmingham entrepreneur Joseph F. Johnston on the first ballot. Oates's campaign against Kolb competed for newspaper coverage with Governor Jones's use of troops to put down the prolonged strike of Birmingham coal miners. Kolb and his Populist and Republican allies turned their fire against Jones, while Oates ran as the "One-Armed Hero of Henry County," foe of anarchy and disorder, defender of white supremacy.

In the August 1894 election, Oates defeated Kolb by a count of 111,875 to 83,292 votes. As in 1892, Democratic victory was partly the result of stuffed ballot boxes in the Black Belt. The decline in the number of ballots was probably the result of the Sayre election law of 1893, which changed registration and voting requirements in ways that disfranchised many illiterates. Kolb and many of his supporters refused to accept the official returns, but their protests were to no avail in the absence of an effective election contest law. Undeterred, Kolb declared himself the victor and on inauguration day, December 1, took an oath of office from a Montgomery justice of the peace. With his band of loyal followers he marched up Dexter Avenue to the capitol grounds, where under the noses of Governor Jones and incoming governor Oates, who were protected by state troops, he was forced onto a side street. Kolb delivered an "inaugural" address to his angry supporters, but Oates was peacefully and officially sworn in as governor for a single term.

The 1894–95 legislature pitted Populists against Democrats, Bourbons against reform Democrats, and hard-money men against silverites. The Populists constituted a substantial minority whose first objective was the passage of a retroactive election contest law. Eventually the legislature passed a contest act that, though not retroactive, was supported by Joseph C. Manning and other Populist leaders as the best legislation they could obtain. The legislative session was marked by constant efforts on the part of the Populists to draw the federal government into an investigation of Alabama's 1892 and 1894 election outcomes. Oates and his allies defeated the Populists at every turn.

125
◇

Oates's chief concern as governor was the financial stability of the state. Previous administrations had successively lowered the rate of ad valorem taxation from 7.5 mills in 1876 to 4 mills in 1889, while state expenditures had doubled. In the depressed early 1890s Governor Jones had been forced to borrow money to keep the government in operation and had approved a half-mill tax increase in 1893. Even so, in 1894 he projected a deficit of nearly $700,000 by September 1896. Oates's allies in the legislature rushed through another half-mill tax in December over the opposition of Populists, who hoped to see the Oates administration short of funds. In February 1895, after considerable debate, the legislature passed bills that provided more state control over tax assessment and authorized Oates to seek refinancing of the state's bonded indebtedness. In the same month, at the governor's request, the lawmakers repealed Jones's plan to phase out the convict lease system, thus preserving a vital source of revenue for the state and a convenient form of labor control for industrialists.

William C. Oates
1894–1896

In March 1895 Oates traveled to New York to meet with the state's creditors about Alabama's bonded debt. There he was ambushed by Joseph Manning and Populist congressman Milford W. Howard, who were in town to publicize the need for ballot reform in the South. They denounced Oates as governor by fraud, head of a bogus and unjust regime. Whether because of negative publicity or unsettled business conditions, Oates was unable to make satisfactory fiscal arrangements and returned to Alabama in a poor state of health and nerves. Over the next year hard times persisted, and Oates was forced to borrow money for the state from bankers in New York, Selma, and Mobile. In the midst of these difficulties he must have taken comfort in the knowledge that Populist efforts to overturn the 1894 election had failed; by May 1896 it was clear that Congress would conduct no investigations into Alabama's election process.

In 1896 the Oates wing of the Democratic Party had troubles of its own. The silverites were in the ascendancy, and Oates, who was not a candidate for reelection, could not prevent the prosilver candidate, Joseph F. Johnston, from winning the Democratic gubernatorial nomination. With his term drawing to an end, the "One-Armed Hero" still dreamed of a Senate seat. A vacancy was due to be filled in 1897, and Oates campaigned for it, but without success. The position was given to Edmund W. Pettus, a supporter of free silver. Oates, a Bourbon bulldog of great value to the Democrats when audacity and confrontation were needed for victory, was no longer useful in more peaceful times.

On leaving office, Oates returned to his legal practice, interrupting it in 1898 to serve as brigadier general of volunteers in a company stationed at Camp Meade, Pennsylvania, during the Spanish-American War. He also played a role in the constitutional convention of 1901, criticizing some of the disfranchisement measures introduced, particularly the "grandfather clause." He thought that provision might be found unconstitutional and added, characteristically, that not all of the Confederate grandfathers in question had served honorably. Nevertheless, the former governor strongly supported ratification of the 1901 constitution.

Thereafter Oates applied himself increasingly to Confederate reunions and to writing a well-received account of the war, *The War between the Union and the Confederacy* (1905). He died on September 9, 1910, a classic example of the conservative self-made man who soldiered to the last for the causes he embraced.

References

Huggins, Carolyn Ruth. "Bourbonism and Radicalism in Alabama: The Gubernatorial Administrations of Thomas Goode Jones, 1890–1894." Master's thesis, Auburn University, 1968.

Perry, Mark. *Conceived in Liberty: Joshua Chamberlain, William Oates, and the American Civil War.* New York: Viking, 1997.

Pruitt, Paul M. Jr. "Joseph C. Manning, Alabama Populist: A Rebel against the Solid South." Ph.D. thesis, College of William and Mary, 1980.

Rogers, William Warren. *The One-Gallused Rebellion: Agrarianism in Alabama, 1865–1896.* Baton Rouge: Louisiana State University Press, 1970.

Sparkman, John. "The Kolb-Oates Campaign of 1894." Master's thesis, University of Alabama, 1924.

Joseph F. Johnston, 1896–1900

MICHAEL PERMAN

JOSEPH Forney Johnston was elected governor for two terms, just as the challenge from the Populists and from the Jeffersonians led by Reuben F. Kolb began to ebb in the late 1890s. Once in office, he tried to redirect the Democratic Party toward a course of reform through the incorporation of most of the electoral base and policies of these two dissenting organizations. But his intentions were foiled by his opponents who controlled the party machinery as well as by the movement for disfranchisement, which Johnston himself had hoped could be an agent for reform but rather became the primary obstacle preventing its attainment.

Johnston was born on March 23, 1843, in North Carolina and grew up on the family farm. In 1860 he moved with his parents to Alabama. He was an eighteen-year-old attending school in Talladega when the Civil War broke out. Right away, Johnston enlisted in the Confederate army; he rose from the rank of private to captain and was wounded on four separate occasions. After the war, he decided to become a lawyer and was admitted to the bar in 1866. Moving to Selma in 1867, he practiced law in the Black Belt city for the next seventeen years. He also became active in the Democratic Party of Dallas County, playing an important part in its opposition to Reconstruction and soon becoming influential in party affairs at the state level. From 1878 to 1882, he led the party as chair of the state executive committee. Then in 1884 he left Selma and the law to embark on a career as a banker in the booming new town of Birmingham.

Johnston

After three years as president of the Alabama National Bank, Johnston became president of the city's largest manufacturing firm, the Sloss Iron and Steel Company. His remarkable accomplishments in business were paralleled by his political achievements. Already successful as a party manager, he began to link his Black Belt connections with the banking and steel barons in Birmingham, thereby aligning himself with the twin pillars of Alabama's Democratic Party in the late nineteenth century. Johnston had thereby positioned himself to play a pivotal role in Alabama politics in the 1890s, a decade that proved to be possibly the most turbulent in the state between the Civil War and the civil rights movement one hundred years later.

In the first half of the decade, Johnston was a leading figure in the Democrats' triumph over Reuben F. Kolb and the agrarians. In 1890 he was one of four Democratic gubernatorial contenders who participated in a scheme at the party's convention to deprive Kolb of the nomination by combining all the other candidates behind Thomas G. Jones. At the next state election two years later, Kolb decided to run as an independent. As chair of the platform committee at the Democratic convention, Johnston was responsible for the critical thirteenth plank, which directed the assembly to enact legislation to secure "the government of the State in the hands of the intelligent and the virtuous." Although Johnston had initially intended that a constitutional convention be called for this purpose, the legislature produced instead the notorious Sayre law of 1893, a simple yet devastatingly effective remedy that made voting so difficult that thousands of the Democrats' opponents in 1892 found themselves disfranchised two years later.

Johnston again sought the party's gubernatorial nomination in 1894 but was defeated by the seven-term congressman from the Black Belt, William C. Oates. In contrast to the profoundly conservative Oates, Johnston was the leader of an emerging element in the party that advocated free silver and was willing to adopt some of the reforms proposed by Kolb and his splinter party, the Jeffersonians, as well as by the Populists. Fearing that the Democrats were becoming too conservative and inflexible when confronted by the revolt of the farmers and by a series of strikes in 1894 among the state's coal miners and steel operatives, Johnston urged his party to consider reform. Meanwhile, Oates defeated Kolb by a greater margin than Jones had in 1892, though with fifty thousand fewer votes cast.

In 1896, when the Populists fused with the Democrats in the presidential election, Joe Johnston ran as the reform, free silver candidate for the Democratic gubernatorial nomination and defeated the "goldbug" congressman Richard H. Clarke. He went on to the governorship by beating Albert T. Goodwyn, the leader of the Populist-Republican coalition, in the general election. With the national party favoring free silver and nominating William Jennings Bryan for president and with the state party opening up its primaries ("letting down the bars" was the contemporary phrase) so that former Kolb supporters could return and participate again, Johnston's plans for a broader-based and liberalized

◇

Democratic Party seemed within reach. He won the governorship in 1896 by a larger margin—128,541 to 89,290—than Oates in 1894, and the majority of his votes came from outside the Black Belt. Although he benefited from the customary ballot-box stuffing in the Black Belt counties, he had not needed them to carry the state. Consequently, Johnston came into office independent of the Black Belt machine and at the head of a broad coalition that included Birmingham industrialists, reform-minded regular Democrats, former Kolb supporters, and farmers from the white counties of north Alabama.

To satisfy the various elements of his emergent coalition, Governor Johnston recommended a wide array of legislative proposals. He encouraged northern capital to enter the state and offered tax exemptions to manufacturing firms to promote industrial development. To ensure that this development was orderly and regulated, he proposed an elective railroad commission, modeled on Georgia's, with power to set freight rates and punish roads that failed to comply. He recommended creation of a state tax commission to bring assessment and collection under more centralized control and to ensure that large landowners as well as corporations were appropriately evaluated and their taxes properly levied. In addition, corporations were to be subject to a franchise tax on both their property and the market value of their stock, a levy its opponents decried as a double tax, which they then proceeded to defeat in the legislature. Another reform measure was Johnston's plan to investigate the convict lease system, though the bill that the legislature produced lacked any enforcement mechanism and applied only to counties, not the state government. The governor also proposed to build more roads and to plan and finance them more effectively. He increased the budget for the state's public schools by adding more than $100,000 and an extra one mill ad valorem tax.

All of these reform proposals did not, however, produce dramatic change. Many of them encountered stiff opposition from the railroads and from Johnston's factional rivals within the party, and so they were often either restricted or defeated. Furthermore, the governor's own proposals, such as his approach to convict leasing, were overly cautious and limited. Finally, Johnston's ability to marshal support for his measures was frequently constrained by the diversity of his coalition and incompatibility among its elements.

One reform that Johnston proposed was to plague him. In his first message, the new governor urged the legislature to call a convention to rewrite Alabama's 1875 constitution, which, he complained, "crippled and dwarfed enterprise, education and progress." For example, it restricted government aid to the state's emergent industries while its limitations on taxation prevented such growing cities as Birmingham and Anniston from raising funds needed to finance development and expansion. The most important reason for a convention, however, was to restrict the right of suffrage, an issue that preoccupied Johnston since 1892. Not only would disfranchisement eliminate black voters whose qualifications for the suffrage he doubted, but "pure elections" were expected to be obtainable once the electorate was, as noted earlier, limited to the "intelligent and the virtuous."

The constitutional revision issue proved, however, to be the nemesis of Johnston's attempt to realign the Democratic Party because opposition to a new constitution arose primarily from within his own coalition. In the 1896–97 legislature, a convention bill passed the house, only to fail in the senate where former Kolbites and Populists voted against a proposal they feared would disfranchise poor and illiterate whites. Seeing that his own supporters were hostile, the governor reversed his position in the next legislature. Democratic legislators insisted on a convention, however, and, after placating the doubters by imposing four restrictions on the convention's action (prohibiting removal of the state capital from Montgomery, continuing to base representation in the state legislature on population, protecting military veterans from being disfranchised, and keeping the 1875 constitution's state tax rate), the legislature approved the initiative by 18–11 in the senate and 52–41 in the house.

Although Johnston signed the convention bill, he was alarmed at the turn of events. North Alabama's opposition seemed undiminished, and his enemies in the conservative "goldbug" wing of the party secured many of the nominations for delegate at large and seemed likely to win significant influence in the convention. When the Democratic leadership tried to make the convention call a party loyalty issue, Johnston decided he had to stop the juggernaut in its tracks. At a state convention in March 1899, he and his supporters intervened to head off the party test. When they failed, Johnston embarked on an unprecedented and remarkably risky maneuver. He called a special session of the legislature and insisted that the convention bill be repealed. In effect Governor Johnston had broken with his party on an issue of vital importance to the future of the Alabama Democracy. Because the governor was attempting to reverse the party's decision to disfranchise the black electorate, the Democratic leadership mobilized all its forces, including the state's U.S. senators, Edmund W. Pettus and John Tyler Morgan, to get the legislators to stand firm. Despite the pressure, a slim majority of lawmakers supported repeal. The *Birmingham Age-Herald*, the leading newspaper in the state and one that Johnston had once owned, was aghast. The governor's confrontational strategy was "a remarkable personal and executive triumph," the paper exclaimed; "he displays an audacity in politics unexampled in this state for many a long year."

For the next three years, Johnston acted as the leader of the rank and file, organized around his north Alabama–reform coalition, in a massive struggle against the party organization based on an alliance forged between the Black Belt and big business. This dramatic contest was fought out in the upcoming election for the U.S. Senate in 1900 as Johnston took on the four-term incumbent, John Tyler Morgan. That Morgan had been an advocate of free silver and also Johnston's patron in earlier years — he once told Johnston that he had "never done a better work for Alabama" than in helping him win the governorship in 1896 — mattered little now as both men fought over the future composition and course of the white man's party in Alabama.

Shortly after Johnston announced his candidacy for the Senate, Alabama's major newspapers charged that the governor was involved in a scandal related to the University of Alabama. Serious ethical questions were raised about Johnston's efforts to get the university to sell four thousand acres of coal lands to his old firm, Sloss Iron and Steel. Indeed, the governor had called a secret meeting of the university board of trustees in 1899 and pushed for the sale to Sloss for the absurdly low price of $12.50 per acre. Although evidence later showed that Johnston no longer owned stock in the steel company and had little to gain from the sale, Morgan exploited the issue in an attempt to undermine Johnston's claims to be a reformer. The charges hurt Johnston, but the main issues in the campaign revolved around disfranchisement and the future direction of the Democratic Party. The election results decided both questions. Morgan's reputation as the elder statesman of Alabama politics and his control of the party machinery provided him with an overwhelming victory. A convention to achieve disfranchisement was now virtually inevitable.

As expected, the convention was called, and, as Johnston feared, it was dominated by the Black Belt–big business alliance. On suffrage and representation as well as on economic issues, their imprint on the emerging constitution was unmistakable. Hoping to prevent the imposition of such a conservative and antidemocratic document as well as to revive his reform coalition, Johnston once again rallied the opposition in an attempt to defeat ratification of the proposed constitution. Once again, however, he suffered a significant defeat, his second in just twelve months. Even though Johnston's rearguard action was supported by few of the leading Democratic politicians, a majority of voters in thirty-two of the state's sixty-six counties voted against the constitution. As usual, the Black Belt saved the day by stuffing the ballot boxes with false returns.

The following year, Johnston made a third and final attempt to keep his coalition alive when he demanded that the 1902 gubernatorial contest be conducted under a direct primary. As a counter to the party's election managers and convention wirepullers, the primary was often advocated by turn-of-the-century reformers and protoprogressives such as Johnston. Although initially saying that he would not run for governor himself, he changed his mind after the State Democratic Executive Committee capitulated to the widespread pressure for a primary. Nevertheless, he was unable to capitalize on his success. With the electorate reduced by the new constitution's suffrage provisions as well as by his opponents' control of the registration process, Johnston was easily defeated—in effect, counted out—in a poll of 57,491 to 31,745.

Despite these successive electoral defeats at the hands of the party's establishment, Johnston, nonetheless, remained a figure of influence. In 1906, when the Democrats held a strange and unprecedented primary—called the "dead shoes" primary—to select successors to the state's two octogenarian U.S. senators, Morgan and Pettus, Johnston was the second-highest vote getter behind John H. Bankhead Sr. With the death of Pettus in July 1907, just a month after Morgan, Johnston attained the position he had sought in 1900. He served out Pettus's term and then was elected to a full term in 1909. His own death on August 8, 1913, prevented him from completing it.

Joseph F. Johnston's detractors called him a political chameleon and attributed his complicated maneuvering primarily to an insatiable personal ambition. Some former Populists and Kolbites charged him with emasculating their movement for political and agrarian reform by his doomed attempt to incorporate its elements into the Democratic Party. Whatever his critics might say, however, there was considerable political shrewdness and vision in Johnston's scheme to make the Democratic Party a party of reform. With his evident political skill and ingenuity, Johnston had a chance of pulling it off. Yet he failed. Rather than marking the start of a reform party and the transition to the Progressivism of the early twentieth century, Johnston's initiative proved to be a dead end. Perhaps the Black Belt–big business alliance would have reasserted itself anyway as soon as Johnston challenged it frontally. Still, the movement for a new constitution proved to be the rock on which Johnston's ship foundered. Although set in motion by Johnston himself in 1897, the idea of a disfranchising convention soon developed a momentum that was unstoppable. Despite his desperate attempts on four different occasions, Johnston's reform initiative was undermined by the campaign for constitutional revision, and its base of support was swept away by the resulting constitution itself. Not until the Comer administration of 1907–11 would the Democrats seriously consider reform again.

References

Fry, Joseph A. *John Tyler Morgan and the Search for Southern Autonomy.* Knoxville: University of Tennessee Press, 1992.

Hackney, Sheldon. *Populism to Progressivism in Alabama.* Princeton: Princeton University Press, 1969.

McMillan, Malcolm C. *Constitutional Development in Alabama, 1798–1901: A Study in Politics, the Negro, and Sectionalism.* 1955. Reprint, Spartanburg, S.C.: Reprint Co., 1978.

Rogers, William Warren, Robert David Ward, Leah Rawls Atkins, and Wayne Flynt. *Alabama: The History of a Deep South State.* Tuscaloosa: University of Alabama Press, 1994.

Webb, Samuel L. *Two-Party Politics in the One-Party South: Alabama's Hill Country, 1874–1920.* Tuscaloosa: University of Alabama Press, 1997.

IV

The Progressive Era through World War II, 1900–1945

Between the years of 1900 and 1945, the United States
experienced a Progressive Era, two world wars, the "Roaring
Twenties," and the Great Depression and New Deal eras.
Alabamians began to elect, off and on, more progressive
leaders who used government to address the state's need for
improved education, better roads, and increased social services
for its population. The word "Bourbon" was dropped from
the political vocabulary, and "conservative" and "progressive"
began to be used. But such labels are confusing. Would a
"conservative" be against prohibition? Could a "progressive"
be an active member of the Ku Klux Klan? Not surprisingly in
the fascinating world of Alabama politics, the answer to both
was "yes."

During the New Deal, the word "liberal" came into vogue,
and politicians bearing that label gained popularity in the state.
World War II factories and industries ended the depression and
also the domination in Alabama of an agricultural system that
had held the state's poor people bound since the Civil War.
As a broader middle class began to grow and when organized
labor, backed by Mr. Roosevelt's administration, began to flex
its muscles in Alabama, a backlash pushed against the rising

tide of liberalism. Little but the names of the players changed
in the age-old battle between those who feared big government
as a threat to liberty and those who wanted to use government
to make things fairer.

William J. Samford, 1900–June 1901

MARLENE HUNT RIKARD

WILLIAM James Samford died on June 11, 1901, only six months after assuming office as the thirty-second governor of Alabama. Samford was a lawyer-politician who rose rapidly in Alabama politics during the turbulent and complex post–Civil War era, but his short tenure in the office left him little chance to make a mark on the state.

Samford was born on September 16, 1844, in Greenville, Georgia, to William Flewellyn Samford and Susan Lewis Dowdell Samford. His father was professor of English literature at Emory College in Georgia before he studied law and was admitted to the bar in 1840. He moved his family to Chambers County, Alabama, in 1846 and became a planter and then editor of several Alabama newspapers. The elder Samford lost the Democratic gubernatorial nomination to Andrew B. Moore in 1857 and ran again, unsuccessfully, as an in-dependent in 1859, charging Moore with negligence in defending the principle of states' rights. Known as the "penman of the Civil War in Alabama," Samford was an ardent secessionist who continued to write extensively on the political issues of the day throughout his life. Young William James was shaped by his father's ardent support of states' rights and his interest in literature, law, writing, and oratory and by his mother's cultured upbringing and spiritual devotion.

Samford

William James Samford began his education at age seven at the Classical School in Oak Bowery in Chambers County and continued in the public schools of Tuskegee and Auburn. He worked after school as a typesetter at his father's Tuskegee newspaper. Samford attended the East Alabama Male College (now Auburn University), then transferred to the University of Georgia, but his education was cut short by the Civil War. Only seventeen years old in May 1862, Samford enrolled as a private in the Forty-sixth Alabama Regiment and rose through the ranks to become first lieutenant of Company G. Captured in May 1863 at the battle of Baker's Creek, he was incarcerated at Johnson's Island on Lake Erie, where he encountered his old schoolmaster from Oak Bowery, Major W. F. Slaton.

During his eighteen-month confinement, he resumed his studies in classics and mathematics. Released in a large prisoner exchange in January 1865, he rejoined his regiment and, at war's end, returned to his Auburn home a Confederate hero.

Despite parental warnings about their reduced circumstances in the aftermath of the war, he and Caroline Elizabeth Drake, the eighteen-year-old daughter of Dr. John Hodges Drake and Polly Drake of Auburn, were married in October 1865. They moved to a farm near Auburn and eventually had nine children. A devout Christian, Samford was a licensed preacher in the Methodist Episcopal Church South and served regularly as a delegate to the Alabama annual conference.

Samford worked his farm by day and read law in the evenings, earning admission to the bar in 1867. He opened a practice in nearby Opelika in 1870, but his meager earnings of $200 in the first year forced a return to farming for another season. He reopened his office in 1872 and moved his family to Opelika, where they endured austere conditions as he established his reputation as an attorney and orator.

In 1872 Samford began his political career as an Opelika city alderman. Moving swiftly into state politics, in the same year he served as a delegate to the state Democratic Party convention and as an alternate elector on the Horace Greeley ticket. Although he thought the selection of Greeley was a mistake, he supported the party, a pattern of compromise that marked Samford's political career. As a member of the Lee County Executive Committee of the Democratic and Conservative Party, Samford used his oratorical talents on the stump to win the Third District for gubernatorial candidate George S. Houston in 1874. With conservative Democrats in control, he supported the call for a constitutional convention and, at age thirty, was elected the youngest delegate of the convention. Serving on the Finance Committee, he was instrumental in limiting the taxing power of the state legislature in the Bourbon 1875 constitution. That device, however, also limited the ability of the state to market itself to northern businesses or to foster and support social services.

In 1878 Samford won the nomination of his party to the U.S. Congress from the Third District. In his single term as a congressman, he held conservative positions on states' rights and centralized power, but his agrarian background led him to support the unlimited coinage of silver, a position later taken by reform-minded Populists. He also supported the unsuccessful Reagan bill, which would have given the federal government the power to regulate railroads. Missing his family, he declined to run for reelection and returned to Opelika.

After resuming his law practice, Samford again plunged into state politics, earning a reputation as one of the state's finest orators. Elected to represent Lee County in the Alabama House of Representatives in 1882, Samford moved to the state senate for terms in 1884–88 and 1892–96, serving two years as president of that body. Reflecting his growing statewide reputation, in 1896 he was appointed a trustee of the University of Alabama. In 1899 Samford finally reached the top rung of state politics, winning the Democratic nomination for governor on the third ballot.

Samford's rise in state politics occurred during tumultuous years in Alabama. After "redeeming" the state from Republican control, conservative "Bourbons" and the Democratic Party controlled state politics through the party caucus and by intimidation and manipulation of the votes of blacks in the Black Belt counties. In the 1880s and 1890s Greenbackers and Populists, mainly from the hill counties of north Alabama, denounced the political alliance between Black Belt planters and urban industrialists but with little lasting success. Samford's immediate predecessor, Joseph Johnston, won the gubernatorial election as a reformer and succeeded in bringing many Populists back into the Democratic Party. The state's more conservative Democrats distrusted Johnston and were angry at him for refusing to call a convention to write a constitution that would disfranchise black voters. They pushed for a candidate who would support such a convention and succeeded in returning the governorship to a Bourbon when they nominated Samford as the Democratic candidate for governor in 1900.

Samford endorsed the party platform, which called for suffrage changes if white voters were not disenfranchised. He easily won the governorship in the general election over token opposition from Republicans and Populists. During the campaign, Samford's fragile health from a degenerative heart condition became increasingly apparent. The legislature met in November to organize itself and elect a president of the senate who could take over as governor should Samford die. They also approved a bill for a popular vote on calling a constitutional convention, pledging that the constitution would be submitted to voters for ratification.

As the time neared for his inauguration, Samford was too ill to travel to Montgomery for that event. Sworn in while on his sickbed by his son, Samford asked the recently elected president of the senate, Williams Dorsey Jelks, to serve as acting governor until he recuperated. During Jelks's December tenure, he approved Samford's appointments to the railroad commission, and both he and Samford expressed concerns over legislative spending that put the state's treasury in the red. Samford finally took the reigns of office on December 26, 1900, and personally decried the growing debt of the state. Urging fiscal restraint, Samford recommended that state railroad commissioners also serve as the state's pardons board at no additional pay.

In April 1901, 155 delegates to a constitutional convention were elected on the same apportionment as the state legislature, assuring control of the

139
◇

convention by the Black Belt and south Alabama. The delegates convened in Montgomery on May 23, 1901, but Samford died less than a month later after attending a University of Alabama trustees' meeting in Tuscaloosa. In addition to endorsing the call for a constitutional convention, the only other substantive accomplishment of his short days in office was creation of the Alabama Department of Archives and History to house the public records and artifacts of the state. On Samford's death, Jelks assumed the governorship and the responsibility of implementing the new constitution that was ratified on November 11, 1901 — again with fraudulent votes from Alabama's Black Belt region. The provisions of the new constitution not only effectively eliminated the votes of black Alabamians but also diminished the vote of poor whites in future years.

References

Owen, Thomas M. *History of Alabama and Dictionary of Alabama Biography.* 4 vols. Chicago: S. J. Clarke, 1921.

Rogers, William Warren, Robert David Ward, Leah Rawls Atkins, and Wayne Flynt. *Alabama: The History of a Deep South State.* Tuscaloosa: University of Alabama Press, 1994.

Samford, William J. Typescript biographical sketch. Samford University Special Collections, Samford University, Birmingham, Alabama.

Smith, George Hudson. "The Life and Times of William J. Samford." Master's thesis, Samford University, 1969.

Sobel, Robert, and John Raimo, eds. *Biographical Directory of the Governors of the United States, 1789–1978.* Westport, Conn.: Meckler Books, 1978.

William D. Jelks, December 1900, June 1901–1907

DAVID E. ALSOBROOK

WHEN he left office in 1907, William Dorsey Jelks had been governor of Alabama longer than anyone, and this record remained intact until Bibb Graves surpassed it. Jelks was also the first Alabamian to serve as temporary governor due to the illness of a sitting governor, the second to succeed a governor who died in office, and the first governor elected to a four-year term. He was the last in a line of "Bourbon" governors, known for their archconservatism in fiscal and racial matters.

Jelks was born on November 7, 1855, at Warrior Stand in Macon County, Alabama, to Joseph William Jelks and Jane Goodrum Frazer Jelks. Jelks's father, a Confederate army captain, died in 1862 from wounds incurred in the war. Widowed with four young children, Jane Jelks married Major Robert Green Wright of Union Springs in January 1865.

Growing up in Union Springs, young William Jelks helped support his family with odd jobs and with the fish and game he brought in from the surrounding countryside. Rising from this hardscrabble background, the ambitious young man displayed such exemplary work habits and academic potential that patrons from Union Springs awarded him a scholarship to Mercer College in Macon, Georgia. At Mercer, Jelks developed the writing skills that laid the groundwork for his future career in journalism. He is also said to have been converted on that Baptist campus, but he was a member of no church as governor.

After earning his degree at Mercer in 1876, Jelks returned to Union Springs, served on the town's council, his first elective office, and acquired co-ownership of the *Union Springs Herald and Times* with his future brother-in-law, Edward H. Cabaniss. In August 1880, with the support of Congressman William C. Oates, Jelks purchased the *Eufaula Times and News*, and Eufaula became his home for the remainder of his life. In June *Jelks* 1883 he married Alice Keitt Shorter, whose father was a wealthy Eufaula attorney and president of the state railroad commission. Alice, who bore Jelks a daughter, was also the niece of Civil War governor John Gill Shorter and the cousin of Populist leader Reuben Kolb. This marriage solidified Jelks's niche in the state's social and political hierarchy.

Jelks transformed the Eufaula newspaper into one of Alabama's most influential periodicals. To that weekly publication he added the *Eufaula Daily Times*, which he marketed to more than ten thousand subscribers in ten counties throughout southeast Alabama. In eighteen years as the *Daily Times* editor, Jelks became well known for his powerful commentaries on southern education, agricultural diversification, industrialization, the penal system, lynch law, and the "Negro Question." The editor seldom strayed from his readers' prejudices or the Bourbon credo of white supremacy and fiscal austerity.

Racial control was one of Jelks's lifelong obsessions. In editorials that ran between 1882 and 1885 he labeled the black man "an ignorant devil, . . . a foul blot, a blight upon the land . . . , little short of a savage." As early as 1883 he advocated transporting blacks to other locations in the United States as a means of "cleansing" the political arena and encouraging "industrious" white immigrants from western Europe to settle in Alabama and other southern states. The future governor argued that lynching was "a cure and an effective one" and suggested that every potential black rapist should be forewarned that "his neck will be broken without the benefit of judge, jury, or clergy" if he attacked a white woman. Later, when he understood how such barbaric acts tarnished the state's image and discouraged economic investment in Alabama, Jelks moderated his public utterances and adopted an antilynching stance.

Through his newspaper, Jelks built a broad political base and made influential friends among Alabama's congressional delegation, state legislators, and urban business elite. With support from family, friends, and readers of the *Daily Times*, he won a two-year term in the state senate in 1898. During his first term, Jelks sat on the legislative committee that proposed a statewide referendum on whether Alabama should have a constitutional convention to write a document to disfranchise poor white and black voters, and he helped to guide that measure through the senate in late 1898. Earlier in the decade, Populist efforts to create an alliance with blacks had threatened the political control held by the planter–Birmingham business coalition. Jelks stressed "the necessity of relieving the Black Belt of the incubus resting upon it," or as a colleague put it with much less delicacy: "We are here to get rid of the nigger [vote]." The opposition of Governor Johnston led legislators to reject the convention in 1899, but the constitution issue was far from dead and affected the governor's race in 1900. When Confederate hero and former congressman William J. Samford won the nomination, obstacles to a constitutional convention were cleared.

Shortly after his election, Samford was stricken with acute heart disease, which touched off a political crisis in the state because the 1875 constitution included no provision for a lieutenant governor. The president of the senate was again first in line of succession to the governorship, and selection of a senate president became the leading issue when the new legislature convened in November 1900. Jelks had been reelected to the legislature, and he was expeditiously chosen senate president. Over incumbent governor Johnston's opposition, legislators also rushed through a succession bill that provided for the senate president to become temporary governor if the governor could not assume office because of illness, resignation, or absence from the state for more than twenty days.

On December 1 Governor Johnston formally relinquished his office to Samford, and two days later the ailing governor asked Jelks to "take temporary control of the office." Jelks served as acting governor for twenty-three days. During that period he forwarded Samford's recommendations for several appointments to state commissions and boards to the senate and joined him in expressing alarm that the legislature was spending money the state did not have. On December 11, 1900, Jelks signed into law the bill authorizing a constitutional convention in 1901. It was his last official deed as acting governor.

In late December 1900, after Samford reassumed his duties as governor, Jelks confessed that his temporary service had not been "a pleasing thing." He had been torn between carrying out Samford's wishes while trying not to appear to be "a mere figurehead, an automaton." If he was to be governor at all, he preferred to be "governor in fact." He returned to the senate presidency, where he expressed frustration at Samford's style, complaining to a friend: "The governor never promises anything: He will hardly 'commit' himself to the Ten Commandments." On June 11, 1901, Samford died, and Jelks became "governor in fact." He served out the remaining eighteen months of Samford's term, a period consumed by emotional debate over the proposed new constitution and a bitter factional fight within the Democratic Party during the political campaign of 1902.

Jelks watched with satisfaction as voters, on November 11, 1901, approved the new constitution containing proposals to disfranchise poor and illiterate voters. Proponents of ratification argued that disfranchisement would usher in a new era of political reform and "clean government." Yet, during the legislative session of 1901–2, the house and senate rejected bills to regulate child labor, to guarantee compulsory school attendance, and to insure minimum funding for education.

The new constitution increased the term of elected state officials from two to four years, and in 1902 Jelks sought a full term. Former governor Joseph F. Johnston, who opposed the 1901 constitution, also sought another term. During the summer and autumn of 1901, Johnston's forces backed a statewide direct primary only for white voters to replace the party convention process controlled by an elite. Noting the popularity of the primary, Jelks endorsed the proposal, effectively undercutting Johnston's attempt to style himself the reform candidate. The primary was adopted, and both men ran as reformers. Jelks reminded voters that he supported "the new order of things— for white supremacy by law, clean primaries and honest elections" and that under his leadership the convict leasing system had netted the state $100,000 in one year, more than the Johnston administration had received in its four years. Johnston's campaign was poorly organized and did little more than attack the "machine" of Black Belt and Birmingham politicians who, he said, still governed the state.

The primary assumed a new dynamic when the industrialist Braxton Bragg Comer injected the issue of an elected state railroad commission into the campaign. He and others argued that Alabama's railroad freight rates were higher than surrounding southern states, which damaged the state's economy. Comer partisans attempted to extract a commitment from Johnston and Jelks to support an elective railroad commission and were surprised when Johnston refused. Jelks quickly vowed to sign any "proper bill" for an elected commission, and Johnston then voiced similar sentiments, but Comer refused to endorse either candidate.

On August 25, 1902, Jelks easily won the Democratic nomination, with

Johnston carrying only four of the state's sixty-seven counties. Almost 50 percent of the qualified voters did not participate in the primary, and thousands were disfranchised by the poll tax and other suffrage restrictions of the new constitution. Jelks's well-financed organizations in each county, his close alliance with Alabama's congressional delegation, his apparent support of railroad regulation, and his manipulation of the issue of white supremacy served him well. He and Dr. Russell M. Cunningham, who won the lieutenant governor's nomination (the office of the lieutenant governor was constitutionally reestablished in 1901), carried the November election easily against weak Populist-Republican opposition.

As governor in his own right, Jelks focused on policies and programs designed to bolster the state treasury. With the state debt at $9.4 million in 1903, the governor launched an ambitious program to refund the debt by getting the legislature to adopt a series of bond issues. By the end of Jelks's term his efforts on this issue yielded positive results, and when he left office the state had a surplus of almost $2 million.

The governor also believed that state programs such as education and convict leasing should be administered along "strict business lines" to produce substantial savings for taxpayers. Ironically, his narrowly focused approach ultimately produced some limited reforms. For example, to abolish bribes and kickbacks in the convict leasing program and to make the system more efficient, Jelks ordered state prison officials to devote more attention to the feeding, clothing, and medical care of convicts. The horrors of convict leasing persisted in Alabama until 1927, but Jelks's policies eliminated some of the worst evils and corruption inherent in the system. In 1906 the governor proudly announced that the state had collected $400,000 in convict fees in that year alone.

With regard to education, Jelks generally supported the status quo in funding the state's public schools, and he actually reduced appropriations for educating deaf and blind children. In 1903 he signed the Uniform Textbook Act, which brought efficiency and considerable cost savings to the distribution of books to schools across the state. Despite Jelks's parsimonious attitude, funds for education increased during his term, primarily because of his success in reducing the state's bonded indebtedness, leaving additional revenues for education.

Despite his promise during the campaign to support an elective railroad commission, Jelks offered no backing to legislators who enacted a bill requiring the election of three commissioners to begin serving four-year terms in 1904. The new law also pressured the railroads to justify their rates but provided no adequate enforcement power to the commission. Jelks appointed two prorailroad men to the commission before he signed the bill, and the legislature later delayed the process of electing railroad commissioners until 1906.

Again with scant attention from Jelks and largely through the efforts of reformers Edgar Gardner Murphy and Irene Ashley McFayden, the 1903 legislature passed a limited child labor law, which established a minimum age of twelve for factory workers and prohibited night jobs for youths under the age of thirteen. As with the railroad legislation, this law lacked a factory inspection provision and any mechanism for enforcement. The antilabor cast of the Jelks administration became more evident when it supported the Anti-Boycott Act of 1903. The law, a clear effort to stop Alabama's growing labor movement, created fines and imprisonment for inducing others not to do business with any firm or corporation.

In the spring of 1904 Jelks contracted tuberculosis and traveled to the New Mexico Territory for treatment. He then developed a viral infection requiring surgery and did not return to his office for nearly a year. Lieutenant Governor Cunningham served as acting governor until Jelks's return in early March 1905. During his absence, Jelks became deeply despondent but corresponded frequently with Cunningham about pending bond issues, appointments to office, politics, and personal family matters. Soon after his return to Montgomery in 1905, he became ill again and spent several more weeks recuperating out of the state. Returning again, although weakened physically and emotionally, he plunged back into his busy schedule. Unfortunately, his governorship was soon distracted by Jelks's own racist obsessions.

In the early part of his governorship, Jelks had distanced himself from his intemperate editorials about lynching as a means to deter rape. In fact, between 1903 and 1905 Jelks gained national attention in the press as an antilynching crusader. He reminded legislators that avenging black assaults on white women was no longer a reasonable excuse for lynchings because Alabama juries and judges generally sentenced the accused to death. The real horror of lynching, Jelks thought, was that innocent men were occasionally murdered. Journalists proclaimed his bravery in the face of mob violence as exemplifying a new progressive spirit in the South.

In a revealing interview with a Memphis newspaper in 1905, however, the recovering Jelks restated his old belief that lynching accused black rapists was justified. "For this crime against women," he said, "no southern judge, court, or governor can expect to convict those who have avenged the wrong." Equally shocking were the governor's remarks in 1906 as he shared a platform with the distinguished Booker T. Washington at Negro Day at the state fair. Jelks used that opportunity to denounce all education for blacks because he believed it took them from their labors in the field and led to idleness, vagrancy, and crime.

On more than one occasion Jelks called out the state militia to prevent a lynching, but an incident in Mobile in October 1906 demonstrated that he was capable of ignoring the clear danger represented by racist mobs. While visiting the port city to survey hurricane damage, Jelks received urgent calls from Mobile's black community to help the county sheriff protect two black defendants charged with the rape of a white woman. Instead of calling out the militia, Jelks reacted by lecturing blacks on the need to "hunt down the rapists; ostracize them in your societies and consign them to eternal damnation from your pulpits." Later, when a mob overpowered the sheriff and lynched the two men, Jelks seemed shocked. He was "perfectly astounded to know the feeling that existed on the part of the very best class of citizens in that staid old city."

After leaving the governorship, Jelks did not seek public office again. He served as Alabama's representative on the Democratic national committee from 1912 to 1916 and advised Governor Charles Henderson on various financial matters. He put most of his energy into private business, establishing the Protective Life Insurance Company in Birmingham in 1907. He wanted his new company to decrease the northward flow of capital from the state and keep it where it could be used to expand Alabama's growth and development. By the time Jelks retired in 1929, the company had branch offices in six other southern states and more than $7 million in assets. On December 15, 1931, Jelks died of a heart attack in Eufaula at the age of seventy-six.

Jelks was Alabama's last Bourbon governor, a typical nineteenth-century Black Belt leader who managed the state's financial problems well but struggled ineffectually with complex social and political issues such as education, railroad regulation, child labor, and race relations. Many white Alabamians, at least those in positions of power, were not ready for substantive reforms during the Jelks administration, and the governor simply reflected their biases. Once again in the state's history, the predominant force of racism overshadowed the governor's fiscal actions and consigned him to relative obscurity between the more progressive administrations of Governors Johnston and Comer.

146
◇

References

Alsobrook, David E. "William Dorsey Jelks: Alabama Editor and Legislator." Master's thesis, West Virginia University, 1972.

Clayton, Henry D., Jr. Papers. University of Alabama, Tuscaloosa, Alabama.

Jelks, William Dorsey. Official Papers, 1901–6. Alabama Department of Archives and History, Montgomery.

———. Biographical File. Alabama Department of Archives and History, Montgomery.

Morgan, John Tyler. Papers. Library of Congress, Washington, D.C.

Russell M. Cunningham, April 1904–March 1905

MARLENE HUNT RIKARD

URING Governor William D. Jelks's recurrent illnesses and recuperations out of the state, Lieutenant Governor Russell McWhorter Cunningham served as acting governor. Born on August 25, 1855, in Mt. Hope, Lawrence County, Alabama, to Moses W. Cunningham and Caroline Russell Cunningham, Russell received his education in the public schools of the county. He financed his continued education by teaching school (beginning at age seventeen) and by farming, a skill he learned from his parents. He initiated his medical studies with Dr. John M. Clark of north Alabama, attended the Louisville Medical College in 1874–75, and completed his studies in medicine at Bellevue Hospital Medical College in New York City in 1879. In 1876 he married Sue L. Moore of Franklin County, where he established his first medical practice, and she bore him one son. After his first wife died, Cunningham married Annice Taylor of Birmingham.

147
◇

Cunningham entered the political arena as a way of furthering his medical career, successfully offering himself as a Democratic candidate for the state house of representatives from Franklin County in 1880. In his autobiography, he wrote, "It was my desire to go to the Legislature that I might get acquainted with influential men throughout the State, and in this way get an introduction to some locality more advantageous for the practice of my profession. I confess that I had no burning ambition to serve the people of my county or State; notwithstanding after election I did that to the very best of my ability." Cunningham represented Franklin County in the 1880–81 session but did not seek elective office again until 1896.

Cunningham

In 1881 Cunningham was appointed physician of the state penitentiary and moved to Wetumpka, where he also established a private practice. He began to compile the first reliable statistics on prison mortality rates in Alabama, and his recommendations concerning health, sanitation, and work hours reduced the death rate among Alabama convicts from 18 percent per annum to 2.83 percent per annum by October 1884. In 1883, when prison reform legislation required him to establish his residence where the largest number of state convicts were employed, he moved to the Pratt mines' Birmingham industrial district.

Russell M. Cunningham
1904–1905

In 1885 he became physician and surgeon at the Pratt mines and at the Ensley division of the Tennessee Coal, Iron, and Railroad Company, the largest industrial concern in the district and one of the major leasers of convicts. He became the company physician at the Alabama Steel and Ship Building Company; established a private infirmary at Ensley; served as county health officer; and held numerous positions of leadership in local, state, and regional medical associations. In October 1894 he and eight other Birmingham physicians opened a proprietary school in which he taught physical diagnosis and clinical medicine. The establishment of the medical school in Birmingham set off a rivalry with the previously established public institution in Mobile, a competition that Birmingham ultimately won.

Also active in community affairs, Cunningham was president of the school board in Ensley and held numerous offices in Masonic organizations. In 1896 he reentered politics, drafted by "friends of bimetallism" to run for the state senate against a "gold standardist." As such, he supported William Jennings Bryan, the free silver Democratic candidate for president. Although Cunningham claimed to be opposed by his own social and economic set—"the banks, the corporations, and the business interests generally"—he won election and represented Jefferson County from 1896 to 1900, serving as president of the senate in 1898. His activity in Democratic Party politics grew. In 1900, when ill health made it impossible for William J. Samford to continue his speaking engagements, Cunningham was chosen by the State Democratic Executive Committee to fulfill those commitments.

Elected as a delegate to the 1901 constitutional convention, Cunningham helped to design the measures that disfranchised black voters in the state. Through speeches and editorials, Cunningham went to great lengths to justify his position. Quoting unnamed philosophers, he argued that the "highest and best civilizations" had a "fellowship" in blood, language, religion, and custom. He believed that political equality would lead to partial social equality and interracial marriage. "Therefore," he stated in his autobiography, "it is neither unjust nor inequitable to disfranchise the great bulk of an inferior race."

The new constitution reestablished the office of lieutenant governor and extended the term of elected state officials from two to four years. In 1902 Cunningham ran for lieutenant governor on the Democratic ticket, supporting the gubernatorial candidacy of William D. Jelks, the incumbent governor. Cunningham and Jelks won easily both in the primary and in the general election.

On April 25, 1904, when Governor Jelks left the state to recuperate from tuberculosis, Cunningham took over his duties and served almost a year. While serving as governor, Cunningham attempted to bring greater regulation of railroad rates, an issue that had affected the 1902 election and would reemerge in the 1906 governor's race. He assisted Jelks in devising reforms in the convict lease system in what he thought were some of the "best works" of his public career. A member of the Committee on Temperance in the 1880s and a Baptist, Cunningham supported local option (whereby each county decides whether to support prohibition), later campaigned for a statewide prohibition amendment, and endorsed the Eighteenth Amendment to the U.S. Constitution. On other issues, he expressed an interest in adequate funding for education and in fair and honest elections, and he actively pressed for safety and sanitation inspections of coal mines.

Because the new constitution did not allow elected officials to succeed themselves, Cunningham was expected to be the next governor. He announced his candidacy for the Democratic nomination, stating that he had "learned to like the job during Governor Jelks's absence" and "hoped that no other gentleman will announce this time." His hopes were not fulfilled. Braxton Bragg Comer, a businessman and textile mill owner from Birmingham and the sole elected representative on the state's railroad commission, seized on the regulation issue and announced his candidacy.

In 1902 the State Democratic Executive Committee agreed to a direct primary election for officials to choose who were elected statewide. The Democratic primary would soon be the most important election held in Alabama, far more critical than the November election. Cunningham was backed by many of the leading newspapers in the state, whereas Comer enjoyed the support only of the *Birmingham News*. The main issue, according to Comer, was railroad rate reform. He had been elected president of the state railroad commission in 1904, and his reform efforts were thwarted by the votes of the two prorailroad commissioners who had been appointed by Governor Jelks. Comer soon decided the only real power to effect change resided in the governor's office.

Although Cunningham was considered the candidate of the conservative wing of the party, his platform was, in many ways, as "progressive" as that of Comer, who wore that title. Cunningham praised Comer's work on the railroad commission but reminded voters that he had sent a letter to the commission's members urging regulatory action and threatening to encourage the governor to convene a special session of the legislature if no action occurred. Comer called this the "11:55 letter," a meaningless gesture mailed out on the day of Jelks's return to office. Both candidates supported increased spending for education, pensions for the state's Confederate veterans, and road improvements. Cunningham stressed the continuing need for reform of the convict lease system, but Comer emphasized railroad regulation to the exclusion of almost all other issues.

In a contest that lasted almost a year, Cunningham spoke in every county in the state and held several debates with Comer. Cunningham favored a stronger child labor law than his opponent, and the *Montgomery Advertiser* attempted

149
◇

to discredit Comer by pointing out that he employed children in his Avondale textile mill. Even this charge failed to stem the rising popular support for Comer. Cunningham lost the Democratic nomination bid in August 1906, and a new era was launched in Alabama as Comer supporters also won a majority of seats in the state's legislature.

Cunningham, the doctor turned politician, returned to his medical practice in Jefferson County. He made a brief notation about the ill-fated campaign for governor in his autobiography: "In 1906 I ran for the office of Governor and was defeated, which was the best thing that ever happened to me in politics." Cunningham died in Birmingham on June 6, 1921.

References

Alabama Official and Statistical Register, 1903.

Cunningham, Russell M. "Address of Dr. R. M. Cunningham: Candidate for Governor to People of Alabama." Cunningham File, Alabama Department of Archives and History, Montgomery.

———. Autobiography (typescript). Cunningham File, Alabama Department of Archives and History, Montgomery.

———. *Historical Interpretation.* Montgomery: Alabama Historical Society, reprint no. 30, 1905.

Doster, James F. "Alabama's Gubernatorial Election of 1906." *Alabama Review* 8 (1955): 163–78.

Holley, Howard L. *The History of Medicine in Alabama.* Birmingham: University of Alabama School of Medicine, 1982.

Owen, Thomas M. *History of Alabama and Dictionary of Alabama Biography.* 4 vols. Chicago: S. J. Clarke, 1921.

150
◇

Braxton Bragg Comer, 1907–1911

DAVID ALAN HARRIS

HISTORIANS have claimed that a new, progressive era in Alabama politics began with the governorship of Braxton Bragg Comer. Scion of a well-to-do family, this successful industrialist and planter spent four stormy years as Alabama's governor, years marked by progress in education, railroad regulation, tax funding, and conservation. This same person used strong-armed tactics toward labor and demonstrated a lack of genuine concern for children in the labor force. Comer's brand of progressivism—which sought to serve the new industrial-urban interests while not disturbing the traditions of the old plantation system — brought numerous collisions with powerful interests.

Comer was born at Spring Hill in Barbour County, Alabama, on November 7, 1848, to John Fletcher Comer and Catherine Drewry Comer, who moved from Virginia to Georgia before finally settling in the southeastern section of Alabama's Black Belt in the 1840s. John Fletcher Comer was a county judge in Georgia, and in Alabama he planted cotton and ran a lumber mill. He gave his son a good private education, and in 1864 young B. B. Comer entered the University of Alabama, *Comer* where he remained until Union forces burned it in 1865. He subsequently attended the University of Georgia and received bachelor of arts and master of arts degrees from Virginia's Emory and Henry College in 1869. Three years later he married Eva Jane Harris of Cuthbert, Georgia, who bore him eight children. The Comers were committed members of the Methodist Episcopal Church South.

After college Comer prospered as a planter at Comer Station in Barbour County where, like most of his class, he opposed Alabama's Reconstruction Republican government. Republicans were narrowly defeated statewide in the pivotal 1874 election that ended Reconstruction in Alabama, and by many accounts, election shenanigans by Comer and his brothers in Barbour County played a major role in that defeat.

Like many postwar planters, Comer branched out into merchandising. In 1885 he used the money he made as a merchant-planter in Barbour County to become a partner in a wholesale grocery business in the New South city of Anniston, Alabama. He sold his interest in the firm in 1890 and moved to Birmingham, where he became president of the City National Bank and the owner of corn meal, flour, and textile mills. Comer achieved his greatest business success in the development of Avondale Mills, a textile venture that grew into one of Alabama's largest industrial enterprises.

While in Anniston, Comer learned that his Atlanta competitors could undersell his and other Alabama businesses because of Georgia's lower freight rates. By the time he had built Avondale Mills, Comer was the state's most vocal advocate of controlling Alabama's railroad rate structure. The Birmingham Commercial Club, which Comer helped to organize in 1893, and the Birmingham Freight Bureau, also led by Comer, both investigated freight rate discrimination and recommended that rates be controlled by expanding the powers of the state railroad commission. Comer's organized efforts failed to persuade legislators of the need for reform during the 1890s, but he and his allies renewed their efforts at the constitutional convention of 1901, where they campaigned to include in the document an elective railroad commission with extensive powers to regulate rates. When that effort failed, the reformers compromised and accepted a provision in the document that gave the legislature sweeping authority over railroad rates.

If the railroads had continued to dominate all branches of government as they did in the 1890s, the new legislative power over railroad rates would have meant little. But the disfranchisement movement and direct primary made it possible for popular forces to challenge entrenched power groups without fear of black voter manipulation. In 1903 urban reformers failed to get the railroad commission to lower rates. As a result, Comer decided to seek the commission presidency, which the legislature had made elective. He profited from the new primary system and won nomination and then election to the commission.

Comer found that being president of the commission gave him little power. The two appointed incumbents who held the other commission seats supported the railroads. When they made decisions favoring the railroads in 1905, Comer decided that he had to run for governor to achieve change. "From my associates' decision against the people," he asserted, "there is no appeal except to the ballot." Comer knew that he must win not only the Democratic nomination for governor but also control of the legislature. Legislative candidates began to align with or against him.

The 1906 gubernatorial campaign in the Democratic primary—complicated by the nonbinding selection of candidates to replace Alabama's two elderly and ill U.S. senators should they die in office before the next legislative session—was one of the most memorable in Alabama's history. The Democratic Party dropped the word "Conservative" from its formal name, demonstrating that it was now comfortable with a more progressive platform. The state's railroads supported Comer's chief opponent, Lieutenant Governor Russell Cunningham, but the line between progressives and conservatives was not clearly drawn. On issues other than railroad rates Cunningham was as progressive as Comer, who came under severe criticism for his opposition to child labor reform. Comer was a better campaigner and orator than Cunningham, and his verbal attacks on the railroad villains so aroused Alabama audiences that he won the primary with 61 percent of the vote and the November election with 85.5 percent. A majority of the legislators elected were committed to rate reform, and with this sympathetic legislature to enact and implement his programs, Comer proved to be one of Alabama's most effective governors.

The new governor devoted much of his inaugural address to the issue of railroad reform and requested the legislature to pass twenty separate laws to give the railroad commission strong rate-making and enforcement powers. His program was enacted with few changes by March 1907. This legislation thoroughly reorganized the commission; gave it increased power and authority to regulate passenger and freight rates; and increased its jurisdiction to cover express, steam packet, terminal, telegraph, and long-distance telephone companies. In an effort to keep railroads from obtaining federal court injunctions to stop state court enforcement of the new laws, lawmakers added a provision that any corporation bringing suit in federal court on any issue already before a state court would have its state business license revoked.

Despite this effort to protect state rules from conservative, probusiness federal judges, it was inevitable that the railroads would appeal to federal courts. A highly publicized legal fight ensued in the federal district court in Montgomery presided over by former governor Judge Thomas Goode Jones. The legal sparring with the railroads, led by the Louisville and Nashville, led to personal animosity between Governor Comer and Judge Jones, who had once served as chief legal counsel for the powerful L and N. The president of the L and N, Milton Hannibal Smith, and the governor were already long-standing enemies, which led to a stubborn unwillingness to compromise on both their parts. Smith called Comer a "socialist" and aligned himself against the governor on other issues as well. Judge Jones sided with the railroads on every decision, and he enjoined the enforcement of several portions of the new railroad commission acts. Efforts to reverse some of his decisions in the higher courts took several years, and it was 1914 before the state of Alabama and the railroads reached a compromise, long after Comer had left the governorship. Comer is credited, nonetheless, with winning the war to give the state increased regulatory power over railroad freight rates.

153
◇

Even though B. B. Comer seemed obsessed with the railroad rate question and was accused of being a one-issue candidate, in actuality he supported a broad platform of reforms while governor. His efforts to increase revenue to the state through more accurate assessment of property brought him in conflict with large-property owners including, again, the railroads. He succeeded in creating a state tax commission and a state board of equalization, but despite the rise in the assessed value of property in the state, state tax revenues were less than disbursements in every year of Comer's administration, requiring the state to rely more heavily on the income it received from convict leasing.

Stating that education was "the most successful foundation for the future of the state," Comer and the legislature doubled the general appropriation for public schools and in a path-breaking measure mandated that there be a public high school in every county. His administration was generous with its appropriations for higher education, and several of the state's colleges demonstrated their appreciation by placing his name on new campus buildings.

Comer expanded the boys' reform school and encouraged humane treatment of Alabama's convict population. Appropriations to support better public health services increased, and the legislature established a tuberculosis commission and sanitarium. When President Theodore Roosevelt suggested that the nation's governors should join him in conserving the country's natural resources, Comer and the legislature established the Alabama Soil Conservation Department to oversee a public park system in Alabama. The legislature passed and the people approved an amendment to the 1901 constitution authorizing the state to help finance public roads. Furthermore, the governor advocated abolition of "bucket shops," where gambling on stock market prices occurred; supported a local option liquor bill, which allowed each county to decide for itself whether to have prohibition; and wanted to expand the use of direct primaries.

Comer's supporters finally prevailed on him to support a stronger child labor law despite his previous history of lobbying against legislation that might either end or severely restrict the use of child labor. Comer employed children in his mills and argued that this practice was not improper because the children worked at their parents' behest. During the Jelks administration, anti–child labor legislation was derailed by Comer and his friends in favor of a compromise measure that limited children under age fourteen from working more than sixty hours a week. Finally, in a half measure, Comer approved legislation that raised the age of night work from thirteen to sixteen and mandated children under the age of sixteen to attend at least eight consecutive weeks of school, thereby being unavailable for work.

154
◇

It was paradoxical that Comer believed that liquor was a "fearful influence for crime and family destruction" yet was less concerned about the damage to families and children overworked in his textile mills. On the issue of liquor control, which divided progressives of the era, Comer shifted his position. In the early days of his administration, the governor supported the state's local option liquor law. Misreading public sentiment, he reversed his position and ended his term as governor with a crusade for statewide prohibition. In 1906 the Democratic Party had reacted to the Anti-Saloon League's advocacy of statewide prohibition by putting local option into its platform. By 1908 local option elections had succeeded in drying up fifty of the sixty-seven counties of the state, but the fact that seventeen counties remained wet created enormous difficulties for law enforcement agencies. The Anti-Saloon League had demonstrated its considerable clout, and Comer cast his lot with them. The state was quickly divided into wets and drys, and the prohibition issue dominated the gubernatorial elections of 1910, 1914, and 1918. It was impossible not to take a stand on the issue, and whatever position Comer took was certain to create enemies. Pressure from interest groups led Comer to call a special session of the legislature in 1909 for the purpose of adopting statewide prohibition. Legislators passed a law that made the state dry, but, not content with a mere statute, they also proposed a constitutional amendment to end the sale of liquor. Even those who had supported the "bone dry" law divided over whether prohibition should be in the state constitution. Comer's decision to support the prohibition amendment diminished the popular standing he had won with the electorate during his struggle with the railroads. The governor stumped the state in support of the amendment, but the groups who opposed him on other issues united to defeat it. This defeat ended Comer's reform efforts.

The governor's progressive instincts did not extend to organized labor. From the Civil War until World War II, Alabama's industrial base was dominated by coal mining, which was central to the success of the iron and steel industries in the state. In Jefferson, Walker, Shelby, Bibb, and Tuscaloosa Counties, coal mining became the occupation of thousands of workers and the basis of new fortunes. Alabama's miners were poorly paid, worked in dangerous conditions, and were forced to compete for their jobs with convict labor. These conditions led a growing movement of miners into the United Mine Workers (UMW) and other labor groups. Many Progressive Era reformers wanted to ameliorate the workers' plight, but Comer was not among them.

In 1908, when the Tennessee Coal, Iron, and Railroad Company, Alabama's leading coal mine employer, reduced its work force and ordered miners to take a 10 percent pay cut, the UMW called for a strike that soon swept across the state's coal fields, affecting an estimated eighteen thousand workers. The governor was asked to take action to keep order in an increasingly volatile situation, and he sent the Alabama National Guard into the coal fields. Comer claimed to be neutral in the strike, but his actions proved otherwise. Guardsmen were soon escorting trainloads of strikebreakers brought into the state by the companies, and desperate striking workers responded with violence. Dynamite explosions were set off, and one black worker, accused of being a dynamiter, was lynched by company men. Comer hurried to Birmingham to be near the center of the crisis. Using health regulations as a pretense, Comer ordered guardsmen to cut down tents erected just outside company property by workers who, displaced from company housing, had no other place to live. With Comer's help the strike was broken, and the Tennessee Coal, Iron, and Railroad Company emerged from the struggle with even more control over its workers than it had previously exercised.

Prohibited by the 1901 constitution from succeeding himself in 1910, Comer ran for reelection in 1914 and was defeated by a strange coalition of enemies who included the railroads, organized labor, and supporters of local option. He did not run for public office again, but in 1920 when Senator John Hollis Bankhead died in office, Governor Thomas E. Kilby appointed Comer to serve out the senator's term—a period from March 5, 1920, to November 2, 1920. Comer then returned to Alabama to manage his textile mills, where he initiated reforms in the treatment of the workers in his "company towns." Comer died in Birmingham on August 15, 1927.

Comer's administration as governor had a profound impact on Alabama. Entering the position, as he put it, "a plain man with a grievance," Comer used government to aid both the general public and business interests. His successful antirailroad campaign protected industry—especially cotton mills—from paying excessive rates, and control of the rates also protected consumers. His administration made great strides in education, public health, road building, and conservation of the state's resources. On the other hand, Comer's attempt to bring prohibition to the state failed, and his lukewarm approach to child labor was not laudable. He discussed reform of the convict leasing system but ended up simply trying to find ways to make the system bring more revenue to the state. His actions in the coal strike of 1908 demonstrated that his view of labor had changed little from his plantation days. Comer was a progressive, but he was a conservative one.

References

Comer, B. B. Papers. Southern Historical Collection, University of North Carolina at Chapel Hill, 1967.

Comer, James M. *Braxton Bragg Comer (1848–1927): An Alabamian whose Avondale Mills opened new paths for Southern Progress.* New York: Newcomen Society of England, American Branch, 1947.

Doster, James F. *Railroads in Alabama Politics, 1875–1914.* University: University of Alabama Press, 1957.

Going, Allen J. "The Governorship of B. B. Comer." Master's thesis, University of Alabama, 1940.

Hackney, Sheldon. *Populism to Progressivism in Alabama.* Princeton: Princeton University Press, 1969.

Harris, David A. "Racists and Reformers: A Study of Progressivism in Alabama, 1896–1911." Ph.D. diss., University of North Carolina at Chapel Hill, 1967.

Journal of the [Alabama] Senate, 1909.

Emmet O'Neal, 1911–1915

R. B. ROSENBURG

LIKE his father Edward, Emmet O'Neal was president of the state bar association, framer of a state constitution, presidential elector, and governor of Alabama. Born on September 23, 1853, in Florence, Alabama, Emmet attended Florence Wesleyan University (now the University of North Alabama) and the University of Mississippi before graduating in 1873 from the University of Alabama. In July 1881 he married Lizzie Kirkman in Tuscaloosa, and they had three children, two of whom survived him. Emmet studied and practiced law with his father until 1882, when he managed his father's first campaign for governor. Two years later he was on the campaign trail again, canvassing the state on behalf of his father's reelection and running as presidential elector for Grover Cleveland. In 1892 O'Neal garnered his own political patronage for the first time when he was appointed U.S. attorney for north Alabama, a position he held from 1893 to 1897. He supported William Jennings Bryan in the 1896 presidential race, and he was serving as a city alderman in 1901 when he was elected a delegate to the state's constitutional convention.

At that convention, O'Neal served as chairman of the Committee on Local Legislation and on the Committee on Suffrage and Elections, which disfranchised blacks and poor whites and decided to disallow women voters in state elections. "The paramount purpose of this Convention," declared O'Neal, "is to purify and elevate the political conditions in Alabama [by] secur[ing] permanent white supremacy in this State." On the issue of women's suffrage, which the constitution did not include, O'Neal asserted: "Women are now our superiors, and when you pass a law of this kind you bring them down to the level of a man. . . . The women of the State have not demanded the vote. . . . They would not exercise it if you granted it to them."

Emmet O'Neal

Five years later, while campaigning for lieutenant governor, O'Neal included a "purity of the ballot" plank in his platform and portrayed himself as a reform candidate. He advocated railroad rate regulation, liberal funding for education, and better highways. He denounced insurance companies as "a body of freebooters dividing their spoils among their henchmen" and called for campaign finance reform and changes in the primary laws. At the same time, O'Neal favored conservative causes, including increased aid to Confederate veterans, local option liquor laws, and immigration restrictions placed on persons of the "wrong sort"—paupers, criminals, anarchists, lunatics, and especially the Chinese. O'Neal lost the election for lieutenant governor, but the contest provided him statewide name recognition.

Despite that defeat, O'Neal remained active in politics and was elected president of the Alabama Bar Association from 1909 to 1910. During that period, he led the opposition forces against ratification of a constitutional amendment that prohibited the manufacture and sale of intoxicating liquors in Alabama. The state was already a dry state effective January 1, 1909, through legislative statute, an act that O'Neal and others believed to be unconstitutional and a failure as well. O'Neal labeled the constitutional amendment an even worse encroachment on personal liberty, one that would put in danger the private actions of people within their own homes. "If this amendment is ratified," asserted O'Neal, "it means the legislature can invade the home. . . . The sanctity of the home must be kept inviolate." On November 29, 1909, Alabamians agreed with O'Neal and rejected the amendment.

In January 1910 O'Neal announced his candidacy for governor. He attacked Comer's "diabolical" prohibition amendment but pledged to enforce all laws, including the prohibition statute, until the people voted to revise, modify, or repeal them. O'Neal also provided voters with a rehash of the same platform of "reasonable" ideas he had offered in his race for lieutenant governor. He left no doubt, however, that the prohibition issue was foremost in his campaign, declaring: "I believe in temperance and sobriety. I do not believe in force as a moral agent. . . . I believe that if you want liquor in your home that is your affair and not mine. Let every man be his own prohibitionist." O'Neal easily won both the Democratic primary and the November general election races to become Alabama's thirty-sixth governor.

O'Neal believed the outcome of the election of 1910 reflected the voters' protest against "unwise, extreme and radical legislation," and was a "demand for the restoration of that spirit of conservatism which, while wisely progressive, refuses to embark the State upon novel, untried and half-considered legislative experiments or dangerous innovations." In his message to the legislature on January 16, 1911, the new governor raised every social, economic, and political problem confronting Alabama, but he devoted more than twenty-five pages of his speech to prohibition. He called for the restoration of local option as the "best solution" to the problem. Furthermore, he recommended creation of county excise boards to control liquor traffic, an increase in liquor licensing fees, and the passage of a law that allowed the manufacture of liquor in cities with populations over thirteen thousand. He also advocated new restrictions on "soft drinks" that contained cocaine, caffeine, and other "injurious chemicals or habit-forming drugs."

In other matters, O'Neal recommended both fiscal restraint and increased revenues from an inheritance tax he advocated to meet the state's $1.5 million debt. "The business of the State should always be so managed as to make its income equal to its expenditures—our salvation demands the rigid application of plain, sensible, and house business methods." He offered remedies to address defects in the ward system of city governments and supported revision of municipal codes. He supported the creation of a law enforcement department to deal with a disturbing increase in crime in the state.

Governor O'Neal called for the appointment of an education commission to supervise and unify curriculum in the public schools of the state and advocated giving county school boards greater autonomy. He recommended uniting the separate boards of trustees of the state's normal schools and colleges into one governing body, which he believed would help to minimize needless duplication in higher education. "The State has now nine normal schools. . . . The State no more needs nine normal schools than it does nine universities."

As O'Neal continued his wide-ranging speech before the legislature, he declared himself in favor of the creation of a state highway commission to be funded by a license tax on motor vehicles, the establishment of a centralized board to oversee charitable institutions, appointment of a state forester to super-vise conservation efforts, a state chemist to assist farmers, and more-restrictive child labor laws. He recommended expanding the railroad commission to allow it to regulate the intrastate rates of telephone and telegraph companies. He sought to increase the number of mine safety inspectors and their frequency of inspections, and he recommended reforms in the primary election laws of the state.

Before the legislature adjourned, many of the governor's initiatives had been enacted; most notably, the legislature repealed the statewide prohibition act that was passed during the Comer administration and replaced it with a local option law. Important changes were also made in election procedures. Corporate donations to candidates were limited, and candidates were required to file expense statements and were prohibited from serving drinks or food on election day within one hundred yards of polling places. The legislature provided procedures whereby cities could replace the ward system of govern-ment with the more "progressive" commission government. As the legislative session continued, on April 8, 1911, an explosion at the Banner Coal Mine in Birmingham killed 128 miners, 123 of whom were convict laborers. This accident underscored the governor's call for improved mine safety measures and prison reform. Six days later the legislature enacted a mine safety law and established a board of mediation and arbitration to handle labor-management controversies.

The legislature appropriated an additional $500,000 for Confederate pensions and purchased an official residence for the governor that O'Neal and his family moved into in 1912. Legislators also appropriated $100,000 to construct a north wing onto the capitol building.

Not all of O'Neal's policies were enacted, however. The legislature approved the creation of the state highway commission but rejected a tax to fund public highway construction and drivers' examinations and licensing. The legislature treated the charge of driving while intoxicated only as a misdemeanor. Lawmakers were willing to create an oyster commission and a board of dental examiners, but they did not want to expand the railroad commission into a public utilities commission. Child labor was not addressed, nor did O'Neal win his proposal to allow district school taxes. Legislators did establish a rural library system, adopt a standard course of study for white students only, and create a central board of trustees for the state's normal schools. Moreover, during O'Neal's tenure as governor the state appropriated almost $9 million for public education, nearly $2 million more than during any previous administration.

As with previous and subsequent governors, O'Neal gained national attention for his controversial views on various issues. While attending the third annual Governors' Conference hosted by Governor Woodrow Wilson of New Jersey in September 1911, O'Neal ridiculed initiative, referendum, and recall and in a later speech accused those who embraced these ideas of being "guilty of heresy, if not of high treason." At the fourth Governors' Conference in 1912, O'Neal offered a resolution supporting the enactment of national legislation to prohibit interracial marriage. O'Neal's racial sentiments became even more clear when he chose Alabama Polytechnic Institute (now Auburn University) over the Tuskegee Institute and the Huntsville State Colored Normal School (now Alabama A and M) to receive $10,000 in federal funds received annually through the Smith-Lever Act for demonstration and cooperative agriculture extension work. He justified this decision by asserting that Auburn officials fully appreciated the "needs of [the black] race and, as the funds develop, every effort will be made to render all assistance possible" to black farmers. Yet, O'Neal stood firmly against mob violence against blacks. When asked to pardon a white man guilty of having killed "only a Negro," O'Neal replied that the "open season for killing Negroes closed" when he became governor. He encouraged prosecution of those engaged in lynchings to the "full extent of the law" and added, "I know of no distinction between a murder committed by a mob or a single individual." The *Montgomery Advertiser* reflected on O'Neal's term as governor and wrote that Alabama was "having more legal hangings and fewer lynchings than ever before since the Days of Reconstruction."

O'Neal's reputation for law and order was seriously damaged in the second year of his term. While he attended Woodrow Wilson's inaugural as president in

March 1913, a scandal broke involving James G. Oakley, president of the Convict Board, and his chief clerk, Theophilus Lacy. Although the state received more than $1 million from convict leasing in 1913 alone, more than in any previous year, an audit discovered at least $115,000 missing, and Lacy soon disappeared with $90,000 drawn from a Montgomery bank. Lacy was finally arrested in 1914 and claimed that a portion of the money had been paid to O'Neal. The governor vehemently denied this charge, calling it politically motivated and "the most diabolical libel that was ever instigated by cowardly conspirators." Lacy, who later retracted his accusation, was convicted of embezzlement and grand larceny and was sentenced to sixteen years of imprisonment. Oakley was removed from office, arrested, charged with embezzlement of state funds, and tried twice but acquitted. O'Neal, although not guilty of theft, appeared guilty of mismanagement. His enemies used this scandal to discredit his administration, and he spent most of the remainder of his term conducting investigations, defending himself, and trying to explain the various acts of fraud and embezzlement.

Even after he left office, further allegations against the governor were made. A legislative investigative committee suspected that money set aside for maintenance of the governor's mansion had been squandered. There were additional charges of irregularities and mismanagement of funds in the attorney general's office, the Military Department, and the Department of Agriculture, where two men were later found guilty of embezzlement. Investigators conducted a thorough scrutiny of O'Neal's personal finances and business affairs, but no formal charges were brought against him. O'Neal claimed the probings were illegal and politically motivated by the "Comerites." He ultimately had the satisfaction of having the *Montgomery Advertiser* state in a January 19, 1915, article that O'Neal "is as clean a man as ever sat in the executive chair of Alabama." If he had a flaw, the paper continued, it was that he "was a greater master of issues than a judge of men. . . . He was disposed to trust some of his friends too far."

After his tenure as governor, O'Neal was appointed a federal referee in bankruptcy for the Birmingham district, earning considerably more than he had as governor. He interrupted his brief hiatus from politics in 1920 when he campaigned for the U.S. Senate on the slogan "The Public Welfare Demands the Least Governmental Interference" and on a platform of state sovereignty and "equal and exact justice to all men." He spoke against the recently ratified Nineteenth Amendment—ratified without Alabama's approval—and argued that "the States have plenary power to grant to women the right of suffrage, and hence the amendment is unnecessary[,] . . . unwise, useless and harmful." O'Neal lost the primary race to J. Thomas Heflin of Birmingham, who used the ex-governor's 1914 pardon of a black man who had killed a white man to arouse voters against him.

O'Neal died in Birmingham on September 7, 1922, and was buried in Florence. He never wore the progressive label but advocated a number of progressive measures. His fiscal policies and strong views on limited government at every level placed him squarely within the conservative faction of his party. On race, he reflected the accepted ethos of the times. He was fairer than many of his contemporaries when racial tensions created law-and-order issues, but he was strictly white supremacist in every other area.

References

Edwards, Inez N. "Emmet O'Neal: Alabama Governor, 1911–1915." Master's thesis, Auburn University, 1956.

Ellis, Mary L. "Tilting on the Piazza: Emmet O'Neal's Encounter with Woodrow Wilson, September 1911." *Alabama Review* 39 (April 1986): 83–95.

Jones, Allen W. "Political Reforms in the Progressive Era." *Alabama Review* 21 (July 1968): 163–72.

Sellers, James B. *The Prohibition Movement in Alabama, 1702–1943.* Chapel Hill: University of North Carolina Press, 1943.

Ward, Robert D., and William W. Rogers. *Convicts, Coal, and the Banner Mine Tragedy.* Tuscaloosa: University of Alabama Press, 1987.

Charles Henderson, 1915–1919

LEE N. ALLEN

IF ANYONE deserved the title of "business governor" of Alabama, it was Charles Henderson. His experience as the leading businessman of Troy, Alabama, affected his actions as governor. During his administration the principles of economy and efficiency were his faithful guides.

Henderson was born to Jeremiah Augustus Henderson and Mildred Elizabeth Hill Henderson on April 28, 1860, at the family farm at Gainer's Store, an area now know as Henderson, twelve miles south of Troy. Jeremiah Henderson represented Pike County at the Alabama secession convention and served in the Fifty-seventh Alabama Regiment during the Civil War. He then moved to Troy and became one of the wealthiest men in southeast Alabama.

Young Charles was educated in the private schools of Pike County where one of his teachers was a former Southern Baptist missionary, R. W. Priest, who had a great influence on the young man. Henderson enrolled at the Baptist-affiliated Howard College (now Samford University), then located at Marion, but remained only two years because his father's death compelled him to return home to manage the family business. Because he was only seventeen, an act of the state legislature was required to relieve him of the disability (as a business proprietor) of being underage. With two brothers, he entered the mercantile business known as Henderson Brothers, a phenomenally successful concern that spelled prosperity for the Henderson family and for Troy. At the time of his death during the depths of the Great Depression, Henderson's estate was estimated to be worth $3 million.

Henderson

Henderson and his brothers sold this business to an uncle in 1890, and the future governor established the Charles Henderson Wholesale Grocery Company. In addition to that venture, he was majority stockholder and president of both the Pea River Power Company and the Standard Telephone and Telegraph Company. In addition, Henderson was a director and stockholder in the Farmers and Merchants Bank of Troy, the Standard Chemical and Oil Company, the Troy Compress Company, and the Alabama Warehouse Company. When he became governor, he owned an estimated three thousand acres in Pike County.

Henderson entered local politics at the urging of some of the younger men of Troy who asked him to run for mayor of that city. He served three terms before withdrawing from public life to devote himself to his flourishing business empire. After a brief respite, he agreed to run again and served a total of thirteen years as mayor. During his tenure the town established a public school system, and he helped to establish Troy State Normal College, now Troy State University, where he served as a trustee.

One of the teachers who was employed in the new city school system was Laura Montgomery of Raleigh, North Carolina, a graduate of the prestigious St. Mary's Seminary. She caught the eye of the twenty-seven-year-old bachelor mayor, and they were married on November 7, 1887. The Hendersons had no children, and Laura joined her husband in numerous civic and cultural affairs.

Henderson's career took another direction in 1906 when he was elected to his first statewide office on the Alabama Railroad Commission. He was appointed president of the commission and served two terms from 1907 to 1915. Using his membership on the commission as a stepping stone to higher office, Henderson ran for governor in 1914, defeating former governor B. B. Comer in a Democratic Party runoff. He easily defeated Republican, Progressive, and Socialist Party candidates in the November general election.

When Henderson took office in January 1915, the state was deeply in debt, with dim prospects for balancing the budget. With the outbreak of war in Europe in July 1914, the price of cotton plummeted, and the economy of the state was devastated. Within two years, however, the economic picture turned, and the state began to share in the nation's wartime prosperity. Wages for Alabama workers increased and neared the national average; federal monies flowed into the state for the Muscle Shoals munitions development and training camps. Henderson paid off the outstanding debts of the state and left a small surplus in the treasury for his successor. Having seen the result of an economy based on one crop, Henderson devoted much of his remaining life to encouraging agricultural diversification.

Governor Henderson also faced the continued problem of prohibition. As an Episcopalian, he was less committed to total abstinence than the Baptists and Methodists, who made up the bulk of the state's population. He, like former governor O'Neal, favored local option, but the majority of the legislature favored absolute statewide prohibition. Henderson vetoed a new statewide prohibition law, only to have his veto overridden. Thus, Alabama was dry before national prohibition was instituted, with Alabama's approval and ratification, by the Eighteenth Amendment in 1919.

After the United States declared war on Germany in 1917, Congress passed conscription legislation. The process of drafting young men into the armed services revealed that a disproportionately large number of Alabamians were rejected because of poor health or for illiteracy. Henderson called on the legislature to provide additional funding for the state's Department of Health and for public schools. The legislature permitted school districts to levy a three mill tax for local schools, and many took advantage of this legislation to increase community funding for schools.

Although Henderson was clearly a representative of the conservative wing of the Democratic Party, he encouraged progressive causes where he saw a need. He commissioned the Russell Sage Foundation to study conditions in the state. That report, issued late in 1918, declared Alabama's educational, public health, child services, and prison systems to be woefully inadequate. It affixed blame for the substandard programs on the state's inequitable tax system, a contentious subject to this day. Although Henderson advocated reform, it was left to Governors Kilby and Graves to act on most of the issues raised by the Sage Foundation report.

Henderson did propose reform of the court system, but when the legislature delivered only a part of his request, he vetoed their measure. He succeeded in passing a primary election law that established procedures for certification of candidates and for setting the dates for such elections. Prison camps were reduced in number and their supervision improved. Henderson supported the state's highway commission, and Alabama was among the first states in the Union to qualify to receive funds from the federal Bankhead Good Roads bill. Henderson's administration was marked by a workable blend of conservative economy and mild, but important, progress.

Following his term as governor, Henderson returned to Troy to manage his business affairs, but he continued in public service. Governor W. W. Brandon appointed him to the new Alabama State Docks Commission and made him a trustee of Auburn University. He received an honorary degree from the University of Alabama in 1923, and an armory in Troy was named for him posthumously, as was a World War II battleship.

When he was seventy-seven, Henderson contracted influenza and then had a slight stroke. His condition worsened, and he died in Troy on January 7, 1937. He provided trusts for his wife and sister, but the remainder of his estate was placed into a trust for the public good. For twenty years the proceeds went to the construction of school facilities in Troy, and later monies were used for a Troy hospital for crippled children. Twenty of his nephews and other relatives attempted to break the will, but its validity was upheld by the supreme court of Alabama in two separate cases. Through this notable donation and his steady tenure as governor, Henderson's legacy survives.

References

Farmer, Margaret Pace. "Governor Charles Henderson." *Alabama Review* 9 (October 1956): 243–50.

Henderson, Charles. Folder. VF Miscellaneous Clippings (SG 6999). Alabama Department of Archives and History, Montgomery.

———. *Speech of Charles Henderson at Troy, Alabama, August 14, 1913.* Montgomery: N.p., n.d.

Moore, Albert B. *History of Alabama and Her People.* 3 vols. Chicago: American Historical Society, 1927.

Owen, Marie Bankhead. *The Story of Alabama: A History of the State.* 5 vols. New York: Lewis Historical Publishing, 1949.

Owen, Thomas M. *History of Alabama and Dictionary of Alabama Biography.* 4 vols. Chicago: S. J. Clarke, 1921.

Stewart, John Craig. *The Governors of Alabama.* Gretna, La.: Pelican Publishing, 1975.

Thomas E. Kilby, 1919–1923

MICHAEL A. BREEDLOVE

PERHAPS remembered most for having his name placed on a new and ultimately famous Alabama prison, Thomas Erby Kilby was born on July 9, 1865, in Lebanon, Tennessee, to Peyton Phillips Kilby and Sarah Ann Marchant Kilby. His family moved to Atlanta, Georgia, where in the public grammar schools of Atlanta Kilby received his early and only education. He began his business career in 1887 as Anniston, Alabama, agent for the Georgia-Pacific Railroad. In 1889 he entered the steel business with Horry Clark, who owned Clark and Company, and soon he was made a partner in the renamed Clark and Kelly Company. Over the next decade the company evolved into a major operation renamed the Kilby Steel Company. The future governor also founded the Alabama Frog and Switch Company, and he served as president of both it and the Kilby Steel Company. Kilby, an Episcopalian, married Mary Elizabeth Clark on June 5, 1894, and they had three children.

166

◇

    In 1911 Kilby foresaw the potential profits to be made in cast iron pipe and organized the Alabama Pipe and Foundry Company. By 1921 he had consolidated some dozen independent plants into the company, creating a large and profitable business that he controlled until his death in 1943. Kilby extended his industrial business success into banking in 1902 when he became president of the City National Bank of Anniston, a position he held until he became governor and to which he returned as chairman after his governorship.

Kilby

    Kilby was elected to the Anniston City Council in 1898 and was influential in saving the city from bankruptcy by convincing those who held city debt to accept payment at a lower rate of interest. The meagerly educated Kilby also served on the city's school board, where he acquired a lifelong commitment to education. In 1905 Kilby ran unopposed for mayor of Anniston and served two successive terms during which he maintained conservative fiscal, probusiness, and prodevelopment policies. Despite fiscal restraint, Kilby demonstrated strong progressive tendencies as he increased the monies spent on prisoners for meals and medical treatment, constructed sanitary sewers, appointed a milk inspector, enforced gambling laws, and provided greater oversight of local water rates.

At the conclusion of his second term as mayor, Kilby traveled to Europe to study state and municipal governments there. He returned to Alabama and, in 1910, won election to the state senate representing Calhoun County. In the legislature he was a strong proponent of statewide prohibition and helped to write a new revenue bill. In 1915 he was elected lieutenant governor, and his term was marked by the restoration of appointive powers for legislative committee assignments from the governor back to the lieutenant governor. Having won that power, Kilby saw that every legislative committee had a majority of prohibition supporters, insuring the passage, over Henderson's veto, of a "bone dry" statewide prohibition law. Kilby's disgust with the legislature for delaying enactment of revenue bills until the last moment propelled him to run for governor in 1918.

Kilby's campaign aimed to reform the way the legislature enacted budgets and raised revenue for the state's business. He refused all campaign donations, and the contest was a quiet one, in part, because the United States was still at war in Europe. Kilby's platform proposed an executive budget system that included an audit of state finances, increased support for public education, revision of state tax laws, increased pay for jury duty, abolition of the convict lease system, and support for the Eighteenth Amendment to create national prohibition.

Kilby defeated William W. Brandon and was inaugurated in January 1919. The war in Europe was over, soldiers were returning home, and the inaugu- ration was lively and filled with more excitement than usual. Kilby made a brief speech in which he advocated increased support for education and public health, more attention to law enforcement, and good roads. Then, in a new event for gubernatorial inaugurals, he received the public for about two hours in the capitol.

Kilby benefited from a brief period of postwar prosperity in 1919, but he also inherited a large bonded indebtedness and had to deal with postwar inflation and increased cost of services. Kilby proposed a balanced budget to the legislature, endorsed a graduated income tax, and recommended an excess profits tax on businesses to bring in needed revenue. He proposed a tax on the products of mines and forests, asserting that the natural resources of the state were being depleted and that such taxes would repay the state for its loss. In addition, Kilby promoted administrative reforms. He recommended abolishment of county boards of equalization in favor of a person in each county appointed by the governor to equalize taxes. He created a Board of Control and Economy to purchase supplies for all departments of the state, manage the charitable and educational institutions of the state, and oversee the Convict Department. A budget commission was created, with the governor, attorney general, and state auditor comprising its membership. When the income tax bill was declared unconstitutional by the state supreme court, Kilby attempted to raise ad valorem taxes. The governor managed to pay off more than $1 million in floating indebtedness, retire more than $500,000 in bonds, and pay off more than $1.5 million in unpaid warrants inherited from previous administrations. Nevertheless, he, too, left a debt for his successor.

Kilby justified his tax increase proposals by linking them to humanitarian benefits. He had run for governor on a program of social reform. He advocated prohibition, a "reform" he believed would destroy saloons, lessen the crime and prostitution that occurred around them, and benefit family life and the workplace as well. Kilby campaigned on keeping Alabama "bone dry" and advocated ratification of the Eighteenth Amendment in 1919. He also wanted to end convict leasing, but his efforts were unsuccessful, and the system was not eliminated until late in 1927, making Alabama the last state in the nation to abandon it. Nonetheless, Kilby's activism brought better sanitation and sleeping arrangements at the convict camps, and a new prison facility that carried the governor's name was built, boasting a dairy, hog farms, and a spinning mill in which prisoners worked. He expanded services to the mentally ill and increased funding to Bryce Hospital. He obtained additional funds for the Boys Industrial School and for the State Training School for Girls. One of his most lasting accomplishments was the creation of the Child Welfare Department in 1919, which began enforcing laws regulating the employment of children and supervising institutions that cared for children.

168
◇   Kilby displayed even greater passion for improving education in the state. Under his prodding, the legislature authorized a commission of experts, led by U.S. Commissioner of Education P. P. Claxton, to make recommendations for the Alabama school system. They suggested more streamlined administration and increased funding, and the legislature concurred. A new school code was enacted in 1919, vesting more power in the state board of education. Vocational education received new emphasis as well, and spending for education increased more than 100 percent, rising from $3,750,000 in 1919 to $8,269,596 in 1922.

Ratification of the Nineteenth Amendment to the U.S. Constitution was a controversial issue in the 1919 legislative session. On this issue Kilby took no stand, although after the vote he expressed regret that the woman's suffrage ratification was defeated in the state. In 1920, after national ratification was completed and women won the vote, Kilby called a special session of the legislature to provide for the registration of women to vote in Alabama.

Kilby was involved with other social issues as well. He increased appropriations to the Public Health Department. Workers' compensation in the state became law in July 1919. The budget for farm demonstration agents was quadrupled. Confederate veterans received an increase in their pensions, and Kilby secured a $50,000 appropriation from the legislature to support construction of the Alabama World War Memorial Building, which was to house the

Department of Archives and History and the Department of Education. He also led the movement to sell $25 million in state bonds in order to earn matching funds under the 'Good Roads Act that Alabama senator John Bankhead Sr. sponsored in Congress.

Kilby's attitude toward upholding the law was exemplified in two disparate ways. In 1919 he used the power of his office to insure that the lynchers of a man in Baldwin County were arrested and convicted. Likewise, he used his executive powers to protect nonstriking miners during a 1919 strike in the Birmingham coal fields. The essential issue in this case was whether mine owners would be forced to recognize the union. When shortages of coal began to occur, Kilby sent in units of the state's National Guard to end the strike, and nonunion laborers replaced the strikers, effectively, if only temporarily, destroying the United Mine Workers in Alabama. Social and economic equity held little appeal for Kilby, especially because many of the striking miners were black. His numerous efforts at social progress are overshadowed by his actions during this and other strikes.

Kilby's progressivism was that of the businessman. He set the state's finances on a businesslike footing, enforced accountability, and streamlined government while increasing services and benefits to deserving citizens. He understood that government action could be the engine of economic expansion and that education was essential to economic and social success.

Kilby won no other political offices after his term as governor. He ran for the U.S. Senate in 1926 and in 1932 but lost to Hugo Black both times. In the first race, Kilby treated Black condescendingly and concentrated on debating and defeating his other opponent, John Bankhead Jr. As they hurled insults at one another, Black moved up with the voters. Kilby finished last in a field of five candidates in 1926 and fared little better against the incumbent Black in 1932. He returned to his business pursuits in Anniston and died there on October 22, 1943.

References

Howington, Arthur F. "John Barleycorn Subdued: The Enforcement of Prohibition in Alabama." *Alabama Review* 23 (July 1970): 212–21.

Kilby, Thomas Erby. Administrative files, 1919–1923. Alabama Department of Archives and History, Montgomery.

National Cyclopaedia of American Biography. S.v. "Kilby, Thomas Erby." New York: James T. White and Co., 1926.

Owen, Emily. *Thomas E. Kilby in Local and State Government.* Anniston, Ala.: Birmingham Publishing Co., 1948.

Owen, Thomas M. *History of Alabama and Dictionary of Alabama Biography.* Vol. 2. 1921. Reprint, Spartanburg, S.C.: Reprint Co., 1978.

Rogers, William Warren, Robert David Ward, Leah Rawls Atkins, and Wayne Flynt. *Alabama: The History of a Deep South State*. Tuscaloosa: University of Alabama Press, 1994.

Straw, Richard A. "The United Mine Workers of America and the 1920 Coal Strike in Alabama." *Alabama Review* 28 (April 1975): 104–27.

William W. Brandon, 1923–1927

LEE N. ALLEN

W HEN "Plain Bill" Brandon entered the race for governor in 1922, it was said that he was so popular that virtually no one wanted to run against him. After four years in office, he was the only governor to leave the capital as popular as when he entered. Yet Brandon's career as governor of the state was not his primary legacy. That came in the realm of political lore. As chairman of the Alabama delegation to the Democratic National Convention of 1924, it fell his lot to cast the state's vote. Only five feet, one inch tall, he had to stand on a chair to be seen. With no electronic amplification but with a booming, stentorian voice, he had no trouble being heard as he proudly announced, "Alabama casts twenty-four votes for Oscar W. Underwood." In fact, the lone microphone on the speaker's podium, which carried the proceedings to a small radio audience in the eastern portion of the nation, picked up the vote. Later in the proceedings, which required 103 ballots, visitors in the balcony and eventually other delegates as well began to join with Brandon as he rhythmically cast the Alabama vote. For many years, his voice and his vote were remembered and repeated by scores who followed politics.

170
◇

Brandon

William Woodward Brandon was born in Talladega on June 5, 1868, to Franklin Thomas Jefferson Brandon and Caroline Woodward Brandon. His father was a Methodist minister, subject to frequent reassignments. Brandon received his early education at Cedar Bluff Institute in Cherokee County and was graduated from high school in Tuscaloosa. He took a law course at the University of Alabama in 1891 and opened his practice of law in Tuscaloosa in 1892. In 1900, he married a widow, Mrs. Robert N. Nabors, nee Elizabeth Andrews, whose first husband had been a Methodist minister and by whom she had two daughters. The Brandons had no additional children. When she became the state's First Lady, Mrs. Brandon initiated the popular custom of receiving friends and visitors at the governor's mansion every Tuesday afternoon.

Prior to his political career, Brandon in 1886 joined the local Warrior Guards, a part of the National Guard, and was elected lieutenant two years later and captain in 1894. In 1894 he began a military journal, "The Citizen Soldier," for his troops. With the outbreak of the Spanish-American War in 1898, Brandon joined the Second Alabama Volunteers, was promoted to major, and was dispatched to Florida, where his unit remained until the brief war ended. In 1899 he was appointed state adjutant general by Governor Joseph F. Johnston and was reappointed by Governors Samford and Jelks, serving until 1907. During his tenure as commander of the state's military forces, Brandon followed the national mandate and implemented reorganization and modernization policies. Although his career moved in other directions after 1907, when the United States entered World War I in 1917, Brandon offered his services to President Wilson. In 1938 the National Guard armory in Tuscaloosa was dedicated as Fort William W. Brandon.

Brandon became interested in public life at an early age. He was elected city clerk of Tuscaloosa in 1891 and served three terms. In 1892 he was appointed justice of the peace in Tuscaloosa, and in 1896 he was elected to the state legislature. During his three terms in the state house, he became known as "Warwick of the Warrior" for his legislative skill. He was at various times a member of the State Democratic Executive Committee and served as reading clerk at the 1901 constitutional convention.

Brandon's career was moving inexorably toward the governorship, which had long been his ambition. He was elected state auditor in 1907, a minor position that was often used in this era as a stepping stone to more prominent state offices. As state auditor, he introduced a system of accounting practices that earned plaudits from the state examiner of accounts. While serving as state auditor, he was also elected probate judge of Tuscaloosa County. In 1918 he made his first run for the governorship, coming in a close second to Thomas Kilby. He continued to campaign vigorously during the next four years and was elected governor in 1922 by a margin of three to one over Bibb Graves, who was making his first bid for the high office. The new governor was elected on a platform of economy in government, no new taxes, and defense of the convict lease system.

Brandon's modest accomplishments as governor were made possible by prosperity. Inheriting a substantial debt from Kilby, the Brandon administration, through a combination of good economic fortunes and strict fiscal restraints, passed on a small surplus to the next governor. Although he had spoken in campaign speeches of the need for more support for education, no new initiatives were undertaken during his economy-minded term as governor. He used bond money authorized during the Kilby administration to improve

Alabama's roads, a crying need as the automobile rapidly supplanted the horse and buggy. Brandon promoted this issue both as governor and afterward in the United States Good Roads Association, serving a term as its president. In another small and noncostly move, the Forestry Commission initiated efforts to use nonagricultural lands more profitably and encouraged wood-using industries to locate in Alabama.

Perhaps the most notable achievement of Brandon's administration was the creation of the Alabama State Docks Commission. A $10 million bond issue financed improvements, which included deepening the port and enhancing facilities. These improvements made it possible for the state's industries to use Mobile rather than New Orleans for its incoming and outgoing products, saving Alabama industries millions of dollars in costs over the next several decades and turning Mobile into a major gulf port.

In defending the convict lease system, Brandon asserted that it was not inhumane, that it provided work for otherwise idle hands, that it put a small sum of spending money in the pockets of the prisoners, and that it relieved the state of a heavy expense while generating needed revenues. He was generous with paroles for convicts despite a storm of protest throughout the state. Brandon reflected his Christian rearing, which had taught him to think the best of people and to believe that lives could be redeemed and turned around. In speeches he often cited the Salvation Army slogan, "A man may be down, but he is never out."

172 ◊   At the conclusion of his single term as governor, Brandon returned to the office of probate judge under appointment of his successor, Bibb Graves. He remained active in Democratic politics, and in 1928, when Alabama Democrats split over the candidacy of Al Smith — the first Roman Catholic nominated for president by a major political party — Brandon remained loyal to the national ticket. His popularity and loyalty helped to carry the state for the Democrats despite opposition from such stalwarts as Senator Tom Heflin. Despite declining health, Brandon announced his candidacy for delegate at large to the 1932 Democratic National Convention, causing the *Birmingham News* to comment editorially: "Sick or well, this old warhorse of Democracy could hardly resist the call of battle." After initially opposing Franklin D. Roosevelt, Brandon jumped on the New Yorker's bandwagon and was elected a delegate to the national convention, pledged to FDR. He was once again chosen to chair the Alabama delegation, but poor health and age had tarnished his silver, sonorous tones of 1924 as he again intoned, "Alabama casts twenty-four votes for Roosevelt."

Brandon died in a Tuscaloosa hospital on December 7, 1934, and was buried by his wife in Tuscaloosa Memorial Park cemetery. Although the Brandon administration was free of scandal, it was also marked by little noteworthy or constructive legislation and represents a quiet period the people of that era wanted between the activity of Governors Kilby and Graves.

References

Brandon, William W. Folder. VF Miscellaneous Clippings (Box SC 7000). Alabama Department of Archives and History, Montgomery.

———. *Statement of Gov. W. W. Brandon on Convict System Appearing in the Press of June 10, 1923.* Montgomery, 1923.

Kelley, Richard B. Collection (Box SG 2285). Alabama Department of Archives and History, Montgomery.

Moore, Albert B. *History of Alabama and Her People.* 3 vols. Chicago: American Historical Society, 1927.

Owen, Marie Bankhead. *The Story of Alabama: A History of the State.* 5 vols. New York: Lewis Historical Publishing, 1949.

Owen, Thomas M. *History of Alabama and Dictionary of Alabama Biography.* 4 vols. Chicago: S. J. Clarke, 1921.

Bibb Graves, 1927–1931, 1935–1939

WAYNE FLYNT

173

B IBB Graves was one of the most important and controversial Alabama governors of the twentieth century and the first to serve two four-year terms in office. His alliance with the Ku Klux Klan helped to win him the governorship in 1926 but tarnished the reputation he later earned as a liberal.

Graves

Born at Hope Hull in Montgomery County, Alabama, on April 1, 1873, Graves grew up in Texas and Montgomery. He attended the University of Alabama, where he earned a degree in civil engineering in 1893 and was elected to Phi Beta Kappa. He then studied law for two years at the University of Texas and transferred to Yale, where he earned his bachelor of laws degree in 1896. Graves began a law practice in Montgomery, and in 1900 married his first cousin Dixie Bibb. They had no children.

The future governor entered politics in 1898 when he was elected to the state house of representatives, to which he was reelected in 1900. He allied himself there with progressives who supported the policies of reform governor Joseph F. Johnston, and he joined the former governor in opposing ratification of Alabama's constitution of 1901. In 1904 Graves was defeated when he ran against the incumbent Democratic congressman from the Second Congressional District, and he did not seek elective office for another decade. An officer in the state National

Guard since the 1890s, Graves was named adjutant general of that body in 1907 by Governor Braxton Bragg Comer, whom he had served as Montgomery County campaign manager. In 1914, Graves won the chairmanship of the State Democratic Executive Committee in a unique primary election. Instead of choosing its own chairman, as was usual, the committee asked voters to select one in the primary, and Graves won his first statewide political race.

In 1914, when Comer ran for a second term as governor, he won a plurality but was forced into a runoff in which he was defeated. An angry and disappointed Chairman Graves collaborated in writing a new election law that abolished runoffs and provided that in races with three or more candidates, each voter could, but was not required to, cast a first- and a second-choice vote. Candidates with a majority of first-choice votes were nominated, but if no candidate secured a majority the nomination went to the one receiving the largest combination of first- and second-choice votes. This new system remained in effect during the 1918, 1922, 1926, and 1930 gubernatorial elections, and Graves became its major beneficiary.

During World War I, Bibb Graves commanded an Alabama regiment that saw action in France. He rose to the rank of colonel and was thereafter addressed as "Colonel Graves." The "Colonel" helped to organize Alabama's chapter of the American Legion and became a champion of war veterans, who furnished him with a powerful political base. Graves first sought the governorship in 1922 but was badly beaten by William W. Brandon. Brandon's lopsided victory and a lack of support for Graves from the state's urban newspapers led pundits to write him off in the 1926 governor's race. Retiring governor Brandon endorsed his lieutenant governor, Charles S. McDowell of Eufaula, who became the front-runner. Nonetheless, Graves won a shrill campaign by mobilizing one of the strangest coalitions in Alabama's political history. Many prohibitionists and women backed him because they considered him a friend of temperance and women's rights. Graves's wife, Dixie, helped bring recently enfranchised Alabama women into the alliance through her impressive record of civic work and her statewide network of female friends. Organized labor approved of Graves's workingman platform, his pledge to abolish the convict lease system (which kept the wages of free labor down), and his goal to improve social services. His promise to establish a minimum seven-month school term statewide (forty-four counties had shorter terms in 1926) and to increase education funding won him backing from educators.

To these supporters Graves, the Grand Cyclop of the Montgomery Klavern, added the membership of the Ku Klux Klan. Klan support was crucial in the joint victories of Graves and Hugo L. Black, candidate for the U.S. Senate in 1926 and also a Klansman. In many states the Klan was conservative and antilabor, but in Alabama it allied with labor and temperance groups in opposition to the

Black Belt planters and urban corporations that dominated state government. Graves managed the narrowest of victories. He won less than 30 percent of first-choice votes in the 1926 primary but had more combined first- and second-choice votes than any other candidate and thus became the Democratic nominee. He ran strongest among rural voters in north Alabama and weakest in the Black Belt, where planters generally opposed him.

As Alabama's fortieth governor Graves compiled an impressive record of accomplishment. He had hardly taken his oath of office when he began to remove state convicts from Alabama's coal mines. The legislature passed Graves's proposal to end the convict lease system in Alabama late in 1927, the last state in the nation to do so. Graves transferred convicts to road construction or prison cotton mills or put them to work making auto tags and road signs at the new Kilby prison facility.

Graves's aggressive highway program generated jobs for convicts. The governor endorsed a $25 million bond issue for good roads and a $5 million sale of bonds for toll bridges, both financed by driver's license fees and gasoline taxes. As a consequence of these state initiatives, Alabama won even greater quantities of matching federal highway monies. By 1930 the state's hard-surfaced roads had grown from five thousand miles to more than twenty thousand. Expenditures for roads increased from $1 million in 1921 to $20 million in 1928, and the number of automobiles registered in Alabama climbed steadily from 74,637 in 1920 to 277,147 in 1930.

175
◇

Graves was also as good as his word in providing adequate funding for education. He asked legislators to pass an emergency appropriation to fund his ambitious expansion of the school year to seven months, and they responded with the largest appropriation for education thus far in Alabama's history. The state's universities and the Alabama Education Association agreed to a four-year budget of $25 million, compared with a $9.9 million budget under Governor Brandon. Additional funds for education came from taxes on tobacco products and corporations. The presidents of Alabama Polytechnic Institute (Auburn University), the University of Alabama, and Alabama College (University of Montevallo) made the taxes more palatable by agreeing to coordinate their programs and eliminate wasteful duplication.

Furthermore, Graves presided over a complete revision of Alabama codes dealing with education. The state Department of Education added a Division of Negro Education in 1927 with a black director partly supported by the Rosenwald Fund, a national philanthropic foundation. The state paid the full salary of another black staff member. The state department continued the controversial work of consolidating rural schools and steadily increased the per capita expenditure on education. Teacher salaries increased from an average of $689 per year in 1926–27 to $761 in 1929–30. In 1929 the normal schools at

Florence, Jacksonville, Livingston, and Troy were designated as state teachers' colleges, authorized to grant the bachelor of science degree. Illiteracy rates remained high, teacher salaries were below national levels, and expenditures per child were still inadequate. The state, nonetheless, made major progress in all phases of education compared with prior administrations.

Public and mental health services also received Graves's attention. During his governorship, legislators authorized a new 225-bed hospital for blacks at Mount Vernon, a 200-bed addition at Bryce Hospital in Tuscaloosa for white patients, and major improvements at the Institute for the Blind at Talladega. State appropriations doubled for child welfare, and the state health departments expanded operations into fifty-four of Alabama's sixty-seven counties, reaching nearly 90 percent of the state's population and becoming a model for the nation. The Graves administration spent $2.25 million for public health, as compared with $820,000 spent during the Brandon years. Alabama actually spent 25 percent more per capita on public health than the national average. Child welfare services also expanded into all but one county, and fifty-three counties employed a social worker to deliver these services. Rates of child labor plunged as a result of this careful supervision.

A booming state economy made this remarkable progress possible. Industrial growth and tax reform legislation produced substantial new state revenue during the initial years of Graves's first term. Yet even with this windfall, the tremendous increase in state expenditures resulted in budget problems. The 1929 stock market crash and ensuing depression devastated Alabama's economy and punished the state for acquiring so much bonded indebtedness. Graves's "spend now, pay later" philosophy of floating bonds may have made popular policy during years of prosperity, but its fallout plagued the state during the 1930s. By the end of his first term, commentators accused Graves, with some accuracy, of political cronyism, fraternizing with the Klan, and being a spendthrift.

Conservatives in and out of the legislature had vigorously opposed Graves's policies. Centered among Black Belt planters and Birmingham businessmen who disliked Graves's association with labor, small farmers, and the Klan, this opposition would have made reelection difficult for him even if the 1901 constitution had allowed gubernatorial succession. Because it did not, his opponents were relieved when conservative Democrat Benjamin M. Miller was elected in 1930. But they had not seen the last of Bibb Graves, as they soon discovered.

Miller criticized the extravagance of the Graves years but soon found himself embroiled in the consequences of his own conservative alliances. Powerful financial interests that had supported his election defeated many of his attempts to enact tax increases to keep public schools operating. As a consequence, virtually the entire public school system closed down in the winter of 1933. Angry voters grew nostalgic about the prosperous if profligate Graves years and easily reelected him governor in 1934. His Democratic primary victory over conservative Birmingham attorney Frank M. Dixon presented a classic case of Alabama's political bifactionalism. Organized labor, small farmers, and New Dealers supported Graves, but small business, big industry, and planters favored Dixon. Dixon's attacks on Graves's Klan ties seemed irrelevant to a people more concerned with their economic woes than issues of intolerance. The second-choice voting system had been temporarily abolished, majorities were required for nomination, and Graves was forced into a runoff. He carried fifty-six counties on his way to a 157,000 to 135,000 victory over Dixon in a campaign characterized by deep class divisions. He became the first governor elected to a second four-year term since the 1901 constitution lengthened the tenure of governors.

During the campaign Graves coined a term for his big business enemies, calling them "Big Mules." He said they reminded him of a farmer who had harnessed a small mule to a wagon heavily loaded with corn. Behind the wagon he had hitched a big mule who munched contentedly while the smaller animal strained every muscle to pull the load. The imagery was memorable, and many ordinary Alabamians became convinced that the wealthiest and most powerful citizens were not pulling their fair share of the load. During his second term, Graves responded to the "smaller mule" constituency that had elected him.

A textile strike, the largest in American history to that time, began in Alabama during the summer of 1934, and it, as well as organizing drives by the United Mine Workers, had polarized the state's voters in the Democratic primary. Graves created a new state Department of Labor in 1935 and appointed Robert Moore, a member of the Bricklayers' Union and president of the state Federation of Labor, as its director. The department contained a Child Labor Division, headed by Daisy Donovan, and a Conciliation Division, which was headed by labor activist Mollie Dowd, who had been secretary to the Alabama League of Women Voters, an official of the retail clerks union, a leader of the National Women's Trade Union League, and an organizer for the United Textile Workers. As an administrator in the new state labor department, Dowd worked to prevent strikes by assuring fairer treatment of labor and suggested a laundry list of prolabor legislation: tougher safety laws, a shorter work week, higher minimum wages, and stiffer child labor laws.

Not only did Graves open important government positions to women and labor leaders in an unprecedented fashion, but he also turned a deaf ear to business demands that he use the National Guard to break strikes, a practice that had been used regularly even by progressive governors. When Graves refused to send troops to quell disturbances in Huntsville's textile mills in 1937, he was booed and heckled by a delegation of mill owners and Huntsville officials. On other occasions, he used mediators from his labor department to settle strikes around the state, and the emergence of a vigorous, healthy, and politically influential labor movement in Alabama owed much to Graves.

On racial matters, however, Graves adhered to the orthodox conservatism of his constituents. A dispute that marred his second term involved the "Scottsboro Boys." In the early 1930s nine black men were convicted of having raped two white women near Scottsboro, Alabama. Evidence against the men was, at best, flimsy, and people from all parts of the world protested against the prosecution. A courageous Alabama judge granted new trials for some of the men on the basis that the evidence could not sustain a guilty verdict, and the U.S. Supreme Court ultimately overturned convictions of other defendants. Graves was repeatedly implored to grant the men a pardon or parole, but even in the face of a private appeal to do so from President Franklin D. Roosevelt, he refused to alleviate this injustice.

On other matters, however, Graves demonstrated his strong support for Roosevelt and his New Deal. He responded to the passage of the Social Security Act in 1935 by creating the Alabama Department of Public Welfare from the older State Child Welfare Department. County almshouses were closed, and the revenue previously used to support them was now used to match federal funds for old-age pensions. The state also pioneered unemployment insurance during the second Graves administration.

178
◇   Perhaps Graves's greatest contribution came in education reform. Having inherited from Miller a school system in shambles, he sponsored the Minimum Foundation Program law that sought to equalize educational opportunity for students no matter which county they lived in. This was unprecedented, and the minimum program has continued to serve as a standard of equity. The institutions of higher education that had been on probation regained their accreditation under Graves. The state began providing free textbooks for the first three grades, and the seven-month minimum school term was guaranteed and fully funded in part through the state's first sales tax. The passage of the sales tax was a signal moment in Alabama's history. Graves proposed that the legislature fund his educational reforms by passing a gross receipts tax on business, but the Big Mules took the burden off their own backs and pushed through the sales tax. Graves signed the measure, and it became the basis of a regressive tax system that continues to place an undue burden on people with low or fixed incomes and funds education from a constantly fluctuating and uncertain financial base.

Other achievements of the Graves administration included the transformation of the state's capitol complex, aided by vigorous New Deal federal public works spending. New buildings included space for the highway department, supreme court, and state archives. Tolls on bridges funded in the Miller administration were eliminated, and more miles of roads were paved than in all but two other states. Graves signed the Alabama Alcoholic Beverage Act, creating a system of state stores to sell liquor and providing critical state revenue from the twenty-four counties that voted wet during these years.

Alabama's share of federal funds was proportionately high due to the state congressional delegation's strong support of Roosevelt. Alabama's congressional delegation was regarded as the South's most liberal, with William and John Bankhead, Hugo Black, Henry Stegall, and others giving full support to Roosevelt's policies from their seats in the Congress. In 1937, when Roosevelt appointed Senator Hugo Black to the Supreme Court, Graves appointed his wife, Dixie, to complete Black's term, making her the state's first female senator. She, too, supported Roosevelt's initiatives but declined to run when her term expired.

Frank M. Dixon, a cautious and pragmatic conservative, became governor in 1939, although most pundits believed that Graves could have won a third term if the law had not banned gubernatorial succession. Instead, Graves impatiently endured the four-year interval and prepared to run in 1942. He almost certainly would have been reelected, but his health failed, and he died in March of that year. His death left his liberal-labor-New Deal coalition splintered in the gubernatorial campaign, some compromising on conservative Chauncey Sparks while more liberal labor and farm elements backed the colorful but largely unknown maverick James E. "Big Jim" Folsom.

Graves's private life was not so colorful as his public career. He was a member of the Disciples of Christ (Christian) denomination, which he served for years as elder. His public service was recognized by Baptist-affiliated Howard College (Samford University), which awarded him a doctor of humanities degree, and by his alma mater, the University of Alabama, which granted him a doctor of laws degree.

Graves's legacy was a strange mixture. Taking office as one of the state's brightest and best-educated governors ever, he held membership in the Klan, was financially extravagant, and used political patronage to help his cronies. On the other hand, his efforts on behalf of labor, his unparalleled promotion of women to government positions, his education reform programs, his support of public welfare agencies, and his roads, bridges, and public building programs won him the support both of liberal activists and of ordinary Alabamians. He was clearly one of Alabama's most successful and popular governors. With Big Jim Folsom, who owed much of his own success to the political coalition Graves forged, the "Colonel" was arguably one of Alabama's most liberal twentieth-century governors.

References

Alabama Official and Statistical Register: 1915.

Carter, Dan J. *Scottsboro: A Tragedy of the American South.* Baton Rouge: Louisiana State University Press, 1969.

Benjamin M. Miller
1931–1935

Gilbert, William E. "The First Administration of Governor Bibb Graves, 1927–1930."
   Master's thesis, University of Alabama, 1953.
Montgomery Advertiser.
Rogers, William Warren, Robert David Ward, Leah Rawls Atkins, and Wayne Flynt.
   Alabama: The History of a Deep South State. Tuscaloosa: University of Alabama
   Press, 1994.

Benjamin M. Miller, 1931–1935

G L E N N A . F E L D M A N

ENJAMIN Meek Miller served as governor of Alabama during the worst years of the Great Depression. A large, bespectacled, dignified man, Miller had a long legal career before and after his term as governor of a state that was among the most severely affected by the depression. In that difficult era, the man and the times did not perfectly meet.

Miller, called "Meek" by his friends, was born in Oak Hill, Wilcox County, on March 13, 1864, to Sara Miller and Reformed Presbyterian minister John Miller. He attended public schools at Oak Hill and Camden after his father took a pulpit there, which he held for thirty-one years. In 1884, at the age of

twenty, Miller was graduated with his bachelor of arts degree with class honors from Erskine College in South Carolina and became a high school principal, a position that ideally suited his sober and dignified appearance if not his ambition. He left that position in 1887 to enter the University of Alabama School of Law and earned his degree in 1889. While still a law student, Miller was elected to the Alabama House of Representatives from Wilcox County and served from 1888 to 1889. Upon graduation, he established a law office in Camden, and in 1892 he married Margaret Otis, who bore him two children.

Miller

For the better part of the next four decades, Miller practiced law, served in various judicial capacities, and oversaw his family's large land holdings in Wilcox County—holdings so vast that Miller once boasted: "A man could walk six miles in a straight line and never leave Miller land!" Miller won his second elective political office in 1904 when he was chosen judge of Alabama's Fourth Judicial Circuit. In 1920 he was elected to serve as associate justice of the Alabama Supreme Court but was defeated for reelection in 1926.

180
◇

It was during the bitter and divisive 1928 presidential election between Protestant Republican Herbert Hoover and Catholic Democrat Al Smith that Miller made his political name. New York's Governor Smith was not Miller's choice, but bolting the Democratic party jeopardized the solid hold Democrats had long held over the South. At the core of party regularity was the loyalist Democratic concern with maintaining white supremacy and political power. Miller and other party loyalists invoked the race issue as they opposed the Hoovercrat "bolt," which was led in Alabama by U.S. senator Tom Heflin and Birmingham attorney and gubernatorial aspirant Hugh Locke. "[T]here was not a seat for a [single] nigger at Houston," Miller declared in a speech describing the Democratic National Convention. "No nigger helped nominate Smith. He was nominated by more than 900 Anglo-Saxons."

Smith narrowly took the state, but fallout from the rancorous 1928 campaign haunted Alabama politics for a time. A fierce struggle within the State Democratic Executive Committee for control of the party's machinery in 1929 led to the ouster of Senator Heflin and Judge Locke as retribution for their parts in leading the bolt. The expulsion movement was considered mandatory punishment for the two politicians whose action placed solid Democrat control and white supremacy at risk. Locke and Heflin were refused places on the 1930 Democratic primary ballot, so they joined others to form an independent movement and announced themselves for state office as Jeffersonian Democrats, a conscious attempt to rekindle Populist memories.

181

◇

Miller declared himself a candidate for governor in the Democratic primary and made opposition to the waning Ku Klux Klan and its "loose-spending" governor, Bibb Graves, the centerpiece of his campaign. He promised fiscal responsibility and the firing of state employees known to have KKK associations. "[I]f you are satisfied with the rule of the Ku Klux Klan," Miller announced, "don't vote for me. Vote for any of my opponents." Miller's opposition to the Klan, like that of other wealthy white supremacists, had little to do with racial liberalism and more to do with maintaining political power. The planter-industrialist coalition, of which Miller was a part, eventually rejected the 1920s version of the Klan because it represented a direct threat to their power over poorer and middle-class whites. Many Alabama Klansmen participated in violence and terror during the decade, but the Klan also made itself influential by forming political coalitions with farmers, prohibitionists, women, and unions. These alliances threatened the control that planter-industrialists had exercised in Alabama politics.

The sixty-six-year-old Miller also used his vaunted personal and political economy as a campaign issue and was not at all embarrassed when it became widely known that he still used oil lamps instead of electricity on his Wilcox plantation in order to save money. A staunch prohibitionist, Miller was fond of quoting Proverbs as an argument against repeal of the Eighteenth Amendment: "Wine is a mocker, and strong drink is raging; and whosoever is deceived thereby is not wise." Editor Grover C. Hall swung the *Montgomery Advertiser's* full weight behind Miller with an editorial describing the judge as "the sturdy oak of Wilcox." Miller promised no new taxes, better roads, improved public health, and added child welfare, all within the vital pledge of strict fiscal responsibility. In August 1930 Miller narrowly defeated a field of five other candidates to win the Democratic primary.

For the first time since the Populist revolt of the 1890s, the Democratic primary did not end the gubernatorial campaign. The general election featured some of the dirtiest campaigning since that era. Even Wilcox's dignified Judge Miller found himself getting down in the political dirt of 1930. He accused his opponents of favoring alcohol, being tools of the Klan, and benefiting from graft and corruption in Graves's administration. Miller easily defeated his third-party opponent, Judge Locke, in a general election that drew more voters than usual to the polls.

Once in office, Miller's well-known parsimony remained the most prominent aspect of his early days as governor. His inaugural parade featured only two automobiles in order to conserve gasoline, and he brought his favorite cow to the capital from Wilcox County in order to provide the governor's mansion with milk and butter. By the time he took office in 1931, the Great Depression had settled across the state, and its starving urban populations and habitually impoverished farmers desperately needed government services. As a fiscal conservative battling a mountain of debt and fears of even more debt, however, Miller was reluctant to add to the state's financial difficulties by any act that might, in retrospect, be considered reckless. Nonetheless, after campaigning against Graves's propensity for debt, Miller immediately borrowed $500,000 to keep the state's social service agencies functioning, and he advocated raising the state's borrowing limits. The governor coupled new debt with a commission of the Brookings Institution to study Alabama's finances and governmental systems. The study called for an almost complete overhaul of state government and recommended increased property taxes to meet a state debt the institution estimated to be in excess of $18 million. During Miller's tenure, however, the legislature refused to adopt various reform measures drawn from this study.

In an attempt to balance the state's budget, Miller eliminated hundreds of state jobs and limited the use of state automobiles. His "no new taxes" pledge soon evaporated in the arid financial climate of the Great Depression. He sought a two-cent hike in the gasoline tax, which eventually passed as a one-cent increase. To the surprise of many, Miller opposed a sales tax because it was regressive and would harm the poorer consumer. His opposition to this form of taxation demonstrated that the governor was not the absolute tool of the conservative Democratic oligarchy that had put him into office. "[The proposed sales tax] should be called the consumer's tax," Miller argued. "The consumer now, as a rule, is battling for bread, hunting for food, seeking clothes; and . . . tens of thousands of them are idle, hungry and begging for the necessities of life. To raise taxes we should go to those who have made money, who have money, who have the ability to pay and where profits and incomes have never been taxed in Alabama."

Miller recommended a constitutional amendment to allow a graduated income tax to generate needed revenue for the state. He stumped the state for passage of the income tax amendment even though many of his strongest supporters opposed it. After bitter defeats in referendums by voters in 1931 and 1932, Miller finally won his income tax in 1933. As an incentive to get voters to ratify the income tax amendment, the legislature enacted the Budget Control Act of 1932, and Alabama became one of thirty-plus states in the nation to require revenue to be in the state's treasury before it was expended. In 1933, lawmakers sent to the voters an amendment to the state's constitution that insured that this "balanced budget" measure would be difficult to eliminate. Voters approved both the income tax and the balanced budget amendments and added their ratification to the Twenty-first Amendment repealing prohibition, an action the "dry" Miller decried.

In the midst of Miller's term, Democrats in the state reunited to help elect Franklin Delano Roosevelt president of the United States in 1932. The new president's programs dramatically and permanently affected Alabama and its population. Even before the New Deal, Miller had reduced the salaries of state employees and was paying teachers in state paper (IOUs) known as "scrip," which many landlords, grocers, and others were unwilling to accept in lieu of money. County schools moved to shorter terms, and some closed altogether.

As with his predecessors' terms of office, Miller's administration met charges of cronyism. The governor rewarded Grover Hall for his editorial support by appointing him probate judge of Montgomery County. Even Julian Hall, Grover's nephew and editor of the *Dothan Eagle*, published a "Shame Sheet of Alabama" listing the most prominent beneficiaries of Miller's largesse, including the Dothan editor's own future bride.

Another black eye for Miller was his administration's laxness in dealing with vigilantism. Although he intervened to prevent two lynchings in 1931, Miller allowed a particularly gruesome event to occur in 1934. With police connivance, public approbation, and official approval, an interstate mob tortured Claude Neal, an accused black rapist who was moved from Pensacola, Florida, to Brewton, Alabama, for safekeeping. They cut off parts of Neal's body and forced him to eat them. Newspapers advertised the lynching for several days in advance, yet neither Miller nor his Florida counterpart sent militia to prevent the torture and murder. Instead, Miller sent the state guard to Brewton to quash black protests over the incident. In another case that drew negative national attention to the state, the governor repeatedly denied state protection to the various Communist attorneys representing Alabama's "Scottsboro Boys" even though mob hysteria surrounded the courthouse. He and his successor, Bibb Graves, refused to commute the sentences of these men because of the involvement of Communists who supported them.

Miller was an avowed opponent of organized labor and did little to endear himself to plain folk with insensitive remarks such as: "[A] dollar a day [is] enough for any working man." In 1933 and 1934 Miller responded to intense pressure from Alabama coal mine owners, iron companies, and textile mills by repeatedly using the state militia to crush labor strikes. Birmingham executives enjoyed close cooperation and assistance from state government in their efforts to defeat union organizers, whom they called "invaders," "communists," and "outside agitators."

Miller returned to his law practice at the end of his term as governor. Ten years later, on February 6, 1944, he died at the age of eighty at his daughter's home in Selma. Miller's legacy as governor is one shared by many of the state's governors. He was unable to see that the same consumers he defended in his fight against a state sales tax might be equally hurt by an unyielding fiscal conservatism that did not adequately value or fund social services and programs. Nor did he understand that his unyielding opposition to trade unionism denied ordinary citizens a tool to balance the power of big business. The conservative ideal of fiscal responsibility and corporate profit at the expense of virtually all else places Miller's administration among those of numerous like-minded Alabama governors. One important reform that Miller and the state legislature did accomplish, with the governor's strong support, was the abolition of the first- and second-choice voting systems in Alabama's Democratic primaries. Beginning in 1934, and in every primary since, gubernatorial candidates have been nominated by a majority of the voters.

References

Dobbins, Charles G. "Alabama Governors and Editors, 1930–1955: A Memoir." *Alabama Review* 29 (April 1976): 133–54.

Feldman, Glenn. *From Demagogue to Dixiecrat: Horace Wilkinson and the Politics of Race.* Lanham, Md.: University Press of America, 1995.

Flynt, Wayne. "The New Deal and Southern Labor." In *The New Deal and the South,* edited by James C. Cobb and Michael V. Namorato, 63–96. Jackson: University Press of Mississippi, 1984.

Moore, Albert B. *History of Alabama*. 1934. Reprint, Tuscaloosa: Alabama Book Store, 1951.

Rogers, William Warren, Robert David Ward, Leah Rawls Atkins, and Wayne Flynt. *Alabama: The History of a Deep South State*. Tuscaloosa: University of Alabama Press, 1994.

Frank M. Dixon, 1939–1943

GLENN A. FELDMAN

FRANK Murray Dixon, Tidewater Virginian, provided executive leadership for the state of Alabama during the early watershed years of World War II. A handsome man and skilled orator, Dixon allied himself early and often with Alabama's Big Mule coalition of Birmingham entrepreneurs and Black Belt planters that controlled state politics during much of the early twentieth century.

Dixon was born on July 25, 1892, in Oakland, California, the son of the Reverend Frank Dixon and Laura Dixon. Dixon's father was one of a long line of poor farming Dixons from the North Carolina piedmont who made a career from the Baptist pulpit and irregular lecturing. The boy's uncle was the Reverend Thomas Dixon—lawyer, preacher, state legislator, and best-selling author of several novels, including *The Clansman* (1905), which was later the basis for *The Birth of a Nation*, the first silent film to treat a serious subject.

185

◇

Dixon's writings offered a powerful depiction of the Reconstruction era as a period of corruption in which the South was forced to endure the rule of ignorant blacks, rapacious carpetbaggers, and scoundrel scalawags. Thomas Dixon's work undoubtedly had a powerful influence on his young nephew.

Dixon

Although born in California, Frank Dixon spent the majority of his youth in the Tidewater region of Virginia. He received his early education in the public schools of Virginia and Washington, D.C., and was graduated from the prestigious Phillips Exeter Preparatory School and then Columbia University. He took his law degree at the University of Virginia in 1916 and soon thereafter married Juliet Perry of Greene County, Alabama, with whom he had a son and a daughter.

Upon graduation from law school, he accepted employment with the prestigious Birmingham law firm of Captain Frank S. White and successfully managed White's run for the U.S. Senate. Dixon then resigned from the firm to join the fighting in World War I as a volunteer with the Royal Canadian Air Corps. He was commissioned a second lieutenant and assigned to the French escadrilles as an aerial observer and machine gunner. In July 1918 the enemy shot down Dixon's plane over Soissons, France, and he was seriously wounded, requiring doctors to amputate his leg. The French government awarded him the Croix de Guerre with palm, made him a chevalier of the French Foreign Legion, and promoted him to major. During the 1920s Dixon helped to organize the American Legion in Alabama and served as its state commander and twice as Birmingham's chapter post commander, service that earned him the loyalty of veterans across the state.

When he returned to Birmingham, Dixon formed his own law partnership, Bowers and Dixon, and became a successful corporate lawyer. He served as assistant solicitor of Jefferson County from 1919 to 1923 and wrote a legal treatise titled "The Local Laws of Birmingham." He became more involved in politics during the 1920s, taking an active role in winning Alabama's electoral votes for the controversial 1928 Democratic candidate for president, New York governor Al Smith. Like so many other Democratic loyalists in this event, Dixon warned that "bolting" the party to vote for Republican Herbert Hoover would reconstitute Reconstruction-like "Negro rule" and bring "the black heels of the ex-slaves down on the throats of Southern men and women."

186 ◇   Although Dixon was an open advocate of white supremacy, he and other Birmingham executives joined planters in the state in opposing the 1920s version of the Ku Klux Klan as a political force. The Klan represented a plain people's challenge to the hegemony of the Birmingham industrialists and their allies in the Black Belt. Along with the terror and intolerance of many Klansmen, the organization allied itself with the aspirations of union supporters and other working class Alabamians.

In 1934 Dixon attempted to succeed the conservative Benjamin Meek Miller as governor. Despite solid support from the planter-industrialist oligarchy and charges of Ku Kluxism against his opponent, Dixon lost the primary election to former governor Bibb Graves. Four years later, in a process that repeated itself regularly during this era of Alabama politics, Dixon profited from the constitutional mandate that forbade a governor from succeeding himself in office and easily defeated Chauncey Sparks to become governor of the state. Ironically, Dixon attracted union leaders, younger voters, and other progressive Alabamians to his standard by pledging his desire to abolish the poll tax, to push for reapportionment of the legislature, and to reorganize state government.

Dixon's successes as governor were not accidental; he prepared for his term as few others have. In the months between his election and his inauguration, Dixon met with departing governor Graves, traveled to Washington to secure the advice of public administration experts and even President Roosevelt on his plans for changes in state government, and skillfully courted the press in Alabama. To secure legislative support for his programs, he held closed-door, presession conferences with twenty lawmakers at a time to hear their views on his plans for administrative reform. He also placed his supporters in key leadership posts in both the state house and senate.

Dixon launched a program to streamline Alabama's government, basing his actions on the Virginia model of government and the advice of University of Alabama political scientist Roscoe C. Martin, an expert in the field of administrative and civil service reform. In his effort to rid the state of waste, inefficiency, duplication, and excess, the focused governor eliminated twenty-seven government agencies, largely by consolidating related and overlapping duties within one department. For example, the Department of Finance oversaw fiscal affairs by assuming the full duties of four agencies and the partial duties of six others. A new Department of Corrections replaced two older agencies; a single Department of Industrial Relations replaced six agencies including Bibb Graves's Department of Labor; the Conservation Department subsumed the functions of five agencies; and the Commerce Department took over those of three more.

Agencies under the leadership of committees were placed under a single individual accountable to the governor, thus centralizing power in the office of the governor. He ordered the termination of all state employees who were added to state payrolls after May 3, 1938, the date he was nominated for governor, as well as every employee who had no specific and clearly assigned duties. In significant milestones for public school teachers, he helped push through a teachers' retirement system and a teacher tenure law. Dixon's most visible accomplishment was the establishment of a state civil service system requiring merit-based hiring of state employees. He was the first, and the last, twentieth-century governor to make an effort to eliminate duplication, inefficiency, and waste in the state's bureaucracy.

187
◇

Furthermore, Dixon reformed the way in which property taxes were assessed throughout the state. He and others in the "good government" reform movement objected to the county appointment of property tax review boards whose members, they maintained, deliberately kept assessments at low levels, resulting in inadequate support for school districts and municipal services. Dixon's reform bill provided for local boards to be replaced by three-person boards appointed by the governor from a pool of names submitted by the county commission, county board of education, and representatives of the county's largest municipality. Although this measure passed, a second bill calling for state funds to be tied to a county's willingness to increase its assessments was later withdrawn.

In 1939, as World War II began in Europe, prosperity slowly returned to the nation and state. By 1942 more than one-half of the voluntary enlistments into the military for the entire country came from the South, putting formerly unemployed citizens to work. The governor oversaw a wartime reorganization of the Alabama State Docks at Mobile, resulting in a 400 percent increase in barge traffic. The war also brought a mushrooming shipbuilding and ship repair industry to the Gulf Coast and the establishment of a major supply and repair post at the U.S. Army's Brookley Field. Alabama enjoyed tremendous economic benefits from the industrial and military buildup associated with the war, and military bases and industries brought full employment and middle-class sensibilities to the state.

For all his achievements Dixon was said to be "cold and inaccessible" in his style, conservative in his appointments, and fiercely anti–New Deal. The governor openly opposed Franklin Roosevelt's third and fourth campaigns and made opposition to Roosevelt's 1942 Fair Employment Practices Committee and other prolabor New Deal measures a notable feature of his administration. The state's Congress of Industrial Organizations newspaper denounced him as a "peg-legged bigot whose creaking cork leg is moved to take each step at the command of Birmingham's industrial barons." One close student of the state's politics has written that the state legislature could never "pass enough anti-labor bills to please him." Dixon was a member of "Christian Americans," thought by progressives to be a semifascist, "anti-labor KKK." Beyond his antilabor stance, Dixon also joined Grover Hall and others in Alabama to oppose the New Deal's Wagner-Costigan federal antilynching bill, a measure that called for steep fines and jail terms for policemen who lost their prisoners to mobs, additional fines against counties that hosted a lynching, and long sentences for county officials who conspired in such actions. The governor opposed it as "dangerous . . . unwarranted . . . and unwise." When Fort Deposit whites lynched a black man for arguing with his white employer in early 1942, Dixon turned a blind eye and warned that the Klan might ride again if the federal government did not allow southern states a free hand in controlling their black populations.

The exigencies of war and the needs of a wartime people may have muted Dixon's fundamental racism, but his postwar role as one of the primary architects of the 1948 "Dixiecrat" revolt, however, fully revealed his bigotry. Although Dixon declined to serve as the presidential standard-bearer of the Dixiecrats, he delivered the keynote address at its national convention in Birmingham. The Dixiecrat or States' Rights Party organized in response to the civil rights package in the Democratic Party platform of 1948, which recommended four pieces of legislation: abolition of the poll tax, a federal antilynching law, desegregation, and a permanent Fair Employment Practices Commission. President Truman fully supported these goals, which promised the greatest federal intrusion into the South since Reconstruction, a frightening thought for those who shared Dixon's leanings. The rump party eventually polled more than a million votes and carried five states in the 1948 general election. Some have suggested that Dixon and his confederates were attempting to restore the South to its former place of influence within the Democratic Party, a place Dixie had lost after the 1936 repeal of the rule requiring that Democratic presidential and vice presidential nominees receive two-thirds of the delegate votes at the Democratic National Convention. These high-minded ends may have played into the actions of the governor and his associates, but their overarching goal was to guarantee and maintain the racial status quo in the South.

During the 1950s and early 1960s, the former governor returned to the practice of corporate law and served as a lobbyist for conservative causes in the state legislature. In particular he devoted much of his time to fighting labor's attempts to overturn the state's "right-to-work" law (a measure that forbade making union membership a condition for employment) that was passed during Governor Gordon Persons's administration. The former governor also spoke against the economic and sometimes racial liberalism of Governor "Big Jim" Folsom.

Dixon died in Birmingham on October 11, 1965. Many of the reforms he instituted as governor are among the most significant in the state's history. Nonetheless, in an era when Alabama's congressional delegation was among the nation's most liberal, Dixon may be remembered primarily as an archconservative who opposed the New Deal, turned his back on organized labor, and expressed a more virulent form of racism than many of the leading Alabama politicians of the era.

189
◇

References

Alabama Magazine, 1939–1943.

Dobbins, Charles G. "Alabama Governors and Editors, 1920–1955: A Memoir." *Alabama Review* 29 (April 1976): 135–54.

Feldman, Glenn. *From Demagogue to Dixiecrat: Horace Wilkinson and the Politics of Race.* Lanham, Md.: University Press of America, 1995.

Permaloff, Anne, and Carl Grafton. *Political Power in Alabama: The More Things Change—.* Athens: University of Georgia Press, 1995.

The Public Life of Frank M. Dixon: Sketches and Speeches. Montgomery: Alabama Department of Archives and History, Historical and Patriotic Series, no. 18, 1979.

Roller, Daniel C., and Robert L. Twyman, eds. *The Encyclopedia of Southern History.* Baton Rouge: Louisiana State University Press, 1979.

Wilson, Charles Reagan, and William Ferris, eds. *The Encyclopedia of Southern Culture.* Chapel Hill: University of North Carolina Press, 1989.

Chauncey M. Sparks, 1943–1947

HARVEY H. JACKSON III

C HAUNCEY Sparks became governor during the height of World War II. He inherited full employment and a surplus in the state treasury from his predecessor. Although he was considered to be fundamentally conservative as he entered the governorship, Sparks was surprisingly progressive on a number of issues.

Sparks was born on October 8, 1884, in Barbour County, Alabama. His parents were George Washington Sparks and Sarah E. Castello Sparks, natives of Georgia. His father died when Chauncey was two, and the family moved back to Georgia, where the future governor attended local schools in Quitman County. He worked his way through Mercer University in Macon, Georgia, often having to drop out to earn the money to continue. That institution awarded him the bachelor of arts in 1907 and a law degree in 1910.

That same year Sparks returned to Barbour County, passed the Alabama State Bar exam and opened a law office in Eufaula. A few months later he was appointed judge of the Barbour County inferior court by Governor Emmet

Sparks

O'Neal, a position that gave him a steady source of income and a title that followed him the rest of his life. He remained on the bench until 1915, when he returned to law practice. In 1919 he was elected to the legislature, where he supported Governor Thomas E. Kilby's school program and became Kilby's assistant floor leader in the house. He chose not to stand for reelection and in 1923 returned to his law practice and to his farm, where he experimented with livestock and poultry as alternatives to growing cotton.

A bachelor, Judge Sparks resided with his sister and her family and lived a life during the 1920s that was described as "quiet, careful, and hardworking." Then in 1930, to the surprise of many, he announced again for the legislature and was elected. Sparks became an important member of what was described as the "economy bloc," a group of representatives who fought both income and state sales tax proposals. Furthermore, he sponsored a constitutional amendment to limit salaries of state officials to $6,000 a year, and, it was said, "preached against waste and prayed for a balanced budget." His leadership in this group earned him the title the "Barbour Bourbon."

In 1938 Judge Sparks ran for governor against Frank Dixon and came in second, but he declined a runoff. Still, the race gave him statewide exposure, and, building on this, he prepared to make another run for the executive office. Declaring his candidacy in 1942, Sparks faced a number of opponents, including former governor Bibb Graves, who was considered the front-runner, and a young, but little known, James E. Folsom. Almost by default, Sparks found himself the conservative choice, but there was little enthusiasm for his campaign until, not long after the qualifying deadline passed, Graves died. Sparks, now the best-known candidate left, immediately became the favorite, and though some liberals tried to rally around Folsom, they were not able to mount a successful challenge. Chauncey Sparks was elected.

The expectation in Montgomery was that Governor Sparks would, according to one newspaper, "padlock the state treasury," but, to the surprise of many, the Barbour Bourbon became something of a progressive. America was at war, and at home the economy was booming. Tax revenues were up, and with wartime restrictions on what the state could do—no big manpower jobs such as highways could be undertaken—the governor and legislature were faced with the unique problem of how to spend the surplus. Rejecting efforts by such groups as the Farm Bureau to use the money to reduce property taxes, Governor Sparks launched a series of initiatives that resulted in a host of programs to improve the quality of life for all Alabamians.

During the Sparks administration the state appropriation for education was doubled, the school term was lengthened from seven to eight months, appropriations for medical education were doubled, and the University Medical College was moved to Birmingham and expanded to a four-year program. A School of Forestry opened at Alabama Polytechnic Institute (Auburn University), and the Tuskegee Institute received an increase in state funding. In addition, appropriations for agricultural programs doubled, and new farm experiment stations opened. Work began on the coliseum in Montgomery, and the state Department of Labor—created by Governor Graves and eliminated by Governor Dixon—was reestablished to deal with wartime labor problems. All of this was achieved while reducing the state's bonded indebtedness by 25 percent. Along with these accomplishments, a constitutional amendment was passed that required the state legislature to meet every two years instead of quadrennially.

Like so many of his contemporaries, Sparks was, according to state historian Marie Bankhead Owen, an outspoken opponent of "federal encroachments on the rights of states, particularly in such domestic affairs as race relations," and he was frequently quoted as saying that "we don't want federal handouts with strings attached." Toward the end of Sparks's administration, the legislature passed the Boswell Amendment, which aimed to limit the increasing number of black voters in the state. The amendment gave county registrars the power to deny suffrage to voters who, in the view of the registrars, did not understand constitutional issues. Governor-elect James E. ("Big Jim") Folsom spoke out vigorously against its ratification, but to no avail. In a separate issue, Sparks actively fought against the freight rate structure that allowed railroads to discriminate against Alabama and the South.

Always a frugal administrator, the governor delighted and amused Alabamians when they discovered that he was charging his niece, who served as his official hostess, rent for her family's lodgings in the governor's mansion. Sparks, although not a drinker himself, kept fine liquors in the mansion for special occasions, liquors that were hard to find and purchase during wartime. He jealously guarded the supply and is said to have stopped one of his cabinet members who was trying to slip a bottle out of the mansion after a party, making him return the stolen goods.

Sparks left office in January 1947. Prohibited by the constitution from succeeding himself as governor, he nevertheless remained active in politics and the next year represented the state as a delegate to the Democratic National Convention. When the "Dixiecrats" walked out of that convention in protest of its racially liberal platform, Sparks refused to join them. To him the Dixiecrat movement was "ill-starred, ill-conceived, ill-supported and stillborn." Remaining with him was a young George Wallace, a fellow Barbour County politician whom Sparks had given his first political job as an assistant state attorney general. Sparks and Wallace remained close friends over the years, and, according to those who knew them, the former governor was "like an uncle" to his young friend.

In 1950 Sparks made another attempt at the governor's office but finished far back in a large pack of candidates. His loyalty to the Democratic Party in 1948 may have hurt him in the Black Belt, where he had previously enjoyed strong support. He remained in Eufaula and devoted the rest of his life to his law practice and to following the Wallace rise to power. He died there on November 6, 1968.

Summing up his career in a 1957 interview, Sparks concluded, "I ran for governor three times but won only once. I don't think that's much of a record." If he could have read his eulogies he might have thought differently. Although writers could not decide if he was a "liberal conservative or a conservative liberal," they all agreed that, as governor, he set aside parochial interests and did what he could for the people of the state. This was a man, it was noted, who "swung from a plantation-owning Whig viewpoint to a New Deal apostle." For this change, Sparks asked no pardon but simply explained that "it was different representing Barbour County in the legislature and looking out on the whole state from the Capitol steps."

One of the most "bookish" and reflective governors in Alabama's history, some suggested that he wrote his own epitaph when he said: "Orthodoxy is o.k., but it is the unorthodox who bring in fresh breezes, stimulating ideas, and progress. In a world of so many new and newer ideas one is foolish to remain stationary." For much of his life and career Sparks was a man of his time and circumstance. But for four years as governor of Alabama, given his earlier career, the "Barbour Bourbon" was truly unorthodox.

References

Alabama. *Official and Statistical Register*, 1931, 1948.

Gray, Daniel Savage. *Alabama: A Place, A People, A Point of View.* Dubuque, Iowa: Kendall-Hunt Publishing Co., 1977.

Owen, Marie Bankhead. *The Story of Alabama: A History of the State.* 5 vols. New York: Lewis Historical Publishing, 1949.

Sparks, Chauncey. Folder. Alabama Department of Archives and History, Montgomery.

V

Post–World War II to 1987

New Deal programs and, to a greater degree, World War II brought prosperity to the nation and made Alabamians more affluent. As poor white Alabamians made economic strides they began to see the federal government less as their savior and more as an enemy to their autonomy. A cold war supplanted the hot one, and the result, for a time, was continued economic good times combined with an unsettling fear of enemy missile attacks. After Russian-made sputniks orbited the earth, the federal government began to invest large sums of money in public education and in the space program at Huntsville, Alabama, and elsewhere. This beneficent government, however, also began to insist on integration of the races in publicly financed schools and other public areas. States' rights and racism were again as large on the scene as they had been in the pre–Civil War era.

On the national scene, Republicans most often held the presidency while Democrats consistently controlled Congress. In Alabama, however, Democrats continued to hold the governor's chair and large majorities in the legislature. One man dominated the state's politics from 1962 to 1986 and gave Alabama's population perhaps more publicity than they wanted.

Indeed, it took a "family feud" within the Democratic Party to finally place a Republican in the governor's chair, the first to hold that position since Reconstruction. Since then, the state has moved steadily toward a highly competitive two-party system.

James E. Folsom, 1947–1951, 1955–1959

CARL GRAFTON AND ANNE PERMALOFF

JAMES E. "Big Jim" Folsom, Alabama's second governor to serve two four-year terms, looked like a leader. He was six feet, eight inches in height, had broad shoulders, and a striking face. Folsom exuded genuine friendliness and warmth toward Alabama's plain people, both black and white, and beguiled them with his colorful sense of humor that sometimes masked his serious aims. He challenged the Black Belt–Big Mule coalition of planters and businessmen that controlled state government, tried to extend the fruits of democracy to blacks and women, and courageously addressed some of Alabama's most pressing problems. The increasing dominance of the race issue in state politics and Folsom's inability to control his personal weaknesses left his achievements far short of his promise.

Folsom was born on October 8, 1908, in Coffee County near Elba in southeast Alabama's Wiregrass region, the seventh of eight children of Joshua Marion Folsom and Eulala Cornelia Dunnavant Folsom. Jim's lifelong love of politics came from his father, who held county office, led one of two political rings that ruled Coffee County, and was more pragmatic than idealistic. He died in 1919, and Jim became a combination of his political technician father and his more idealistic uncle John Dunnavant, who became a second father to the youngster. Dunnavant had been a Populist who influenced Folsom with romanticized tales of 1890s rebellion.

When Folsom finished high school in 1927 a team effort by the entire family enabled him to attend the University of Alabama that fall. Entering the university was an important step for politically ambitious young men, but in 1929 his college *James Folsom* days ended when he returned to Elba to assist relief efforts that followed a flood of the Pea River. After the flood cleanup, Folsom drifted around the world working and serving in the merchant marine. In 1931 he went home and began to court Sarah Carnley, the daughter of Coffee County probate judge J. A. Carnley. Folsom married Sarah on Christmas Day 1936.

James E. Folsom
1947–1951, 1955–1959

In 1933 Folsom ran as a wet candidate for delegate to the state convention that was to decide Alabama's stand on federal prohibition. He genuinely opposed prohibition, but he ran primarily to gain recognition and was badly beaten. He then won a job as head of the Marshall County Civil Works Administration (CWA), a New Deal relief program. Folsom's work in the CWA reinforced his belief that politics was a struggle between big business and working people, but many of his actions angered the bureaucracy, and he was removed from his position in 1934.

Folsom returned to Elba and ran for Congress against incumbent Henry B. Steagall in 1936. He had little chance to win and so again ran to gain publicity. He attacked the relatively liberal Steagall from the left by advocating programs to lower interest rates on farm loans, provide federal aid to education, pave farm-to-market roads, provide rural electrification, and improve flood control. The campaign lacked funding and was not supported by courthouse rings or other interest groups, but Folsom received 38 percent of the vote, an excellent showing against the popular Steagall. Subsequently, when his family organized an insurance company, the future governor became an agent. Sales trips around south Alabama should have helped in a rematch against Steagall in 1938, but he lost by an even wider margin.

In 1939 Folsom moved to Cullman County in north Alabama to become his insurance company's agent there. This gave him a home county in each end of Alabama, an advantage in a one-party electoral system where statewide races depended more on "friends and neighbors" politics than on lasting political factions. North Alabama's hill country and the southern Wiregrass region were both rural, primarily inhabited by small white landowners and tenant farmers, with relatively few blacks and with strong populist traditions. This sharply contrasted with the Black Belt's large slave-descendant population and planters who wielded vast power in the state's government in concert with corporate interests from Birmingham and other cities. This coalition supported the status quo of low taxes, limited voting rights, and a malapportioned legislature that gave the Black Belt an unfair advantage over other regions.

In 1942 New Dealer Bibb Graves prepared to seek a third term as governor against Black Belt–Big Mule leader Chauncey Sparks and four others. Graves was so ill that liberals feared he would die before the Democratic primary and that the election would go by default to the conservative Sparks. Shortly before the filing deadline, friends convinced Folsom to run. Graves died soon thereafter. The standard way to campaign for governor was to align with as many powerful county rings as possible and to win newspaper endorsements. Folsom enjoyed little ring or newspaper support outside Coffee and Cullman Counties, and he had no funding to counter these deficiencies with advertising. He decided to address voters directly in a grueling schedule of speeches.

Folsom's striking appearance and humorous speeches, honed by three campaigns and years of insurance sales work, made him effective on the stump. His platform was standard New Deal–populism and included old-age pensions, higher pay for teachers, removal of the sales tax on food, improved workers' compensation, and road and bridge construction. His campaign's significance went beyond these proposals, however. He connected with voters, especially the powerless, in ways that confounded political pundits. These voters believed he was one of them and that he understood their problems better than professional politicians with money and organizations. As expected, Sparks won a majority, but Folsom's strong second-place showing with 26 percent of the vote was a surprise. Most observers discounted Folsom's large vote as a fluke.

In 1943 Folsom rejoined the merchant marine, a dangerous activity critical to the nation's efforts in World War II, but his mind remained on politics. In 1944 he filed by postcard to run for delegate at large to the Democratic National Convention and was elected. Then tragedy struck. Sarah died from complications associated with a pregnancy, and Folsom was released from the merchant marine to care for his two daughters. Despite these personal setbacks, he ran for governor a second time in 1946.

Folsom's campaign strategy had not changed. Once again he had little support from newspapers or county rings, but many labor unions joined his effort. His innovative, symbol-filled speeches were preceded with music from a country band called the "Strawberry Pickers." He used a mixture of clever devices on the stump, including his famous corn shuck mop, which he said he would use to clean out the capital, and a "suds bucket" to hold campaign contributions. His major opponents in the Democratic primary were Lieutenant Governor Handy Ellis and Agriculture Commissioner Joe Poole. Ellis, a former legislative leader for liberal governor Bibb Graves, was the clear favorite but ran a close second to Folsom. In the ensuing runoff, Ellis suddenly shifted to the political right in an effort to unite conservatives in a crusade against the ultraliberal Folsom.

Most daily newspapers backed Ellis and criticized Folsom's connections to organized labor, including the Congress of Industrial Organizations (CIO), which they claimed was part of "the Communist fringe." Folsom's response was ideologically charged. "They can't stop us," he said, "by trying to divide race and race, class and class, or religion and religion. We've just finished fighting a war against hatred and violence." His opponents, Folsom charged, were "satisfied with things as they are. They are satisfied for Alabama to be way down at the bottom among the [then] 48 states. They are satisfied for Alabama people to make less." Folsom's landslide victory over Ellis revolutionized state campaigns. It demonstrated that county rings and newspapers could be defeated by effective direct appeals to the voters. After winning the primary election but before he

James E. Folsom
1947–1951, 1955–1959

was inaugurated, Governor-elect Folsom risked some of his popular support by actively campaigning against ratification of the Boswell Amendment, which attempted to restrict black voting in the state. The amendment was narrowly approved but was later declared unconstitutional by a Mobile federal judge.

In his inaugural address Folsom asked for the elimination of voting restrictions that disfranchised poor people and for the state to "open the way for women to have a full share in our government." He argued for a wider distribution of political power in the state, asserting that many people were "frightened by real democracy. They want to keep power in the hands of the few. I am not afraid of too much democracy. I am afraid of what happens to people when they have too little democracy." The legislature was solidly under Black Belt–Big Mule control, and little that Folsom favored stood any chance of passage. In addition, his selection of legislative leaders revealed an inability to judge people, a weakness that plagued his political career. In an attempt to win over his opponents, the governor ludicrously chose a Black Belt senator as his floor leader, but the man vehemently opposed Folsom's program. His choice for house speaker led to similar results. The first major legislative fight of the Folsom administration demonstrated these weaknesses.

When he tried to break up a political coalition between the Alabama Farm Bureau Federation (a Big Mule ally) and Alabama Polytechnic Institute's (now Auburn University) Farm Extension Service agents, Folsom suffered a humiliating defeat. Extension service agents furnished a statewide organization in support of the Farm Bureau's political goals, which coincided with those of the largest landowners and agribusiness interests. Vowing to get the extension service out of politics, Folsom in 1947 nominated four anti–Big Mule members to the ten-person board of trustees of Alabama Polytechnic, convened a special legislative session to confirm them, and asked legislators to approve a constitutional convention to reapportion the legislature on a one-person, one-vote basis. Farm Bureau lobbyists filled the capital to fight Folsom, whose appointees they condemned as left-wing radicals. Senators easily defeated Folsom's nominees and ignored his call for a constitutional convention. During the 1947 regular legislative session, Folsom was again unsuccessful when he asked legislators to eliminate the poll tax.

Before the 1949 legislative session convened, Folsom improved his relationship with the legislature and behaved less like an outsider-revolutionary, but his civil libertarian goals had not changed. In his address to the opening session of the legislature he said: "It is inherent in a democracy that a person who exercises the full rights of citizenship should be allowed to vote. . . . Our population is 60 percent white and 40 percent Negro. We are gradually affording the Negro opportunity to make substantial contributions for the benefit of the total population. We must strengthen the cornerstone of opportunity for them.

We must remember—that which is built upon prejudice or ill will cannot survive in a democracy."

The governor's program appalled the Big Mules. He asked for vastly increased overall spending, $61 million in new taxes, and an $80 million road bond issue and again called for the elimination of the poll tax. These proposals were partly intended as the opening bid in a bargaining process, but he would gladly have accepted them unchanged. Nearly all of fifty-six administration bills were defeated or drastically amended, but the legislature did not win every fight. When it passed a bill requiring an anti-Communist loyalty oath for public employees, Folsom, unlike his liberal counterparts in many northern states, vetoed it on First Amendment grounds. This principled stand was highly unpopular in this era of anti-Communist hysteria. Folsom further angered right-wingers when he appointed voter registrars who favored the registration of blacks.

As if his civil liberties stand and his efforts to extend democracy to blacks and women did not create enough enemies, Folsom also had his first term scarred by scandals. The governor's political appointees were accused of illegally manipulating bids for state contracts and of outright bribery. During the last year of his first term, the number of pardons and paroles of state prisoners so dramatically increased that Folsom asked for the resignation of the officials responsible. Subsequent investigations proved that many prisoners had bought their way out of jail and that others were released because their families had supported the governor. The intensity of wrongdoing may or may not have exceeded that of previous administrations, but Folsom's appointees were unusually inept at shielding their actions from public view. Folsom was not accused of personally participating in or benefiting from any of the wrongdoing.

Many people were also dismayed by Folsom's personal behavior. He actively courted criticism from the state's more genteel elements by engaging in "boyish" high jinks, such as allowing a national magazine to photograph him while he was soaking in a bathtub. He also earned the name "Kissin' Jim" because of his propensity for kissing beautiful young women, but these and other laughable indiscretions merely added to the "Big Jim" legend. Others showed serious irresponsibility.

In March 1948 a woman filed a lawsuit in Cullman County that asked a court to declare that the governor was her common-law husband and the father of her twenty-two-month-old son. Folsom claimed the suit was merely a ploy designed to discredit him, but that was untrue, and years later he admitted that he was the child's father. It was a massive scandal, and newspapers throughout the country carried the story. Folsom's friends paid the woman off, and she dropped the lawsuit. The governor's well-earned reputation for drinking and carousing become more muted in May of 1948 when he married Jamelle Moore, nineteen years his junior. The marriage was an enduring one, and between 1949 and 1970 the couple added seven children to the family that already included Folsom's two daughters.

Folsom briefly toyed with the idea of running for president in 1948 and announced that he would be a candidate for the Democratic nomination, but he failed to gain significant support. When the Democratic National Convention adopted a pro–civil rights platform, neither Folsom nor his legislative supporter George Wallace bolted the party as some other southerners did. The third-party bolters, popularly known as the "Dixiecrats," held a convention in Birmingham, and Governor Folsom graciously welcomed the delegates to the state. Nevertheless, at their departure he supported Truman's reelection and assailed them for their disloyalty to the national party.

State law barred Folsom from seeking reelection, and his handpicked successor, state revenue commissioner Phillip Hamm, was badly defeated in 1950. One of Folsom's last acts as governor was his appointment of Annie Lola Price to a seat on the Alabama Court of Appeals. She took office at a time when women were still barred by law from serving on the state's juries. In 1951 Folsom returned to Cullman and to the insurance business, but in 1952 he briefly made state headlines when he was arrested in Jefferson County on charges of driving while intoxicated. After a trial, he was found not guilty.

In 1954 former governor Folsom was the clear front-runner in a field of seven candidates in the state Democratic primary. Among his opponents were three state senators, the president of the state Public Service Commission, and the lieutenant governor. Folsom conducted another colorful campaign, but this time there was more campaign money. People who wanted to do business with the state gave large contributions to Big Jim's campaign. The "Little Man's Big Friend," as Folsom styled himself, now had some larger friends, and he welcomed the new allies with a slogan, "Y'all Come," that resonated with the voter.

Folsom's 1954 campaign speeches have become legend. When opponents charged that his first administration had been laced with corruption, he responded by saying, "Shore I stole. I stole to build hospitals. I stole to build schools. I stole to build roads." Pointing to members of the audience he said, "I stole for you and you and you." The wealthy interests and the "lyin' newspapers" had tried to persecute him, his family, and "the boys who helped me, and who tried to help you." Folsom advocated the same programs that he had pushed during his first term, including the reapportionment of the state legislature so that no region of the state was placed at a disadvantage. He won the primary, which was tantamount to election, without a runoff, capturing 51.4 percent of the vote. It was a remarkable victory considering the stature and number of his opponents. One week after the primary, the United States Supreme Court delivered its famous desegregation decision in *Brown v. Board of Education of Topeka, Kansas.*

When the *Brown* decision became public, Folsom realized that legislators and their constituents would be obsessed with maintaining segregation and white supremacy and that his hopes for reapportionment of the legislature or for a convention to reform the outmoded 1901 constitution would be too controversial in such an atmosphere. Still, Folsom had helped to elect a substantial number of allies to both legislative chambers, and lawmakers were friendlier in his second term. He toned down his populist rhetoric, and his programs sounded more like those of a conventional business progressive. He managed to get a number of important measures enacted that had widespread support, including road bond issues; increases for health, welfare, and education programs; and the creation of an industrial development commission. Folsom repeatedly called for a constitutional convention to reapportion the legislature on a one-person, one-vote basis, but lawmakers refused to respond.

The farm-to-market road program became the most popular feature of Folsom's second administration. The governor convened a special session of the legislature days after his inauguration, asked for the largest road bond construction program in Alabama's history, proposed a two-cent gasoline tax to pay for it, and used much of the money to blacktop the dirt roads in Alabama's rural counties. Folsom encountered extreme opposition from legislators to certain features of the program but finally convinced them to agree to most of it. The legislation pumped nearly $100 million into the state's highways and left rural Alabamians with their most tangible memory of Big Jim. Even his opponents praised Folsom's effort to take the isolated areas of the state out of the mud and dust and put them into the twentieth century.

Governor Folsom demonstrated a large measure of courage in the face of the prosegregation hysteria that swept across the state in the wake of the *Brown* decision, and he either vetoed or refused to sign all but a handful of anti–civil rights bills that passed the legislature. Perhaps the most notable of the bills was the so-called nullification resolution that declared the *Brown* decision and related rulings by the Supreme Court "null, void, and of no effect" in Alabama. Folsom quipped that the resolution was a lot of "clap-trap" that reminded him of a "hound dog baying at the moon and claiming its [*sic*] got the moon treed."

As Alabama politics became dominated by segregation mania, Folsom began to retreat from his long-standing commitment to civil rights. In 1956 he said, "I was and am for segregation." Such segregationist gestures by Folsom were always delivered in a lukewarm tone or as part of a sarcastic joke. He resisted discussing race and refused to use it as an emotional issue to gain votes. Folsom privately encouraged Dr. Martin Luther King Jr. and others who led the Montgomery bus boycott in 1955–56, but when he got the chance to do something positive for blacks in public he was either silent or absent from his office. His greatest failure in the area of civil rights occurred during an effort to integrate the University of Alabama in 1956.

A black student, Autherine Lucy, was quietly admitted to the university in the winter of 1956, but some white students and other area residents began demonstrations to have her removed from school. Eventually, a riot broke out, and she barely escaped harm. A nervous university board of trustees, instead of trying to restore order, expelled her. At a key moment in the episode Folsom could not be reached because he was enjoying himself at a drunken party on a boat in the Gulf of Mexico. He should have known of the danger to Lucy and of the fears by university officials about what might happen, but he did nothing to uphold the law. It was a failure that would forever haunt him. If he had acted decisively on behalf of Lucy, efforts to defy the law by later Alabama governors might never have happened.

It was the race issue, more than any other, that ended Folsom's political career. When Adam Clayton Powell visited Montgomery during the city's bus boycott, the governor caused a sensation when he invited the controversial black New York congressman to the mansion, where they chatted for half an hour over drinks. The people of the state were appalled; this breach of southern custom was too outrageous even for Folsom. Alabama politics had been captured by racism, and Folsom's brand of liberalism was in decline. When he ran for Democratic national committeeman in 1956, he was badly defeated by a staunch segregationist.

Alcoholism stole over Big Jim during the last three years of his administration, and although he was capable of scaling back consumption on most days when he had to appear in public, it was a severe and besetting problem for him. His embarrassing alcohol-induced antics at certain public functions have become legend. At the 1957 National Governors' Conference he was chairman of the committee on atomic energy, a major issue in the fifties. When the time came for his committee report he told the gathering that he did not know anything about "atom bums," so he would "just retire to the bar." No one was surprised. Folsom achieved little after the early special and regular legislative sessions of 1955, and when he left office in 1959 there were more charges that his friends had used state government for their benefit.

In 1962 Big Jim ran for a third term in office, and his principal opponent was George C. Wallace, who had once been a close Folsom ally. Wallace ran as an extreme segregationist and promised to defy federal court decisions ordering the state to integrate its schools, while Folsom called for "peaceful" relations in the state and chose as his campaign song the old hymn "Peace in the Valley." Wallace's tactics were successful, and Folsom finished in third place in the race after he appeared to be in a drunken condition during a television appearance on the last night of the campaign. He later charged that his enemies had drugged him.

Big Jim lived for twenty-five years after his 1962 defeat, and he ran for office several more times with no success. He started a series of businesses that failed, and he suffered seizures, strokes, and heart attacks that led him, finally, to stop drinking. One stroke blinded him, but he maintained a positive attitude, even attending the Talladega School for the Deaf and Blind, where he learned to read braille. Those who saw him in his later years noted that his good humor and liberal convictions never faded. He died on November 21, 1987.

One of the most memorable of all of the state's governors, Folsom is not remembered for programs initiated during his administrations except for his farm-to-market roads. He was important for offering an alternative to the Big Mule approach to governance, and he pointed the way to a different Alabama, one not obsessed with or held back by racial or gender discrimination. He was guilty of oversimplifying and undersupervising approaches to welfare, education, and road construction, and like many liberals of the era he was content to throw money at problems in ill-conceived and corruption-ridden programs. Still, if the legislature had adopted the policies he recommended during his first term, Alabama could have avoided future federal court orders on reapportionment and voting rights. Folsom will be remembered for his drinking, his antics, his humor, and the cavalier approach he took to the corruption that often went on around him, but he will also be remembered for his good-hearted efforts to represent the dispossessed and the powerless.

References

Barnard, William D. *Dixiecrats and Democrats: Alabama Politics, 1942–1950*. University: University of Alabama Press, 1974.

Grafton, Carl, and Anne Permaloff. *Big Mules and Branchheads: James E. Folsom and Political Power in Alabama*. Athens: University of Georgia Press, 1985.

Sims, George. *The Little Man's Big Friend: James E. Folsom in Alabama Politics, 1946–1958*. University: University of Alabama Press, 1985.

Gordon Persons, 1951–1955

S. Jonathan Bass

ALABAMA'S forgotten governor of the post–World War II era, Seth Gordon Persons is often overshadowed by his flamboyant predecessor and successor, James E. Folsom. Persons's public persona—amiable, quiet, and dignified—presented a stark contrast to Folsom's more outrageous manner. Serving as governor from 1951 to 1955, the congenial Persons was a calming influence in the years following the Dixiecrat revolt and Folsom's turbulent relations with the legislature.

Persons was born on February 5, 1902, in Montgomery, where his father owned and operated a corner drug store in their neighborhood. Impatient and ambitious, the younger Persons roared through the streets of Montgomery on a souped-up motorcycle while most boys his age slowly pedaled about town on bicycles. A mediocre student, Persons attended four different preparatory schools during his high school career. After graduation, he enrolled in electrical engineering at Auburn University in 1921, where his most noteworthy achievement was his presidency of the innocuous "Hobo Club," a gathering of students who, as "Boxcar Reds" and "Boxcar Blacks," attended all of Auburn's away

Persons

football games. The organization's name reflected his restless spirit; Persons quit school after one year and moved from job to job for the next several years. He worked for the Farm Bureau, a cotton association, and an IBM factory in Ithaca, New York, and he ran a service station in Montgomery. Persons finally discovered his niche when he recognized the potential for radio in Alabama, opened a radio parts store in Montgomery, and began to sell light crystal sets. His success in radio escalated when, in 1930, he and partner Howard Pill founded Montgomery's first radio station, WSFA. On March 20, 1928, he married Alice McKeithen, and they later had two children, a son and a daughter.

Persons gained his first taste of state politics when Governor Bibb Graves appointed him chairman of the state Rural Electrification Authority (REA) in 1935. After three years on the job, the entrepreneurial Persons formed his own engineering firm and strung more than ten thousand miles of electrical lines in Alabama. By 1940 Persons had earned a small fortune and was a hero to many farmers who benefited from his efforts to bring electricity to families in rural Alabama. While Persons was becoming a key player in the public scene, he was also growing wary of the powerful influences of the Public Service Commission (PSC). "I didn't think it was being operated as efficiently as it might be," Persons once said, "and I felt that maybe I could do something about it." His desire for reform led to his campaign for the presidency of the PSC in 1940. Persons emerged from the election as the apparent winner, but a recount in several counties ultimately gave the victory to his opponent by fewer than two thousand votes. Undaunted, Persons returned two years later and won a seat as an associate commissioner, and in 1944 he was elected president of the PSC.

From this position, Persons made his first bid for the state's highest office in 1946. A serious throat ailment hampered his campaign, and he finished last in the primary race. He continued to lead the PSC—keeping gas, telephone, and electricity rates low and curtailing the influence of powerful utility companies. In 1950 Persons renewed his pursuit of the governor's office but avoided the bruising battle between those who supported the Dixiecrats in 1948 and those who remained loyal to the national Democratic Party. He opened his campaign by pledging loyalty to the national Democratic Party, then quickly dropped the issue for the remainder of the race. During the 1950 campaign, Persons traveled throughout the state in a two-seat helicopter, causing a stir among many rural Alabamians who were seeing such a flying machine for the first time. His whirly-bird campaign made 385 landings, and one of his competitors labeled Persons the "Man from Mars." Voters, on the other hand, found the PSC president to be a down-to-earth choice. On a rainy, overcast day in early May 1950, a heavy voter turnout gave Persons 35 percent of the vote, far ahead of the fourteen other candidates in the primary. His next closest opponent, Phillip Hamm, who was Folsom's handpicked successor, trailed with only 13 percent of the vote. Hamm withdrew from the runoff, giving Persons the nomination. In the November election, Persons swamped his Republican opponent with more than 90 percent of the vote.

The silver-haired Persons brought a no-nonsense business approach to the governor's office. He rejected the usual inaugural parade and black-tie ball for a simple ceremony and no fanfare. "I do not think that either is proper as long as Alabama boys are being killed and wounded in Korea," Persons announced. At the inaugural, he stood on the steps of the capitol for the oath of office in a plain business suit instead of the customary morning coat and top hat. He told the assembled crowd that he had no further political ambitions. "Since I have no political future, " he added, "the decisions I make during the next four years will be for the good of Alabama and not just for myself."

Stocky, good-natured, and quick-witted, Persons had a broad, infectious grin that worked well in his dealings with the state legislature. Unlike the previous four years under Folsom, the new governor's term was marked by harmonious relations with the folks on Goat Hill. "Above all," he said in 1950, "let's have four years of no fussin', no fightin', and no feudin'." His goals and programs were simple, conservative, and ultimately successful: initiate prison reform, increase funding for education, make Alabama's highways safer, and encourage educational television in the state. But his first official act as governor was to call a meeting of the board of trustees at Auburn for the purpose of firing that institution's losing coach. They then hired Ralph "Shug" Jordan, who restored Auburn's winning football program.

In pursuit of his goals Persons quietly and methodically went about the business of governing Alabama. He accepted no speaking engagements during his four years in office, preferring to let his record in office speak for him. Soon after taking office, Persons and the legislature ended fiscal mismanagement in the Department of Corrections and placed the prison system under the control of a new supervisory board. In a vivid public display, Persons burned the straps used to whip convicts in the state. "There'll be no more whipping of prisoners in Alabama," he announced. "Whipping is a sign of weakness on the part of those in authority. It is inhuman and will not be tolerated."

Despite his deeply held convictions on whipping convicts, Persons, ironically, threatened to use the lash on a journalist or two. Perhaps Persons's most

208 controversial action as governor was his callous treatment of Geoffrey Birt, a

◇ reporter for the *Montgomery Advertiser.* At a news conference during the summer of 1951, the usually easygoing Persons exploded at Birt. "I'll whip your ass in five seconds!" the governor promised, accusing Birt of unfairly manipulating his words. Two years later, Persons again threatened to stomp the "dirty son-of-a-bitch" after a Birt article accused the governor of unethical dealings. "You're just a dirty Folsomite!" Persons shouted. The *Advertiser* accused the governor of uncorking his "frenzied Anglo-Saxon billingsgate," but the controversy quickly dissipated.

Despite some negative press, Alabamians still recognized Persons for his positive programs. He increased expenditures for highway construction, and in 1953 he instituted a mandated sixty-miles-per-hour speed limit during the day and fifty at night. "We want tourists," he declared, "but we want them to get into Alabama and leave the state alive." The governor's efforts significantly reduced traffic fatalities in the state.

With his background in radio, Persons was among the first in the nation to see the educational potential that existed through the television medium. Alabama created an Educational Television Commission in 1950, the first state to do so. Persons signed into law a "right-to-work" law that prohibited requiring union membership as a condition for employment. This legislation was possible through a section of the Republican-sponsored 1947 Taft-Hartley

Act and came in the midst of a series of postwar strikes during the Truman administration. Governing in the midst of the McCarthy era, Persons signed a bill that forbade communists from holding public office and required them to register their party affiliation. He also supported a "Little" Boswell amendment that established new ways to disenfranchise blacks as the old ones were being found unconstitutional by federal courts.

Late in Persons's administration and just before a new governor would be chosen, the Supreme Court of the United States handed down the *Brown v. Board of Education of Topeka, Kansas* decision, outlawing racially segregated facilities in public schools. Persons hoped to reduce anxiety in the state over this volatile civil rights issue, and a year earlier he had begun studying ways to deal with the long-awaited court decision. A relative moderate on racial issues, Persons had campaigned for governor on a pledge to limit or abolish the poll tax, which eliminated poor voters, both black and white. The legislature passed a compromise measure limiting back unpaid poll taxes to two years and eliminating them entirely for voters over the age of forty-five. As with many of the state's moderates, the governor believed abolishing segregation was unthinkable, but he refused to call a special session of the legislature to maintain segregation in public education. "I stand on my conviction that no intelligent legislation can be passed until that subject is clarified and until the legislature actually knows what it is facing," he asserted.

209
◇

In addition to the uneasiness caused by desegregation, another serious domestic problem faced Alabama. Albert Patterson, who had used his campaign of cleaning up corrupt and dangerous Phenix City to win the Democratic nomination for the state's attorney general slot, was murdered, thrusting his son, John Patterson, into the political limelight. Persons placed Russell County under martial law and sent in National Guard troops to protect citizens from the criminal element that dominated the city.

Persons could not succeed himself as governor, but his political activism was cut even shorter when, just days before Jim Folsom's reelection victory in November 1954, he suffered a serious heart attack. He never returned to his office and designated his executive secretary, Vernon Merritt, to read his farewell address to the legislature. "I will always stand ready to be of service to Alabama in any way as a private citizen," he said. Despite his promise never to return to public office, many considered Persons the front-runner for governor in 1958. A mild stroke, however, prevented another serious bid for Alabama's top job. On May 29, 1965, he suffered a major stroke and died in a Montgomery hospital.

Persons had campaigned for governor on the slogan, "I keep my promises." He did just that by providing four years of sound, conservative government, the last relatively quiet administration for two decades, as Folsom returned to power and the activist phase of the civil rights movement began.

John Patterson
1959–1963

References

Alabama: The News Magazine of the Deep South, January 1950–January 1955.
Birmingham News, 1950–55.
Montgomery Advertiser, 1950–55.
Persons, Gordon. File. Alabama State Department of Archives and History, Montgomery.
Rogers, William Warren, Robert David Ward, Leah Rawls Atkins, and Wayne Flynt. *Alabama: The History of a Deep South State*. Tuscaloosa: University of Alabama Press, 1994.

John Patterson, 1959–1963

ANNE PERMALOFF AND CARL GRAFTON

JOHN Malcolm Patterson was thrust into Alabama's political arena by the brutal murder of his father, attorney general–elect Albert Patterson, in the summer of 1954. Asked by the State Democratic Executive Committee to fill his father's place as the party candidate and to finish his father's work in cleaning up the corruption and vice in Phenix City, Patterson made a young, attractive, and emotionally sympathetic candidate.

Patterson

Patterson was born in Goldville, Alabama, on September 27, 1921. His parents, Albert Love Patterson and Agnes Louise Benson Patterson, were schoolteachers in Tallapoosa and Cullman Counties, and his father later served as a high school principal in Coosa and Clay Counties before settling into a Phenix City law practice. These numerous county contacts would one day give John Patterson a healthy support system in Alabama's "friends and neighbors" politics.

Patterson entered the army in 1940 as a private and left five years later as a major and holder of a Bronze Star. He saw active duty again during the Korean conflict from 1951 to 1953. In 1947, between the two wars, he married Mary Jo McGowin and began a family that included two children, a son and a daughter. In 1949 he received his law degree from the University of Alabama and began to practice law with his father in Phenix City.

In 1954 Patterson's father, Albert, won the Democratic Party nomination for attorney general. He campaigned against the gambling, prostitution, and drug trafficking that were rampant in Phenix City. Less than a month after winning the nomination, Albert Patterson was murdered by Phenix City criminals. John

Patterson acceded to the request of the State Democratic Executive Committee to replace his father on the Democratic ballot, met no Republican opposition in the November election, and became attorney general in January 1955.

Patterson's service as attorney general is known for three areas of activity: the cleanup of Phenix City; investigations into corruption in the second Folsom administration; and legal maneuvers against desegregation efforts following the 1954 *Brown v. Board of Education of Topeka, Kansas* decision of the Supreme Court. These areas of concern served as the cornerstone of his successful gubernatorial campaign four years later. Although he completed his father's fight against corruption and rid Phenix City of the worst of its criminal element and activity, Patterson was less successful in finding any direct connection between Governor Folsom and the corruption that marked his administrations.

It was Patterson's actions in support of maintaining segregation in the state that brought him the most widespread publicity and support. The National Association for the Advancement of Colored People (NAACP) was one of the most active civil rights organizations in the nation, as well as the best known and most financially sound. In 1956 Patterson sought and received a restraining order against the NAACP, barring it from operating in the state on the basis that the organization had not registered as an out-of-state corporation as required by state law. In a separate move, the attorney general sought a court order compelling the NAACP to reveal its membership. The organization refused, believing that the information would be used to retaliate against the members. In July 1956, the circuit court of Montgomery found the organization in contempt and issued a $100,000 fine. When the Alabama Supreme Court refused to review the decision, the NAACP appealed to the U.S. Supreme Court, which countermanded the citation and fine in 1958. Nonetheless, the restraining order against NAACP operation in the state remained in effect until 1964, when it was lifted by another U.S. Supreme Court decision.

Not content with attacking the NAACP, Patterson also filed suit against the Tuskegee Civic Association, a civil rights group that organized a boycott against Tuskegee merchants. Begun in 1957, the boycott protested one of the most elaborate gerrymanders in American history, which removed four hundred black residents from the city limits in order to protect white control of local government. The black citizens of Tuskegee won their case in federal court in 1958.

The 1958 campaign for governor saw Patterson, Judge George C. Wallace of Barbour County, and Bay Minette newspaper publisher Jimmy Faulkner as the front-runners against eleven other candidates. The campaigns of all three focused heavily on maintaining segregation. Only Patterson, however, could claim actual success against desegregation as well as against crime and corruption. He connected the crime, corruption, and segregationist themes by arguing that outside forces—namely, gangsters and the NAACP—were pouring money into the state to stop him. Another theme in the Patterson campaign was his support for such populist programs as higher pensions for the elderly, better schools, and farm aid, and he portrayed himself as the more prolabor candidate. George Wallace had not yet achieved fame as a segregationist and was perceived as a racial moderate. Many voters still identified him as a Folsomite, which meant not only liberal on economic matters but also soft on segregation. The Patterson campaign reminded voters of the corruption of the Folsom administrations and encouraged them to connect that corruption to Wallace. Because of Patterson's role in cleaning up Phenix City and the sympathy attached to him because of the murder of his father, he had become the subject of television and movie features and was viewed more favorably than the others.

Patterson led in the primary with 31.8 percent of the vote, and Wallace placed second with 26.3 percent. During the runoff campaign, a revived Ku Klux Klan supported Patterson, which Wallace and his supporters unsuccessfully attempted to exploit. In a vote that suggested that his antidesegregation attitude and actions resonated with much of the Alabama public, Patterson easily won the runoff with 55 percent of the vote. He was only thirty-eight years old. Reliable observers reported that on learning of his loss in the election, Wallace asserted: "John Patterson out-niggered me, and boys, I'm not going to be out-niggered again."

As governor, Patterson continued to block desegregation. In perhaps the nadir of his term as governor, he excused attacks on black and white civil rights demonstrators known as "freedom riders" who violated local segregation ordinances as they traveled through Alabama. In May 1961 freedom riders were taken from their buses and beaten in separate attacks near Anniston and in Birmingham. Patterson placed full blame for these incidents on the civil rights activists, observing: "We can't act as nursemaid to agitators. They'll stay at home when they learn nobody is there to protect them. The state of Alabama can't guarantee the safety of fools, and that's what they are."

In resisting desegregation, the young governor always used two lines of argument to justify his actions. First, segregation was part of state law and the state constitution, which Patterson claimed his oath of office required him to uphold. Second, Patterson asserted that legal tactics were used to avoid conflict with the federal government and to delay the inevitable desegregation process so that the public had time to adjust to change gradually. Whatever his justifications, during his tenure first as attorney general and then as governor, Alabama endured more racial bombing of black churches and private dwellings than any other state in the nation.

On other issues Patterson, a self-proclaimed populist, governed with varying degrees of success. He supported but did not achieve reapportionment of the state legislature because of the wide rift that now stood between the old Black Belt and its former Jefferson County allies. Patterson warned of impending federal court intervention if the legislature did not act. He toughened lending laws and limited the activities of loan sharks. Old-age pensions were expanded. In a show of frugality, Patterson sold off five of the state's airplanes, but later purchased new ones.

Patterson's upbringing as the son of two schoolteachers predisposed him to support public education, and his campaign travels exposed him firsthand to the deplorable condition of the public education system of Alabama. Urban schools were overcrowded due to the migration of population from Black Belt counties. The physical plants of hundreds of schools were in appalling condition, with an estimated $340 million needed to repair rotting floors and leaking roofs and to replace inadequate plumbing and heating systems. More than one hundred schools had failed to attain accreditation standards and were on probation. Serious underfunding led to actual and threatened loss of accreditation for several programs on the college and university levels. Property taxes, the major source of local support, were so low that public school funding was inadequate. Reports from a blue-ribbon Commission on Alabama Education created by a legislative act in 1957, a legislative interim committee, and group meetings of educational leaders outlined actions to be taken. From these recommendations, Patterson forged a "rescue" reform package, which he presented to a special session of the legislature in June.

Patterson's plan contained a tax package designed to raise $42 million per year in additional revenues beyond current educational funding levels. Increased revenue was to come from higher taxes on the sale of automobiles, reductions in exemptions for personal income tax, and increases in corporate income tax rates. In addition, he proposed a $75 million bond issue for school construction with two-thirds of the funds to be allocated to public schools and one-third to higher education. In order to build legislative support, Patterson identified specific allocations in the plan for each school district and for each university and college and advertised them before the special session met. Patterson lobbied community leaders, bankers, county commissioners, and school board members—urging them to pressure their legislators into supporting the legislation. He contacted legislators personally and attempted to use highway construction monies to gain leverage.

Virtually every interest group of any consequence organized to protect itself in the tax battle, and each proposed a host of new tax measures to force others to assume the burden. Most of the externally suggested revenue sources were regressive and were opposed by Patterson. A revised package that increased funding for education passed the legislature, but it raised only half the money needed, and the revenue sources were regressive. Still, this amount, added to the $75 million bond issue, represented a substantial increase in spending for education. The budget for education in Patterson's first year as governor was the largest allocated in the state's history, and teachers were given a 15 percent pay increase—only to have 10 percent of it stripped from them when revenues lagged. In the process of fighting for the education package, Patterson used most of the political capital available to a new governor, thus limiting other possible accomplishments. Patterson's program succeeded and began a period of improvement in the state's public education system.

Related to the education battle was Patterson's campaign for property tax equalization. Each county had a board of equalization whose job was to hear appeals from property owners who believed their property had been assessed unfairly. The state revenue commissioner appointed members to a four-year term but had to select them from a list submitted by the county commission, county board of education, and county commissioner of revenue. County boards of equalization rarely raised an assessment and frequently lowered them. Furthermore, although Alabama's 1901 constitution called for property taxes to be assessed at 60 percent of their fair market value, this was never done in any county. In 1950 the Alabama Supreme Court overturned the 60 percent rate, noting that actual assessments tended to run at 5 to 15 percent of fair market value with high population counties such as Jefferson and Mobile having their property assessed at higher rates.

Patterson's revenue commissioner, Harry Haden, a former University of Alabama law professor of Patterson's, led the administration attack on the assessment system. He calculated that if all residential property in the state were assessed at 30 percent of fair market value, more than $30 million a year in added revenues could be raised. He and Patterson actively recruited individuals to serve on the equalization boards who would implement Haden's plan. Although the governor again lobbied appropriate groups who were supportive of more equitable assessment, it was an uphill fight from the beginning, and it was a losing one. Opposition to the tax plan was immediate and ferocious; it came from rural counties and urban business interests, as well as from individuals. Eventually, in a compromise, Patterson had to agree to end his equalization efforts, and opposition lawmakers agreed not to strip the revenue commissioner of his powers.

Patterson found it somewhat easier to convince the legislature to act on other issues. Within weeks of taking office, he called two special sessions. During the first, the legislature passed a $60 million bond issue for highway construction and maintenance. A second special session passed legislation that addressed loopholes in the state's sales tax law and added a two-cent tax to packages of cigarettes and a 10 percent tax on liquor—all earmarked for education, old-age pensions, and mental health projects. Despite the increased revenue, Patterson's was not an inexpensive administration, and he left his successor a deficit of more than $2 million.

The state was changing as Patterson prepared to leave the governorship. Its population was growing but more slowly than in other states, and in 1960 Alabama found it was to lose one of its seats in Congress. As the legislature attempted to redraw congressional lines to make eight districts where there had been nine, old sectional rivalries arose. After much rancor, filibustering, and even scuffles in the legislature, the lawmaking body decided that all nine incumbent congressmen would run "at large," and the candidate receiving the fewest votes lost his seat.

When George Wallace was sworn in as governor in 1963, Patterson stayed in Montgomery and returned to the practice of law. In 1965 he and other political hopefuls and their supporters in the legislature actively participated in the successful senate fight to stop the constitutional amendment that would allow Wallace to succeed himself. Patterson planned a comeback in 1966 and did not want to face an increasingly popular incumbent.

The defeat of the succession amendment resulted in actions that greatly influenced state politics for years. Wallace's wife, Lurleen, ran for governor and won the 1966 Democratic primary against Patterson, Congressman Carl Elliott, and others without a runoff and then easily defeated the Republican candidate, Congressman Jim Martin. In 1972 Patterson ran for chief justice of the Alabama Supreme Court and was, again, defeated. Appointed to the state court of criminal appeals in 1984 by George Wallace, he was elected to a full term and reelected in 1990, finally retiring in January 1997. In 1994 Patterson was one of the judges who upheld the felony ethics conviction of Governor Guy Hunt. He also served as chief judge of the court of the judiciary, the hearing panel authorized to remove, suspend, or censure judges for misconduct or professional wrongdoing. Divorced from his first wife, Patterson married Florentine "Tina" Brachert Sawyer in 1975 and now serves as a supernumerary judge on a part-time basis.

As governor John Patterson attempted to reform the state's property tax system and fund education at an adequate level. These laudable efforts, regrettably, are overshadowed by his irresponsible behavior toward civil rights groups seeking equal rights in Alabama.

References

Engelhardt, Sam. Personal Files. Alabama Department of Archives and History, Montgomery.

Grafton, Carl, and Anne Permaloff. *Big Mules and Branchheads: James E. Folsom and Political Power in Alabama*. Athens: University of Georgia Press, 1985.

215
◇

———. "The Big Mule Alliance's Last Good Year: Thwarting the Patterson Reforms."
    Alabama Review 47 (October 1990): 243–66.
Patterson, John. Office Files. Alabama Department of Archives and History, Montgomery.
Permaloff, Anne, and Carl Grafton. *Political Power in Alabama: The More Things
    Change—*. Athens: University of Georgia, 1995.

George C. Wallace, 1963–1967, 1971–1979, 1983–1987

GLENN T. ESKEW

ETWEEN 1963 and 1987 George Corley Wallace held a virtual monopoly on the governor's office in Alabama, a position that enabled him to promote industrial development, low taxes, and trade schools as the key to the state's future. During the same period, Wallace launched four unsuccessful bids for the presidency on platforms opposing the growth of federal power, all the while shifting his racial views to suit the tenor of the times. Alabama voters elected Wallace governor for an unprecedented four terms, in 1962, 1970, 1974, and 1982, and he served as *de facto* governor during the administration of his wife, Lurleen Burns Wallace, from 1967 to 1968.

George Wallace

Praised by some as a populist and denounced by others as a demagogue, the charismatic Wallace appealed at first to a white, lower-middle- and working-class electorate with his antifederal, racist, states' rights message and then to a white liberal and black electorate with promises of state spending. Despite his support for road construction, education, and industrial development, Wallace's virulent resistance to civil rights, his shortsighted economic vision, and his unbridled ambition for higher political office left behind a mostly negative legacy of unresolved problems that saddled the state with political cynicism and a negative reputation nationally and internationally.

A native of Barbour County, Wallace was born in the railroad town of Clio on August 25, 1919, to George C. Wallace and Mozelle Smith Wallace. Both his father, who owned farmland but wasted the rents on drink, and his paternal grandfather, a teetotaler physician who delivered many of the county's babies, were active in local politics. Young George grew up accompanying them on trips to the courthouse in Clayton. He watched politicians "work" social and religious events such as revivals at his Methodist Church. In 1935, he won a position as page in the state senate and spent the

216
◇

summer in Montgomery meeting state lawmakers including Barbour County's representative, Chauncey Sparks. By then the gaunt fifteen-year-old stood his full height of five feet, eight inches and wore his black hair slicked down and combed back.

Too small to be a football standout, Wallace became a boxer, gaining from it pugnacity and perseverance. The 1936 and 1937 Alabama Golden Glove champion would translate lessons learned from the ring to the political arena. Between 1937 and 1942, Wallace boxed for the University of Alabama while taking prelaw and law school courses. After earning his law degree and signing up for the armed services in 1942, Wallace hung out his shingle in Tuscaloosa. He spent his last few weeks in the university town working for the gubernatorial campaign of Sparks, who guaranteed the young man a job after the war. Wallace also spent that summer of 1942 courting Lurleen Burns, a pert sixteen-year-old sales clerk.

In February 1943 Wallace reported for army air force basic training in Miami Beach, then participated in the college program for cadets at Arkadelphia, Arkansas. There he contracted spinal meningitis, which thwarted his chances of piloting a plane. He recovered in Tuscaloosa where, on May 21, 1943, he married Lurleen. The army taught Wallace the mechanics of B-29 multiengines, commissioned him a sergeant, and ordered him to Alamogordo, New Mexico, for final training. Lurleen and their first child, a daughter, joined him there, and they briefly made a home in a converted chicken coop. Wallace's political ambitions burned continuously so that, during his years of military service, he sent home hundreds of Christmas cards to people in Barbour County, many of whom had no idea who he was.

Wallace served under the command of General Curtis LeMay in the Fifty-eighth Wing of the Twentieth Air Force. From a base in the Pacific, he and his comrades launched bombing attacks on the Japanese throughout the summer of 1945. The unnerving air raids and physical exhaustion from long missions caused Wallace to suffer combat fatigue. Following the bombing of Hiroshima, his crew was transferred to California, a move that signaled the end of the war to Wallace. He refused to fly anymore. Doctors diagnosed severe anxiety and confined him to a hospital, where for two months he recuperated and regained his weight. Wallace received an honorable discharge from the army, medals recognizing his service, and a disability check from the Veterans Administration. The twenty-six-year-old boarded a train for Alabama in December 1945 ready to begin his political career.

Dressed in uniform, Wallace marched into the capitol and asked for the promised job. Governor Sparks arranged for him to work as an assistant attorney general, but in February 1946 Wallace took a leave of absence to run for a seat in the state legislature. He moved his family to Clayton, and for the next three months campaigned across Barbour County. Those wartime Christmas cards paid off, and he won the Democratic primary, returned to Montgomery, and resumed his state job. During the seven months before his swearing in as the state's youngest legislator, Wallace—now a player on Goat Hill—cultivated two groups of politicians, the outgoing Sparks crowd and the incoming Folsomites.

During his two terms in the Alabama legislature—from 1947 to 1953—Wallace wrote trade school and industrial development acts that aligned him with the reformist administration of Governor James E. "Big Jim" Folsom. With Marion County representative Rankin Fite, Wallace pushed through the Trade School Act of 1947, which used a tax on liquor to finance the creation of five state vocational schools. He believed technical training was crucial for building a strong industrial economy and to providing employment for his constituency of rural white voters. The Wallace-Cater Act of 1951 attracted many multinational corporations to Alabama to take advantage of the state-built industrial parks for rent at below cost rates and the nonunion white workers for hire at low wages. Yet this updated version of the South's old colonial economy brought few riches while creating a new dependence on minimum wage jobs. Likewise the trade schools proved less successful in preparing Alabamians for the emerging high-tech service economy.

These actions seemed to align Wallace with the Folsom camp, but he never fully endorsed the radical restructuring of Alabama's government promoted by the governor. Big Jim won election challenging the Black Belt–Big Mule alliance of planters and industrialists that had dominated state politics since Reconstruction. He struck at the roots of this alliance's power through his plans for legislative reapportionment, an expanded biracial electorate, an equitable tax structure, and increased social spending. Through Folsom's first term and the administration of his successor, Gordon Persons, Representative Wallace retained friendly relations with Black Belt leaders on racial and reapportionment issues but opposed Big Mule industrialists on economic issues. In 1948 both Folsom and Wallace were delegates to the Democratic National Convention, and both refused to join other southerners in a bolt of the convention over the party platform's civil rights plank.

After six years in the statehouse, Wallace announced his candidacy for circuit judge of the state's Third Judicial District. Campaigning against Preston Clayton—a wealthy, former anti-Folsom state senator and World War II lieutenant colonel—Wallace announced at rallies that officers should vote for his opponent but that "all you privates vote for me." They did, and Wallace's pseudopopulist rhetoric and sharp retorts became his political hallmarks. Finally generating a steady income, Wallace bought a house in Clayton for his family, which now included three children, two daughters and a son. Almost a decade would pass before the birth of the Wallace's last child, a daughter. Although

Judge Wallace swore off the all-day poker games he enjoyed as a legislator, he remained an absentee father, rarely spending time with his children or Lurleen because of his continued involvement in state politics. Wallace directed Folsom's south Alabama reelection campaign in 1954, using that opportunity to learn political ploys from a master showman and to build his own political base. Soon after Folsom's second term began in 1955, however, Wallace made it clear that he disagreed with the governor's lukewarm support for racial segregation.

This open break with Folsom was part of Wallace's strategy as he prepared to run for governor in 1958. Of the thirteen candidates Wallace faced in the May 1958 Democratic primary, Attorney General John Patterson was the most formidable. Patterson, who had received national attention from his vindication of the murder of his father, ran as a strong segregationist. Wallace, by comparison, seemed more moderate and ran on his legislative record, promising to maintain segregation. When he denounced Patterson's Klan ties, Wallace received the unwanted endorsement of the NAACP and was soundly defeated in the runoff. Wallace later remarked, "John Patterson out-niggered me, and boys, I'm not going to be out-niggered again."

Following this defeat, Wallace returned to the circuit court bench to complete his term and to face the federal government in the first of many showdowns. He had previously earned high marks for fairness from black attorneys who argued cases before him, but he had also used the bench for political gain. Wallace turned a federal judge's demand for voting records in nearby Georgia as an opportunity to grandstand over states' rights, threatening to arrest any federal official who tried that in his jurisdiction. When he realized that this ploy won him publicity and popularity, Wallace sought new confrontations with agents of the federal government.

The U.S. Civil Rights Commission requested Barbour County and Bullock County voting records, and Wallace, who took them from the grand juries for alleged safekeeping, refused to release them to federal agents, threatening to "lock up" anyone who tried to take them. Federal district judge Frank Johnson, a former law school classmate of Wallace, cited the circuit judge with contempt of court for hindering the work of the commission. Faced with jail, Wallace met with his old friend and offered to turn the records back over to the grand juries to give to the commission. Johnson agreed. Wallace then publicly proclaimed that he had "stood up" to the federal government by not personally handing over the records. Irked by this false claim, Judge Johnson criticized Wallace's conduct in an opinion read in open court, but Wallace's empty gesture appealed to many Alabama voters who saw it as a meaningful attack on an ever-encroaching federal government into local affairs.

Against the backdrop of civil rights protests and federal court orders, Wallace organized his 1962 gubernatorial campaign around increasingly ugly rhetoric, calling Judge Johnson "a low-down, carpetbaggin', scalawaggin', race-mixin' liar" and promising to stand in the schoolhouse door to defy federal court orders on desegregation. To shut out the reelection bid of the hard-drinking but still popular Folsom, Wallace vowed that he would never serve liquor in the governor's mansion. Because of drunken antics by Folsom in the last days of the campaign, state senator Ryan deGraffenried edged out the former governor for a spot in the runoff against Wallace. Wallace responded to deGraffenried's racial moderation by emphasizing his own uncompromising opposition to desegregation, and the self-described "Little Fightin' Judge" won the primary with the largest number of votes ever received by a gubernatorial candidate.

Wallace peppered his inaugural speech with demagogic phrases: "I draw the line in the dust and toss the gauntlet before the feet of tyranny. And I say, Segregation now! Segregation tomorrow! Segregation forever!" Such self-serving challenges to federal authority signaled that he would waste state resources fighting the inevitable and sully the image of Alabama. Yet Wallace, although reactionary on race, was progressive or "populist" in his view of the role of state government to help average citizens. He attracted nearly $350 million in expanded and new industries to Alabama, which added nineteen thousand new jobs in 1963 alone. During his first year in office, teachers received a substantial increase in pay, and state employees were given added fringe benefits. His administration expanded the program of providing free textbooks to include the state's high schools. The governor sold $116 million in state bonds to benefit Alabama's colleges and universities and not once meddled in administrative matters or teacher instruction issues, thereby winning the approval of many members of the Alabama Education Association (AEA). Although Wallace was liberal with funding, he never identified a stable formula or source to support public education. He funded new expenditures by increasing the state's regressive sales tax from three to four cents, raising the state's bonded indebtedness, and depending on increased revenues from expansion of the state's industrial base.

The new governor appeared to enjoy campaigning more than administering the state's affairs, and he left many matters in the hands of political appointees who often used their positions for personal gain. Graft abounded as friends won lucrative state contracts and bought state surplus at discount while making large political donations to Wallace's numerous campaigns. The state's technical schools and junior colleges became political plums, placed in counties as payoffs or incentives for votes rather than according to student demand or need. To the twelve schools that existed in 1962, Wallace and the legislature added twenty more, with each member of the state board of education receiving one in his home town. The governor's petty politics were further observed in the construction of the state's interstate highway system.

Wallace used huge amounts of federal funds to pave these modern roadways through rural areas but refused to build them in or around Birmingham, the state's most populous city, because a majority of its voters did not support him.

Wallace administration intervention in civil rights conflicts exacerbated racial tensions in Alabama during his first term as governor. The governor brought the Alabama state patrol under executive control and renamed them the Alabama state troopers, attiring them in uniforms decorated with Confederate battle flags and placing them under the command of hard-nosed and impulsive Colonel Al Lingo. Wallace's mean-spirited rhetoric heightened anxieties during Birmingham's demonstrations that won national attention in the spring of 1963, and the governor interfered with local law enforcement officials by sending Lingo to Birmingham to disrupt the negotiated settlement. On the night of May 11, Wallace's troopers viciously attacked angry blacks who had filled the streets to protest bombings in their community.

When federal courts ordered the desegregation of the University of Alabama, Wallace participated in an elaborate charade that played across the nation's televisions. In an agreement worked out with the U.S. Department of Justice, the feisty governor was allowed to "stand in the schoolhouse door" and backed down only to Alabama adjutant general Henry Graham, who acted on orders of President Kennedy and whose state troops had been federalized to force the registration of two black students. Many observers believe that Wallace's defiant attitude on race encouraged violence. Following his "standing up" to the federal government, Klansmen bombed the Sixteenth Street Baptist Church in Birmingham, killing four young black girls. Wallace's minimal investigation led to no arrests, and no one was convicted for the offense until 1977.

The governor continued to interfere with efforts by local officials to carry out federal desegregation orders. In 1964 Judge Johnson ordered Macon County schools desegregated, and the local school board came up with a plan to implement the order. Wallace forced the board to rescind the plan and sent state troopers to the county to stop integration. Judge Johnson now had clear evidence that state officials controlled local school boards and concluded that he should move forward with a statewide desegregation order. Thus Wallace's uninvited participation in local county affairs actually speeded desegregation in Alabama.

Despite a consistent record of losing his battles with the federal government, through these confrontations Wallace gained national attention, and he decided to enter the 1964 Democratic presidential race. The governor traveled north, and his speeches before Ivy League audiences demonstrated his considerable political savvy. He tempered his racist prose and engaged in playful repartee as he referred to students as "You left-wing, pinko liberals." He claimed that his fight was not about race but about the rise of an all-powerful central government. Wallace won over doubtful audiences with his defense of local voters: "You have the right to run your schools, your businesses, your lives as you see fit" without "bearded beatnik bureaucrats" or "social engineers" telling you what to do. Having claimed that a vote of 15 percent would "shake the eye teeth" of Washington liberals, the Alabama governor seemed victorious when he polled 43 percent in Maryland and carried one-third of the votes in both the Indiana and the Wisconsin Democratic presidential primaries. With a powerful Democratic incumbent sure to win the nomination, Wallace soon gave up his presidential effort. But the 1964 run whetted his appetite for future national campaigns.

Events in Alabama, however, threatened his national image. During a campaign to gain voting rights, black demonstrators joined by white supporters massed for demonstrations in Selma, Alabama, in the early months of 1965. They hoped to dramatize their goals by marching from Selma to the "cradle of the Confederacy," Montgomery. Colonel Lingo won national enmity when he allowed state troopers to beat black and white activists as they crossed the Edmund Pettus Bridge on their way to the capital. Wallace was severely criticized for this incident and, under orders from Judge Johnson, was forced to protect the participants on the rest of their march to Montgomery. Congress passed the 1965 Voting Rights Act as a direct result of the Selma events, fundamentally altering the South's election processes by adding hundreds of thousands of black voters to the rolls. Again, Wallace's defiant actions, rather than saving segregation, hastened the demise of Jim Crow.

Despite these events, Wallace's ambition for the presidency was undiminished, and he needed to hold on to the governor's office as his launching pad. As governor he could demand large campaign contributions from people doing business with the state government and use the perquisites of the office for campaign purposes. Forbidden by the state's 1901 constitution from succeeding himself, Wallace made a bold move when he allowed his legislative lieutenants to introduce a constitutional amendment that would allow future governors, including the incumbent, to succeed themselves. The governor claimed he had no hand in this effort, but when seven state senators engaged in a filibuster that ultimately killed the bill, Wallace attacked each one by name in a statewide television address. Then Wallace hit on the idea of running his wife and serving as her chief advisor. Lurleen, who had recently fought a bout with cancer but appeared to be recovered, agreed to serve as a stand-in candidate so that her husband could "expand his fight" against the "centralization of power by the federal government." The couple campaigned together telling folks to "Stand Up for Alabama," a coded reference to Wallace's choreographed, but unsuccessful, attempt to thwart integration at the University of Alabama.

Lurleen won in an unprecedented landslide, and the people of the state amended the constitution in 1968 to allow future governors to succeed themselves. George moved from the governor's office to one across the hall, and staff personnel began referring to them as Governor Lurleen and Governor George. His wife's 1966 campaign set the stage for Wallace's 1968 presidential race. The theme in both was that "there isn't a dime's worth of difference" between national Democrats and Republicans and that a new, fearless, independent voice was needed to save the country.

In June 1967 Lurleen was discovered to again be battling a virulent cancer. Her friends complained that Wallace's presidential campaign caused him to neglect his wife during her illness, but he was at her bedside with their children when she died on May 7, 1968. The grief-stricken family moved out of the governor's mansion, and Lieutenant Governor Albert Brewer took over the affairs of state. Wallace pledged to support Brewer in the 1970 governor's race. Five weeks later the widower returned to the presidential campaign trail as a candidate for president on the American Independent Party ticket.

Wallace decided to run as an independent candidate for president in 1968, hoping to gain enough electoral votes to throw the election into the U.S. House of Representatives. Although he used many of the same anti–federal government themes that had characterized his previous campaigns, the widespread protests over the Vietnam War and the rise of the "counterculture" furnished him with new material. Wallace, who had counseled defiance of federal law and resistance to legally mandated racial integration, now used the new theme of "law and order." He mocked antiwar demonstrators and used vituperative and sarcastic language to describe the personal lifestyles of those who "dropped out" of the American economic system. Wallace's flag-waving, pro-middle-class rhetoric endeared him to hard-working people all over the country who believed that the rebellious atmosphere of the 1960s was tearing the nation apart. Although polls in September indicated he might draw as much as 20 to 25 percent of the vote, when his vice presidential running mate, General "Bombs Away" Curtis LeMay, advocated using atomic weapons to end the war in Vietnam, Wallace's support began to shrink. Wallace finished with 13 percent of the vote and carried only five southern states, a devastating defeat for him. Unlike the 1964 campaign, the 1968 battle did not strengthen Wallace at home. His constant forays outside the state had begun to embarrass and bother some who had once supported him.

No sooner were the 1968 votes counted than the perennial candidate made plans to again use the governor's office to his advantage in the 1972 presidential race. Wallace ignored his promise to Governor Brewer and announced his candidacy for governor in 1970. This move ignited one of the nastiest gubernatorial races the state had ever witnessed. Brewer, who had served as Wallace's speaker of the house, was a racial moderate favored by progressives in the state. He positioned himself as Alabama's "full time" governor and, therefore, a clear alternative to Wallace's incessant campaigning. Brewer polled a plurality in the primary, but failed to win the necessary majority, forcing a runoff with the former governor. Wallace's presidential ambitions had made him wish to avoid race as an issue in this campaign. But stunned by his second-place finish, he struck back with the proven tactics of racism and dirty tricks. Because of Brewer's strong support from black voters, Wallace's campaign ran advertisements cautioning Alabamians that a vote for the incumbent threatened to turn the state over to the "Black Bloc Vote." Wallace partisans circulated a picture of a young white girl surrounded by black boys under the caption, "This Could Be Alabama Four Years from Now! Is This the Image You Want?" Wallace consistently called the young governor a "sissy-britches" and spread rumors that Brewer's wife was an alcoholic. Perhaps the biggest lie was Wallace's promise that he had no higher political aspirations and that he would be a full-time governor. Brewer attempted to ignore the slander and refused to make race the issue of his campaign, but bigotry, racism, and outrageous lies again succeeded in Alabama politics, and Wallace was returned to the governor's chair.

Wallace brought a new, young wife to his second term as governor. The striking and gregarious Cornelia Ellis Snively first met Wallace in 1947 when, as the niece of Governor Jim Folsom, she and her mother lived for a time in the governor's mansion and attended parties frequented by state legislators. Twenty years his junior, Cornelia married Wallace after the general election but before the inauguration so that she could participate in the festivities. Cornelia replaced Wallace's dark undertaker suits, white shirts, and narrow ties with fashionable color-coordinated ensembles. His hair was now puffed up and sprayed rather than greased. To match the 1970s look, Wallace modified his language to fit a tempered presidential candidate. Because desegregation was a reality, Wallace expressed a slightly less strident approach to court-ordered busing to achieve desegregation while denouncing this as the most recent example of "unconstitutional" federal involvement in state affairs.

In the first months of his second administration, a rebellious state legislature —still under the influence of Brewer—resisted Wallace's initiatives and adjourned without passing a budget. Wallace used his statewide support drummed up by his antibusing rhetoric to force a special session, and this time a chastened legislature approved the budget. It also established the Alabama Office of Consumer Protection and increased both old-age pensions and unemployment compensation. In 1973–74 Wallace won legislative approval of a record educational appropriation and continued his first term's energetic pursuit of new businesses for the state. He also continued his penchant for ignoring most of the daily details of running the state, leaving that in the hands of cabinet members.

In the fall of 1971 Richard Nixon's Justice Department was threatening to prosecute Wallace's brother, Gerald, on charges that he had rigged state bid procedures, received illegal campaign contributions, and accepted kickbacks and payoffs on which he neglected to pay taxes. A Wallace advisor, Seymour Trammell, had been convicted on similar charges and was serving a term in jail. He later charged that "Nixon and Wallace made a deal" whereby Wallace announced he would not run in 1972 as the candidate of the American Independent Party but would seek the Democratic nomination instead. In response, the Nixon Justice Department declared that it was closing its investigation of the Wallaces. Wallace entered the 1972 Democratic presidential primaries and forced the political debate to the right as Nixon and several of the contenders for the Democratic nomination began to echo versions of Wallace's anti–federal government attack. Neglecting his job back home, the Alabama governor spent fifty-two of the seventy-five days before the Florida primary campaigning in that state. He won 42 percent of the vote in Florida, sweeping past his rivals. Wallace placed second in the Wisconsin, Pennsylvania, and Indiana primaries. Although the delegate system put in place by national party rules limited Wallace's ability to broker a deal, his popular showing was something else for both political parties to consider.

On May 15, 1972, Wallace traveled to Maryland for a campaign appearance at a strip mall parking lot in Laurel. It was the last day of that state's primary campaign. There, would-be assassin Arthur Bremer waited until Wallace finished his speech and moved into the crowd before firing five shots into the governor. Wallace fell to the pavement, never to walk again. Surgery revealed that a bullet had bisected several nerves that controlled his lower bodily functions, and he was left in constant pain. The next day Wallace won the Maryland and Michigan primaries as voters continued to register their opposition to busing and their concerns about crime. His absence from the campaign trail led to his defeat in future primaries, and liberal Democrat George McGovern was nominated. During Wallace's recuperation in Maryland, Lieutenant Governor Jere Beasley became acting governor of Alabama. Released from the hospital to attend the Democratic National Convention in July 1972, a wheelchair-bound Wallace received an ovation when he addressed the delegates, but they ignored his pleas to adopt more moderate stances and to move the party to the center.

Where once his caretaker government ran Alabama while he was out of state campaigning, now it managed affairs while he sought treatment for his painful paralysis, recurrent peritonitis, or one of the other complications that came in the wake of the shooting. Wallace suffered deep depressions and turned to faith healers, became a born-again Christian, and tried acupuncture and experimental treatments. His prior good health, a strict regimen of physical therapy, and learning that many believed he was washed up politically brought him back fighting. A year after the assassination attempt, he stood strapped to a podium and addressed the state legislature on local issues. It was an amazing and emotional event that secured his political comeback. In 1974 he won reelection, the first person in the state's history to be elected to a third term. To secure his election Wallace greased the system with plenty of pork, especially in black neighborhoods, which suddenly saw their local roads paved by the state. Several black leaders jumped on board the Wallace campaign, and he won reelection with 65 percent of the vote, the largest margin ever posted in a primary. Approximately 25 percent of black voters cast their ballots for Wallace in the Democratic primary of 1974.

In his third term as governor, Wallace stepped up his efforts to reconcile the races while laying the groundwork for a final bid at the presidency. His 1975 inaugural featured a black choir, and Wallace promised to represent "all our citizens . . . black or white." He joined his old civil rights nemesis, the Reverend Ralph David Abernathy, in accepting honorary degrees from the historically black Alabama State University, which, in a bizarre revision of history, cited Wallace for his "good judgment and official restraint" during the 1960s. When Wallace explained to a black audience at Montgomery's Dexter Avenue Baptist Church that his past actions had not been racially motivated but federally provoked, the congregation responded by singing the "Battle Hymn of the Republic." The governor met with the Reverend Martin Luther King Sr. and expressed his sorrow over the murder of King's son. Few could have anticipated such a transformation on the race issue, but Wallace's neglect of state government changed very little.

Although he consistently supported pay increases for Alabama's public school teachers and deserves much of the credit for moving their salary levels near the national average by the mid-1980s, the state still languished near the bottom of the nation in per student spending through all of Wallace's administrations. Commissions that study state governments and other observers uniformly recommended raising the state's property tax to meet the revenue shortfall, but Wallace refused to consider this alternative until late in his fourth term. The state's general fund, from which the noneducation functions of state government were financed, also lacked a stable funding source. When faced with budget shortfalls or emergency funding crises, the governor and legislature resorted to stop-gap measures that merely postponed the problem.

Within this framework in 1971 and again in 1975, when the general fund received far less revenue than lawmakers had appropriated for highways and other state programs, the governor attempted to redirect money from the state's educational fund in order to resolve the problem. Certain state taxes are earmarked for education only, but Wallace recommended that a portion of these designated revenues be placed in the general fund. He abandoned the plan in 1971 when legislators and the teacher's lobby of the AEA lined up in opposition. Four years later, the governor engaged in a heated battle over the same issue, appearing on statewide television to attack the AEA for its opposition to his scheme. Despite the low level of school funding, Wallace claimed that a huge surplus existed in the education fund that could be used elsewhere. In a special legislative session the teachers' group finally agreed to a compromise allowing a small portion of the education revenues to be redirected, but it amounted to far less than the governor sought. In a related event, the 1975–76 fiscal year began on October 1 without the legislature appropriating funds to meet the state's essential functions. Wallace used an opinion from the state's attorney general to begin spending money to keep state government running. When a state court judge declared his actions an unconstitutional violation of the separation of powers, he appealed the decision to the state supreme court and lost. A special session of the legislature finally resolved the impasse.

A number of federal court orders affected Wallace's second and third terms. On March 12, 1971, federal judge Frank M. Johnson ordered the state to provide adequate and effective treatment to all patients being held in Alabama's mental health facilities. Subsequent rulings from Johnson's court forced Wallace's administrations to increase significantly the funding for mental institutions.

Another federal court order mandated an end to the state's discriminatory property tax system, required equalization of those taxes, and demanded a rational basis for any differences that were left in Alabama's property tax rates. In 1972 the legislature responded to the ruling by adopting a new system of property assessment that valued individually owned, residential property at 15 percent of real market value and allowed huge tracts of valuable forest and agricultural lands to be assessed at a similarly low value. Not content with these low assessments, in 1978 the Alabama Farm Bureau and the Alabama Forestry Association—private lobbying groups who represented large landowners— pushed through a "current use" concept that allowed the assessment of land to be based on how it was used rather than on its real market value. Thus, the tax burden on large landowners declined while state and local sales taxes levied on all Alabamians without regard to their ability to pay increased. The need to fund education through an adequate and predictable source such as property tax revenues was ignored, leaving the state to pay most of the cost of its educational services through inconsistent, unpredictable, and unfair sales tax revenues.

In January 1976, Wallace's old nemesis, Judge Frank Johnson, declared that Alabama's prison system was operating in a manner that violated the "cruel and unusual punishment" section of the Bill of Rights. Johnson ordered remedial measures that required huge outlays of money. Infuriated by the order, which embarrassed Wallace during his 1976 presidential campaign, the recurrent candidate returned to an old theme: "Thugs and federal judges" had taken control of state government and were attempting to create a "hotel atmosphere" in the prisons that would make them "a vacation resort." Wallace postponed action until the order could be appealed to the U.S. Supreme Court. Late in 1978, the high court upheld Johnson, although it was left to the next governor, Fob James, to deal with this problem. Johnson had issued so many orders forcing the state government to meet its constitutional duties that some wags began to call him "the real governor" of Alabama.

Despite all the problems at home, Wallace made a final bid for the presidency in 1976, running under the slogan "Trust the People" and on a repackaged version of his 1968 platform, which had opposed busing, promoted law and order, favored lowered taxes for the middle class, and promoted a beefed-up military. With Wallace's heath in question, voters turned to another southerner and Washington outsider, Jimmy Carter. Wallace threw his support to Carter, and in a speech to the Democratic convention again exhorted the party and the nation: "The monster bureaucracy is driving people in this country nuts. It should get off their backs and out of their pocketbooks."

Wallace closed his third term as governor by divorcing his wife after a bitter public dispute with her. Unable to prove her contention that he had hidden millions of dollars, Cornelia was awarded $75,000, which the court had determined was one-third of his verifiable assets in 1978. Wallace was not rich, and as he left the governor's office, the University of Alabama at Birmingham offered him a position as a consultant and fund-raiser. He lectured there and occasionally at Auburn University, but academe did not suit him, nor did political retirement. He considered running for the U.S. Senate but feared the isolation from his family and friends and the distance from his doctors. In 1981, he married again, this third time to a thirty-three-year-old blond divorcee, Lisa Taylor, the daughter of a Walker County coal mine owner. Lisa, with her sister, had once formed the Mona and Lisa duo that entertained crowds during Wallace's 1968 presidential race. Boasting a new and much younger wife, Wallace once more hit the campaign trail.

Black voters provided the margin that reelected Wallace for an unprecedented fourth term as governor in 1982. Times were bad in Alabama as the Carter recession rolled into the Reagan administration. Promising to be a friend of the poor, Wallace ran against Reaganomics, a powerful platform in a state suffering 15 percent unemployment. He received one-third of the black vote in the initial primary and increased that support to defeat Lieutenant Governor George McMillan in the Democratic primary runoff by a breathtakingly close 1 percentage point. In the general election, Wallace carried 90 percent of the black electorate, which he linked with rural voters and members of the Alabama Education Association to form a coalition that easily defeated a Republican challenge by Montgomery mayor Emory Folmar.

His 1983 inaugural seemed light years away from his first one that occurred two decades earlier. A black Alabamian led the Pledge of Allegiance, and another gave the benediction. There were no parades, and a band's playing of "Dixie" was the only relic from the Confederacy or the "old" Wallace. Despite the governor's declining physical condition, his last term may well have been his most productive. Wallace worked out an agreement with trial lawyers and business and labor leaders to create new workplace liability rules for job-related injuries. Improvements in Alabama's prisons and mental health facilities led the federal government to phase out its control over these programs. In one of the most important actions of his last term as governor, the aging and often ailing Wallace won passage of a constitutional amendment that created the Alabama Trust Fund that protected the corpus while investing the interest derived from offshore leases on Alabama oil and natural gas into the general operating fund of the state.

Stating that he wanted the main focus of his fourth term to be "jobs, jobs, jobs," Wallace continued to appeal to multinational corporations to locate their businesses in the state. He demonstrated his "born-again" status by appointing more than one hundred blacks to advisory panels. Wallace increased funding for education through a $310 million bond issue, but he, too, was forced to prorate education budgets during periods when income did not match planned outlays. Although Wallace enjoyed support from some of the state's most powerful factions—the AEA, organized labor, black political organizations, and trial lawyers, his late and weak attempt to get the legislature to provide a more stable source of funding for education through increased property or income taxes failed.

Wallace's health deteriorated, and his pain increased, causing him to be hospitalized on numerous occasions during his fourth and final term. He regularly used painkillers and took antidepressants but feared leaving office and longed to run again. This time his advisors discouraged the notion. In a tearful, emotional appearance before the media, the political Wallace bade Alabama a "fond adieu." A month after leaving office in January 1987, he and his third wife were divorced. He accepted a sinecure with Troy State University and, over the next decade, settled into the life of the retired elder statesman, investing his energies into the political career of his son and namesake, George Wallace Jr. After numerous hospitalizations, Wallace died in a Montgomery hospital on September 13, 1998, and was buried in the capital city's Greenwood Cemetery.

There is an irony about Wallace as governor. It is possible, indeed likely, that because of his constant forays into presidential politics Wallace may have spent less time at actually running the state than anyone else previously in the position. Nonetheless, he is unquestionably the most significant of the state's governors. He entered office during a period of social transition, and, instead of endorsing the fundamental changes taking place, he chose to defend a dying system. After encouraging a violent atmosphere, he became violence's victim. Wallace recanted and repented, seeking forgiveness from those he had wronged. Yet his conservative influence was widespread; his antigovernment rhetoric and demonization of the federal government had affected the language and policies of both national political parties. Certainly in Alabama the indelible images of the racist Wallace, like the phantom pains he felt in his body after being shot, continue to haunt the state.

References

Carroll, Peter N. *Famous in America: The Passion to Succeed: Jane Fonda, George Wallace, Phyllis Schlafly, John Glenn.* New York: Dutton, 1985.

Carter, Dan T. *The Politics of Rage: George Wallace, the Origins of the New Conservatism, and the Transformation of American Politics.* New York: Simon and Schuster, 1995.

Frady, Marshall. *Wallace.* New York: World Publishing, 1968.

Lesher, Stephan. *George Wallace: American Populist.* Reading, Mass.: Addison-Wesley, 1994.

Permaloff, Anne, and Carl Grafton. *Political Power in Alabama: The More Things Change—.* Athens: University of Georgia Press, 1995.

Rogers, William Warren, Robert David Ward, Leah Rawls Atkins, and Wayne Flynt. *Alabama: The History of a Deep South State.* Tuscaloosa: University of Alabama Press, 1994.

Lurleen B. Wallace, 1967–May 1968

GLENN T. ESKEW

WHEN Governor Lurleen Burns Wallace died from cancer after a short sixteen months in office as the stand-in for her husband, George Corley Wallace, Alabamians genuinely mourned the loss of not only the first woman to be elected to the position but also someone with whom many of the state's average citizens could relate. Never a politician, Mrs. Wallace ran for governor in 1966 to facilitate her husband's run for president in 1968. Like her husband, she defiantly denounced federal court-ordered desegregation. The Lurleen Wallace administration is not remembered for great amounts of important legislation, although she did succeed in drawing attention to the state's deplorable treatment of the mentally ill and the need for more state parks and recreational facilities. Sadly, she is remembered most for the time and energy she spent seeking treatment for the cancer that claimed her life.

Lurleen Wallace

Lurleen Wallace was born into a working-class family on September 19, 1926, and had she not been smitten by a charismatic attorney, she probably would have remained in that environment. Although the family occasionally farmed, her father, Henry Morgan Burns, worked as a bargeman in Northport on the Black Warrior River and later as a crane operator in wartime Mobile while her mother, Janie Estelle Burroughs Burns, managed the household. Something of a tomboy as a child, the attractive, green-eyed, and slightly built five-foot, two-inch tall woman had a lifelong passion for fishing. After completing her formal education at Tuscaloosa County High School in 1942, she began working as a sales clerk in the local Kress five-and-dime store, where she soon met George Wallace. He was just graduated from the University of Alabama's School of Law and was awaiting induction into the armed services. After a brief courtship, George left for basic training but returned to Tuscaloosa to recuperate from meningitis. He and Lurleen married on May 21, 1943, while he was on furlough; he was twenty-four, and she was sixteen.

During the war, the couple moved in and out of rooms they rented near army bases in Texas and at Montgomery and Clayton, Alabama. After the war, Lurleen supported George's run for the state legislature from Barbour County by becoming the sole breadwinner of the family and by writing campaign letters for him, even though she was too young to vote. After two terms in the state legislature George won election as state circuit judge for the Third Judicial District. This position provided enough income to allow the Wallaces to purchase a home in Clayton for their growing family. The job of raising the children—two daughters and one son at that time—fell to Lurleen because, even as a judge, Wallace remained consumed by politics and was often absent as a father. Her loneliness was filled by her best friends and closet confidants in Clayton, Mary Jo Ventress, a home economics teacher, and Catherine Steineker, a homemaker who later served as her personal secretary.

Ever the dutiful wife, Mrs. Wallace assisted George in his many campaigns. She accompanied him during his first governor's race in 1958 but remained reticent and shy of crowds. After his defeat in that election and the loss of his judicial position, George moved the family to Montgomery to begin working on his 1962 gubernatorial campaign. When she became aware of George's adultery, the long-suffering Lurleen threatened him with divorce, an act that would surely have ruined his political career. He convinced her to remain married, and on George's election as governor in 1962 Lurleen Wallace assumed the responsibilities of First Lady. Although she maintained that role, the shy Lurleen disliked playing hostess and declined invitations to join social clubs. In public she always appeared smartly dressed in tailored outfits of blazers and turtlenecks, knit skirts, or dress suits. In private she smoked cigarettes, drank abundant amounts of coffee and an occasional beer, and preferred to dress in hunting pants.

After Governor George Wallace's schoolhouse stand in 1963 and an aborted presidential bid in 1964, it was clear that Wallace intended to run for president again in 1968. Kept from succeeding himself as governor by provisions of the 1901 constitution, Wallace would soon lose the perks of office that facilitated his presidential aspirations. He resolved to hold on to the position by running his wife for the office in his stead and to become her "$1 a year chief advisor." Mrs. Wallace had already undergone treatment for cancer, and many believed she agreed to run for governor out of misguided loyalty and at her own peril.

As the 1966 campaign began, Lurleen Wallace would say a few carefully prepared remarks before she introduced her husband, who then lectured the crowd on federal abuses. As the campaign lengthened, she grew more brave and began to speak off the cuff, sometimes giving whole talks in George's absence. She became a candidate in her own right, remembering key people, shaking hands, and making promises. In an almost unprecedented demonstration of popularity, Mrs. Wallace won the Democratic primary without a runoff. She had defeated nine male opponents, including former governors Folsom and Patterson, Congressman Carl Elliott, Attorney General Richmond Flowers, and others. She went on to defeat easily the Republican candidate, Congressman Jim Martin of Gadsden, Alabama, in the November general election to become the first, and so far only, woman governor of Alabama and only the third woman governor in America's history to that time.

For the first five months of her administration, Mrs. Wallace was healthy enough to act as the actual governor of the state. Yet many observed that George's entire administration remained in place despite, as a female journalist noted, "some little womanly touches, a moment's silent prayer for the boys in Vietnam, and sentences beginning with 'as a wife and mother.'" George Wallace took an office across the hall from his wife, and the staff referred to them as Governor Lurleen and Governor George.

Nonetheless, Mrs. Wallace brought to her governorship concerns that sometimes differed from those of her husband, and hers was not simply rule by proxy. Her first executive order directed the state treasurer to deposit state revenues only in banks that agreed to pay at least 2 percent interest on funds on deposit for more than thirty days. She continued the state's fight against federal control of education and promised to use every legal weapon to resist the guidelines for racial integration of schools issued by the U.S. Department of Health, Education, and Welfare. In a move with import for her spouse, the legislature finally passed and the people ratified an amendment to the 1901 constitution allowing future governors to succeed themselves.

After touring the Bryce and Partlow mental institutions in Tuscaloosa in February 1967, a visibly shaken governor recommended more spending to renovate the old hospital and school and to increase the staff and number of beds. She proposed a $15 million bond issue that the legislature passed in March and voters approved in December. Governor Lurleen enlisted the popular football coaches from Auburn and Alabama to head a drive to raise funds to build a chapel for the facilities. She advocated improving state parks and providing for the elderly, but she wanted most to be remembered as the governor "who did something about mental health."

Admiration and respect for the delicate Lurleen grew during her months as governor as she brought to the office a charm that allayed most opposition and a bravery that enabled her to face a horrific death. Evidence of cancer had first appeared during the caesarean delivery of her fourth and last child in 1961. Although George was informed of the questionable tissue, Lurleen was never told, and no follow-up treatment was done. With the diagnosis of uterine cancer in November 1965, doctors prescribed six weeks of radiation treatments and then performed a hysterectomy, which the George Wallace administration reported as a "female operation." Mrs. Wallace recovered to run for office, but only five months after becoming governor she told a close friend: "I won't be here a year from now." The pain had returned. By late June, the governor's office reported that tests confirmed a recurrence of cancer. Her doctors recommended that she consult at the M. D. Anderson Clinic in Houston, Texas. There, surgeons removed a metastasis from her colon and began radiation treatments that caused cramps and nausea. In her long absences, a caretaker government managed affairs of state, and George campaigned for president.

A frail governor briefly returned to her office in late summer but was back in Houston by mid-September for seven more weeks of radiation. Despite her desperate weakness and pain, she joined George in California in November 1967 as he succeeded in getting his name on that state's ballot as an independent candidate for president of the United States. Mrs. Wallace was home for Christmas, but in early January 1968 doctors recommended betatron radiation to destroy the numerous tumors they had discovered. In an attempt to relieve the excruciating pain, surgeons performed a colostomy in February, a surgery that left the already weakened governor bedridden. She at first refused morphine but by month's end accepted the doses offered. Throughout the spring of 1968, the governor underwent repeated surgical procedures at St. Margaret's Hospital in Montgomery and received spiritual comfort from the minister of the St. James Methodist Church. On April 13, 1968, she returned to the governor's mansion to die. Only family and close friends were allowed to visit; she was reduced to a weight of less than eighty-five pounds. High school bands serenaded her with "Dixie" outside her window. For much of those last weeks of her life, George was campaigning in Arkansas and Texas, yet when told that she had another abscess that needed draining, she asked, "Well, what does George think about that?" She died at the age of forty-one on May 7, 1968, with her family surrounding her.

The body of Governor Lurleen Burns Wallace lay in state in the capitol rotunda, an honor previously afforded only to Jefferson Davis, and more than thirty thousand Alabamians passed by in respect. Once again, George overrode Lurleen's desires and, against her wishes to have a closed casket, ordered it opened. The Poor People's Campaign, assembled on the outskirts of Montgomery, canceled its scheduled protest in the city. Mourners who gathered at St. James Methodist applauded Georgia's segregationist governor Lester Maddox as he arrived for the funeral. Such reminders that Lurleen Wallace served the state during the momentous upheaval of the civil rights era seemed incongruous with the "modesty and humility" eulogized by the Reverend John Vickers. Her life struck a deep chord among many of the state's working-class population who admired her devotion to family, loyalty to an often disloyal husband, and unpretentious good nature. It is little wonder that her popularity had increased throughout her term. Lurleen Burns Wallace was not the most important governor of the state, but she may well have been its most loved.

234
◇

References

Carter, Dan. *The Politics of Rage: George Wallace, the Origins of the New Conservatism, and the Transformation of American Politics.* New York: Simon and Schuster, 1995.

House, Jack. *Lady of Courage: The Story of Lurleen Burns Wallace.* Montgomery: League Press, 1969.

Smith, Anita. *The Intimate Story of Lurleen Wallace: Her Crusade of Courage.* Edited by Ron Gibson. Montgomery: Communications Unlimited, 1969.

Albert P. Brewer, May 1968–1971

GORDON E. HARVEY

I
N MAY 1968 Governor Lurleen Wallace lost her long and valiant struggle
against cancer, and Lieutenant Governor Albert Preston Brewer was thrust
into the governor's chair. Brewer, the only governor in Alabama's history
to hold the offices of speaker, lieutenant governor, and governor in succession,
had a personal style that was different from the Wallaces'. In his thirty-three
months as governor of Alabama he established by executive order Alabama's
first code of ethics for state employees, decreased the power of special interests
in the capital, and formed a constitutional reform commission. Brewer brought
to the office a zeal for efficiency and economy in state government and a desire
to make Alabama's public education system worthy of national respect.

Brewer was born on October 26, 1928, in Bethel Springs, Tennessee, to
Daniel Austin Brewer and Clara Alberter Yarber Brewer. While Albert was
still a child, his father relocated the family to Decatur, Alabama, in order to
work for the Tennessee Valley Authority. Albert remained in Decatur until 1946
when he enrolled in the University of Alabama, where he carried a double
major in history and political science and worked at a local
drugstore. In 1952 Brewer was graduated from the University of
Alabama School of Law, where he had become close friends
with other students who became major figures in Alabama's
history during the last half of the twentieth century. These
friendships proved invaluable to Brewer during his years in
government.

235
◇

Brewer returned to Decatur and established a law practice. In 1954 Morgan County's state representative retired, and
Brewer was prodded by local business and community leaders to
run for the vacant seat. He was initially reluctant to run because   *Brewer*
he had married Martha Farmer, was now the father of one child,
and needed to put his practice on its feet. But the potential for new clients,
visibility, and a desire to pursue his interest in public service convinced him
to run.

Brewer won and entered the legislature in 1955, where he joined many of
his old law school pals. This core of young, professional, enthusiastic legislators
held progressive ideas on education, reapportionment of the state legislature,

modernization of rules for the legal profession, highway improvements, and economic development. Elected in 1958 and 1962 to second and third terms, in 1963 the thirty-four-year-old Brewer defeated better-known candidates to become one of the youngest speakers of the state house in Alabama's history. He enjoyed Governor Wallace's stamp of approval, and his congenial and urbane demeanor made him popular with other legislators.

Although considered a "Wallace-man," Brewer was able to remain relatively independent of Wallace, who enjoyed running for office but according to Brewer, "didn't want to be bothered with governing." By 1966, with Wallace unable to succeed himself, Brewer considered a run for governor but gave up that idea with the entry of Lurleen Wallace into the race. Brewer held no illusions that he could win if she ran. He decided, therefore, to run for lieutenant governor, and—with support from Wallace's close political friends, organized labor, and urban areas—he defeated his opponent by a vote of more than four to one. As lieutenant governor, Brewer supported Governor Lurleen Wallace and, on his own, initiated establishment of a state educational study commission that later provided the framework for his educational reform package as governor. During early 1968, Lieutenant Governor Brewer, along with other Alabama attorneys, went into northern states to help former governor George Wallace get his name on state ballots as an independent candidate for president.

At Lurleen Wallace's death on May 7, 1968, Brewer became governor, the first lieutenant governor to take the office in this manner under the 1901 constitution. He replaced only a few of Wallace's aides with his own and gave all who worked for him just one directive: "Get the job done, eliminate waste, provide service." One of the first differences people noticed about Brewer as governor was his different style and disposition from George Wallace. The *Anniston Star* described Brewer as a man with a "neat, open, 'nice guy' appearance," who used light wit and irony to get a message across. Nonetheless, many Alabamians continued to perceive Brewer as a Wallace man and wondered whether he could become his own person. Three of Brewer's initial actions as governor moved him away from Wallace's style of governing. He established a state motor pool and cut in half the use of personal state vehicles, saving the state more than $500,000 a year. He centralized departmental computers into one unified system, which saved the state another $1 million annually. Finally, Brewer left vacant many of the "crony" jobs in the governor's cabinet, positions that had long been awarded to political operatives.

Brewer's greatest contribution came in the area of education. In 1969 he moved through the legislature one of the most successful education reform packages ever passed in Alabama. During the previous year, Alabama had funded education at $200 less per child than the national average and $81 less than the southeast average, with only Mississippi providing less. Alabama's teachers' salaries ranked forty-sixth in the nation. Brewer called a special session of the legislature and held presession meetings with ten to twenty legislators at a time to hammer out details of the package and to flatter them with his personal attention. In a tribute to his hands-on attention and his skill at governing, his reform package passed. The Alabama Commission for Higher Education was established, and the Alabama Education Study Commission was given permanent status. State support for school districts was equalized, education appropriations were increased more than $100 million over the next two years, and teachers received a pay increase of 12.9 percent with a conditional appropriation for another 8.2 percent raise to be implemented a year later. In a brief tenure of many successes, this was Brewer's finest moment.

Brewer believed that federal court–ordered integration guidelines were causing white flight from public schools and a growth in private education that, over time, eroded public support for the tax base that supported public education in the state. Viewed as a racial moderate, the young governor supported the right of parents to choose their children's schools, actively resisted federal court orders, and appealed for patience and time from the courts in order to ease the state into integration. The courts had run out of patience, and the state had run out of time because of the rancorous shenanigans of Brewer's predecessors. During his brief, two-plus years as governor, Brewer, with his soft-spoken, nonconfrontational manner, allowed race relations in the state to improve. More blacks held public office, and racial confrontations declined.

Despite his less-belligerent style, Brewer displayed familiar conservatism in certain areas. A lifelong Baptist, he attempted to enforce Alabama's 1907 obscenity law, which banned nudity outside of art galleries, and he ordered the closing of drive-in movies showing X-rated films. In an action popular with most "patriotic" Alabamians, he backed the decision of Auburn University's president to ban Reverend William Sloane Coffin from appearing on campus because of his open advocacy of draft evasion during the Vietnam War.

Confident of his popularity and believing that Wallace was not going to seek the governorship again, in 1969 Brewer announced his decision to run for a full term. Shortly before the filing deadline, Wallace declared his candidacy. In a hard-fought campaign, Brewer ran on his record as governor, asserting that the state needed a "full time governor" and reminding voters of Wallace's constant campaigns, which kept him out of the state. With support from a coalition that combined blacks, upper-class whites, and educated middle-class whites, Brewer shocked Wallace by running first in the Democratic primary. News of Wallace's second-place finish circled the world. In the runoff campaign, the contest turned vicious. The Wallace camp whispered claims—ultimately proved true—of Republican support for Brewer's candidacy, spread vicious and untrue rumors about Brewer's family, and doctored photographs to show Brewer in friendly poses with controversial black activists. Wallace supporters covered Brewer bumper stickers with their own that read, "I'm for B & B: Brewer and the Blacks." Brewer refused to attack the Wallace administration until near the end of the runoff campaign. It was too little, too late. Playing both the race and class cards, Wallace defeated Brewer by thirty-four thousand votes, dashing any hopes that Alabama might enter the "New South" era that other southern states were enjoying.

Brewer returned to the practice of law and ran for governor one last time in 1978. He was confronted in that campaign with evidence that his 1970 political operatives had secretly accepted more than $400,000 in contributions from Richard Nixon's Committee to Re-Elect the President (CREEP). Nixon, who had barely won the presidency in 1968 because of Wallace's run as a third-party candidate, badly wanted Wallace defeated by Brewer in 1970 so that he would have no base from which to run again for president in 1972. As this connection between the Nixon and Brewer campaigns became known during the Watergate hearings and with Nixon forced from office, Brewer's political support eroded. Despite his clear reform credentials, Alabama voters rejected Brewer and gave the Democratic nomination to nonpolitician and businessman Fob James.

Brewer is presently Distinguished Professor of Law and Government at Samford University's Cumberland School of Law. He enjoys the status of respected elder statesman and is often called on to serve on commissions that make recommendations to the governor and legislature. In *The Transformation of Southern Politics*, authors Jack Bass and Walter DeVries assert that Alabama's political development was frozen by the influence of George Wallace. Albert Brewer was the state's best chance to bring on a much-needed thaw, and his brief tenure as governor provided the state with a glimpse of what Alabama might be after the Wallace ice age.

References

Anniston Star.

Bass, Jack, and Walter DeVries. *The Transformation of Southern Politics: Social Change and Political Consequence since 1945.* New York: Basic Books, 1976.

Birmingham News.

Brewer, Albert. Papers. Alabama Department of Archives and History, Montgomery.

Brewer, Albert Preston. Interview by Gordon E. Harvey. Birmingham, Alabama, October 15, 1997. Transcript in possession of author.

Montgomery Advertiser.

Rogers, William Warren, Robert David Ward, Leah Rawls Atkins, and Wayne Flynt. *Alabama: The History of a Deep South State.* Tuscaloosa: University of Alabama Press, 1994.

Jere Beasley Sr., June–July 1972

MARGARET E. ARMBRESTER AND SAMUEL L. WEBB

I N JULY 1972 after several weeks in a Maryland hospital, George Wallace was recovered enough from the would-be assassin's gunshot wounds to attend the Democratic National Convention in Miami. Rather than fly directly to Florida, Governor Wallace ordered his plane to land for mere minutes on a strip at the Montgomery airport. He was on a mission. In accord with the state's constitution, Lieutenant Governor Jere Locke Beasley had become acting governor of Alabama for a five-week period because of Wallace's long absence from the state. By touching down, Wallace regained the governorship.

Beasley's brief service as chief of state appeared to give him a natural lead in future races for governor. Fate is fickle, however, and he joined Albert Brewer and Bill Baxley as one of the "Three B's" who lost to the lesser-known Fob James in the 1978 Democratic primary. The candidate returned to his private practice of law and does not include his service as governor in a list of accomplishments provided by his office.

239
◇

Beasley was born on December 12, 1935, in Tyler, Texas, to Browder Locke Beasley and Florence Camp Beasley. His family moved to Alabama during the depression to make a living at farming and managing a mom-and-pop grocery. Beasley was graduated from Clayton High School in 1954 and completed a major in economics from Auburn University in 1959. During a brief hiatus from his studies, he joined the army and ultimately earned the rank of captain in a military police company. In 1958 he married Sara Baker of Adamsville, Alabama, and they subsequently had three children, two daughters and a son. Beasley earned his law degree from the University of Alabama School of Law in 1962, finishing first in his class. After brief tenures in Tuscaloosa and Clayton law firms, in 1965 the young lawyer opened his own office as a single practitioner, and in 1966 others joined him to create the firm of Beasley, Williams, and Robertson with offices in the Barbour County cities of Clayton and Eufaula.

Beasley

In 1968 Beasley managed the election campaign of Senator Jim Allen with such success that he decided to run for office himself. He was immediately successful and in 1970 won the Democratic primary for lieutenant governor

Jere Beasley Sr.
1972

during George Wallace's second term. Beasley had been a close associate of Wallace and was thought to be favorable to his fellow Barbour Countian's governorship. As lieutenant governor, however, he organized the state senate in such a fashion that he, and not the governor, controlled that body. Not surprisingly, this led to animosity between the two.

In 1972, while campaigning for president on the Democratic ticket, Wallace was shot at close range by Arthur Bremer. His recuperation in Maryland kept the governor out of the state more than the proscribed twenty days set by the 1901 constitution. Beasley became acting governor for a matter of weeks in 1972, and nothing substantive occurred during that time. As soon as he was able, Wallace returned to the state—literally for minutes only—to regain his position as governor of the state.

At the end of his term as lieutenant governor, Beasley remained in Montgomery, where he opened a law office and planned his losing 1978 run at the governor's chair, which ended his political career. In recent years the fill-in governor has concentrated on building his law practice and has earned national notoriety for the large settlements his firm wins for its clients. An active member of local and national associations of trial lawyers, he remained in the news as an opponent of tort reform efforts in Alabama during the 1980s and 1990s. He has not sought public office since his defeat in the 1978 governor's race.

240

◇ References

Beasley, Jere Sr. Information provided by Beasley's law firm to authors.
Montgomery Advertiser.
Who's Who in America, 1973.

VI

The Post-Wallace Era

At the end of the twentieth century, the United States faced new challenges. The iron curtain came down, and the cold war ended, but smaller and more complicated ethnic and village wars broke out, requiring units of Alabama's National Guard to serve in the Persian Gulf, Bosnia, and Somalia. In 1992 a patrician Republican was defeated by a popular Arkansas governor who became the first Democrat since Franklin D. Roosevelt to serve two full terms as president and the second in the nation's history to survive the impeachment process.

The state of Alabama also faced new challenges. The post-Wallace era was marked by the election of two Republican governors, with the felony conviction and removal from office of one and the antics and antifederal threats of another. Alabamians in the heart of the Bible Belt elected a Democratic governor apparently on the sole issue of creating a state lottery to support public education, then surprised him by refusing to vote for a lottery. Old issues of federal intrusion into state affairs were revisited in the 1990s, and "everything old seemed new again."

History requires distance, and we are not yet sure of the significance of any of the state's more recent governors. We are certain that the past informs the future, that Alabama politics continues to engage interesting participants, and that the state continues to reflect its own peculiar set of priorities and values.

Forrest ("Fob") James Jr., 1979–1983, 1995–1999

WILLIAM H. STEWART

ORREST Hood ("Fob") James Jr. has the distinction of being the only person ever elected governor of Alabama first as a Democrat and then as a Republican. In this respect he is an appropriate transitional figure in Alabama as state politics moved from being dominated by the Democratic Party to a competitive two-party system.

Fob James was born on September 15, 1934, in Lanett, Alabama, to Forrest Hood James and Rebecca Ellington James. He and his father (and his son and grandson) bear the names of the Confederate generals Nathan Bedford Forrest and John Bell Hood. The elder James was also nicknamed Fob. Young Fob attended public schools in Lanett and West Point, Georgia, before transferring to the private Baylor Military Academy in Chattanooga, Tennessee, when he was a sophomore in high school.

A talented football player, James returned to Alabama in 1952 for college and won Movietone and International News Service's All-American status as a member of Coach Ralph "Shug" Jordan's Auburn (Alabama Polytechnic Institute at the time) Tigers squad. He received his bachelor of science degree in civil engineering in 1956. On August 20, 1955, before he entered his senior year at Auburn, he eloped with the school's homecoming queen, Bobbie May Mooney of Decatur.

Following his graduation, James played professional football for the Montreal Alouettes in the Canadian Football League for one year during the 1956 season. At the termination of his brief football career, the future governor served two years as a lieutenant in the U.S. Army Corp of Engineers. Late in 1958 he and his family moved to Montgomery, where he worked as an earthmoving engineer. The Jameses had four sons, including their second born, Greg, who was diagnosed in 1959 with cystic *James* fibrosis and later died at the age of eight in 1967. In need of additional money to pay Greg's medical bills, James left Montgomery in 1960 to take a job as construction superintendent with a road paving company in Mobile. Then in 1961 James, just twenty-seven years old, made his most important career move.

Forrest ("Fob") James Jr.
1979–1983, 1995–1999

He decided that profits could be produced from a process that manufactured plastic-coated barbells. With financial support from his father and a wealthy attorney friend, Jacob Walker Jr. of Opelika, the three incorporated Diversified Products in 1962. Starting small, James worked the filling machines himself, and over the next fifteen years the company experienced tremendous growth. When Diversified Products was sold to the Liggett Group of Durham, North Carolina, in 1977, it had three plants and sales amounting to about $1 billion annually. James continued a formal association with the company until he was elected governor in 1978.

Politically, James always seemed a nonpartisan conservative who was usually attracted to the Republican Party. Bobbie James was actually the first in the family to go on a ballot, running unsuccessfully on the Republican ticket in 1970 for a post on the state board of education. Her husband, after serving briefly as a member of the State Republican Executive Committee, switched to the Democratic Party in 1977. It was the expedient action of a man who had decided to run for governor in a state that had not elected a Republican in a century.

James set his sights high and, when he made known his aspirations for the Democratic gubernatorial nomination early in 1978, was given little chance of success. George Wallace, who was finishing his third term as governor and his second successively, was constitutionally barred from seeking another term. Therefore, most political observers thought that the next governor would be one of the "three B's"—former governor Albert Brewer, Lieutenant Governor Jere Beasley, or Attorney General Bill Baxley. In the first balloting on September 5, 1978, however, James's extensive media advertising paid off, and he easily led the ticket, followed by Baxley, who lagged by some eighty-five thousand votes. In the September 26 runoff, James won the Democratic nomination by an even wider distance. In the general election in November, which was little more than a formality, James defeated former Cullman County probate judge Guy Hunt by a nearly five-to-one margin.

Alabama's new governor was inaugurated for his first term on January 15, 1979, and won immediate and widespread approval when he declared in his inaugural address that he "claim[ed] for all Alabamians a New Beginning [his campaign theme] free from racism and discrimination." During his first term as governor he named Oscar W. Adams to fill a vacancy on the Alabama Supreme Court, the first black chosen for such a position. In addition, he appointed other blacks to cabinet positions, including Gary Cooper as director of the Department of Pensions and Security, the first black to be named to head a major state agency in Alabama in a century.

Despite such auspicious beginnings, James's lack of experience was immediately observable. He did not attempt to organize the legislature as previous governors had done and often found himself defeated by the "unmanaged" body. Nor did he focus on a limited agenda; instead, he attempted to push through numerous programs simultaneously. The legislature rejected his proposal for a new constitution and also turned down his recommendation that they stop earmarking state funds, the process by which legislators assigned specific tax revenues for particular projects. James's first administration inherited serious economic problems from a deep national recession during the late 1970s, and the business-trained governor wanted a freer hand in deciding where state revenues would be expended. With declining revenues, he consolidated state agencies and cut a number of employees from the state payroll. During his first term, the governor angered some and was praised by others because he chose to emphasize funding for the kindergarten through twelfth-grade (K-12) levels over that for Alabama's colleges and universities. As the state's economic circumstances worsened, James was forced to prorate both the general and education budgets. Proration is a phenomenon in Alabama that occurs when tax revenues fall short of appropriated amounts. Under the state's balanced budget requirement, funds are cut, forcing schools to complete the academic year with less revenue than anticipated.

James was also thwarted when he asked legislators to decentralize state government and give home rule to counties and cities so that they could determine their own futures. Frustrated and not given to compromise, James reacted to these legislative defeats with outbursts of anger. Still, he was often his own worst enemy, and his inattention to detail led to embarrassing mistakes. A package of twenty anticrime bills, which he persuaded a special session of the legislature to enact in 1982, did not become law because his office failed to deliver them to the secretary of state within the required ten-day period. Later court decisions upheld the strict interpretation of this requirement for prompt delivery.

In other areas, however, James was more successful. Early in his first administration, the governor won praise from beyond Alabama's borders by the cooperative stances he frequently took in relation to the federal government, a sharp contrast to the confrontational Wallace style. James was more sympathetic to federal judicial efforts in the areas of mental health and prisons and to federal executive efforts to ensure the viability of the Medicaid program than was George Wallace.

The issue of religion in the public arena, which figured so prominently in James's second gubernatorial term, was also prominent in the first. In 1982 the legislature passed a bill to encourage voluntary prayer in the state's public schools, and it included a suggested prayer written by the governor's son Fob James III. James's official biographer, Sandra Baxley Taylor, reported that James "was pushed" into his proreligion crusades by his wife, whom Taylor identified as a "religious activist." James's efforts regarding prayer in public schools were thwarted but did not dissuade him from similar battles on the subject during his second term.

James's decision not to run again for governor in 1982 eased the way for George Wallace to return to office for a fourth and final term. Out of office, James began to yearn for a return to the governorship, and in 1986 and again in 1990 he ran in the Democratic primary but was badly defeated in both races. Living a semiretired life while out of office, he was associated with his sons in several businesses, including a marina, a solid-waste disposal firm, and a company concerned with preventing coastal erosion. In the spring of 1994, James's desire to be governor led him to switch parties one more time, and he qualified at the last moment as a Republican candidate. In the June 7 first balloting, state senator Ann Bedsole of Mobile forced James into a runoff, but on June 28 he defeated her decisively. In the November general election, James ran against the incumbent Democratic governor, Jim Folsom Jr., who had succeeded to that office on the ethics conviction and forced removal from office of Governor Guy Hunt. James stressed ethics and repeatedly reminded voters that Folsom and his associates were under investigation for alleged illegal conduct. He also pledged that he would support no new taxes if he were given another term of office. Folsom, on the other hand, stressed economic development, especially his leadership in attracting the Mercedes-Benz company to Alabama. With integrity as an issue, low voter turnout in rural Democratic strongholds, and unusually high voter turnout in Republican suburbs, James defeated Folsom by a narrow margin and won his second term as governor, this time as a Republican. James also benefited from the national Republican landslide that gave the GOP control of Congress for the first time in forty years.

James had been out of office for twelve years and was only the second Republican governor in modern times. In some areas the governor replicated the policies of his first administration, appointing Aubrey Miller, a black Alabamian, to head the Alabama Bureau of Tourism and Travel. He stressed again what he called "fundamental American values" and pressed his consistent support for K-12 education. The legislature joined him in passing an educational reform package known as the James Educational Foundation Act. This important legislation required local school systems that were not already at a minimum level of support to raise local property taxes to 10 mills, and it increased the number of credit hours in academic subjects that students were required to have in order to graduate. This legislation also empowered the state superintendent of education to take control of schools that scored poorly on national achievement tests. It was a remarkable and important feat for James and, more important, for the state. Unfortunately, in his quest to improve K-12 education, he stripped funding from the state's colleges and universities, and the bad feeling between those in higher education and the governor's office intensified.

James took a predictable "get tough" position on crime and criminals when he and his prison commissioner, Ronald Jones, reinstituted chain gangs for Alabama's prison inmates. The governor approved other strict policies instituted by Jones but balked at the commissioner's suggestion that chain gangs be extended to include female prisoners. Alabama's chain gangs attracted national attention, and a number of other states followed Alabama's lead in this area. In the summer of 1995 James signed into law a bill that ended Alabama's requirement that rape victims pay for their own medical examinations, making Alabama the last state in the nation to end this practice. Yet, James's reputation for distracted and eccentric behavior often overshadowed his positive actions. In a widely reported incident James remarked that he wished the state's government ran as well as the Waffle House Restaurants he enjoyed frequenting. Editorial observers responded by suggesting that running a state was significantly more complicated than running a restaurant.

Reversing the moderate posture of his first term, James began to reflect an individualistic states' rights attitude. He refused to accept federal monies from the U.S. Department of Education's Goals 2000 program because, said James and several other governors, accepting the money would lead to increased federal involvement and control over the state's schools. When Secretary of Education Richard Riley promised that the Department of Education would not interfere in the use of the funds, Alabama's state board of education ignored the governor's role and voted to accept the funding and use it to purchase computers for K-12 classrooms. In a similar act, James "seceded" from the National Governors' Conference and was the only head of a state to refuse to attend this organization's meetings.

James's longest and most publicized battle with the federal government came during the controversy surrounding the posting of the Ten Commandments and the offering of a daily prayer in the courtroom of Etowah County judge Roy Moore. In a suit brought by the American Civil Liberties Union, U.S. district court judge Ira DeMent, an appointee of President George Bush, ordered removal of the commandment plaque and cessation of the prayers because they violated the First Amendment guarantee of separation of church and state. Judge Moore appealed the decision, and James supported his position, threatening for a brief period to mobilize the Alabama National Guard and use force if necessary to prevent the removal of the Ten Commandments plaque from Moore's courtroom. In October 1997 Judge DeMent issued another sweeping and controversial order forbidding certain religious practices in DeKalb County's public schools. James verbally attacked DeMent's order as yet another illegitimate intrusion by federal courts into local affairs. The judge's order was, in part, reversed shortly after James left office, allowing students—on their own—to hold religious meetings on school grounds.

Forrest ("Fob") James Jr.
1979–1983, 1995–1999

Despite controversial statements and actions, James's standing in public opinion appeared to benefit from the prosperity being enjoyed by the state and nation. When he qualified for a third term as governor in March 1998, the state's unemployment rate was at its lowest point ever. But the business community and others who had supported James during earlier campaigns were disgruntled with his lack of interest in economic development issues and with his silly antics and provocative language. On various public occasions, he had scratched himself like a monkey, suggested that lobbyists were like French poodles who occasionally needed a "kick in the ass," and recommended a "good butt-whupping and then a prayer" as the solution to teen crime. The business community blamed his flip-flopping and inattention for the failure to get strengthened tort reform enacted.

James struggled through a bitter Republican primary runoff with Montgomery millionaire businessman Winton Blount III and had little money left to finance the general election campaign. Lieutenant Governor Don Siegelman, on the other hand, easily won the Democratic primary on the sole issue of establishing a state lottery to provide college scholarships for the state's young people. James opposed the lottery but had no focused agenda to offer and was defeated. He returned to semiretirement, saying he wanted to spend more time with his children and grandchildren.

248 ◇ James entered politics and was elected governor the first time as an idealistic progressive who sought fundamental reforms of Alabama's constitutional system. Yet he was, on the whole, an inept politician and did not succeed in getting most of his agenda through the legislature. During his second term, James — like George Wallace — seemed distracted from the real issues of economic development and providing adequate funding for education by battles with the federal courts he could not possibly win. His momentous reform of K-12 education seems to be making some improvement in the education provided to the state's children, but sadly this success is obscured by his futile battles with the federal government.

References

"James, Forrest Hood (Fob) Jr." Webpage, Alabama Department of Archives and History.

Labash, Matt. "God and Man in Alabama." *Weekly Standard*, March 2, 1998, 19–25.

Raimo, John W., ed. *Biographical Directory of the Governors of the United States, 1978–1983*. Westport, Conn.: Meckler Publishing, 1985.

Sack, Kevin. "Alabama's GOP Governor Follows His Own Vision of New South." *New York Times*, August 29, 1997.

Taylor, Sandra Baxley. *Governor Fob James: His 1994 Victory, His Incredible Story*. 1995. Reprint, Mobile: Greenberry Publishing, 1995.

Guy Hunt, 1987–April 1993

William H. Stewart

Harold Guy Hunt was the first Republican elected governor of Alabama since the Reconstruction era. He became the first to be removed from that office in 1993 following his conviction on ethics charges involving misuse of funds donated for his inaugural expenses. The ethics law dates only from 1973, and many Republicans believed Hunt was treated unfairly. On March 31, 1998, the Alabama Board of Pardons and Paroles, in a controversial action, pardoned him on grounds that Hunt was innocent of the charges brought against him.

Guy Hunt was born on June 17, 1933, in Holly Pond, a rural Cullman County community. His parents were William Otto Hunt and Frances Holcombe Hunt. At an early age he joined the Mt. Vernon Primitive Baptist Church, and church and home became critical influences on Hunt, who expected to continue his family's farming tradition.

Less than a year out of high school and only seventeen years of age, Guy Hunt married Helen Chambers on February 25, 1951. They had four children, three daughters and a son. During the Korean War, Hunt served both in the 101st Airborne and the 1st Infantry divisions of the U.S. Army and earned a certificate of achievement for outstanding performance of military duty and the distinguished service medal. After military service, Hunt returned to his farm at Holly Pond and in 1958 was formally ordained as a minister in the Primitive Baptist Church.

In the early twentieth century, Cullman County had an active Republican presence, but during the New Deal era it became solidly Democratic and remained so until the 1960s. Guy Hunt, however, seems never to have been in any doubt regarding his party affiliation and was willing to go against long odds to uphold the Republican cause. In 1962 he was

Hunt

an unsuccessful Republican candidate for the state senate. He was again on the Republican ticket in 1964 and this time benefited when Alabamians in massive numbers voted the straight GOP ticket for Barry Goldwater and other Republicans. Hunt, who was running for probate judge of Cullman County, was swept into office and was reelected without Goldwater's coattails in 1970.

249
◇

Guy Hunt
1987–1993

In 1976 Hunt led Alabama's delegation to the Republican National Convention and sought unsuccessfully to replace incumbent president Gerald Ford with Ronald Reagan as the party's standard-bearer. Two years later he made the first of his three campaigns for governor but was overwhelmingly defeated by Fob James, then a Democrat, in the general election. In 1980, Hunt served again as state chairman of the Alabama delegation to the Republican National Convention, which this time nominated Ronald Reagan for president. When Reagan was elected, Hunt was rewarded for his loyalty when he was appointed state executive director of the Agricultural Stabilization and Conservation Service. He held this job for four years, resigning in 1985 to prepare for another attempt at the governorship.

Hunt easily won his party's nomination in the June 1986 primary. Only about thirty-three thousand Alabamians voted in this primary, however. The Democratic contest was more hard fought and more significant because everyone, probably including Hunt, thought the next governor would be one of the better-known, long-time politicos squaring off in the Democratic primary. In that party's runoff election on June 24, Attorney General Charlie Graddick narrowly defeated Lieutenant Governor Bill Baxley. Graddick, the state's chief law enforcement officer, was accused in a federal court suit of having encouraged and allowed Republicans to vote in the Democratic primary, thereby diluting the votes of black voters and violating the provisions of the 1965 Voting Rights Act. The state Democratic Party was ordered to either designate Baxley as its nominee or hold a new primary. Party leaders gave the nomination to Baxley, creating a furor among Alabama voters who believed a party elite had stripped them of their power to elect the governor of their choice.

When Graddick aborted a write-in candidacy, Hunt, originally viewed as the Republican sacrificial lamb, saw his chances against the Democratic nominee improve. Baxley ridiculed Hunt as unqualified because he had not attended college and worked as an Amway products distributor and chicken farmer in addition to being a part-time Primitive Baptist preacher. A rumor floated that Hunt was asked to leave his federal job because he had solicited campaign contributions from his employees. Hunt stressed economic development issues and the need for conservative Democrats who had been abandoned by their party to join his team. The humble farmer benefited from the stench of "dirty Democratic" politics and was elected by a decisive 56 percent to 44 percent margin on November 4, 1986. He was the first Republican to hold this office since David Peter Lewis in 1872.

Hunt was inaugurated on January 19, 1987, and, despite his lack of state-level experience, he enjoyed some early successes. Within six months, the legislature passed a tort reform package supported by the governor. This group of laws was passed in response to claims that Alabama juries were too liberal in their verdicts for plaintiffs in their civil disputes against companies, and the reform package sought to restrict such verdicts. The legislation was largely gutted, however, by Alabama Supreme Court decisions that upheld large settlements and declared that the enacted laws restricted the rights of citizens to unfettered trial by jury.

Hunt established a tax reform commission to review ways to restructure the state's revenue-raising system and increase funding for education, but the legislature refused to adopt its recommendations. He also created several commissions to study educational reform and from their work made numerous proposals for improving education. Again, little came from those proposals. During the last full year of his first term, a lawsuit was filed against Hunt and other state officials by education leaders in fourteen poorer counties of the state, charging that education appropriations were both inadequate and inequitable. Montgomery County circuit judge Gene Reese agreed and ordered the state to move toward providing equitable education funding to all counties.

Alabamians were pleased and not a little surprised when Hunt, in his first year in office, was identified by *U.S. News and World Report* as one of America's best governors. Far more than Fob James, Hunt took a personal interest in industrial recruitment and relished the governor's role as leader of his political party, enthusiastically welcoming converts from the Democratic Party to the Republican fold.

When Hunt ran for reelection in 1990, his Democratic opponent was Alabama Education Association leader Paul Hubbert, a formidable force in Alabama politics for two decades. Hunt again stressed industrial development, and Hubbert presented himself as Alabama's opportunity to elect a "New South" governor. Republicans were successful in casting Hubbert as sympathetic to the liberal "national Democratic" agenda, which they labeled as pro-gay and pro–big government, and in a controversial decision they circulated photographs of Hubbert with various black politicians. Hunt defeated Hubbert by a 52 percent to 48 percent margin.

In his second inaugural speech Hunt reemphasized education reform. He proposed testing new teachers for their competence, providing and mandating kindergarten, lengthening the school year, strengthening graduation require-ments, and increasing school choice options for students and parents to force accountability and improvements to the schools that were not fit. Many of Hunt's proposals were included in the Alabama Education Improvement Act, which passed the legislature in July 1991. The law was mostly symbolic, however, because funds to implement its policies were not provided. The effects of a national recession caused revenue shortfalls for Alabama, and Hunt was forced to prorate state budgets early in 1991.

Controversy began to surround Hunt that summer. The governor's use of state planes to fly to religious events in neighboring states was made public.

Because Hunt accepted "love offerings" for preaching while on these trips, his use of planes for nonpublic purposes was attacked. In response to the criticism, he agreed to stop using the planes and reimbursed the state for earlier trips. The Alabama Ethics Commission, however, did not let the matter drop and in September 1991 recommended that Democratic attorney general Jimmy Evans prosecute Hunt. Hunt and state Republicans believed that the attack on him was partisan, and they may have had a point because Alabama's political culture had never previously been one that insisted on the highest ethical standards for its officeholders.

On December 28, 1992, Hunt was indicted on thirteen felony counts, most of which were ultimately dropped. The charge that stuck was that he had taken $200,000 from a 1987 inaugural fund, which included no tax or state funds, for his own personal use. Hunt vigorously denied that he had done anything illegal and again claimed a Democratic plot existed to force him from office. It was reported in the state's press early in 1993 that attorneys for Hunt had sought an agreement that would allow him to plead guilty to a misdemeanor prior to the December felony indictments, but Attorney General Evans would not consent. Prior to the trial, circuit judge Randall Thomas had urged Evans and Hunt's lawyers to settle the criminal case against the governor, but they were unable to do so.

On April 12, 1993, Guy Hunt stood trial on the inaugural fund diversion charge. The governor argued that any money he had taken was repayment for loans he had made to his unsuccessful 1978 campaign. The trial proceeded through six days of largely technical testimony, and most political observers believed that a jury would be disinclined to convict the governor. On April 22, 1993, however, after deliberating a total of only two hours, the jury rendered a verdict of guilty. Alabama law required Hunt's immediate removal from office, and within hours Jim Folsom Jr., the Democratic lieutenant governor and eldest son of former governor "Big Jim" Folsom, was sworn in as Alabama's new chief executive. Hunt's sentencing came on May 7 when Judge Thomas, ignoring Attorney General Evans's arguments that Hunt should be jailed, limited Hunt's formal punishment to a $211,000 fine, one thousand hours of community service, and five years' probation.

In June 1997 Hunt won his first victory on the road back to rehabilitation when the Alabama Board of Pardons and Paroles approved a pardon for him on grounds of innocence. For the pardon to be valid, however, it needed to be signed by a judge or district attorney, and no one could be found who was willing to perform that act. Even the recently elected Republican attorney general, Bill Pryor, refused to sign the pardon, arguing that he did not believe his office held that right or power. Then in a stunning defeat, when Hunt requested that probation be terminated shortly before it was due to expire in

1998, circuit judge Sally Greenhaw extended it for five more years because Hunt had been able to pay only $4,200 of the fine and court costs assessed against him. On March 30, 1998, however, Hunt's probation was lifted when his attorney presented a check to the court for the entire balance. Sympathetic Alabamians, both Democrats and Republicans, had helped Hunt to raise the needed funds. The next day, the Board of Pardons and Paroles again pardoned Hunt on grounds of innocence, and because probation had been terminated, no affirming signature was needed. The following day, Hunt qualified to run for the Republican nomination for governor against incumbent governor Fob James and three other contenders. Hunt failed to make the runoff and supported Winton M. Blount III against Fob James, who won the 1998 Republican runoff. Hunt returned to his Holly Pond farm and preaching assignments.

Hunt became governor of Alabama as a result of a squabble within the Democratic Party that offended Alabama voters, and few people expected him to achieve great success in that office. He surprised many people with his serious approach to governing and his efficient administration of the state's agencies. His successes, however, will always be marred by his conviction and removal from office.

References

Birmingham News.
Birmingham Post-Herald.
Montgomery Advertiser.
Mullaney, Marie M. *Biographical Directory of the Governors of the United States, 1988–
    1994.* Westport, Conn.: Greenwood Press, 1994.
Tuscaloosa News.
Who's Who in America, 45th (1988–89) and 47th (1992–93) eds.
Who's Who in American Politics, 1993–1994. 14th ed. New Providence, N.J.: R. R. Bowker,
    1994.

James E. Folsom Jr., April 1993–1995

WILLIAM H. STEWART

J AMES E. Folsom Jr. is the only governor ever to assume that office due to the felony conviction of his predecessor. He is also one of only two father-son gubernatorial combinations, the other being Edward and Emmet O'Neal.

Jim Folsom was born in Montgomery on May 14, 1949, to Governor James Elisha "Big Jim" Folsom Sr. and Folsom's second wife, Jamelle Dorothy Moore Folsom, during the elder Folsom's first term as governor. "Little Jim" began public school in Montgomery during his father's second term as Alabama's chief executive. When Big Jim left the governorship in 1959, Little Jim transferred to the Cullman system and was graduated from Cullman High in 1967. He began college at the University of Alabama but stayed there only one year. Jim joined the National Guard and, a year later, in 1970, entered Jacksonville State University. Working at a local post office and yarn mill to help finance his way through school, he was graduated from Jacksonville State in 1974. In 1977 he married Marsha Guthrie, daughter of a former Cullman state senator and close ally of Big Jim, and they had two children, a son and a daughter.

James Folsom Jr.

The younger Folsom's first postcollege job was with the Alabama Department of Industrial Relations, where he worked from 1974 to 1976. Then he worked briefly as the southeastern public affairs representative for Reynolds Aluminum Company in Muscle Shoals. In 1976 he was defeated in his first political race, an ill-considered bid to unseat veteran congressman Tom Bevill in the Democratic primary. In 1978 Folsom launched a more realistic bid for public office when he ran successfully for a seat on the Alabama Public Service Commission. Midway through his first Public Service Commission term, Folsom detected a chance to move quickly to a higher political office. The U.S. Senate seat formerly occupied by the late James B. Allen was now held by Donald Stewart whom Folsom correctly perceived to be vulnerable. He successfully challenged Stewart in the fall 1980 Democratic primary. In the November general election, however, Ronald Reagan was the Republican nominee, and state Republicans had nominated Admiral Jeremiah Denton, a courageous former prisoner of war in North Vietnam, as their

254
◊

senatorial candidate. Reagan carried Alabama easily, and his coattails helped Denton to defeat Folsom by a closer margin.

Little Jim continued to serve on the Public Service Commission and was reelected to a second term without difficulty in 1982. In the 1986 state elections, Folsom was elected lieutenant governor, winning the Democratic nomination and then the general election. As a result of this election, both the new governor, Guy Hunt, and the lieutenant governor were from Cullman County. Folsom won election with support from groups his father had long opposed, especially the conservative businesspeople called the "Big Mules." Presiding over the state senate, he helped steer a limited tort reform package through the legislature in 1987, but he did not attempt to dominate the upper chamber. He and Hunt were reelected to their posts in 1990, but circumstances changed dramatically for Folsom on April 22, 1993.

On that date a Montgomery jury found Governor Hunt guilty of a felony violation of the state ethics act, causing the immediate removal of the governor from office. A few hours after the jury's verdict was rendered, Folsom took the oath of office as Alabama's fifty-third governor. Six days later, the new governor directed that the Confederate battle flag not be flown again above the capitol dome when its renovations were completed. The controversial flag had been placed above the capitol in the early 1960s by Governor John Patterson during the era of civil rights confrontations. Folsom drew praise and outrage by that act. There was less notice taken by some as Folsom began to staff his administration with blacks and women in several key posts. In August 1993 Folsom called a special session of the legislature to consider ethics and campaign reform. The assembly passed only weak reform bills, which Folsom chose not to sign into law because they offered little improvement over existing laws.

In the area of education, Governor Folsom made an effort to comply with two state court rulings that required adequate and equitable education for Alabama's schoolchildren. In June 1993 he named a task force that ultimately recommended an education reform plan that, if implemented, would have cost the state an estimated $1 billion annually. To the surprise of few, the governor could identify no politically expedient funding mechanisms to support this plan, although increased property taxes and gambling casinos such as neighboring Mississippi's were suggested. Thus, no meaningful changes occurred in the state's education system. Folsom did successfully collaborate with another son of a famous governor, state treasurer "Little George" Wallace, to provide a plan whereby Alabama parents could prepay the college tuition of their children at a great savings over the predicted real costs of four years at a state institution of higher learning.

The brightest spot in Folsom's brief administration of one year, eight months, and twenty-four days occurred in September 1993 when Alabama

James E. Folsom Jr.
1993–1995

landed the Mercedes-Benz automobile plant in a competition that included numerous states across the nation. In late summer, the legislature, at Folsom's urging, passed a financial incentive package that provided tax advantages to firms such as Mercedes who were seeking new plant sites. Folsom had traveled to Germany personally to woo Mercedes officials into selecting Alabama as the location for the $300 million sports-vehicle assembly plant that was expected to provide as many as fifteen hundred jobs for Alabama workers.

Folsom, like his predecessor Guy Hunt, was also the target of ethics complaints. While gambling legislation was under consideration in the state senate and Folsom was serving as lieutenant governor, he and his family flew to the Cayman Islands for a vacation on the personal jet of gambling magnate Milton McGregor. A lengthy investigation of this matter dragged on and no doubt had an effect on the outcome of the 1994 governor's race.

Folsom waged a vigorous campaign in the Democratic primary for a full term as governor in 1994. He won handily over his opponent, teachers' union chief Paul Hubbert, and ran an equally vigorous campaign against Republican nominee Fob James. Most Alabamians seemed to be pleased with Folsom's performance in office, and he was expected to win. James, however, helped by a national Republican landslide that gave the GOP control of both houses of Congress for the first time in forty years, narrowly won the governorship.

256
◇ The ethics investigation by the state attorney general's office ended without any ethics charges being brought against Folsom, although several Folsom associates were convicted of improprieties. Early in 1998 U.S. attorney Redding Pitt, who had been looking into possible federal violations by Folsom, publicly stated that no federal criminal charges would be filed against the former governor. Folsom then called for an investigation of his accusers, specifically Governor James and former Republican attorney general Jeff Sessions, who had since been elected by Alabama voters to the U.S. Senate. Nothing came of his request.

Folsom and his family returned to private life in Cullman, where he is involved in an investment business. He has been urged to run for various public offices but thus far has declined.

References

Birmingham News.
Birmingham Post-Herald.
Encyclopedia American Annual. Various editions.
Montgomery Advertiser.
Mullaney, Marie M. *Biographical Directory of the Governors of the United States, 1988–1994.* Westport, Conn.: Greenwood Press, 1994.
Tuscaloosa News.

Don Siegelman, 1999–

Samuel L. Webb and Margaret E. Armbrester

IN NOVEMBER 1998 Don Eugene Siegelman won a landslide victory over incumbent Republican Fob James and became the first Democrat to win the governorship since 1982. He came into office touted as the state's first "New South" governor, focusing most of his rhetoric on endorsing a state lottery to raise money for education and avoiding racial and religious questions that Alabama candidates have traditionally used to stir the electorate.

Siegelman was born on February 24, 1946, in Mobile, the son of Leslie Bouchet Siegelman and Andrea Schottgen Siegelman. He was graduated from Mobile's Murphy High School in 1964 and entered the University of Alabama at Tuscaloosa that fall, where he was elected president of the Student Government Association in his junior year and earned his bachelor of arts degree in 1968. He then attended Georgetown University in Washington, D.C., where he worked his way through law school and received a doctor of law degree in 1972.

257
◇

That summer Siegelman returned to Alabama to coordinate the state campaign of Democratic presidential candidate George McGovern. Identified as an extreme liberal, McGovern was badly defeated in Alabama, and young Siegelman learned an important lesson. He retreated from the liberalism of his youth and moved toward a more moderate approach to public issues. After a brief period at Oxford University, where he studied international law in 1973, he came home for good. He went to work for the Alabama Democratic Party and was named executive director of the State Democratic Executive Committee, a position he held until 1978. In 1980 Siegelman married Lori Allen of Birmingham, and they became the parents of two children, a daughter and a son.

Siegelman

While working for the Democratic Party in Alabama, Siegelman coordinated efforts to streamline Alabama's outmoded voting laws. In 1978 he became the state's chief election official when he was elected secretary of state of Alabama, a position he won again in 1982. Near the end of his second term as secretary of state, Siegelman decided to run for state attorney general. Despite his law degree, his qualifications for the job were slim; he had never practiced law or tried a single case before a jury. Nonetheless, he won both the Democratic primary and the general election.

Don Siegelman
1999–

After four relatively quiet years as attorney general, in 1990 Siegelman joined a crowded field seeking the Democratic nomination for governor, a group that included former governor Fob James, Alabama Education Association leader Paul Hubbert, and Congressman Ronnie Flippo. Siegelman received only 25 percent of the vote, but it was enough to move him into a runoff with Hubbert. During the runoff, the attorney general recommended a state lottery and increased property taxes on state timber lands to fund education and social services. He accused Hubbert of playing a part in stripping Charles Graddick of the Democratic nomination for governor in the 1986 election. These themes failed to galvanize the electorate, and Hubbert took 53.6 percent of the runoff vote. It was Siegelman's first political defeat.

No longer in public office, Siegelman opened a law office in Montgomery but began immediately to prepare for another statewide political race in 1994. He decided not to challenge incumbent governor Jim Folsom Jr. and Hubbert for governor and opted instead to run for lieutenant governor. With support from many of the same groups that supported Hubbert—teachers, unions, trial lawyers, and black political organizations—Siegelman won his runoff campaign and easily defeated former attorney general Charles Graddick, the Republican nominee, in the general election.

The most controversial aspect of his term as lieutenant governor revolved around tort reform legislation to limit the size of civil jury verdicts. The business community in the state believed that state juries were being manipulated by plaintiffs' trial lawyers into giving outsized verdicts against companies accused of negligently injuring people. These verdicts, they argued, made national headlines and thwarted economic development in the state. Trial lawyers argued that limitations on the size of verdicts interfered with the sanctity of the jury system and the rights of those who suffered severe injuries. Siegelman, who had appointed all of the state senate's committee chairpersons, exercised enormous power over the flow of legislation to the floor of the senate. When supporters of tort reform were unable to get their bills brought up for a vote, business leaders held Siegelman responsible. His support for stronger laws against drunk drivers was far less controversial and enjoyed universal support. Siegelman and his wife had been the victims of an accident caused by a drunk driver in which his wife was severely injured.

By late 1997, business leaders, although irritated with the lieutenant governor for killing tort reform, had grown weary of Fob James's lackadaisical and erratic approach to governing the state. Siegelman took advantage of James's loss of popularity and began to meet with strategic business leaders in the state, even promising them some level of tort reform legislation. He easily won the Democratic primary on a platform of bringing a lottery such as neighboring Georgia's to the state to finance college scholarships for students with B averages. Governor James, on the other hand, endorsed no clear program and used most of his campaign funds on a primary runoff battle that he won narrowly. James had little money remaining to finance his campaign against Siegelman and depended on the growing unpopularity of the Democratic Party among white voters to gain him reelection.

Democratic defeats in the gubernatorial elections of 1986, 1990, and 1994 were caused by the slow erosion of support for the party among white middle-class voters who decided that their old party had deserted them in order to curry favor with minorities and other special-interest groups. Democrats, they believed, no longer cared about their concerns. Siegelman, taking a cue from a fellow southerner in the White House, determined to win back these voters. His lottery idea appeared to hit a responsive note with this middle-class population. That, plus voter weariness with Fob James, led to Siegelman's election with 57 percent of the vote. Voter interest was so high that more ballots were cast for Siegelman than for any gubernatorial candidate in Alabama's history.

Siegelman was the first person to have been elected to each of the state's top three constitutional offices—governor, lieutenant governor, and attorney general—and he was the first lieutenant governor since Thomas E. Kilby to be elevated by voters from that post to the governor's chair. He is the first governor born and reared in the city of Mobile and the first Catholic, and his wife became the first Jewish woman to serve as Alabama's First Lady.

In his inaugural address Siegelman stayed with his campaign proposal and emphasized the need for a lottery to support education needs. The legislature passed the necessary amendment to allow a lottery, but on October 12, 1999, the people of the state rejected that proposal by a 56 percent to 44 percent margin. In response to this defeat, Siegelman declared himself determined to continue to seek ways to improve education in the state but vowed that it must be done without new taxes or any diminution of existing programs.

Before that vote, however, Siegelman surprised many in his own party by supporting and personally pushing tort reform through the legislature. This legislation was promised as part of the state's package of incentives that prompted Honda to locate a major manufacturing plant in Alabama just weeks earlier. Honda was an economic boost for the state and an early feather in Siegelman's hat.

As the governor deals with the need for increased revenues and other issues, he appears willing to compromise and work with disparate forces. It is too soon to know Siegelman's impact on the state as governor. Before taking office in January 1999, he used his position as lieutenant governor to change senate rules, severely limiting the power of the incoming Republican lieutenant governor and insuring that control over committee chairs and legislative calendars was with the Democratic majority. In articles printed less than six months after he

Don Siegelman
1999–

took office, newspapers in the state suggested that Siegelman was not to be Alabama's first New South governor. He promised early on that he planned no new taxes for education, offered no remedy for tax reform in the state, and uttered the hope that he could lower taxes in Alabama, the least taxed state in the Union. There is nothing new in that stance.

References

Birmingham News.
Birmingham Post-Herald.
Siegelman, Don. Resume and other information provided by Governor's Office, Montgomery.

APPENDIX

Governors of Alabama

Party designations are significant during the territorial period (1798–1819) because territorial governors were appointed by the president of the United States. Party designations in the early state period have little or no meaning until the 1828 presidency of Andrew Jackson, who was the first president to call himself simply a Democrat. After the Civil War and Reconstruction from 1874 until 1987, all of the state's governors were Democrats.

Name	Party	Dates in Office
Winthrop Sargent	Federalist	1799–1801
William C. C. Claiborne	Democratic-Republican	1801–1805
Robert Williams	Democratic-Republican	1805–1809
David Holmes	Democratic-Republican	1809–1817
William Wyatt Bibb	Democratic-Republican	1817–1820
Thomas Bibb	Democratic-Republican	1820–1821
Israel Pickens	Democratic-Republican	1821–1825
John Murphy	Democratic-Republican	1825–1829
Gabriel Moore	Democratic	1829–March 1831
Samuel B. Moore	Democratic	March–November 1831
John Gayle	Democratic	1831–1835
Clement Comer Clay	Democratic	1835–July 1837
Hugh McVay	Democratic	August–November 1837
Arthur P. Bagby	Democratic	1837–1841
Benjamin Fitzpatrick	Democratic	1841–1845
Joshua L. Martin	Independent (Democratic)	1845–1847
Reuben Chapman	Democratic	1847–1849
Henry W. Collier	Democratic	1849–1853
John A. Winston	Democratic	1853–1857
Andrew B. Moore	Democratic	1857–1861
John Gill Shorter	Democratic	1861–1863
Thomas H. Watts	Democratic	1863–May 1865
Lewis E. Parsons (appointed)	Unionist Democrat (former Whig, Know-Nothing)	June–December 1865
Robert M. Patton	Unionist Democrat	December 1865–March 1867
Wager Swayne (military governor)	Republican	March–December 1867
William Hugh Smith	Republican	July 1868–December 1870
Robert B. Lindsay	Democratic	1870–1872

David P. Lewis	Republican	1872–1874
George S. Houston	Democratic	1874–1878
Rufus W. Cobb	Democratic	1878–1882
Edward A. O'Neal	Democratic	1882–1886
Thomas Seay	Democratic	1886–1890
Thomas G. Jones	Democratic	1890–1894
William C. Oates	Democratic	1894–1896
Joseph F. Johnston	Democratic	1896–1900
William J. Samford	Democratic	1900–June 1901
William D. Jelks	Democratic	December 1900, June 1901–1907
Russell M. Cunningham (acting)	Democratic	April 1904–March 1905
Braxton Bragg Comer	Democratic	1907–1911
Emmet O'Neal	Democratic	1911–1915
Charles Henderson	Democratic	1915–1919
Thomas E. Kilby	Democratic	1919–1923
William W. Brandon	Democratic	1923–1927
Bibb Graves	Democratic	1927–1931
Benjamin M. Miller	Democratic	1931–1935
Bibb Graves	Democratic	1935–1939
Frank M. Dixon	Democratic	1939–1943
Chauncey M. Sparks	Democratic	1943–1947
James E. Folsom	Democratic	1947–1951
Gordon Persons	Democratic	1951–1955
James E. Folsom	Democratic	1955–1959
John Patterson	Democratic	1959–1963
George C. Wallace	Democratic	1963–1967
Lurleen B. Wallace	Democratic	1967–May 1968
Albert P. Brewer	Democratic	May 1968–1971
George C. Wallace	Democratic	1971–1979
Jere Beasley Sr. (acting)	Democratic	June–July 1972
Forrest ("Fob") James Jr.	Democratic	1979–1983
George C. Wallace	Democratic	1983–1987
Guy Hunt	Republican	1987–April 1993
James E. Folsom Jr.	Democratic	April 1993–1995
Forrest ("Fob") James Jr.	Republican	1995–1999
Don Siegelman	Democratic	1999–

SELECT BIBLIOGRAPHY

Abernethy, Thomas Perkins. *The Formative Period in Alabama, 1815–1828*. University: University of Alabama Press, 1965.

Barnard, William D. *Dixiecrats and Democrats: Alabama Politics, 1942–1950*. University: University of Alabama Press, 1974.

Barney, William L. *The Secessionist Impulse: Alabama and Mississippi in 1860*. Princeton: Princeton University Press, 1974.

Bartley, Numan V., and Hugh D Graham. *Southern Politics and the Second Reconstruction*. Baltimore: Johns Hopkins University Press, 1975.

Bass, Jack. *Taming the Storm: The Life and Times of Judge Frank M. Johnson and the South's Fight over Civil Rights*. New York: Doubleday, 1993.

Bass, Jack, and Walter DeVries. *The Transformation of Southern Politics: Social Change and Political Consequences since 1945*. New York: Basic Books, 1976.

Black, Earl, and Merle Black. *Politics and Society in the South*. Cambridge: Harvard University Press, 1987.

Brantley, William H. *Banking in Alabama, 1816–1860*. 2 vols. Birmingham: Birmingham Printing Co., 1961.

———. *Three Capitals: A Book about the First Three Capitals of Alabama: St. Stephens, Huntsville, and Cahawba, 1818–1826*. 1947. Reprint, University: University of Alabama Press, 1976.

Brewer, Willis. *Alabama: Her History, Resources, War Record, and Public Men, from 1540 to 1872*. Montgomery: Barrett and Brown, 1872.

Carter, Dan T. *Scottsboro: A Tragedy of the American South*. Baton Rouge: Louisiana State University Press, 1969.

———. *When the War Was Over: The Failure of Self-Reconstruction in the South, 1865–1867*. Baton Rouge: Louisiana State University Press, 1985.

———. *The Politics of Rage: George Wallace, the Origins of the New Conservatism, and the Transformation of American Politics*. New York: Simon and Schuster, 1995.

Claiborne, John F. H. *Mississippi as a Province, Territory and State, with Biographical Notices of Eminent Citizens*. 1880. Reprint, Baton Rouge: Louisiana State University Press, 1964.

Dodd, Donald B., and Wynelle S. Dodd. *Historical Statistics of the South, 1790–1970*. University: University of Alabama Press, 1973.

Dorman, Lewy. *Party Politics in Alabama from 1850 through 1860*. Historic and Patriotic Series, no. 13. Montgomery: Alabama State Department of Archives and History, 1935.

Doster, James F. *Railroads in Alabama Politics, 1875–1914.* University: University of Alabama Press, 1957.

Dupre, Daniel S. *Transforming the Cotton Frontier: Madison County, Alabama, 1800–1840.* Baton Rouge: Louisiana State University Press, 1997.

Fitzgerald, Michael R. *The Union League Movement in the Deep South.* Baton Rouge: Louisiana State University Press, 1989.

Fleming, Walter Lynwood. *Civil War and Reconstruction in Alabama.* New York: Columbia University Press, 1905.

Flynt, J. Wayne. *Poor but Proud: Alabama's Poor Whites.* Tuscaloosa: University of Alabama Press, 1989.

Frady, Marshall. *Wallace.* New York: World Publishing, 1968.

Fry, Joseph A. *John Tyler Morgan and the Search for Southern Autonomy.* Knoxville: University of Tennessee Press, 1992.

Garrett, William. *Reminiscences of Public Men in Alabama for Thirty Years.* Atlanta: Plantation Publishing, 1872.

Going, Allen J. *Bourbon Democracy in Alabama, 1874–1890.* University: University of Alabama Press, 1951.

Grafton, Carl, and Anne Permaloff. *Big Mules and Branchheads: James E. Folsom and Political Power in Alabama.* Athens: University of Georgia Press, 1985.

Grantham, Dewey W. *The Life and Death of the Solid South: A Political History.* Lexington: University of Kentucky Press, 1988.

———. *Southern Progressivism: The Reconciliation of Progress and Tradition.* Knoxville: University of Tennessee Press, 1983.

Gray, Daniel Savage. *Alabama: A Place, A People, A Point of View.* Dubuque, Iowa: Kendall-Hunt Publishing Co., 1977.

Hackney, Sheldon. *Populism to Progressivism in Alabama.* Princeton: Princeton University Press, 1969.

Hamilton, Virginia Van der Veer. *Hugo Black: The Alabama Years.* Baton Rouge: Louisiana State University Press, 1972.

———. *Lister Hill: Statesman from the South.* Chapel Hill: University of North Carolina Press, 1987.

Havard, William C. *The Changing Politics of the South.* Baton Rouge: Louisiana State University Press, 1972.

Key, V. O. *Southern Politics in State and Nation.* New York: Alfred A. Knopf, 1949.

Kousser, J. Morgan. *The Shaping of Southern Politics: Suffrage Restriction and the Establishment of the One-Party South, 1880–1910.* Princeton: Princeton University Press, 1974.

Lamis, Alexander. *The Two-Party South.* New York: Oxford University Press, 1984.

McMillan, Malcolm Cook. *Constitutional Development in Alabama, 1798–1901: A Study in Politics, the Negro, and Sectionalism.* 1955. Reprint, Spartanburg, S.C.: Reprint Co., 1978.

———. *The Disintegration of a Confederate State: Three Governors and Alabama's Wartime Home Front, 1861–1865.* Macon, Ga.: Mercer University Press, 1986.

Moore, Albert Burton. *History of Alabama.* 1934. Reprint, Tuscaloosa: Alabama Book Store, 1951.

Mullaney, Marie M. *Biographical Directory of the Governors of the United States, 1998–1994.* Westport, Conn.: Greenwood Press, 1994.

Norrell, Robert J. *Reaping the Whirlwind: The Civil Rights Movement in Tuskegee.* New York: Alfred A. Knopf, 1985.

Nuermberger, Ruth Ketring. *The Clays of Alabama: A Planter-Lawyer-Politician Family.* Lexington: University of Kentucky Press, 1958.

Owen, Thomas McAdory. *History of Alabama and Dictionary of Alabama Biography.* 4 vols. Chicago: S. J. Clarke, 1921.

Owsley, Frank L. *Plain Folk of the Old South.* Baton Rouge: Louisiana State University Press, 1949.

Permaloff, Anne, and Carl Grafton, *Political Power in Alabama: The More Things Change—.* Athens: University of Georgia Press, 1995.

Perman, Michael. *The Road to Redemption: Southern Politics, 1869–1879.* Chapel Hill: University of North Carolina Press, 1984.

Perry, Mark. *Conceived in Liberty: Joshua Chamberlain, William Oates, and the American Civil War.* New York: Viking, 1997.

Pickett, Albert James. *History of Alabama, and Incidentally of Georgia and Mississippi, from the Earliest Period.* 1851. Reprint, Birmingham: Birmingham Book and Magazine Co., 1962.

Raimo, John W., ed. *Biographical Directory of the Governors of the United States, 1978–1983.* Westport, Conn.: Meckler Publishing, 1985.

Rogers, William Warren, and Robert David Ward. *The One-Gallused Rebellion: Agrarianism in Alabama, 1865–1896.* Baton Rouge: Louisiana State University Press, 1970.

Rogers, William Warren, Robert David Ward, Leah Rawls Atkins, and Wayne Flynt. *Alabama: The History of a Deep South State.* Tuscaloosa: University of Alabama Press, 1994.

Rogers, William Warren Jr. *Black Belt Scalawag: Charles Hays and Southern Republicans.* Athens: University of Georgia Press, 1993.

Roller, Daniel C., and Robert L. Twyman, eds. *The Encyclopedia of Southern History.* Baton Rouge: Louisiana State University Press, 1979.

Rowland, Dunbar, and Albert Godfrey Sanders, eds. *Mississippi Provincial Archives, 1701–1729: French Dominion.* 5 vols. Jackson: Mississippi Department of Archives, 1929.

Sellers, James B. *Slavery in Alabama.* University: University of Alabama Press, 1950.

———. *The Prohibition Movement in Alabama, 1702–1943.* Chapel Hill: University of North Carolina Press, 1943.

Sims, George. *The Little Man's Big Friend: James E. Folsom in Alabama Politics, 1946–1958.* University: University of Alabama Press, 1985.

Sobel, Robert, and John Raimo, eds. *Biographical Directory of the Governors of the United States, 1789–1978.* Westport, Conn.: Meckler Books, 1978.

Stewart, John Craig. *The Governors of Alabama.* Gretna, La.: Pelican Publishing, 1975.

Select Bibliography

Summers, Mark W. *Railroads, Reconstruction, and the Gospel of Prosperity: Aid under the Radical Republicans, 1865–1877.* Princeton: Princeton University Press, 1984.

Thornton, J. Mills, III. *Politics and Power in a Slave Society: Alabama, 1800–1860.* Baton Rouge: Louisiana State University Press, 1978.

Tindall, George B. *The Emergence of the New South, 1913–1945.* Baton Rouge: Louisiana State University Press, 1967.

Trelease, Allen. *White Terror: The Ku Klux Klan Conspiracy and Southern Reconstruction.* New York: Harper and Row, 1971.

Ward, Robert David, and William Warren Rogers. *Convicts, Coal, and the Banner Mine Tragedy.* Tuscaloosa: University of Alabama Press, 1987.

———. *Labor Revolt in Alabama: The Great Strike of 1894.* University: University of Alabama Press, 1965.

Webb, Samuel L. *Two-Party Politics in the One-Party South: Alabama's Hill Country, 1874–1920.* Tuscaloosa: University of Alabama Press, 1997.

Weiner, Jonathan M. *Social Origins of the New South: Alabama, 1860–1885.* Baton Rouge: Louisiana State University Press, 1978.

Wiggins, Sarah Woolfolk. *The Scalawag in Alabama Politics, 1865–1881.* University: University of Alabama Press, 1977.

Wilson, Charles Reagan, and William Ferris, eds. *The Encyclopedia of Southern Culture.* Chapel Hill: University of North Carolina Press, 1989.

Woodward, C. Vann. *Origins of the New South, 1877–1913.* Baton Rouge: Louisiana State University Press, 1951.

Wooster, Ralph A. *The People in Power: Courthouse and Statehouse in the Lower South, 1850–1860.* Knoxville: University of Tennessee Press, 1969.

Yarbrough, Tinsley E. *Judge Johnson and Human Rights in Alabama.* University: University of Alabama Press, 1981.

CONTRIBUTORS

LEE N. ALLEN Ph.D. Pennsylvania, is professor of history and university historian at Samford University and the author of several books, including *Boaz Heritage* (with Catherine B. Allen, 1999).

DAVID E. ALSOBROOK Ph.D. Auburn, is director of the Clinton Presidential Materials Project in Little Rock, Arkansas, and is the author of several books, including *Let Me Live Again: The Morning after the Storm* (1998).

MARGARET E. ARMBRESTER M.A. Vanderbilt, is assistant professor of history and curator of the Samuel Ullman Museum at the University of Alabama at Birmingham and the author of several books, including *Samuel Ullman and "Youth": The Life, The Legacy* (1993).

LEAH RAWLS ATKINS Ph.D. Auburn, is director emerita of the Center for the Arts and Humanities at Auburn University and author of several books, including *The Valley and the Hills: An Illustrated History of Birmingham and Jefferson County* (1981).

HUGH C. BAILEY Ph.D. Alabama, formerly professor of history at Samford University, is president of Valdosta State University and the author of *Edgar Gardner Murphy: Gentle Progressive* (1968).

WILLIAM L. BARNEY Ph.D. Columbia, is professor of history at the University of North Carolina at Chapel Hill and the author of numerous books, including *The Secessionist Impulse: Alabama and Mississippi in 1860* (1974).

S. JONATHAN BASS Ph.D. Tennessee, is assistant professor of history at Samford University and the author of *Blessed Are the Peacemakers: Martin Luther King, Jr., Eight White Religious Leaders and the "Letter from Birmingham Jail"* (2001).

MICHAEL A. BREEDLOVE Ph.D. American University, is an archivist with the Alabama Department of Archives and History and the author of several published articles on the history of Alabama.

ALBERT P. BREWER J.D. University of Alabama, was governor (1968–71), lieutenant governor (1967–68), and speaker of the state house of representatives of Alabama (1963–67), author of *Alabama Constitutional Law* (with Charles D. Cole, 1997), and is presently distinguished professor of law and government at Cumberland School of Law, Samford University.

KIT CARSON CARTER III Ph.D. Alabama, is professor emeritus of history at Mississippi University for Women, currently on the history faculty at Troy State University, and compiler of *The Army Air Forces in World War II: Combat Chronology, 1941–1945* (with Robert Mueller, 1991).

Contributors

HARRIET E. AMOS DOSS Ph.D. Emory, is associate professor of history at the University of Alabama at Birmingham and the author of *Cotton City: Urban Development in Antebellum Mobile* (1985).

DANIEL S. DUPRE Ph.D. Brandeis, is associate professor of history at the University of North Carolina at Charlotte and the author of *Transforming the Cotton Frontier: Madison County Alabama, 1800–1840* (1997).

GLENN T. ESKEW Ph.D. Emory, is associate professor of History at Georgia State University and the author of *But for Birmingham: The Local and National Movements in the Civil Rights Struggle* (1997).

GLENN A. FELDMAN Ph.D. Auburn, is assistant professor with the Center for Labor Education and Research at the University of Alabama at Birmingham and the author several books, including *Politics, Society, and the Klan in America: 1915–1949* (1999).

MICHAEL W. FITZGERALD Ph.D. UCLA, is associate professor of history at St. Olaf College and the author of *The Union League Movement in the Deep South* (1989).

WAYNE FLYNT Ph.D. Florida State, is distinguished university professor at Auburn University and the author of several books, including *Alabama Baptists* (1998).

CARL GRAFTON Ph.D. Purdue, is professor of political science at Auburn University at Montgomery and coauthor of *Big Mules and Branchheads: James E. Folsom and Political Power in Alabama* (1985).

DAVID ALAN HARRIS Ph.D. North Carolina, is associate professor emeritus of history at Old Dominion University and the author of *Racists and Reformers: A Study of Progressivism in Alabama, 1896–1911* (1967).

GORDON E. HARVEY Ph.D. Auburn, is assistant professor of history at the University of Louisiana at Monroe and is completing a manuscript on twentieth-century New South governors.

HARVEY H. JACKSON III Ph.D. Georgia, is professor and chair of the Department of History at Jacksonville State University and the author of several books, including *Rivers of History: Life on the Coosa, Tallapoosa, Cahaba, and Alabama* (1995).

JOHN R. MAYFIELD Ph.D. Johns Hopkins, is professor and chair of the Department of History at Samford University and the author of several books, including *The New Nation: 1800–1845* (1982).

MARY JANE MCDANIEL Ph.D. Mississippi State, is professor of history and chair at the University of North Alabama and the author of several published works, including *Study Guide for Liberty, Equality, and Power* (2000).

HENRY M. MCKIVEN Ph.D. Vanderbilt, is associate professor of history at the University of South Alabama and the author of *Iron and Steel: Class, Race, and Community in Birmingham, Alabama, 1875–1920* (1995).

ANNE PERMALOFF Ph.D. Minnesota, is professor of political science at Auburn University at Montgomery and the coauthor of *Big Mules and Branchheads: James E. Folsom and Political Power in Alabama* (1985).

MICHAEL PERMAN Ph.D. Chicago, is professor and chair of the Department of History at the University of Illinois at Chicago and the author of several books on the post–Civil War South, including *The Road to Redemption: Southern Politics, 1869–1879* (1984).

PAUL MCWHORTER PRUITT JR. Ph.D. William and Mary, is assistant law librarian at the Bounds Law Library, University of Alabama, and the author of several published articles related to the history of Alabama.

MARLENE HUNT RIKARD Ph.D. Alabama, is professor of history at Samford University and the author of several published articles on Alabama history.

WILLIAM WARREN ROGERS Ph.D. North Carolina, is professor emeritus of history at Florida State University and the author of several books on the history of Alabama, including *The One-Gallused Rebellion: Agrarianism in Alabama, 1865–1896* (1970).

WILLIAM WARREN ROGERS JR. Ph.D. Auburn, is associate professor of history at Gainesville College and the author of *Black Belt Scalawag: Charles Hays and the Southern Republicans in the Era of Reconstruction* (1993).

R. B. ROSENBURG Ph.D. Tennessee, is associate professor of history at the University of North Alabama and the author of several books, including *Forgotten Confederates: An Anthology about Black Southerners* (1995).

WILLIAM H. STEWART Ph.D. Alabama, is professor emeritus of political science at the University of Alabama and the author of several books, including *Alabama State Constitution: A Reference Guide* (1994).

J. MILLS THORNTON III Ph.D. Yale, is professor of history at the University of Michigan and the author of *Politics and Power in a Slave Society: Alabama, 1800–1860* (1978).

ROBERT DAVID WARD Ph.D. North Carolina, is professor emeritus of history at Georgia Southern College and the author and coauthor of several works on Alabama history, including *Labor Revolt in Alabama: The Great Strike of 1894* (1965).

SAMUEL L. WEBB Ph.D. Arkansas, is associate professor of history at the University of Alabama at Birmingham and the author of *Two-Party Politics in the One-Party South: Alabama's Hill Country, 1874–1920* (1997).

SARAH WOOLFOLK WIGGINS Ph.D. Louisiana State, is professor emerita of history at the University of Alabama and the author of *The Scalawag in Alabama Politics: 1865–1881* (1977).

INDEX

Abbeville, Alabama, 122, 123

Adams, John, 7, 8

Adams, John Quincy, 20, 35, 41

Adamsville, Alabama, 239

ad valorem taxation, 125, 129, 168

Africans, 44

agrarianism, 119

agrarian movement, 115

agrarian reform, 124

Agrarians, 128

Agricultural Commissioner, 118

agricultural diversification, 141

Agricultural Stabilization and Conservation
Service, 250

agriculture, 55

airplanes, 213

Alabama A&M (Huntsville State Colored
Normal School), 160

Alabama Alcoholic Beverage Act, 178

Alabama & Chattanooga Line, 89, 91, 104

Alabama and Tennessee River Railroad, 67

Alabama Attorney General, 161, 210, 211, 227, 258

Alabama Board of Control and Economy, 167

Alabama Board of Health, 103

Alabama Board of Pardons and Paroles, 249, 252

Alabama Bureau of Tourism, 246

Alabama Child Welfare Department, 168

Alabama circuit court, 87

Alabama Commission for Higher Education,
237

Alabama Congressional districts, 43, 53

Alabama Constitution: constitution of 1819,
12, 22, 25, 29, 34, 36; Reconstruction
constitution, 81, 84, 87; constitution of 1875,
97, 105, 129, 142; constitution of 1901, 3, 126,
131, 140, 148, 157, 173, 177, 212, 214, 222, 240;
proposal for new constitution during James
administration, 245

Alabama Constitutional amendment for term
limits, 223

Alabama constitutional convention: convention
of 1819, 12, 15, 16, 22, 35, 39; Committee of

Fifteen, 22, 35; convention of 1861, 94, 123;
of 1865, 65; convention of November 1867
(Reconstruction Constitution), 81, 85, 88;
convention of 1875, 107, 110; convention of
1901, 120, 139, 140, 142, 143, 148, 157, 171; state
referendum to have 1901 constitutional
convention, 142; proposed constitutional
convention under Jim Folsom, 200

Alabama Convict Department, 167

Alabama Court of Appeals, 202

Alabama Democracy, 130, 200

Alabama Democratic Party, 46; caucus, 46;
Jacksonian wing, 45

Alabama Department of Agriculture, 161

Alabama Department of Archives and History,
140, 169

Alabama Department of Education, 169

Alabama Department of Industrial Relations,
254

Alabama Department of Public Welfare, 178

Alabama Education Association (AEA), 175, 220,
227, 228, 229, 251, 258

Alabama Education Improvement Act (1991),
251

Alabama Education Study Commission, 237

Alabama Ethics Commission, 252

Alabama Farm Bureau, 227

Alabama Federation of Labor, 177; Child Labor
Division, 177; Conciliation Division, 177

Alabama First Cavalry, 87

Alabama Forestry Association, 232

Alabama Fourth Judicial District, 180

Alabama Frog and Switch Company, 166

Alabama House of Representatives, 22, 27, 28,
31, 35, 66, 77, 78, 79, 87, 90, 94, 101, 138,
147, 173, 180, 186; Speaker of the House,
32, 41, 66, 118, 223–24, 235, 236; Judiciary
Committee; Ways and Means Committee,
32

Alabama Infantry Divisions: 2nd Infantry, 118; 8th
Alabama; 9th Alabama Infantry, 110; 15th
Alabama, 123; 17thAlabama regiment, 74;

Index

26th Alabama Infantry, 110; 46th Alabama, 137; 48th Alabama, 123; Infantry, 65; 57th Alabama Regiment, 162
"Alabama Land Fever," 14, 18
Alabama League of Women Voters, 177
Alabama legislature, 15, 26, 39, 58, 74, 80, 118, 152, 195, 207, 218, 235, 245, 250, 259
Alabama National Bank, 19, 127
Alabama National Guard, 1, 155, 171, 173–74, 177, 209, 241, 247, 254; adjutant general of, 174; 2nd Alabama Volunteers during the Spanish-American War, 171
Alabama newspapers, 137
Alabama Office of Consumer Protection, 224
Alabama Pipe and Foundry Company, 166
Alabama Platform, 61
Alabama political maps: 1855, xiv; 1802, xv; 1946, xvi; 1990, xvii
Alabama Provisional Governor, 78
Alabama Public Health Department, 168
Alabama Public Service Commission, 254, 255
Alabama Railroad Commission, 163
Alabama railroad securities, 92
Alabama reform coalition, 130
Alabama Republicans, 86, 87, 88, 95, 97
Alabama River, 10, 15, 25, 26, 45, 67
Alabama school system, 168
Alabama secessionist convention, 74
Alabama Secretary of State, 245
Alabama Senate, 22, 40, 47, 74, 91, 114, 142, 148, 186; judiciary committee, 96
Alabama Soil Conservation Department, 154
Alabama soldiers in Civil War, 51
Alabama state auditor, 171
Alabama state bar association, 157, 158, 190
Alabama State Board of Education, 168
Alabama state bonds, 19
Alabama state chemist, 159
Alabama State Child Welfare Department, 178
Alabama State Commerce Department, 187
Alabama State Commissions: tax commission, 153; Board of Equalization, 153; public park system, 154
Alabama State Conservation Department, 187
Alabama state debt, 82, 125
Alabama State Department of Agriculture, 112
Alabama State Department of Corrections, 187, 208
Alabama State Department of Education, 175; Division of Negro Education, 175
Alabama State Department of Finance, 187
Alabama State Department of Health, 164
Alabama State Department of Labor, 187

Alabama State Docks, 188
Alabama State Docks Commission, 165, 172
Alabama state forester, 159
Alabama State Highway Commission, 159, 160
Alabama statehood, 5, 14, 15
Alabama state militia, ix, 68, 75, 76, 118, 145, 146, 184
Alabama State Penitentiary system, 26, 43, 119, 227
Alabama State Prison at Wetumpka, 43, 50, 147–48; physician for, 148
Alabama State Public Service Commission, 202, 207
Alabama State Republican Executive Committee, 244
Alabama State Teachers' Colleges, 176
Alabama State Treasury, 63, 139, 144, 190
Alabama state troopers, 221
Alabama State University (Normal School for Colored Students), 115, 226
Alabama Steel and Ship Building Company, 148
Alabama Supreme Court, 26, 32, 35, 49, 58, 165, 180, 211, 215, 244, 251
Alabama Territory, 11, 14, 21, 25, 41, 57, 74; part of Mississippi Territory, 10; territorial legislature (Assembly), 12, 11, 35
Alabama troops: seizure of federal installations, 68
Alabama Trust Fund, 229
Alabama Unionists, 94
Alabama Warehouse Company, 163
Alabama World War Memorial Building, 168
alcohol. See liquor
Allen, Jim, 239
American Civil Liberties Union (ACLU), 247
American Independent Party, 223, 225
American Legion, 174, 186
amnesty, 95
Andersonville Prison, 110
Anniston, Alabama, 114, 129, 151, 166, 169
Anniston City Council, 166
Anniston Star, 236
antebellum period, xiii
antiaristocratic factions, 36
Anti-Boycott Act of 1903, 145
anti-Communist oath, 201
anticrime bills, 245
Anti-Saloon League, 154
antisilver policies, 124
antislavery forces, 74, 84
Appomattox, 87, 91, 117
aristocrats, 5, 39
Arkansas, 61, 217, 234, 241

272
◇

armed services, 217
arms and ammunition, 68
Asheville, Alabama, 106
assassination attempt, 226, 239
Athens, Alabama, 48, 101, 102, 105
Atlanta, Georgia, 151, 166
atomic energy, 204
Auburn, Alabama, 137, 138
Auburn University (Agricultural and Mechanical
    College, East Alabama Male College), 112,
    115, 137, 160, 165, 175, 200, 206, 208, 228, 233,
    237, 243; School of Forestry, 191
Autauga County, Alabama, 16, 48
automobiles, 172, 175, 182; tags, 175; tax on, 213
Avondale textile mill, 150, 151

Bagby, Arthur Pendleton, 38, 41–44, 46
Bailey Springs, 60
Baker's Creek, battle of, 137
balanced budget amendments, 183
"Bald Eagle of the Mountains." *See* George
    Smith Houston, 103
Baldwin County, Alabama, 10, 169
ballot box stuffing, 123, 125
Baltzell, Frank, 120
Bankhead Good Roads Bill, 164
Bankhead, John Hollis, 108, 132, 155, 169
Bankhead, John, Jr., 169, 179
Bankhead, William, 179
banking issues, 12, 42, 51, 54, 55, 62
Bank of Alabama, 19, 23, 26, 37, 42, 45, 48, 49, 55,
    64, 66; Mobile Branch, 44; final liquidation
    of, 46
Bank of the United States, 23, 26, 36, 41, 53
bankruptcy, 96
banks, 16, 55
Banner Coal Mine, 159
Baptists, 70, 141, 149, 237; Southern Baptist
    missionary, 162
"Barbour Bourbon," 191, 193
Barbour County, Alabama, 70, 73, 111, 151, 190,
    193, 211, 216, 217, 218, 219, 231, 239, 240
Bass, J. G. (Warden), 108
Bass, Jack, 238
Battle, Mary Ann (Collier), 58
Battle of Brandywine, 13
Baxley, Bill, 239, 244, 250
Baylor Military Academy, 243
Bay Minette, Alabama, 211
Beasley, Browder Locke, 239
Beasley, Florence Camp, 239
Beasley, Jere Sr., 225, 239–40, 244
Beasley, Sara Baker, 239

Beasley, Williams, and Robertson, 239
Beatty, Mary I. (Houston), 101
Bedsole, Ann, 246
beer, 232
Bell, John, 74
Belle Mina, 16
Bell Factory, 32
benevolent societies, 85
Benson, Nimrod E., 45
Berlin, Sir Isaiah, 2
Bessemer, Alabama, 116
Bethea, Tristam B., 104
Betts, E. B. (Judge), 112
Bibb, Thomas, 13–17, 22
Bibb, Captain William, 13
Bibb, William Wyatt, 11, 12, 13–17, 17, 22
Bibb County, Alabama, 16, 155
Bible Belt, 241
"Big Mules," 177, 178, 185, 201, 205, 255
Bingham, Arthur, 114
Bird, Georgena, 117
Birmingham, Alabama, 89, 90, 108, 111, 114, 120,
    124, 125, 127, 129,143, 147, 150, 151, 156, 159,
    161, 177, 184, 185, 186, 188, 189, 191, 202, 212,
    221, 257
Birmingham Age-Herald, 130
Birmingham coal fields, 169
Birmingham Commercial Club, 151
Birmingham Freight Bureau, 151
Birmingham jail, 116
Birmingham News, 149, 172
The Birth of a Nation, 185
Black, Hugo, 169, 174, 179
Black Belt, xiii, 14, 53, 54, 61, 66, 71, 105, 106, 120,
    124, 125, 127, 139, 140, 142, 146, 151, 174–75,
    213
Black Belt-Big Mule coalition, 197, 198, 200, 218
Black Bloc Vote, 224
Black Code Legislation, 82
Black Codes, 84
black convicts, 118
black farmers, 118
black hospital patients, 82
black hospitals, 176
black laborers, 121
black miners, 169
black political organizations, 259
"black Republican," 68
black Republicans, 97, 111
blacks, 11, 33, 81, 90, 95, 100, 104, 120, 160,
    176, 198, 200, 203, 226, 229, 237, 238, 255;
    disenfranchisement, 209; education and
    welfare of, 82, 86, 145; enfranchisement,

79, 81; suffrage, 85, 88, 123; testimony of, in court, 84
black school for the deaf, 115
black schools, 85, 119
black strikebreakers, 120
black students, 221
black voters, 192, 198, 201, 224, 228
Black Warrior River, 15, 231
Blair Education Bill, 115, 124
"bleeding" Kansas. *See* Kansas
Blount, Winton III, 248
Blount College, 34
Blount Springs, 60
Blue Mountain, 67
Board of Convict Commissioners, 113
Board of Dental Examiners, 160
Board of Mediation and Arbitration, 159
bonded debt, 144, 167, 176
born-again Christian, 225, 229
Boswell Amendment, 192, 200, 209
Bourbons, 99, 103,107, 113, 114, 115, 140, 141. *See also* Democrats
boxing, 217
Boys Industrial School, 168
Braham, Jane Locke (Patton), 80
branding, 43
Brandon, Caroline Woodward, 170
Brandon, Franklin Thomas Jefferson, 170
Brandon, William W., 165, 170–72, 174, 176
Breckenridge, John, 74, 91
Bremer, Arthur, 225, 240
Brewer, Albert P., 223, 224, 235–38, 239, 244
Brewer, Clara Alberter Yarber, 235
Brewer, Daniel Austin, 235
Brewer, Martha Farmer, 235
Brewer, Willis, 25
Brewton, Alabama, 183
bribery, 123, 144
Brickell, Robert (Judge), 94
Bricklayers' Union, 177
bridges, 175
Broad and Savannah Rivers, Georgia, 13
Broad River Group, 14, 18, 22, 24, 25, 34
Brown, John, 67
Brown v. Board of Education, 1, 202, 209, 211
Bryan, William Jennings, 128, 148, 157
Bryce, Dr. Peter, 67
Bryce Hospital, 168, 176; mental facilities, 233
Buchanan, James, 47
"bucket shops," 154
Buckner, Simon, 120
budget reform in Alabama legislature, 167
Buford, Jefferson, 122

Bullock, Edward C., 122
Bullock County, Alabama, 219
bumper stickers, 238
Bureau of Refugees, Freedmen, and Abandoned Lands for Alabama, 81
Burns, Henry Morgan, 231
Burns, Janie Estelle Borroughs, 231
Burr, Aaron, 10
Bush, George, 247
business interests, 156
business leaders, 258
businessmen, 169
busing, 224
Butler County, Alabama, 74

Cabaniss, Edward H., 141
Caddo Lake, 27
caesarean delivery, 233
Cahawba, Alabama, 12, 15, 20, 22
Cahawba County, Alabama, 11, 16
Cahawba River, 15, 22
Calhoun, John C., 27, 33, 53, 101
Calhounite Democrats, 37
California, 11, 51, 56, 217
Caller, Mary Parham, 25
Camden, Alabama, 180
Camp Meade, Pennsylvania, 126
Canada, 111
capitol building, 16, 160, 234
carpetbaggers, 88, 95, 97, 103, 220
Carrollton, Alabama, 30
Carter, Jimmy, 228
Carter, Sarah Darrington, 21
Cayman Islands, 255
Cedar Bluff Institute, 170
central Alabama, 14, 72
Central Iron Works, 107, 109
chain gangs, 247
Chambers, Henry, 18, 19
Chambers County, Alabama, 137
chancery court, 43
Chapman, Ann Reynolds, 53
Chapman, Reuben, 46, 53–56, 57, 58
Chapman, Samuel, 53
charitable organizations, 159
Chattahoochee River, 20
Chattanooga, Tennessee, 243
cheap labor, 99
Cherokee, 10, 30, 37
Cherokee County, Alabama, 170
Chickamauga: Battle of, 123
Chickasaws, 10

child labor, 99, 114, 145, 150, 176; laws regarding, 145, 149, 154, 159, 177; reform, 152
Chinese, 158
Choctaws, 9, 11
Chrisman, Jane Ann Boyd McCullough, 77
Christian rearing, 172
Christmas cards, 217, 218
churches, 85
cigarettes, 232
cigarette tax, 214
City National Bank, 151
civil engineering, 173, 243
civil libertarians, 200
civil liberties, 201
civil rights, 84, 87, 89, 96, 97, 128, 203, 209, 211, 212, 215, 216, 218, 219, 221, 226, 255
civil rights bills, 79, 96, 97
civil service, 187
civil service reform, 187
Civil War, 47, 51, 62, 65, 69, 70, 77, 80, 84, 87, 94, 99, 101, 102, 110, 117, 123, 127, 128, 141, 155, 162, 195
Claiborne, Alabama, 31, 41
Claiborne, William C. C., 8, 9; treaty with Choctaws, 9
The Clansman, 185
Clark, Horry, 166
Clark, William A., 122
Clark and Company, 166
Clark and Kelly Company, 166
Clarke, Richard H., 128
Clarke County, Alabama, 11, 21, 23
Claxton, Dr. P. P., 168
Clay, Clement, 25, 34–38, 41, 43, 44, 64
Clay, Clement Claiborne, 74
Clay, Clement Comer, Jr., 58
Clay, Rebecca Comer, 34
Clay, William, 34
Clay County, Alabama, 210
Clayton, Alabama, 216, 231, 239; Clayton High School, 239
Clayton, Preston, 218
clean government, 143
Clemens, Jeremiah, 47, 56
Cleveland, Grover, 115, 124, 157
Clio, Alabama, 216
coal miners, 155
coal mines, 155, 175, 184; safety and sanitation inspections, 149
Coalter, Judge George, 101
coastal erosion, 246
Cobb, Rufus Willis, 106–9
code of ethics for state employees, 235

coffee, 232
Coffee County, Alabama, 197, 198
Coffin, Rev. William Sloan, 237
Colbert Shoals, 23
Cold Harbor, Battle of, 123
cold war, 195, 240
Coleman, Judge Daniel, 94
Collier, Elizabeth Bouldin, 57
Collier, Henry, 47, 54, 55, 56, 57–60, 67, 70
Collier, James, 57
colonial economy, 218
Columbia University, 185
combat fatigue, 217
Comer, Braxton Bragg, xi, 113, 121, 132, 143, 146, 149, 150–56, 158, 174
Comer, Catherine Drewry, 151
Comer, John Fletcher, 151
Comer Foundation, xi
Comer Station, 151
Commissioner of Agriculture, 115
Commission on Alabama Education, 213
Committee of Thirty-three, 102
Committee to Re-Elect the President (CREEP), 238
common law marriage, 201
communism, 119
Communists, 184, 209
Compromise of 1850, 51, 59, 61, 74
computers, 236
Confederacy, 38, 68, 71, 75, 77, 78, 95, 109, 110, 117, 126, 229
Confederate Army, 77, 102, 106, 114, 127
Confederate Attorney General, 73, 76
Confederate Cavalry, 75
Confederate cause, 52, 75
Confederate Congress, 68, 71, 94, 95; Indian Affairs Committee, 94; Patents Committee, 94
Confederate conscription, 72, 76
Confederate Conscription Act of 1862, 75
Confederate Constitution, 71
Confederate deserters, 75
Confederate flag, 68, 221, 255
Confederate impressment, 75
Confederate military forces, 81, 111
Confederate money, 75
Confederate president, 74, 75
Confederate reunions, 126
Confederates, 56, 91, 115, 123, 126, 133, 142, 243; ex-Confederates, 81, 87
Confederate Senate, 47, 74
Confederate soldiers, 69
Confederate Supreme Court, 75

Confederate veterans, 114, 158; pensions for, 160, 171
Congress of Industrial Organization, 188, 199
Connell, Anne Elizabeth, 41
conservation, 150, 154, 159
conservatism, 156, 158
Conservative-Democratic Party, 83, 91, 152. *See also* Democratic-Conservative Party
conservatives, 208, 244
Constitutional Unionist Party, 74
consumer's tax, 183
Convict Board, 161
convict labor, 99, 108, 159, 175; mortality rates, 112; health inspections of, 112
convict leasing, 82, 103, 107, 115, 118, 119, 125, 129, 144, 148, 149, 153, 156, 161, 171, 175; abolition of, 167
convicts, 153, 201
Coosa County, Alabama, 50, 210
Coosa River, 11
corn, 177
corporate capitalism, 46
corporations, 62
cotton, 42, 45, 55, 61, 66, 81, 102, 114, 151, 163, 190, 206; prices, 18, 118
cotton market, 117
cotton mills in prisons, 175
cotton tax, 81
counterculture, 223
court reform, 164
Crawford, William H., 14, 20
Creek Cession in Alabama, 32, 33
Creek Indian removal, 23
Creek Indian Territory, 10, 36, 45
Creek Indian War, 11, 34
Creek Nation, 20
Creeks, 10, 11, 31, 32, 33, 36, 37, 50
crime and criminals, 247
Crisis of 1861, 91
Cuba, 20
Cullman, Alabama, 256, 258; Cullman High School, 255
Cullman County, Alabama, 198, 201, 202, 210, 244, 255
Cumberland College, 61
Cumberland School of Law, x, xi, 238
Cunningham, Annice Taylor, 147
Cunningham, Caroline Russell, 147
Cunningham, Moses W., 147
Cunningham, Russell McWhorter, 143, 145, 147–50, 152
Cunningham, Sue L. Moore, 147
currency, 22

The Daily Picayune, 117
Dallas County, Alabama, 11, 127
Davenport, John G., 29
Davidson, Sophia, 39
Davis, Jefferson, 234
Davis, Nicholas, 30
Dawson, Reginald H., 113
Decatur, Alabama, 97, 235
DeGraffenried, Ryan, 220
DeKalb County, Alabama, 247
Dellet, James, 21, 23
DeMent, Ira (U.S. District Court Judge), 247
Democratic-Conservative Party, 83, 103, 106, 135, 138. *See also* Conservative-Democratic Party
Democratic Executive Committee, State, 181, 210, 211
Democratic gubernatorial primary, 126, 148, 149, 152, 175, 177, 181, 184, 199, 232, 246, 248, 250, 254, 256, 257, 258; in 1974, 226; creation of, 131; "dead shoes primary," 132; 1946 runoff, xiii
Democratic legislative caucus (Alabama), 47
Democratic national committee, 146
Democratic National Convention: convention in Baltimore 1848, 47; convention in Nashville, 1850, 59, 70; convention in Charleston, 1860, 56, 64; convention of 1868, 95; convention of 1924, 170; convention of 1928, 181; convention of 1932, 172; convention of 1936, 189; convention of 1948, 192, 202, 218; pro-civil rights platform, 202; convention of 1972, 225; 1976, 228, 239
Democratic newspaper, 123
Democratic nomination, 143, 163
Democratic Party, 52, 57, 59, 61, 64, 66, 67, 68, 70, 77, 92, 97, 107, 109, 110, 112, 114, 123, 126, 127, 128, 130, 131, 132, 138, 139, 142, 148, 164, 181, 189, 192, 196, 207, 210, 243, 244, 246, 250, 251, 253, 257, 259; "Bourbon" faction, 82, 103, 106, 107, 109, 111, 116, 123, 126, 135; labeled pro-gay and pro–big government, 251; redeemers, 103; states' rights (Chivalry) faction, 57, 59, 61, 67; Unionist (Hunker) faction, 57, 59, 63, 67
Democratic presidential race of 1964, 221
Democratic presidential race of 1972, 225
Democratic State Convention: in Tuscaloosa 1845, 49; convention of 1847, 54; convention of 1870, 110; convention of 1872, 90; 1878 convention in Montgomery, 107; convention of 1886, 114; convention of 1890, 119

Democratic state executive committee, 149
Democrats, 40, 42, 43, 50, 53, 55, 56, 61, 63, 70, 71, 74, 81, 88, 90, 91, 92, 93, 95, 96, 99, 101, 102, 103, 105, 107, 110, 118, 120, 125, 128, 129, 132, 147, 183, 186, 195, 223, 243, 246, 249, 250, 252, 253, 255, 256, 258, 259; Jacksonian Democrats, 62, 65, 101; "Jeffersonian" Democrats, 116, 127, 128, 181; redeemer Democrats, 118, southern Democrats, 102; union Democrats, 102; "Young Democrats," 70
Denton, Jeremiah, 254
Depression of 1837, 41, 45, 49
desegregation, 209, 211, 212, 221, 224, 230
DeVries, Walter, 238
Dexter Avenue, 125
Dexter Avenue Baptist Church, 226
direct primary, 152, 154
Disciples of Christ, 179
discrimination, 244
disfranchisement, 43, 78, 126, 127, 140, 142, 143, 148, 152, 200
Diversified Products, 244
Divine Will, 44, 130
divorce, 25, 61, 215, 228, 229
Dix, Dorothea, 59
"Dixie," 189, 229, 234
Dixiecrats, 186, 192, 202, 206, 207
Dixon, Rev. Frank, 185
Dixon, Frank M., 177, 179, 185–89, 191; awarded Croix de Guerre, 186
Dixon, Juliet Perry, 185
Dixon, Laura, 185
Dixon, Rev. Thomas, 185
doctrine of popular sovereignty in territories, 47
Donovan, Daisy, 177
Dothan Eagle, 183
Douglas, Stephen A., 47, 56, 64, 77, 80, 87, 91, 94
Dowd, Mollie, 177
Dozier, Abraham Giles, 31
draft evasion, 237
Drake, Caroline Elizabeth, 138
Drake, Dr. John Hodges, 138
Drake, Polly, 138
Dred Scott decision, 51
driver's licenses, 175; income from fees, 175
drunk drivers, 258
drys, 154, 158; "bone dry" law, 155, 168
dueling, 25
Dunnavant, John, 197
Durham, North Carolina, 244
dynamite, 155

east Alabama, 70
eastern hill counties, 62
economic development, 236
economic diversification, 59
economic prosperity, 15
economic stringency, 99
Edmund Pettus Bridge, 222
education, 62, 71, 115, 141, 144, 149, 150, 153, 157, 171, 191, 195, 216, 235, 236, 255; at college and university level, 245, 246; compulsory, 153; federal control of, 232; funding for, 175, 214; K-12 education, 245, 246; vocational education, 168. *See also* blacks: education and welfare of; public education
Education Act of 1854, 62
educational reform, 59, 178, 251, 255
Educational Television Commission, 208
Education Commission, 159
Edwards, Jonathan, 77
Eighteenth Amendment, 149, 164, 182
Elba, Alabama, 197
election law, 174
election reform, 174
election run-offs, 174
election violence, 103
electrical engineering, 206
electricity, 181, 207
Elliott, Carl, 215, 232
Ellis, Handy, 199
Elmore, Sarah Terry, 45
Elmore County, Alabama, 45
emancipated slaves. *See* freedmen
embezzlement, 111
emergency war powers, 72
enrolling clerk, 115
Ensley, Alabama, 148; school board, 148
Episcopal Church, 53, 84, 97, 166
Era of Good Feelings, 5
ethics laws, 249, 256
Etowah County, Alabama, 247
Eufaula, Alabama, 70, 73, 122, 124, 141, 146, 174, 190
Eufaula *Daily Times*, 141, 142
Eufaula Regency, 71, 122, 124
Eufaula *Times and News*, 141
Europe, 42, 167, 187
Evans, Jimmy (Attorney General), 252

factory inspection, 145
Fair Employment Practices Committee, 188
Fairfax, Virginia, 9
Fairview Presbyterian Church, 65
Farm Bureau, 191, 206

Index

Farm Bureau Federation, 200
farm demonstration agents, 168
farmers, 24, 39, 114, 116, 118, 122, 177, 181, 207, 232
Farmers Alliance, 116, 118; convention in
     Montgomery, 115
Farmers and Merchants Bank of Troy, 163
farm extension, 200
farming, 147
farms, 81
Faulkner, Jimmy, 211
Faulkner, William, 5
federal army, 89
federal courts, 153, 228
federal forces: 43rd Ohio Volunteer Regiment, 84
federal government, 7, 15, 26, 36, 51, 55, 219, 245,
     248
federal installations: seizure of, 68
federal intrusion, 241
federal land grants, 15
federal military, 32
Federal Military Road, 10
federal troops, ix
felony conviction, 241
Fifteenth Amendment, 90
Fillmore, Millard, 77
fire-eaters, 55, 59
First Amendment, 201, 247
First Lady, 232, 259
fiscal austerity, 141
fiscal conservatism, 184
fiscal restraints, 171
Fite, Rankin, 218
Fitzpatrick, Anne Phillips, 45
Fitzpatrick, Benjamin, 37, 45–48, 57, 66, 78
Fitzpatrick, William, 45
Fleming, Walter Lynwood, 86
Flippo, Ronnie, 258
Florence, Alabama, 39, 40, 80, 101, 110, 113, 115,
     161, 176, 215
Florence Cemetery, 113
Florida, 20, 43, 122, 171, 184, 225
Florida primary, 225
Flowers, Richmond, 232
Folmar, Emory, 228
Folsom, Eulala Cornelia Dunnavant, 197
Folsom, Jamelle Dorothy Moore, 201, 254
Folsom, James (Big Jim), xiii, 179, 191, 192,
     197–205, 206, 208, 209, 211, 212, 218, 224, 252,
     254; fishing trip in Gulf of Mexico, 1, 204;
     and integration of public schools, 1, 164
Folsom, James Jr. (Little Jim), 112, 246, 252,
     254–56, 258
Folsom, Janet Moore, 201

Folsom, Joshua Marion, 197
Folsom, Marsha Guthrie, 254
Folsom, Sarah Carnley, 197, 199
football, 217, 233, 243
Ford, Gerald, 250
Forney's Brigade, 106
Forrest, Nathan Bedford, 243
Fort Confederation, 8
Fort Gaines, 68
Fort Mims Massacre, 31
Fort Morgan, 68
Fort Pulaski, Georgia, 69
Fort Stephens, 11
Fort Stoddert, 10, 31
Fort Sumter, 110
Fort William W. Brandon, 171
Fourteenth Amendment, 82, 85, 95, 119
Fourth Judicial Circuit, 94
France, 9, 103
Franklin County, Alabama, 90, 147
Freedman's Bureau for Alabama, 83, 84, 85
freedmen, 81, 82, 84, 88, 89, 103
freedom riders, 212
free labor, 43
Freeman, Mary, 14
free silver, 128, 131, 148
"friends of bimetallism," 148
furnaces, 99

Gadsden, Alabama, 232; courthouse, ix
Gainer's Store, 162
gambling laws, 166
Garfield, James, 90
Garrett, William, 58
gasoline, 182
gasoline taxes, 175, 182
Gayle, John, ix, 21, 30, 31–34
Gayle, Mary Rees, 31
Gayle, Matthew, 31
General Ticket Bill, 40, 43
geology, 55
Georgetown University, 257
Georgia, 5, 7, 13, 14, 17, 30, 41, 43, 71, 114, 117, 129,
     151, 219, 234; state legislature, 13
Georgia faction in Alabama politics. See Broad
     River Group
Georgia-Pacific Railroad, 166
Germany, 256
Gettysburg, 123
Gist, William H., 68
Gloucester, Mass., 7
Gloucester plantation, 8
Goat Hill, 58, 208, 218

goldbugs, 120, 128, 130
Golden Gloves, 217
gold standard, 124, 148
Goldville, Alabama, 210
Goldwater, Barry, 249
Goode, Sidney M., 66
Good Roads Act, 169
Goodwyn, Albert T., 128
Gordon, John B., 117
governor's residence, 160, 204
Graddick, Charlie (Attorney General), 250, 258
Graham, Henry, 220
Graham, John, 50
grandfather clause, 120, 126
Grange, The 116
Grant, Ulysses S., 79, 91, 96, 123
Graves, Bibb, 140, 164, 171, 172, 173–79, 186, 187, 191, 198, 199, 206
Graves, Dixie Bibb, 173
Great Britain, 9, 11, 27, 28, 42, 71
Great Depression, 2, 135, 163, 180, 182, 239
Greeley, Horace, 138
Green Academy (in Huntsville), 80, 110
Greenback-Independent coalition, 111
Greenback Party, 107, 138
Greene County, Alabama, 30, 32, 113, 114, 185
Greensboro, Alabama, 113
Greenshaw, Sally, 253
Greenwood Cemetery, 229
gubernatorial election of 1837, 38
Gulf of Mexico, 1, 172

Haden, Harry, 214
Hails, Sarah, 21
Hall, Grover C., 181, 183, 188
Hall, Julian, 183
Hamm, Phillip, 202, 207
hard money, 120
Harper's Ferry, Virginia, 67
Harris, Ellen (Swayne), 86
Harris, Eva Jane (Comer), 151
Harrison, William Henry, 33, 42, 43
Hawes, Richard, 116
Hayden, Julius, 85
Haynsworth, Sarah Ann, 31
Haywood, John (Judge), 57
Helena, Alabama, 107
helicopter, 207
Henderson, Alabama, 162
Henderson, Charles, 146, 162–65, 167
Henderson, Charles, Grocery Company, 163
Henderson, Jeremiah Augustus, 162

Henderson, Mildred Elizabeth Hill, 162
Henderson Brothers, 162
Henry County, Alabama, 122
Henry [County] Pioneers, 123
Herndon, Thomas H., 93, 95
Highway Commission, 164
highways, 157; construction, 208, 213, 214; improvements, 236; interstate highway system, 220; highway safety, 208. *See also* roads
hill country, Alabama, xiii
Hiroshima, 217
Hobo Club, 206
Holly Pond, Alabama, 249
Holmes, David, 10, 11
Homestead Bill, 47
Honda, 259
honorary degrees, 226
Hood, John Bell, 243
Hoover, Herbert, 181
Hope Hull, 173
horse and buggy, 172
Horseshoe Bend, 32
hospital for crippled children, 165
Houston, George F., 118
Houston, George Smith, 101–06, 107, 138
Houston, Hannah Pugh Reagan, 101
Houston, John, 101
Howard, Milford, 126
Howard, Oliver O., 84, 85
Hubbert, Paul, xiii, 251, 256, 258
Humphries, David C., 38
Hunt, Frances Holcomb, 249
Hunt, Guy, xiii, 215, 244, 249–53, 255, 256; awarded distinguished service medal, 249; felony ethics conviction of, 215, 254
Hunt, Helen Chambers, 249
Hunt, William Otto, 249
Huntsville, Alabama, 10, 22, 24, 25, 32, 34, 38, 47, 53, 56, 57, 58, 94, 97, 110, 112, 177, 195
Huntsville antibank force, 35
Huntsville Bank, 34, 35
hygiene studies, 112

IBM, 206
illiteracy rates, 115
immigrants, 11, 141
immigration restrictions, 158
impressment of slaves, 123
imprisonment for debt, 43, 118
income tax, 2, 183; exemptions on personal tax, 213; corporate income tax, 213
income tax amendment, 183

Independents, 124
Indian Question, 23
Indian Removal, ix, 43, 51, 53
Indians, 6, 7, 11, 26, 30
industrial development, 216
industrial growth, 176
industrialists, 150
industrialization, 141
industrial parks, 218
industrial-planter interests, 114, 181
industry, 220; big industry, 177
inflation: post-World War I, 167
initiative, referendum, and recall, 160
in-kind taxation, 75
insurance companies, 157, 198, 199
integration, 1, 96, 223, 232, 237
interest rates, 118
internal improvements, 63, 71
Interstate Commerce Act, 124
Interstate 65, xiii
iron and steel industry, 155, 184
iron curtain, 241

Jackson, Andrew, 9, 11, 20, 23, 27, 28, 32, 33, 34, 35, 39, 41, 53
Jackson, Stonewall, 117, 123
Jackson County, Alabama, 28
Jacksonian Democracy, 46, 53
Jacksonian Democrats, 34, 70; radical Jacksonians, 46
Jacksonville, Alabama, 1, 112, 176
Jacksonville State University, 254
James, Bobbie May Mooney, 243
James, Forrest (Fob), ix, 243–48, 250, 251, 253, 256, 258, 259
James, Forrest Hood, 243
James, Greg, 243
James, Rebecca Ellington, 243
James Educational Foundation Act, 246
Jefferson, Thomas, 8
Jefferson College, 8, 17
Jefferson County, Alabama, 148, 155, 159, 186, 202, 213, 214
Jeffersonian Republicans, 7
Jelks, Alice Keitt Shorter, 141
Jelks, Jane Goodrum Frazer, 140
Jelks, Joseph William, 140
Jelks, William Dorsey, 139, 140–46, 154; antilabor attitudes, 145; antilynching efforts, 145
Jesup, General Thomas, 36
Jewish woman, 259
Jim Crow, 222

Johnson, Andrew, 77, 78, 79, 81, 82, 84, 85, 94, 102
Johnson, Frank (Judge), 219, 220, 221, 227, 228
Johnson's Island, 137
Johnston, Joseph Forney, 124, 126, 127–32, 139, 142, 148, 171, 173
Jones, Martha Goode, 117
Jones, Ronald, 247
Jones, Samuel Goode, 117
Jones, Thomas Goode, 116–21, 122, 124, 125, 128, 153
Jones, William G. (U.S. District Judge), 37
Jordan, Ralph "Shug," 208, 243
journalism, 141
judicial reform, 26, 59
junior colleges, 220
juries, 250
jury duty: pay for, 167
justifiable homicide, 61

Kansas: "bleeding" Kansas, 51, 74
Kelly, William (U.S. Senator), 35
Kennedy, John F., 1, 221
Kentucky, 9, 10, 39, 77
Key, Francis Scott, 33
kickbacks, 144
Kilby, Mary Elizabeth Clark, 166
Kilby, Payton Phillips, 166
Kilby, Sarah Ann Marchant, 166
Kilby, Thomas, 155, 164, 166–69, 171, 172, 190, 259
Kilby Prison, 166, 175
Kilby Steel Company, 166
kindergarten, 245, 251
King, Martin Luther, Jr., 203, 226
King, Martin Luther, Sr., 226
King, William Rufus, 47, 58
Knights of Labor, 118
Know-Nothing Party, 56, 63, 67, 74, 77
Knoxville, Tennessee, 34
Kolb, Reuben F., xiii, 115, 118, 119, 120, 124, 127, 128, 141; Kolbites, 128, 130, 132
Korea, 207
Korean War, 210, 249
Ku Klux Klan, 3, 79, 88, 89, 91, 92, 123, 135, 173, 174, 176, 177, 179, 181, 182, 186, 188, 212, 219, 221

labor, 150; contracts, 81; unrest, 111
laborers, 99
labor movement, 145. *See also* black laborers; cheap labor; child labor; convict labor; free labor; organized labor; women, labor issues

Lacy, Theophilus, 161
LaGrange College, 110
laissez faire, 39, 71, 73
Lake Erie, 137
land debt relief, 25
landowners, 81
Lanett, Alabama, 243
Lapsley, J. W., 111
Lauderdale County, Alabama, 11, 39, 40, 80, 101, 114
Laurel, Maryland, 225
law and order, 223
law code of 1799, 8
law enforcement department, 159
Lawler, Levi W., 104
Lawrence County, Alabama, 94
Lawrenceville Academy, 122
League of Women Voters, 177
Lee, Robert E., 118, 123; Lee's Army of Northern Virginia, 110, 117
Lee County Executive Committee, 138
legal profession, 236
LeMay, Curtis (General), 217, 223
Lesdernier, Clara de, 114
Lewis, David Peter, 90, 93, 94–97
Lewis, Dixon Hall, 23, 46
Lewis, Peter C., 94
Lewis, Susan Buster, 94
liberals, 135, 179, 204, 205, 222, 257
libraries, rural system, 160
lieutenant governor, 235, 236
Liggett Group, 244
Limestone County, Alabama, 11, 16, 30, 48, 49, 101, 102
Lincoln, Abraham, 64, 68, 74, 84
Lindsay, Elizabeth McKnight, 90
Lindsay, John, 90
Lindsay, Robert Burns, 89, 90–93, 96, 110
Lingo, Al (Colonel), 221, 222
Lipscomb, Judge Abner Smith, 31
liquor, 182, 192; liquor bill, 154; laws regarding, 158; licensing fees, 158; tax on, 214, 218. *See also* drunk drivers; drys; wets
Lisle, New York, 77
Little Round Top, 123
livestock, 190
Livingston, Alabama, 112, 176
Locke, Hugh, 181
Lockett, Mrs. Napoleon, 68
Longwood, Mary W., 61
lottery, x, 241, 247, 259
Louisiana, 64, 122
Louisiana Purchase, 9

Louisiana Territory, 9
Louisville & Nashville Railroad, 104, 107, 117, 118, 120, 121, 153
Lowther, Alexander (Major), 123
loyalty oath. *See* oath of allegiance
Lucy, Autherine, 1, 2, 204
lumber mill, 151
lynchers, 169
lynchings, 119, 141, 145, 160, 183, 184
lynch law, 141
Lyons, Francis S., 49, 55

Macon, Georgia, 141, 190
Macon County, Alabama, 24, 27, 39, 108, 221
Maddox, Lester, 234
Madison, James, 10, 14
Madison County, Alabama, 10, 36, 39, 53, 61, 94, 110
Magnolia Cemetery, 34
Manifest Destiny, 44
Manning, Joseph C., 119, 125, 126
manufacturing, 116
Maple Hill Cemetery, 97
Mardis, Samuel W., 45
Marengo County, Alabama 49
Marion, Alabama, 65, 67, 69, 162
Marion, Francis, 31
Marion County, Alabama, 218
Marquis de Lafayette, 20
marriage, 9
Marschall, Nicola, 68
Marshall County, Alabama, 111
Marshall County Civil Works Administration, 198
martial law, 209
Martin, Jim, 215, 232
Martin, Joshua Lanier, 37, 48–50, 56
Martin, Louis (Montaigne), 48
Martin, Roscoe C., 187
Maryland, 225
Marysville Road Bill, 36
Maryville, Tennessee, 48
Mason, Mary Gillam, 48
Mason, Sarah Ann, 48
masons, 77, 148
Mathews, General George, 7, 1
McCarthy era, 209
McClung, James W., 110
McDowell, Charles S., 174
McFayden, Irene Ashley, 144
McGovern, George, 225, 257
McGregor, Milton, 256
McKay, Nathaniel, 92

◇

McKee, Robert, 93
McKinley, John, 35
McKleroy, John M., 111
McMillan, George, 228
McVay, Hugh, 30, 38–40
McVay, Polly Hawks, 39
media advertising, 244
Medicaid, 245
medical school, 148
medical studies, 147
medicine, clinical, 148
Meek, Alexander B., 62
Meek, Alexander Beaufort, 29
Memphis, 39, 145
Memphis and Charleston Railroad, 38, 63
mental health, 176, 233, 245; facilities, 229
Mercedes-Benz, 246, 255
Mercer College, 141, 190
merchant marine, 197, 199
merchants, 151
Merchant's Bank of New York, 42
Merritt, Vernon, 209
Metarie Cemetery, 9
Methodist Church, 57
Methodist Episcopal Church South, 138, 151
Methodist ministers, 170
Mexican cession, 56
Mexican War, 50, 53, 56, 57
Mexico, 53, 102, 111
middle class, 135
migration, 104
military bills to equip troops in Civil War, 68
Military Department, 161
Military Reconstruction Acts of 1867, 82, 85, 88
milk inspector, 166
Miller, Aubrey, 246
Miller, Benjamin, 2, 176, 180–84, 186
Miller, John, 180
Miller, Margaret Otis, 180
Miller, Sara, 180
mine safety inspections, 159
mineral district, 68
Minerva, Mary, 27
minimum wages, 177
mining, 16
Mississippi, 5, 7, 9, 11, 14, 39, 61, 237, 255
Mississippi River, 5, 7
Mississippi Territory, 5, 7, 8, 9, 10, 11, 24, 25, 28, 34; militia of, 8; territorial assembly, 11, 24
Mississippi Usury Act, 12, 16
Missouri Compromise, 55
misuse of funds, 249
Mobile, Alabama, 1, 7, 11, 20, 26, 33, 43, 44, 61, 62, 72, 75, 93, 95, 104, 114, 126, 145, 148, 172, 188, 200, 214, 231, 243, 246, 259; black community in, 145
Mobile and Ohio Railroad, 55, 62
Mobile Bay, 14, 68
Mobile Internal Improvements Convention of 1851, 61
Mobile Register, 69, 111
Mobile River, 12
moderates, 257
Mona and Lisa (Taylor sisters), 228
Monroe, James, 14
Monroe County, Alabama, 21, 31, 39, 41
Montgomery, Alabama, 2, 11, 20, 43, 45, 50, 58, 60, 63, 64, 66, 68, 71, 74, 76, 84, 95, 113, 117, 125, 130, 139, 145, 153, 161, 191, 206, 209, 211, 215, 217, 218, 222, 226, 228, 229, 231, 233, 240, 243, 254, 258
Montgomery, Laura, 163
Montgomery *Advertiser*, 124, 149, 160, 161, 182, 208–09
Montgomery bus boycott, 2, 203
Montgomery County, Alabama, 11, 74, 107, 173, 183, 251
Montgomery Klavern (Ku Klux Klan), 174
Montgomery Methodist Church, 59
"Montgomery Regency," 45, 47
Monticello, Georgia, 70
Moore, Andrew Barry, 65–69, 71, 76, 137
Moore, Arthur, 11
Moore, Charles, 66
Moore, Gabriel, 24–28, 64
Moore, Jane Barry, 66
Moore, Letitia Dalton, 24
Moore, Matthew, 24
Moore, Roy (Judge), 247
Moore, Samuel, 28–30
Moore, Thomas, W.B., 66
Morgan, John Tyler (U.S. Senator), 79, 115, 130, 131, 132
Morgan County, Alabama, 53, 235
motor pool (state), 236
motor vehicle license tax, 159
Moulton, Alabama, 94
Mt. Bethel Academy, 31
Mount Vernon, Alabama, 31, 68, 176
Mt. Vernon Primitive Baptist Church, 249
murder, 145, 160
Murphy, Duncan, 21
Murphy, Edgar Gardner, 119, 144
Murphy, John, 20, 21
Murphy, John, Jr., 21

Murphy, Neil, 21
Muscle Shoals, Alabama, 25, 26, 32, 36, 164, 254

NAACP (National Association for the Advancement of Colored People), 211, 219
Nabors, Mrs. Robert N., *nee* Elizabeth Andrews, 170
Nashville, Tennessee, 8, 61, 94
Nashville Convention of 1850, 67
Natchez, Mississippi, 8, 9, 11; as capital of Mississippi Territory, 8
Natchez District, 10
Natchez Trace, 8
Nathan Rothschild and Company, 42
National Bank, 8, 29
national banking system, 6
National Governors Conference, 204, 247
National Republican, 41
National Union Convention, 78, 102
National Women's Trade Union League, 177
natural gas, 229
Neal, Claude, 183
Nea-mathla, 36
Negro. *See* blacks
"Negro Question," 141
New Beginning, 244
New Deal, 135, 177, 178, 179, 183, 188, 189, 192, 195, 198, 199, 249; anti-New Deal, 188
New Mexico, 145
New Orleans, 9, 20, 42, 172
New South, 107, 118, 251, 257, 260
New Spain, 10
newspapers, 149, 199
New York, 42, 126, 172, 186, 204; stock exchange, 20
New York City, 83, 86
Nineteenth Amendment, 161, 168
Nixon, Richard, 225, 238
normal schools, 159
north Alabama, 14, 15, 22, 75, 91, 93, 95, 103, 109; hill country, 198
North Carolina, 5, 9, 24, 58, 90, 114, 127
North Carolina piedmont, 185
nudity, 237
nullification of tariff law, 41

Oak Bowery Classical School (Chambers County), 137
Oak Hill, Alabama, 180
Oakley, James G., 161
Oates, Sarah Sellers, 122
Oates, Sarah Toney, 124
Oates, William, 122

Oates, William Calvin, 119, 120, 122–26, 128, 141; amputation of right arm, 123
oath of allegiance, 65, 78, 81, 95
obscenity law, 237
oil, 229; offshore drilling leases, 229
oil lamps, 181
Oklahoma, 37
old-age pensions, 178, 212, 213, 224
Old South, 99
Old Southwest, 7, 8, 18
Oliver, Samuel W., 41
O'Neal, Edward Asbury, 109–13, 190, 254
O'Neal, Emmet, 112, 157–62, 254
O'Neal, Lizzie Kirkman, 157
O'Neal, Olivia Moore, 110
Opelika, Alabama, 111, 138, 244
orator, 41, 102
oratory, 40
organized labor, 174, 177, 229
Orleans, Territory of, 9
outside agitators, 184
Owen, Marie Bankhead, 191
Owens, Hardaman, 32
Oyster Commission, 160

Panic of 1819, 16, 17, 18, 26, 35, 49
Panic of 1837, 27, 37, 39
Panic of 1873, 92, 96, 107
Panic of 1893, 119
Panola County, Mississippi, 27
paper money, 55
Parsons, Enoch, 36
Parsons, Erastus Bellamy, 77
Parsons, Jennett Hepburn, 77
Parsons, Lewis Eliphalet, 77–80, 83, 84, 87
Partlow mental institution, 233
Patterson, Agnes Louise Benson, 210
Patterson, Albert, 210
Patterson, John, 209, 210–15, 219, 255; awarded Bronze Star, 210
Patterson, Mary Jo McGowin, 210
Patterson, "Tina" Bratchert Sawyer, 215
Patton, Robert Miller, 64, 78, 80–83, 84
"Peace in the Valley," 204
Peace Society, 94
Pea River, 197
Pea River Power Company, 163
Pearl River, 9
Peck, Clarissa Stedman, 33
penal code, 26
penal system, 141; reform of, 144
Peninsula campaign of 1862, 65
penitentiary system, 59, 107, 245

Index

peonage, 118
People's Party, 119
Perry, Sidney S., 61
Perry, Simon L. (Sion), 58
Perry County, Alabama, 65, 66
Persian Gulf, 241
Persons, Alice McKeithen, 206
Persons, Gordon, 189, 206–9, 218
Petersburg, Virginia, 123
Pettus, Edmund W. (U.S. Senator), 126, 130, 132
Phenix City, Alabama, 209, 210, 212
Phi Beta Kappa, 173
physicians, 104
Pickens, Israel, 17–21, 22
Pickens, Jane Carrigan, 17
Pickens, Samuel, 17
Pickens County, Alabama, 30
Pickering County, Mississippi Territory, 8
Pickett, Felicia, 53
Pike County, Alabama, 122, 162, 163
Pill, Howard, 206
Pinckney Treaty (1795), 7
Pinkerton Detective Agency, 111
Pitt, Redding (U.S. Attorney General), 256
plain folks, 184, 197
plantation, 45, 47, 53, 61, 65, 110, 113, 151, 156
planter-Birmingham business coalition, 142
planters, 40, 42, 74, 104, 105, 106, 150, 151, 177, 198
Planters and Merchants Bank of Huntsville, 14,
    18, 19, 22
Pledge of Allegiance, 229
political reform, 143
Polk, James K., 44
poll tax, 200, 209
Poole, Joe, 199
Poor People's Campaign, 234
Pope, General John, 85
Pope, Leroy, 35
Populist Party, 99, 115, 116
populist programs, 212
Populist-Republican coalition, 128, 142
populist rhetoric, 203, 216
Populists, 124, 125, 126, 127, 128, 130, 132, 139, 141,
    142, 181, 197, 198
"populists," 220
post–World War II era, 206
poultry, 190
Powell, Adam Clayton, 204
Powell, Levin, 29
Pratt Consolidated Mines, 108, 115,118, 147
prayer in public schools, 245
Presbyterians, 77, 90
presidency, U.S., 222

presidential candidate, 202, 216, 236
presidential election of 1840, 42
presidential elector, 67, 157
presidential politics, 229
Preston, Albert, xi
price control bill, 72
Priest, R.W., 162
primary election laws, 159
Primitive Baptists, 249, 250
Prison: inmates, 247; prison conditions, 148, 166;
    prison mortality, 148; prison reform, 59, 159,
    208; prison for female inmates, 67. See also
    penal system
Progressive Party, 163
progressives, 173, 186, 220, 247
progressive spirit, 145, 149
progressivism, 132, 135, 150, 152, 156, 159, 162, 164
prohibition, x, 109, 114, 135, 149, 154, 156, 158, 167,
    168, 198; constitutional amendment for, 158
prohibitionists, 174, 181
Prohibition Party, 114
property taxes, 62, 182, 187, 213, 214, 228
proration, 245
Protective Life Insurance Company, 146
Pryor, Bill, 252
Pryor, Luke, 94
public education, 54, 141, 213, 235, 237, 241; high
    school, 153; appropriations for deaf, 144. See
    also education
public health, 153–54, 176
public lands, 26
public roads, 154, 175; hardsurfaced, 175. See also
    highways
public schools, 163, 164, 176, 187
public school teachers, 226, 237
public utilities, 207
Public Utilities Commission, 160
public works, 54
Pugh, James L., 122
Pushmataha, 9

"race mixing," 220
race relations, 146, 162, 178, 191, 237, 257
racial moderates, 224, 237
racism, 117, 145, 148, 188, 195, 230, 244
radio, 170, 206, 208
Railroad Commission, 108, 128–29, 139, 141, 143,
    144, 149, 151, 152, 159, 160
railroads, 6, 62, 63, 65, 82, 91, 92, 96, 104, 105,
    117, 153, 155; bonds, 89; freight rates, 143,
    148, 151, 152, 153, 192; legislation regarding,
    145; regulation of, 108, 146, 149, 150, 157
Raleigh, North Carolina, 163

Randolph County, Alabama, 87, 89
rape, 145; black men accused of, 145, 183–84;
    medical examinations for rape victims, 247
readmission to Union, 82
Reagan, Ronald, 228, 250, 254, 255
Reagonomics, 228
Reconstruction, 1, 64, 78, 79, 83, 84, 85,
    95, 104, 117, 123, 127, 160, 196, 249;
    Congressional Reconstruction, 79, 95;
    military Reconstruction, 48, 78, 85, 87, 88;
    Presidential Reconstruction, 48, 78, 88, 95,
    102; Radical Reconstruction, 65
Reconstruction Acts of 1867, 91, 95
redemption, 76, 110
Reese, Gene, 251
reform school for boys, 153
Relief Act of (June) 1837, 37, 39
religion, 245, 257
Republican government, 110
Republican National Convention, 250
Republican Party, 52, 85, 86, 91, 95, 103, 107,
    163, 186, 244, 250, 256, 258, 259; radical
    Republicans, 76, 102
Republican Primary, 248, 250, 253
Republicans, 68, 74, 84, 85, 88, 89, 90, 92, 93,
    95, 96, 97, 102, 104, 105, 111, 114, 116, 117, 123,
    124, 139, 195, 196, 207, 211, 223, 232, 243, 244,
    246, 249, 251, 252, 253, 256
retail clerks union, 177
Revolutionary War, 8, 13, 53, 65
Reynolds Aluminum Company, 254
Richmond, Virginia, 71, 72, 73, 117
"right-to-work" law, 189, 208
Riley, Richard, 247
Rivers Bridge, South Carolina (battle of), 84
roads, 6, 172; farm-to-market roads, 203, 205;
    improvements of, 149; road bonds, 203;
    road construction, 216. *See also* highways
"Roaring Twenties," 135
Roddey, General Philip, 94
Rodney, Thomas, 9
Roman Catholics, 172, 259
Roosevelt, Franklin D., 135, 172, 178, 179, 183,
    188, 186, 241
Roosevelt, Theodore, 120, 154
Royal Canadian Air Corps, 185–86
"Royal Party." *See* Broad River Group
Rural Electrification Authority (REA), 206
Russell County, Alabama, 32, 209
Russell Sage Foundation, 164

St. Claire County, Alabama, 11, 106
St. James Methodist Church, 234

St. Margaret's Hospital, 233
St. Mary's Seminary, 163
St. Stephens, Alabama, 14, 18
Salary Act, 14
sales tax, 178, 184, 214, 220
Samford, Susan Lewis Dowdell, 137
Samford, William Flewellyn, 67, 137, 171
Samford, William James, 137–40, 142, 148
Samford University (Howard College), xi, 162,
    179; Cumberland Law School, x, xi, 238
sanitary sewers, 166
Sargent, William Fitz Winthrop, 8
Sargent, Winthrop, 7, 9
Sayre Act (1893), 120, 125, 128
"scalawags," 79, 95, 96, 103, 123, 221
scholarships to military schools, 68
School for Deaf and Blind in Talladega, 67, 205
school terms, 174
Scottsboro, Alabama, 178
Scottsboro Boys, 178, 184
scrip, 183
Seay, Anne McGee, 113
Seay, Reuben, 113
Seay, Thomas, 109, 113–16
secession, 29, 38, 47, 51, 64, 67, 68, 71, 73,
    77, 91, 94, 95, 102, 105, 110; antisecession
    (forces), 91; nonsecessionist (forces), 65;
    prosecession (forces), 53, 57, 109, 123
secession convention, 68
Secretary of Education, 247
sectionalism, 12
segregation, 96, 203, 209, 212, 219, 220, 234
segregationists, 1, 204, 212
Selma, Alabama, 126, 127, 184, 222
Selma Argus, 93
Selma Times, 69
Seminole War, 43
separate but equal provisions, 119
Sessions, Jeff, 256
Sevier, John, 8
sharecroppers, 99
Sheffield, Alabama, 114
Sheffield, James Lawrence, 111
Shelby County, Alabama, 11, 106, 107, 109, 155
sheriff sales, 81
Sherman, William Tecumseh (General), 87
Shields, Benjamin G., 59
Ship Island, 114
Shorter, Eli, 70
Shorter, John Gill, 69, 70–73, 75, 76, 94, 141
Shorter, Mary Jane Battle, 70
Shortridge, George, 29, 63
Siegelman, Andrea Schottgen, 257

Index

Siegelman, Don, 248, 257–60
Siegelman, Leslie Bouchet, 257
Siegelman, Lori Allen, 257, 258, 259
"Silverite," 124, 126
Sixteenth Street Baptist Church, 221
Slaton, W.F., 137
slave code, 9, 78
slavery, x, 6, 36, 51, 53, 55, 56, 61, 65, 70, 74, 78, 102; in territories, 45, 70; proslavery, 53, 56, 74; antislavery, 74, 84
slaves, 15, 25, 27, 31, 37, 38, 40, 51, 70, 74, 77, 78, 82, 83, 87, 94, 99; impressments of, 72; insurrection, 36, 43
Sloss Iron and Steel Company, 127, 131
small businesses, 177
Smaw, Ellen, 114
Smith, Al, 181, 186
Smith, Daniel (Senator), 114
Smith, Jeptha Vinnen, 87
Smith, Milton Hannibal, 153
Smith, William Hugh, 85, 87–90, 91, 96
Smith-Lever Act, 160
socialist, 153
Socialist Party, 163
social services, 174
soft drinks, 159
solid-waste disposal, 246
South and North Railroad, 68
South Carolina, 5, 21, 23, 31, 41, 48, 53, 66, 101, 110, 122, 180; state senate, 21
Southern Commercial Conventions, 38
southern land grants to attract industry, 99
southern rights, 59, 64, 67, 71, 74
Southern Rights Party, 60
southern rights radicals,
Southern University, 113, 114
Spain, 5, 7, 11
Spanish-American War, 126, 171
Sparks, Chauncey M., 179, 186, 190–93, 198, 217
Sparks, George Washington, 190
Sparks, Sarah E. Castello, 190
specie, 18, 19, 41, 68
speed limits, 208
Spencer, Senator George E., 88, 89
spoils system, 62
Spring Hill, Alabama, 151
Sputnik, 195
Standard Chemical and Oil Company, 163
Standard Telephone and Telegraph Company, 163
"Stars and Bars." See Confederate flag
state bonds, 92
state debt, 50, 62, 87, 104; repudiation of, 46, 107

state fair, Negro Day, 145
state funds, 62, 63
states' rights, 23, 29, 33, 58, 60, 62, 65, 72, 87, 110, 137, 191, 195, 216, 218, 219, 247
states' rights groups, 58, 59, 60
States' Rights Party, 188
State Training School for Girls, 168
Steagall, Henry B., 198
Steel, Emily, 41
Steele, John (Secretary of Mississippi Territory), 8
Steineker, Catherine, 231
Stewart, Donald, 254
Strawberry Pickers, 199
strict construction of state constitution, 62
strikes, 209; 1894 coal miners, 120, 125, 128; railroad strike, 120
Student Government Association, 257
suffrage, 90, 120, 131, 139
Sumter County, Alabama, 53, 61
Swayne, Noah Haynes, 83
Swayne, Sarah Ann, 83
Swayne, Wager T. (Brigadier General), 81, 82, 83–86, 88; awarded Congressional Medal of Honor, 84
Sweetwater, Alabama, 80, 83
Sylacauga, Alabama, xi

Taft-Hartley Act, 208
Tait, Charles, 14, 16
Talladega, Alabama, 49, 67, 78, 80, 104, 127, 170
Talladega County, Alabama, 77
Tallapoosa County, Alabama, 210
Tallmadge, Frederick, 77
Tanner, John T., 114
tariff, 29, 32, 33, 41, 51, 53; Tariff of Abominations, 23; tariff nullification, 23, 32, 33. See also nullification
taxation, 129; inequitable system, 164
taxes, 216, 226; new, 210; "no new," 171
tax funding, 150, 191
tax laws, 167
tax reform, 176, 251, 260
Taylor, Sandra Baxley, 245
Taylor, Zachary, 44
teacher salaries, 175
Teachers' Union, 265
teaching, 90
technical schools, 220
telegraph, 153, 159
telephone, 159; long distance, 153
television, educational, 208
temperance, 149, 158, 174

tenant farmers, 198
Ten Commandments, ix, 142, 247
Tennessee, 5, 39, 48, 123; state constitution, 8
Tennessee and Coosa Line, 62
Tennessee Coal, Iron, and Railroad Company, 115, 118, 148, 155
Tennessee River, 23, 25, 26, 29, 32, 67
Tennessee River Valley, 10, 11, 15, 18, 26, 36, 40, 61, 62, 80, 101
Tennessee State Supreme Court, 58
Tennessee Valley Authority (TVA), 235
terrorism, 92
Terry, Nathaniel, 49, 54
Terry-Martin bank controversy, 54
Texas, 51, 61, 111, 122, 231, 234; Republic of, 27; annexation of, 44
textbooks, 220
textile mills, 59, 110, 114, 149, 155, 177, 184
textile strike, 177
Third Judicial District, 218, 231
Third Military District, 82, 85
third party, 238
Thirteenth Amendment, 102
thirty-first parallel, 7; as boundary between U.S. and Spain: *See* Pinckney Treaty
Thomas, Randall, 252
Thornton, Mills, 58
Three-Chopped-Way. *See* Federal Military Road
tobacco farms, 13
Toledo, Ohio, 86
Tombigbee River (Tombeckbee River), 10, 11, 12, 14, 18, 32, 49
tort reform, 259
Toulmin, Harry (U.S. Judge), 10
tourists, 208
Trade School Act of 1947, 218
trade schools, 216, 218
"Tragic Era," 52
Trammell, Seymour, 225
The Transformation of Southern Politics, 238
trial lawyers, 229, 258
Troup, George M., 14
Troy, Alabama, 162, 165, 176
Troy Compress Company, 163
Troy State University (Normal School at Troy), 115, 163, 229
Truman, Harry, 188, 202, 209
tuberculosis, 145, 148; tuberculosis commission and sanitarium, 154
Tunstall, Virginia, 58
Tuomey, Michael, 55
Turchin, John Basil, 102
Tuscaloosa, Alabama, 1, 12, 15, 22, 23, 30, 33, 40, 46, 49, 50, 54, 66, 82, 140, 157, 170, 171, 172, 176, 217, 233, 239, 257; as state capital, 58
Tuscaloosa County, Alabama, 11, 155; high school, 232
Tuscaloosa Memorial Park, 172
Tuscumbia, Alabama, 32, 58, 90, 93
Tuskegee, Alabama, 137, 160, 211
Tuskegee Civic Association, 211
Tuskegee Institute, 191
Tuskegee Normal and Industrial School, 109
Tutwiler, Henry, 29
Tutwiler, Julia, 119
twentieth century, xiii, 173, 241
Twenty-first Amendment, 183
two-party system, 196

U. S. News and World Report, 251
Underwood, Oscar W., 170
unemployment, 248
unemployment compensation, 224
Uniform Textbook Act, 144
Union deserters, 75
unionists, 91, 102; southern, 95; Alabamian, 95
Unionist sentiment, 57
Unionist Whig Party, 61, 75
Union League, 85
Union lines, 87
Union Springs, Alabama ("Cradle of the Confederacy"), 76, 141
Union Springs *Herald and Times*, 141
Union troops, 151; 20th Maine, 123
United Mine Workers (UMW), 155, 168
United States, 11, 12
United States Air Force; Brookley Field, 188; 50th wing of the 20th air force, 217
United States Army, 99, 210, 249; 101st Airborne, 249; 1st Infantry, 249
United States Army Corps of Engineers, 243
United States Attorney, 157
United States Civil Rights Commission, 219
United States Commissioner of Education, 168
United States Congress, 5, 11, 23, 25, 35, 36, 49, 55, 80, 85, 95, 101, 115, 124; creation of Mississippi Territory
United States Constitution, 55, 64, 95, 168; proposed amendment of 1860 forbidding Congress to abolish slavery. *See also* Committee of Thirty-three
United States Constitutional Convention, 5
United States Department of Education, 247
United States Department of Health Education and Welfare, 232–33
United States Department of Justice, 221

United States District Court, 33
United States House of Representatives, 8, 14,
    17, 23, 27, 33, 55, 61, 102, 124, 223
United States Justice Department, 225
United States Senate, 9, 14, 25, 27, 37, 44, 46, 47,
    55, 56, 60, 64, 65, 76, 102, 124, 131, 152, 168,
    174, 185
United States Supreme Court, 37, 84, 178, 179,
    202, 203, 209, 211, 228
University of Alabama, 1, 19, 22, 23, 26, 29, 55,
    59, 72, 131, 138, 139, 151, 157, 165, 170, 173,
    175, 179, 187, 197, 214, 217, 221, 222, 233, 235,
    255, 257; integration of, 1, 203, 221, 222; law
    school, 180, 235, 239; medical college, 191
University of Alabama at Birmingham, 228
University of Montevallo (Alabama College),
    175
University of North Alabama (Florence
    Wesleyan), 157
usury, 35

vagrants, 85
Valley Campaign, 117, 123
Van Buren, Martin, 27, 33, 37, 41, 46
Ventress, Mary Jo, 231
Veterans Administration, 217
veto, 62, 63
Vickers, Reverend John, 234
Vietnam War, 223, 237
vigilantism, 183
Vincent, Isaac Harvey ("Honest Ike,"),107, 111,
    112
Virginia, 5, 8, 10, 48, 53, 83, 101, 117, 123, 185
Virginia Legislature, 13
Virginia Military Institute, 117
voting laws, 257
voting rights, 222
Voting Rights Act, 222

Waddel, Moses, 57
Waffle House Restaurants, 247
wages, 164
Wagner-Costigan federal anti-lynching bill, 188
Wakefield, Mississippi Territory, 10
Walker, Chief Justice A. J., 117
Walker, Jacob, Jr., 244
Walker, John Williams, 16, 22, 35
Walker County, Alabama, 155
Wallace, Cornelia Ellis Snively, 224
Wallace, George C., 216
Wallace, George Corley, 1, 192, 202, 204, 215,
    216–30, 232, 233, 234, 236, 237, 238, 239, 240,
    241, 244, 245, 246, 248; stand in schoolhouse
    door, ix, 232
Wallace, George Corley, Jr., 229, 255
Wallace, Gerald, 225
Wallace, Lisa Taylor, 228
Wallace, Lurleen Burns, 215, 217, 219, 222, 223,
    230–34, 235
Wallace, Mozelle Smith, 216
Wallace-Carter Act, 218
Wall Street, 91, 93
The War Between the Union and the Confederacy
    (1905), 126
war hawks, 18
War of 1812, 11, 18, 65
Warrior Guards, 171
Warrior River, 29, 49
Warrior Stand, Alabama, 140
"Warwick of the Warrior," 171
Washington, Booker T., 108, 120, 145
Washington, D.C., 57, 96, 105, 185, 186, 257
Washington County, Alabama, 10, 18; Mississippi
    Territory, 8
Washington Town, 9
water rates, 166
Watts, Thomas Hill, 71, 73–77
Weakly, Gem, 115
Wedowee, Alabama, 87
West, Cato, 9
western Europe, 141
West Point, Georgia, 243
wets, 154, 198
Wetumpka, Alabama, 45, 50, 113
Wetumpka Argus, 43
Wheel, the, 116
Wheeler, General Joseph, 106
Whig Party (Whigs), 23, 33, 36, 37, 40, 41, 42, 43,
    46, 47, 49, 54, 55, 58, 61, 63, 66, 71, 74, 77,
    81, 117
Whig Unionist, 71
whipping, 43, 208
White, Alexander, 77
White, Frank S., 185
White, Judge Hugh, 33, 34
White, Judge John, 49
white flight, 237
white primary, 143
whites, 33, 52, 64, 79, 81, 82, 85, 87, 89, 90, 92, 95,
    97, 100, 103, 104, 105, 118, 121, 190, 200, 216,
    226; middle class, 237; small landowners,
    198
white supremacy, 65, 103, 118, 120, 123, 125, 141,
    157, 162, 181, 186
white teachers, 112

Wilcox County, Alabama, 44, 180, 181, 182
Wilderness, Battle of, 123
Wilkinson, General James, 7, 9, 10
William and Mary College, 8, 13
Williams, George H. (U.S. Attorney General),
   96
Williams, Marmaduke, 15
Williams, Mary McIntosh, 8
Williams, Robert, 9
Williams College, 117
Wilmot Proviso, 51, 53, 54, 55
Wilson, James H., 76
Wilson, Woodrow, 160, 171
Winston, Elizabeth, 9
Winston, John Anthony, 61–65, 91, 103
Winston, Mary Agnes Walker, 61
Winston, Sarah Miller (Lindsay), 91
Wiregrass region, Alabama, xiii, 122, 197, 198
Withers, Susanna Claiborne, 34
women, 174, 181, 197, 200, 201, 230, 255; in
   politics, x; labor issues, 114; suffrage, 157,
   161, 174
Women's Christian Temperance Union, 119

women's rights, 174
Woods, Henry A., 29
Woodville, Alabama, 28
Woodward, G. F., 77
workers' compensation, 168
working class, 231
workplace liability, 229
World War I, 135, 163, 171, 174, 185; Alabama
   Regiment in France, 174
World War II, x, 135, 155, 165, 187, 190, 195, 199;
   Pacific Theater, 217
Wortham, Lucy (Smith), 87
WSFA, 206

X-rated films, 237

Yancey, William Lowndes, 43, 47, 53, 54, 56, 61,
   64, 70, 74, 77
"Yankee Race," 71
Yazoo deals, 7
yellow fever, 104, 112
yeomen, xiii
Young, Elisha, 66

◇